THE RISE OF POPULAR ANTIMODERNISM IN GERMANY

The Rise of Popular Antimodernism in Germany

The Urban Master Artisans, 1873-1896

Shulamit Volkov

Princeton University Press, Princeton, New Jersey

Published by Princeton University Press, Princeton, New Jersey
In the United Kingdom: Princeton University Press, Guildford, Surrey

Library of Congress Cataloging in Publication Data will be
found on the last printed page of this book

This book has been composed in Linotype Caledonia

Printed in the United States of America by Princeton
University Press, Princeton, New Jersey

Contents

Acknowledgments

My interest in social history, in Imperial Germany, and in the fate of the German artisans was first aroused in a graduate seminar conducted by Prof. Hans Rosenberg in Berkeley almost ten years ago. Since then he has continuously directed my efforts with endless suggestions and critical advice. Without his personal support and encouragement I could never have completed this book.

Maura Kealey, whose friendship overcame the geographical distance between us, assisted through years of correspondence in refining this study in many different, subtle ways. Prof. Jürgen Kocka read the entire manuscript with critical care, and his comments proved essential for the final revision. At different stages of the work discussions with Profs. Wolfgang Sauer, Gerald D. Feldman, and G. A. Ritter have greatly helped in clarifying obscure issues. Other colleagues in the United States, in Germany, and in Israel offered critical suggestions throughout these years. Naomi Hendleman in Tel-Aviv and Barbara Westergaard in Princeton did the enormous job of editing my style and correcting innumerable inaccuracies. The responsibility for all the remaining shortcomings of this book is naturally only mine.

A special Graduate Career Prize from the University of California enabled mc to carry on the initial research, and grants from the Institute of International Studies in Berkeley, California, and from the Aranne School of History at Tel-Aviv University helped me complete it.

My daughter, Tal, virtually grew up with this book, and her tact and good sense made the experience of combining motherhood with scholarly work a real pleasure.

Bibliographical Abbreviations

AHR	*American Historical Review*
AHZ	*Allgemeine Handwerker Zeitung*
Am. J. of Soc.	*American Journal of Sociology*
Am. Soc. Rev.	*American Sociological Review*
ASS	*Archiv für Sozialwissenschaft und Sozialpolitik*
DHZ	*Deutsche Handwerker Zeitung*
EHR	*Economic History Review*
GG	*Geschichte und Gesellschaft*
HBS	*Handwörterbuch der Staatswissenschaften*
Int. Rev. of Soc. Hist.	*International Review of Social History*
JCH	*Journal of Contemporary History*
JEH	*Journal of Economic History*
JMH	*Journal of Modern History*
JNS	*Jahrbücher für Nationalökonomie und Statistik*
KZ	*Kreuzzeitung*
PVS	*Politische Vierteljahrsschrift*
Schmollers JB	*Jahrbuch für Gesetzgebung, Verwaltung und Volkswirtschaft im deutschen Reich*
Schriften	*Schriften des Vereins für Sozialpolitik*
St.d.R.	*Statistik des Deutschen Reichs* (New Series)
Steno. Berichte	*Stenographische Berichte über die Verhandlungen des deutschen Reichstags*
VSWG	*Vierteljahrschrift für Sozial- und Wirtschaftsgeschichte*
VZ	*Vierteljahrshefte für Zeitgeschichte*
ZG	*Zeitschrift für Geschichtswissenschaft*
ZGS	*Zeitschrift für die Gesammte Staatswissenschaft*

THE RISE OF POPULAR ANTIMODERNISM IN GERMANY

Introduction

Problem, Method, and Approach

This book attempts to fulfill two interrelated objectives. First, it is an attempt to explain the development of a central ideological trend in late nineteenth-century Germany, the growth of popular antimodernism. It then endeavors to analyze the history of one social group in Germany that developed and adopted this particular ideological-political posture: the small, independent, urban master artisans of traditional crafts.

Opposition to social, economic, political, and cultural manifestations of modernity is not a uniquely German phenomenon. Antimodernism as an intellectual position can be detected in all the industrializing countries of Europe during the second half of the nineteenth and the early twentieth centuries. Furthermore, it infected a number of social movements during that time and was widely felt among various social groups throughout the continent.[1] Only in Germany, however, did *popular* antimodernism become a dominant sentiment determining the ideological and political stand of certain social strata; only there did it combine with other forces to affect the entire course of German history.

Popular antimodernism was not an intellectual trend alone, though it shared its negative attitude toward modernity with "cultural pessimism" and with the ideology of a "conservative revolution," both widespread among intellectuals at the time.[2] It was, rather, a mood prevalent among

[1] See especially Fritz Stern, *The Politics of Cultural Despair*, pp. 5-22, and his useful bibliography, pp. 407-412.

[2] On antimodernism as a cultural-intellectual trend in late nineteenth-century Germany, see in addition to Stern, *Cultural Despair*, Kenneth D. Barkin, *The Controversy over German Industrialization*; Herman Lebovics, " 'Agrarians' versus 'Industrializers' "; Hans Rosenberg, *Grosse Depression und Bismarckzeit*; Fritz K. Ringer, *The Decline of the German Mandarins.*

certain low and lower-middle social elements in German society during the last quarter of the nineteenth century. It grew out of their fear of and hostility toward an emerging new world, and later became the principal determiner of their ideology and politics. Despite the similarity of many of their cardinal beliefs, intellectual and popular antimodernism are two distinct phenomena. Their origins, history, and influence must be analyzed and explained by different methods. While intellectual antimodernism represents a challenge for the historian of ideas, popular antimodernism requires the tools of the social historian. Economic, social, and political factors are not insignificant in explaining the attitudes of men of letters, but they become of primary importance in analyzing the ideological and political position of people who are not normally concerned with ideas as such. Groups composed of such men develop common attitudes primarily as a reaction to specific material circumstances and under the pressures of collective anxiety, fear, and hope.

This is not, therefore, a study in the development of ideas but rather an experiment in social history. In fact it may be viewed as a biography, a biography of a collectivity, a chapter in the history of a social group.[3] Like an individual, a social group may develop its own character, sense of identity, and mentality. It may evolve a special set of relations with other social groups, based on love, hate, or jealousy. When mature, it may create its own pattern of behavior and gain greater or lesser prestige, power, or influence. The analogy, however, has its hazards and limitations, and is often no more than a convenient metaphor. The very existence of a social group needs to be proved: it is often no more than an analytical construct. Not being bound by

[3] The best social group histories available to date are E.P. Thompson, *The Making of the English Working Class* and Jürgen Kocka, *Unternehmensverwaltung und Angestelltenschaft*. For the master artisans, especially during the Weimar Republic, see Heinrich August Winkler, *Mittelstand, Demokratie und Nationalsozialismus*.

a biological life cycle, it has a history fundamentally different from that of an individual. A group, after all, is nothing but a more or less cohesive agglomeration of individual human beings. It sustains itself through a process of self-regeneration, by the birth and death of its members, and through their mobility in and out of it as well as up and down within it. The story of a group is a social history, constantly seeking to sort individuals into categories, without doing violence to their personal uniqueness; to represent their collective nature without obliterating the significant differences among them.

Most histories of modern Germany treat the small masters on two occasions: at the time of the 1848 revolution, and during the early years of National Socialism.[4] The precise place of the master-artisan movement within the political context of the 1848 revolution still needs further investigation. On the face of it the masters played an active role among the various revolutionary forces, eventually convening their own congress in Frankfurt to deliberate simultaneously with the National Assembly. Even then, however,

[4] See e.g. Veit Valentin, *Geschichte der deutschen Revolution 1848-49*, and Jacques Droz, *Les Révolutions allemandes de 1848*. For the artisan problem in particular see Rudolf Stadelmann, *Soziale und politische Geschichte der Revolution von 1848*; Theodore S. Hamerow, *Restoration, Revolution, Reaction*, and "The German Artisan Movement, 1848/49"; P.H. Noyes, *Organization and Revolution*; Rolf Weber, "Die Beziehungen zwischen sozialer Struktur und politischer Ideologie des Kleinbürgertums von 1848/49"; Edward Shorter, "Middle-Class Anxiety in the German Revolution of 1848." The role of the small master artisans in the development of National Socialism has been fully investigated by Winkler in his *Mittelstand*. See also his "Extremismus der Mitte?" and "Unternehmerverbände zwischen Ständeideologie und Nationalsozialismus." Also Karl O'Lessker, "Who Voted for Hitler?"; Michael H. Kater, "Zur Soziographie der frühen NSDAP"; Rudolf Heberle, *From Democracy to Nazism*; Peter Wulf, *Die politische Haltung des Schleswig-holsteinischen Handwerks 1928-1932*; Arthur Schweitzer, "The Nazification of the Lower Middle-Class and Peasants"; David Schoenbaum, *Hitler's Social Revolution*; and Seymour M. Lipset, *Political Man*, especially chap. 5.

they exhibited a mixture of revolutionary and counterrevolutionary attitudes that was later to characterize their position throughout much of the century. From the little reliable evidence on the position of the small master artisans during that time, it appears that they were then still entirely open to a whole range of political alternatives. Their allegiance was not yet definitely established, nor could it be during a period in which social and political divisions in Germany were still only vaguely defined. In contrast, during the late 1920s their stand seems to have lost its ambiguity. By then many of the small masters took a frank and clear-cut political stand, supporting the new National-Socialist party in large numbers. At some point between the revolution of 1848 and the rise of National Socialism, the traditional small masters, as a group, made a choice. They recreated a social and political group consciousness and established a pattern of ideological and political behavior that made them particularly susceptible to National Socialism.[5] This study attempts to identify the period in which this transformation took place and to analyze the various conditions that eventually brought it about.

The translation of social experience into the language of ideas and further into the realm of public action and organized politics, however, is a complex matter for individuals as well as for social groups.[6] Neither economic hardship nor social pressure alone generate specific attitudes or political behavior patterns. The complexity of

[5] On the pre-nineteenth-century group consciousness of artisans, see Rudolf Stadelmann and Wolfram Fischer, *Die Bildungswelt des deutschen Handwerkers um 1800*, chaps. 1-3; Jürgen Bergmann, "Das 'Alte Handwerk' im Ubergang"; Mack Walker, *German Home Towns*, pp. 1-142; and chaps. 3-5 below.

[6] This problem was treated, more subtly than most Marxists today would allow, in Marx's own "The German Ideology," and in his "The Eighteenth Brumaire of Louis Bonaparte." For a non-Marxist perspective see Neil J. Smelser, *Social Change in the Industrial Revolution*, and "Personality and the Explanation of Political Phenomena at the Social-System Level."

human perception and the unexpected manner in which conclusions are drawn and decisions are made play their own role. The connection between material and social conditions and the shaping of group ideas and actions can only be assumed and remain always evasive and uncertain. This transition between the two zones is here presented in as detailed a fashion as possible. An additional analytical stage attempts to expose the master-artisans' psychological and mental state which, springing in a relatively direct way from their socioeconomic and political status in German society, eventually determined their attitudes and the style of their public activity. The relationship between experience and action may in this way lose some, though by no means all, of its mystery and ambiguity.[7]

The central methodological effort in this study is thus directed first toward an integration of social with economic, political, and cultural history. Too often analytical distinctions and the limitations of a linear exposition are allowed to take on the appearance of reality, and in the end a promised new synthesis is not achieved or even attempted. For a study in the history of a social group such a synthesis is crucial, indeed indispensable. The various aspects of a historical period and a unique environment create a total life experience for those who live through and within it. It is this totality alone that evokes the reactions of individuals and groups. Perhaps an attempt to comprehend this overall life experience and an emphasis on the psychological and mental state it produced may help bring the disparate elements of a conventional analysis together into a unified "history of society."[8]

Furthermore, a focus upon a specific social group within

[7] A comparable scheme has been recently suggested in Jürgen Kocka's *Klassengesellschaft im Krieg, 1914-1918*, pp. 4-5; 149-150.

[8] On this concept see E.J. Hobsbawm, "From Social History to the History of Society"; Jürgen Kocka, "Sozial- und Wirtschaftsgeschichte" and "Theorien in der Sozial- und Gesellschaftsgeschichte."

particular national and chronological boundaries may rid social history of the abstractness of sociological analysis. This study has been conducted under the assumption that no general theoretical definition of the position and role of the small master artisans in German society could achieve what a detailed and concrete historical analysis provides. This, therefore, is a social group history, combining an analysis of the economic realities and political struggles of the day in order to portray one social element, while at the same time illuminating from a particular angle some aspects in the development of a whole society, of its material and ideational history alike.[9]

A large number of social historians have repeatedly attempted to find a common denominator among the various aspects of change discernible in the history of many European and non-European countries, Germany included, from the late eighteenth century on. The concept of industrialization and the analysis of the rise of industrial society seemed for a while to serve this purpose. In an effort to break away from the overemphasis on economic factors implied by such a concept, a more general term has now been adopted. Modernization has replaced industrialization as the central theme in many historical studies attempting to comprehend the overall development of the last two centuries.[10] The advantage as well as the disadvantage of the term is its vagueness and all-inclusiveness. It is not

[9] For an overview of German society and politics from 1870 to 1914, see especially H. Rosenberg, *Grosse Depression* and Hans-Ulrich Wehler, *Das Deutsche Kaiserreich 1871-1918*. For earlier studies of certain aspects of this period see Eckart Kehr, *Schlachtflottenbau und Parteipolitik* and his collected essays *Der Primat der Innenpolitik*.

[10] On the use of the concept of modernization see H.-U. Wehler *Modernisierungstheorie und Geschichte*, and the bibliography cited there. The theoretical work on modernization most useful for this study was Leonard Binder et al., *Crises and Sequences in Political Development*. See also C.E. Black, *The Dynamics of Modernization*.

limited to economic and social factors but allows for the inclusion of political and cultural elements as well. However, it perhaps tends to obliterate the uniqueness of certain phenomena that cannot be subsumed under such a sweeping term, and assumes rather than demonstrates ties among all the manifestations of change included within it.[11]

In order to avoid some of the pitfalls of this concept, scholars often rely on a general model in which modernization is characterized as a process of transition between two distinct types of society: a "traditional" and a "modern" one. Within this analytical framework it may be argued that Germany experienced a comprehensive process of modernization beginning in the pre-March era and accelerating after 1850. It underwent a process of change that affected the structure and capacity of its economy, its system of social stratification, the scope and function of its political agents, and the norms and ideals of its culture. A historical survey of German modernization, however, immediately reveals the inadequacy of the simple bipolar approach. At the end of the nineteenth century, and in many respects well into the twentieth, Germany exhibited many traditional features, side by side with modern ones. The modernization of its economy, though impressive in some sectors, remained only partial in others. In its social-stratification system traditional and modern elements continued to coexist and intermingle. The process of national unification did not do away with the autocratic government of the old regime, and many of the traditional values of the old era were preserved despite the intrusion of modern ones. Nevertheless, the direction of the overall process became increasingly evident, and contemporaries came to appreciate its force and comprehensiveness. The way in which *they* evaluated the process of change occurring during their lifetimes supports the approach of a general social history. By the 1890s people

[11] Wehler, *Modernisierungstheorie*, pp. 18-30.

tended to take a stand on the process *as a whole*, to affirm or oppose it, and Germany could then be divided between pro- and antimodern forces. Popular antimodernism emerged as a reaction to the process of modernization, not to one or another of its manifestations. It was an expression of a generalized hostility developed by various elements in German society toward all forces that seemed to weaken the traditional economy and society and threaten old life styles and values. It was a comprehensive attack against a comprehensive process of change.

The emergence of popular antimodernism among the small master artisans can profitably be studied against this general background. The masters were profoundly affected by modernization. They had to adjust to a new structure of government, a changing market economy, restratification of society, and the appearance and growing significance of new social and cultural norms. They formulated their group response during the last quarter of the century, when the effects of gradual modernization were compounded by stresses produced by a period of deflation and severe economic fluctuations, of prevailing pessimism and public anxiety.

While economists and historians often divided industrial development into distinct stages, modernization proved too complex a phenomenon to be treated this way. The latter was indeed a continuous process, with periods of rapid advance and relative regression, often difficult to measure or define in quantitative terms, and not infrequently characterized by internal contradictions. Nevertheless, this study attempts to focus attention on only one phase of the overall process, demarcated by the period known as the "Great Depression." It is a phase distinguishable by the overlap of two phenomena: a continuous, though somewhat decelerated process of economic growth on the one hand, and a prolonged deflation and recurrent economic fluctuations on the other. It is, however, also a phase exhibiting a number of unique social, political, and cultural features, and may therefore also serve as a time unit for a general and not only an economic history of the period."[12]

In fact, the reality of the so-called Great Depression as a distinct economic period has been severely challenged and continues to be debated. Undoubtedly, the term may be misleading when applied to the years between 1873 and 1896, clearly too long a period to be considered a single slump in a regular business cycle. Furthermore, by most economic indices this was not a period of continuous depression. In economic terms it could only be defined as a secular trend, a long economic wave primarily associated with falling prices and declining interest rates. Such a long wave should not be confused with the cyclical booms and slumps occurring along with it. The long-wave phenomenon affected the persistence and severity of the short-term cyclical depressions within it, but it was by no means identical with them.[13] For the sake of economic accuracy the whole period should perhaps be called the "Great Deflation."[14] But in the wider context of German history the old term has its uses and justification. The long-term economic trend was accompanied by a unique state of mind, and it is the

[12] For the methodological, economic, and historical justification of the use of the term "Great Depression" see the discussion in H. Rosenberg, *Grosse Depression*, pp. 1-57, and the titles cited by him. See also Kocka, "Theorien in der Sozial- und Gesellschaftsgeschichte," pp. 25-27, and his "Recent Historiography of Germany and Austria." The term has been applied also in the study of British economic history. See especially W.W. Rostow, *British Economy of the 19th Century* and the earlier article by H.L. Beales, "The Great Depression in Industry and Trade." See also G.D.H. Cole, *British Trade and Industry*, and a host of articles in recent years challenging the reality of a "Great Depression." A summary of the argument and a useful bibliography appear in S.B. Saul, *The Myth of the Great Depression*. For a more balanced view, however, see Peter Mathias, *The First Industrial Nation*, pp. 395 ff.

[13] For a lucid summary of the economic meaning and usefulness of these terms, see Alvin H. Hansen, *Business Cycles and National Income*.

[14] See the comments in Hans Rosenberg, *Die Weltwirtschaftskrise 1857-1859*, pp. XIII-XIV, XXV.

social and sociopsychological dimension that imparts additional connotations to the term "Great Depression." Thus, regardless of the verdict of economists as to the precise nature of the period, it continues to provide a meaningful and convenient time unit for the study of German social history. The Great Depression in its cyclical ups and downs helps to define and explain changes in the social structure of Germany at the time, the functioning of its political system, and the action and mentality of the groups operating within it. It defines a crucial phase in the prolonged process of modernization in Germany, a phase in which ultimately the uniqueness of the emerging state and society was shaped and manifested. The overlapping of a continuing process of economic, social, political, and cultural change with a period of economic hardship and insecurity following the unification of Germany and the political transformations associated with it all combined to endow this period with particular significance in the history of modern Germany.

The years between 1873 and 1896 were punctuated by three cycles of depression and recovery. The period included three short-term slumps (1873-1879; 1882-1886; 1890-1895-96) and two periods of recovery (1879-1882; 1886-1890).[15] For the sake of simplification, and because of the relative mildness of the cyclical movement during the 1880s, the period may also be divided into two severe depressions, separated by a quiet period of recovery, slow at first and then accelerated. These, and not only the long-term period of deflation, provide the general framework within which the development of German society should be analyzed. When social and political criteria are introduced, a roughly corresponding periodization is evident. However, while recurrent economic slumps differ greatly in intensity but are essentially similar in character, social and political events never reproduce themselves in the same

[15] H. Rosenberg, *Grosse Depression*, p. 53; Wehler, *Das Deutsche Kaiserreich*, pp. 41-48, and the introduction to his *Bismarck und der Imperialismus*.

way. Memories, accumulated experience, and the arbitrary nature of the life of both leaders and followers operate to break the neat pattern. If the Great Depression is to serve as a meaningful unit for the history of German society and not merely as a tool for economic analysis, this variation must be taken into account. As the economic prosperity of the foundation years was suddenly brought to a halt, reactions developed only slowly, following the economic manifestations with a considerable lag. In 1890, however, when a severe depression recurred, the lag was considerably shorter, and throughout that cyclical downward movement of the economy, social and political responses were prompt and radical. Ideational and organizational tools were by then available for diagnosing the difficulties, suggesting remedies, and pressing government agencies for action on a host of particular demands. Economic and political fluctuations now reinforced each other, accounting for the militant and often hysterical nature of the first half of the 1890s.

Within this overall framework this study isolates for investigation the social group history of the small master artisans in Germany, and the development of their particular version of popular antimodernism. The masters had had a long history of social and economic "declines." It is, therefore, understandable that they did not immediately recognize the process of modernization for what it actually was. Material difficulties were viewed as yet another temporary crisis and part of the normal but expected fluctuation of the traditional economy. Even the growing estrangement between masters and men was initially regarded as the continuation of a long trend, which might still be reversed.[16] Circumstances, however, were becoming very different as modernization proceeded and acquired additional dimensions. Economic hardship was now the outcome of deep structural changes, unlikely to be reversed. Social strains, familiar as they might have seemed, were aggravated and

[16] See the section on 1848-49 in chap. 3.

made permanent. What was vaguely suspected in the pre-March era became only slowly evident by the end of the boom period in the early 1870s. It took a period of great hope ending in a final blow, however, to bring home the character of the change to the consciousness of many Germans. It took a crisis to make modernization an undeniable reality even for those who directly participated in bringing it about. The master-artisans' antimodernism then gradually emerged. Between 1873 and 1879 old conceptions, beliefs, and alliances were abandoned. Following a period of experimentation and uncertainty during the 1880s, the masters' group consciousness and their hostility to modernity and to the forces that supported and benefited from it were finally shaped during the crisis years of the early 1890s.

The cumulative effect of the various pressures experienced by the small master artisans in Germany during the Great Depression left them with an increasingly acute sense of isolation. On the economic level, this effect was felt as the experience of men left behind by events, pushed from a central into a relatively less important role. On the social level, it was the result of a break between the masters and all the groups most closely associated with them. Suffering a loss of social status and prestige, the masters resented being pushed to the fringe of the new society, left unaided to fend for themselves under increasingly unfavorable circumstances. On the political level, despite a growing reliance upon conservative groups and the bureaucracy, the masters remained essentially alienated from all the political forces in the Reich. It was this overall sense of isolation and lack of belonging that bred their hostility to modernity. Their generalized resentment sprang from a deep sense of collective loneliness.

Parallels to the difficulties faced by small master artisans and their peculiar type of defense and reaction are not difficult to find in other places on the continent. The Austrian experience provides a particularly extreme version of some features of the German.[17] In France, too, since the small artisans had emerged as an active political force toward the end of the nineteenth century, they often displayed tendencies reminiscent of the German antimodern movement.[18] Across the channel, however, an appropriate analogy is sought in vain. There was no "artisan question" in England. In the second quarter of the nineteenth century, the master artisans as a distinct social group do not seem to have existed there at all. While there is no attempt here to offer a full comparison between developments in England and in Germany, a comparative perspective is employed in order to gain a better understanding of the German case. Through it a rough model of two divergent developments emerges. This bipolar scheme represents an undoubtedly simplified view of social reality in both countries, but has proven useful for isolating the major factors that contributed to the emergence of popular antimodernism in one country and not in another, in some regions and not in others, at certain times and not at others. It may thus enhance the under-

[17] It is discussed with much insight in the little known volume by Heinrich Waentig, *Gewerbliche Mittelstandspolitik*. See also H. Rosenberg, *Grosse Depression*, pp. 227-252.

[18] The French handicraft masters played an important role in the French Revolution as well as in the revolutions of 1830 and 1848. See Albert Soboul, *Les sans-culottes parisiens en l'an II*, and its abridged English version *The Parisian Sans Culottes and the French Revolution 1793-4*; George Rudé, *The Crowd in the French Revolution*, especially part 2, and *The Crowd in History*, especially chaps. 6-8. During the last two decades of the ninteenth century the French masters began to show signs of a shift to the extreme right, and their organized movement in the twentieth century was not unlike its German equivalent. For an insight into this issue see Wilhelm Lexis, *Gewerkvereine und Unternehmerverbände in Frankreich*; D.R. Watson, "The Nationalist Movement in Paris 1900-1906," in *The Right in France 1890-1919. Three Studies*, ed. David Shapiro; Stanley Hoffmann, *Le Mouvement Poujade* and "Paradoxes of the French Political Community," in his *In Search of France*; George Lavau, "Les Classes moyennes et la Politique," in *Parties politiques et Classes sociales en France*, ed. Maurice Duverger, pp. 49-54; and Lipset, *Political Man*, pp. 154-165.

standing of antimodernism as a social and political force in Germany and elsewhere during the late nineteenth century, as well as during the era of European fascism and up to the present.

The Master Artisans: A Preliminary Sketch

During the last quarter of the nineteenth century, the small master artisans conceived of themselves as a separate social group and were generally acknowledged as such, explicitly or implicitly, by their contemporaries.[19] Indeed, throughout the latter part of the nineteenth century the existence of the small master craftsmen as a unique social element seems to have been undisputed. The Handwerkerstand (artisans' estate) was a subject of investigation, social policy, and legislation. It was dealt with in speeches and public lectures, in political and scientific journals, in books and propaganda pamphlets. The Handwerkerfrage (artisan question) was repeatedly in the headlines. It was endlessly debated in the Reichstag. It preoccupied the federal Reich government as well as the various state legislatures and the local bureaucracies. Political leaders of all colorings were busy making promises, offering plans, and criticizing each other's proposals for the Handwerker.

Contemporaries, however, devoted little or no attention to the task of explicitly defining the group with which they were concerned. The problem only arose when for legal, institutional, or statistical purposes a distinction had to be made between master artisans and industrialists, or between a craft workshop and a factory. Definitions then were based on such characteristics as the use of skilled labor in the handicraft workshop, the location on the premises of a complete production process, distribution of finished articles made to order within a limited local market, the close

[19] For stylistic purposes the terms small masters, masters, small master artisans, master craftsmen, and small handicraft masters, are used here interchangeably.

connection between the master's shop and his family, and the size of his enterprise.[20] Repeated efforts to revise these definitions attest to their unsatisfactory nature. The continuing process of industrial development and social change produced a great number of borderline cases and frequently forced legislators and administrators to redraw the lines of division.

Yet, outside the legal sphere or when statistical precision was not required, contemporaries apparently had little difficulty identifying the small masters or distinguishing between them and the new industrialists on the one hand, and journeymen and hired workers on the other. Even the organizers of and the participants in the research project of the Verein für Sozialpolitik (VSP, Association for Social Policy), by far the most comprehensive investigation into the conditions of the handicraft trades at the time, virtually ignored the problem.[21] The majority of the individual studies in this large collective enterprise dealt as a matter of course with the economically independent craft workshops and with their owners. Wage-earning craftsmen and masters engaged in domestic industries or in the newly built factories were mentioned mainly for purposes of comparison, or in the context of evaluating the viability of various traditional forms of handicraft production.[22] Moreover, the task of the VSP was considerably simplified by the investigators' explicit emphasis on the fate of the *historical* crafts. Of the 112 individual studies in the project, well over half were devoted to such typical old crafts as carpentry, shoemaking, locksmithery and tailoring, the building crafts, basket and

[20] See Adolph Noll, *Sozio-ökonomischer Strukturwandel des Handwerks*, pp. 27-34.

[21] *Untersuchungen über die Lage des Handwerks in Deutschland.*

[22] See e.g. Franz von Schönebeck, "Die Lage des kleingewerbes in der Kölner Schreinerei," *Schriften* 62 (1895); Paul Voigt, "Das Tischlergewerbe in Berlin," *Schriften* 65 (1895); Hermann Rind, "Die Fleischerei in Leipzig," *Schriften* 68 (1897); Nicolaus Geissenberger, "Die Schuhmacherei in Leipzig und Umgegend," *Schriften* 63 (1895).

barrel making, baking, and butchering. Together they were considered the representatives of a unique economic sector, distinct from both industry and commerce, worthy of special concern and investigation. The Handwerkerstand, a term that had earlier included small and large master artisans together with their journeymen and apprentices, was by the late nineteenth century applied exclusively to men who owned and managed small traditionally run workshops.

The long and complex history of the handicraft masters as a social group, beginning at the time of the medieval guilds, did not seem to obstruct the clear view of contemporaries. For a historian, however, intuition is hardly adequate to the task of defining a group unique to an alien though not so distant a world. It is hoped that a characterization of the small masters as a group will emerge at the end of this investigation, but clarity requires some kind of working definition that avoids both the rigidity of legal and statistical criteria and the vagueness of everyday usage.

Who were the master artisans in the small German town during the last quarter of the nineteenth century? The baker, red faced and plump, sold small buns and fresh-smelling bread at his street-corner shop, while his well-dressed and well-fed wife handed the customers bits of town gossip to go with their oven-hot pastries. The blacksmith at the edge of town welcomed travelers, directing them to appropriate lodgings while he repaired their carriages or shod their horses. The cobbler worked away in the darkness of his cellar flat while his wife rose early every morning to do the laundry for some wealthy households in town. The master brick layer employed a team of five—his son included—prospering with the continuous growth of his native town. The young basket maker, who married the daughter of his own old master and inherited his shop, was well acquainted with the old man's stories about the glories of the past, but knew only poverty himself. The tailor, producing suits to order, was in frequent touch with local bigwigs who disdained ready made garments from the large new stores in the nearby city.

Such an account immediately suggests the source of our difficulty in attempting to move from an impressionistic to a precise definition of the master artisans as a group—the great heterogeneity that characterized them. The Handwerkerstand as it was conceived by the Handwerker and their contemporaries alike did not simply include all owners of small industrial workshops; nor did it include all who possessed a handicraft skill.[23] It was composed of a specific segment among the trained masters of traditional crafts, who were all normally self-employed, and who consciously preserved a common tradition, a common life style, and a common set of social and moral values.

For a handicraft to be considered traditional, it had to be not just an old craft, but to have preserved old methods of production and operation. Throughout the nineteenth century and well into the twentieth, crafts such as shoemaking, carpentry, smithery of various kinds, tailoring, bookbinding, and baking all fulfilled these two essential requirements. In a typical artisan shop in one of these trades, the master was the owner and manager, the supervisor, and the best craftsmen. His few helpers possessed some degree of vocational training normally acquired through the traditional institution of apprenticeship. They worked with little or no machine power, and only a very elementary division of labor. Ideally, the master himself purchased raw or partly finished materials and handled at least some aspects of the marketing. He had constant personal contact with his employees as well as with his customers. With the first he sought to establish a set of relationships patterned after the family, in which he was both father and undisputed master. The latter he encountered daily within a small community and lim-

[23] For studies based on definitions that come closer to identifying handicrafts with the statistical and legal category of "small business" see e.g. Wolfram Fischer, "Die Rolle des Kleingewerbes," and Noll, *Sozio-ökonomischer Strukturwandel*, pp. 27-34.

ited local market. The whole operation entailed a minimal amount of capital and little or no credit facilities. For the late nineteenth century, however, these characteristics delineate only an "ideal type" artisan's workshop. Few masters managed to preserve all these characteristics. In most cases, some features of the typical craft workshop were retained, while others were completely or partially transformed.

Of approximately 3 million people counted by the official German census of 1895 as self-employed owners of small enterprises, only two-thirds were listed in the "mining, industry and building" section.[24] Among these, many were employed in trades that did not belong to the traditional crafts—such as the modern electrical and chemical industries, a host of new mechanical trades, and historical crafts that by the early 1870s had already undergone a transformation that had entirely obliterated their traditional features. This last category included some of the ceramic crafts, printing, soap making, and the major textile trades of spinning and weaving.[25] It may be assumed with some confidence that by the last quarter of the nineteenth century the majority of the men employed in these crafts were no longer a part of the traditional artisan estate.

In 1895, only between 1.2 million and 1.5 million men could still be counted in Germany as self-employed masters of traditional crafts. Over half of them, however, resided in rural areas.[26] Traditionally, town masters considered rural

[24] *St.d.R.* 119, p. 16*. As defined by the German censuses of the nineteenth century, small business included all industrial and commercial enterprises with less than five employees. This limit was used rather consistently until well into the twentieth century, when small business came to mean all enterprises with less than ten employees. Business size can also be determined on the basis of invested capital or volume of production. However, as long as the use of machines was limited, these different criteria were likely to produce similar figures, and the number of employees was in any event by far the simplest measure. Nevertheless, the line of division between small and medium-sized businesses remains partly arbitrary.

[25] See the section on the growth of large-scale industry in chap. 1.

[26] *Erhebung über die Verhältnisse im Handwerk*, part 1. See also

craftsmen intruders and violators of the urban guild monopolies. For all practical purposes, these men were and remained an integral part of the rural, agricultural scene. They often possessed small plots of land and normally developed greater empathy for their peasant neighbors than for their vocational counterparts in town. Moreover, toward the end of the nineteenth century, small peasants frequently took on some handicraft trade in order to supplement their incomes and occupy themselves profitably during the long winter months. The distinction between an artisan with an agricultural sideline and a peasant with a handicraft sideline became increasingly blurred.[27]

Master artisans did not take part in the general migration from country to town characteristic of the time in proportion to their numbers. While between 1858 and 1895 the rural population in Germany declined by one-third, the percentage of rural masters within the general master-artisan population remained unchanged. Their numerical significance in the countryside grew throughout the period. As late as 1895, Germany had 26.7 masters per 1,000 city dwellers and 28.3 per 1,000 country dwellers.[28] Masters in rural areas knew little of the experience of their colleagues in the rapidly growing towns and large urban centers. Changes in the economy, in the character and size of the market, and in the techniques and organization of production had a delayed impact on the rural crafts. In addition, the process of social change and politicization affecting the traditionally apolitical social elements in the towns, reached the rural population only after a considerable lag. The hardships of master craftsmen in the rural environment still had at that time little direct relevance to the over-

---

Wilhelm Stieda, "Die Innungsenquete," *JNS*, p. 7, and Paul Voigt, "Die Hauptergebnisse der neuesten deutschen Handwerkerstatistik von 1895," pp. 1,007 ff.

27 See Hermann Kellenbenz, ed., *Agrarisches Nebengewerbe und Formen der Reagravisierung*, especially pp. 29-37; 155-194.

28 Voigt, "Die Hauptergebnisse," p. 1,009.

whelming problems of modernization and social change the urban masters were forced to tackle.

Excluding the rural masters brings the number of men with whom this study is directly concerned to between 600,000 and 800,000. By 1895 they constituted about 3 percent of the entire labor force in Germany and almost 10 percent of the men engaged in industrial production. With their families they comprised just under 5 percent of the total population.[29] They were mainly employed in the clothing and woodworking trades, in food production and leather work, in the light metal and building crafts.

An enormous variety of skills, working conditions, and personal affluence prevailed among these men. Annual incomes and the property owned by the masters varied greatly both within and between the crafts. Some masters were employers, others were individual self-employed men. Some barely managed to hire one or two trained employees, others gradually enlarged their shops and occasionally progressed to become medium-sized or even big industrial entrepreneurs. Some lived on the edge of starvation, others owned fashionable homes and employed a staff of domestic servants. Some had little shops attached to their living quarters, others had to travel far to their shops, and still others hired out their skills and needed no workshop at all. Furthermore, there was wide variation in the work itself. The watchmaker, concentrating on delicate precision work had a completely different experience from that of a mason or a carpenter at a building site. The butcher's daily routine resembled that of a grocer far more than that of a blacksmith or shoemaker. The bookbinder's customers and the range of his personal interests were in all probability fundamentally

[29] This is calculated on the basis of 4.0 as the average number of people in the handicraft master's family, but it is perhaps a slight overestimation. Gustav Schmoller in his *Zur Geschichte der deutschen Kleingewerbe* used an average family size of 4.1 (p. 95). The average family size of masters, however, was on the decline. For a sample of traditional crafts it was calculated from the *St.d.R.* 2 and 102, to be 3.6 for 1882 and 3.4 for 1895.

different from the tailor's or the basketmaker's. Despite this diversity, however, the bonds that united the small handicraft masters proved powerful enough to overcome divisive forces. By the late decades of the nineteenth century master artisans became increasingly self-conscious as a social group. A common historical memory, a similar life experience, an identical set of social and moral values, and the same real and imaginary enemies all helped to bring together rich and poor masters from various regions and crafts. Their group was often divided against itself, but it never entirely lost cohesiveness and a unique identity.

Perhaps the most powerful link among the small urban craftmasters was the consciousness of their shared past. The memory of the Guild Age was a vital factor in making them into a modern social group. This collective memory had little to do with the actual history of the craft guilds. It was a mythical view of a historical period relegated to an indefinite past. It was faithfully preserved by the master craftsmen, repeated endlessly in public lectures and at artisans' clubs, reiterated in numerous articles in their newspapers and at practically all their local and national meetings. Almost without exception the national congresses of master artisans held during the later decades of the nineteenth century opened with addresses wholly or partially devoted to this topic. Curiously every generation of artisans during the nineteenth century claimed that the ruin of this ideal past was part of its unique experience. Even at the end of the century the masters still insisted that they had experienced something of that glorious time in their youth.[30] This imagined memory was eventually turned into a powerful ideological and organizational tool by men probably deluded by their own propaganda. It may have had little to do with their historical past, but it certainly became a fundamental instrument for shaping their future.

The memory of the Golden Age of the guilds was not

[30] This is well described in Stadelmann and Fischer, *Die Bildungswelt*, pp. 59-61.

restricted to master craftsmen, but was accepted and shared by other social groups in Germany. People of different political persuasions, seeking to exploit the memory for different purposes, drew different and often contrary lessons from it. The glorification of the German past had been an intellectual fashion among the romantics of the first half of the nineteenth century. From mid-century on it had gained new and increasing significance as a propaganda device. Finally, it was used by a conservative elite in an effort to bring nonaristocratic social elements into the conservative political camp.[31] The memory of the Golden Age became part of a general national tradition, and the guilds, as institutions that had transcended the boundaries of the individual German states, served as an instructive component in a newly written national history, so important for the creation and preservation of unity within the new Bismarckian Reich.

Literature on the old guilds was abundant throughout the second half of the nineteenth century, but it was Richard Wagner's *Meistersinger* that was the most successful and popular expression of the public sentiment for the medieval guilds.[32] The work depicted the master handicraftsmen of Nuremberg as prosperous respectable men and most significantly as representatives of a culture of excellence and talent. In his little cobbler shop Hans Sachs, the shoemaker-poet, not only practiced a craft, but also refined his poetic talent and improved his performance skills. With his fellow masters he moved confidently and proudly among journeymen and apprentices, as well as in the company of princes and noblemen. It was dignity of this sort the nineteenth century masters tried so desperately to protect, and its impending loss bound them together.

[31] See the section on social conservatism in chap. 7 and the section on the antimodern ideal in chap. 11. Also Hans-Jürgen Puhle, *Agrarische Interessenpolitik und preussischer Konservatismus*, pp. 98-110.

[32] First published in Mainz in 1862.

The master-artisans' sense of community was further enhanced by the similarity of their life stories. They all engaged in production or in services that required a certain level of manual skill. The diversity of these skills did not decrease the affinity among their practitioners. The various skills were acquired in a similar, if not identical, way; they all required a similar kind and level of education, and they eventually produced a basic resemblance in the overall life experience of the individuals who acquired and practiced them. An 1885 study conducted in Mannheim by the Baden Ministry of Internal Affairs provides some instructive details on the degree of uniformity among the masters in town with respect to education and personal history.[33] Of those who answered the government questionnaires only about 5 percent had had any general education beyond the Volksschule, and only 10 percent had attended vocational schools for a period of between one and three years.[34] Sporadic reports in the literature confirm the impression that the master artisans were on the whole poorly educated. The statisticians in charge of the Mannheim study complained that the majority of masters had been incapable of answering elementary questions concerning their finances because of their ignorance of accounting and bookkeeping.[35] All the reporting artisans in Mannheim, however, had had a formal apprenticeship training for no less than two and no more than four years. At the end of a century of modernization and rapid industrial development the prevalence of the apprenticeship system was still confirmed by all official surveys and academic investigations.[36]

The significance of the apprenticeship years as an element

[33] *Erhebung über die Lage des Kleingewerbes in Baden—Amtsbezirk Mannheim 1885.*

[34] These figures are based on the data provided by the individual questionnaires reprinted in the *Mannheim Erhebung.*

[35] Ibid., p. 12.

[36] E.g., Stieda, "Die Innungsenquete," p. 26, and Voigt, "Die Hauptergebnisse," p. 1,022.

of social cohesion was in providing young masters-to-be with a prolonged training under similar conditions, regardless of craft. The experience of a fourteen-year-old apprentice in a shoemaker's shop was essentially very much like the experience of another in a carpenter's workshop. They were probably both overworked, harshly disciplined, and strictly supervised by the master and his wife. Both apprentices were in an equivocal position in the masters' households, being sons and strangers, workers and servants at the same time. This experience provided the first element in the development of their sense of affinity and common destiny.

Traditionally, the young artisans had been expected to spend a number of years as "tramping journeymen" before they could establish themselves as independent masters. It is difficult to assess the prevalence of this custom during the last quarter of the nineteenth century, especially as the distinction between journeymen furthering their education and skilled artisans seeking employment was easily blurred.[37] According to the Mannheim study, the great majority of the practicing masters in town had spent several years, often as many as ten, wandering from town to town, occasionally even outside Germany. By the time they acquired their own shops very few of them were under thirty, and all had spent the crucial years of their lives being trained and educated by older master craftsmen.

The socialization of the young artisan was a remarkably effective process. The combination of vocational training and general education gave it a unique quality. At the master's home the apprentice and young journeyman acquired not only a handicraft skill but a multitude of social and moral values. This education operated as the major element in perpetuating the life style and norms characteristic of the small master-artisan community. Above all, the new generation of masters was taught to value the "inde-

[37] On this problem see E.J. Hobsbawm, "The Tramping Artisans," in *Labouring Men*, pp. 41-74, and the bibliography cited there.

pendence" they looked forward to.[38] To begin with, the term simply indicated the economic position of the master artisan, his ownership of his own means of production, his relative prosperity, and his personal responsibility in taking decisions pertaining to various aspects of his economic activity. Toward the end of the nineteenth century this "independence" also came to reflect his superior personal character and his role as a stable and reliable citizen. It was by then not merely a descriptive term but a social and moral ideal, associated with the master's position as producer, educator, and head of a family.

The requirements of vocational training enforced by tradition and the limitations of the market created the peculiar age structure of the master-artisan population. By 1882 only 17 percent of the traditional handicraft masters were under the age of 30. In some crafts this figure was as low as 10 percent. Most numerous was the 30-to-40 age group, which included almost 30 percent of the masters in the traditional crafts as a whole. At the same time close to 10 percent of the masters were over 60. The peculiarities of the master-artisan age structure in comparison with other sectors of the working male population in Germany can be observed in the following chart.[39]

Independent master artisans were more likely to be married than other men in the same age category. In 1882 over 80 percent of the masters engaged in typical traditional crafts were married men, and in several trades the percentage was as high as 90.[40] At the same time the average

[38] For the following discussion see especially Noll, *Sozio-ökonomischer Strukturwandel*, pp. 113-118.

[39] The data for these diagrams were collected from *St.d.R.* 2 and 103. The diagram depicting the age structure of traditional handicrafts masters is based on data for the following sixteen crafts: silversmiths, goldsmiths, coppersmiths, locksmiths, cartwrights, bookbinders, saddlers, carpenters, barrel makers, basket makers, bakers, butchers, tailors, shoemakers, bricklayers, and glaziers.

[40] Calculated from *St.d.R.* 2, for the crafts listed in n. 39 above.

A Comparison of the Age Structure of Master Artisans and Other Workers in Germany, 1895

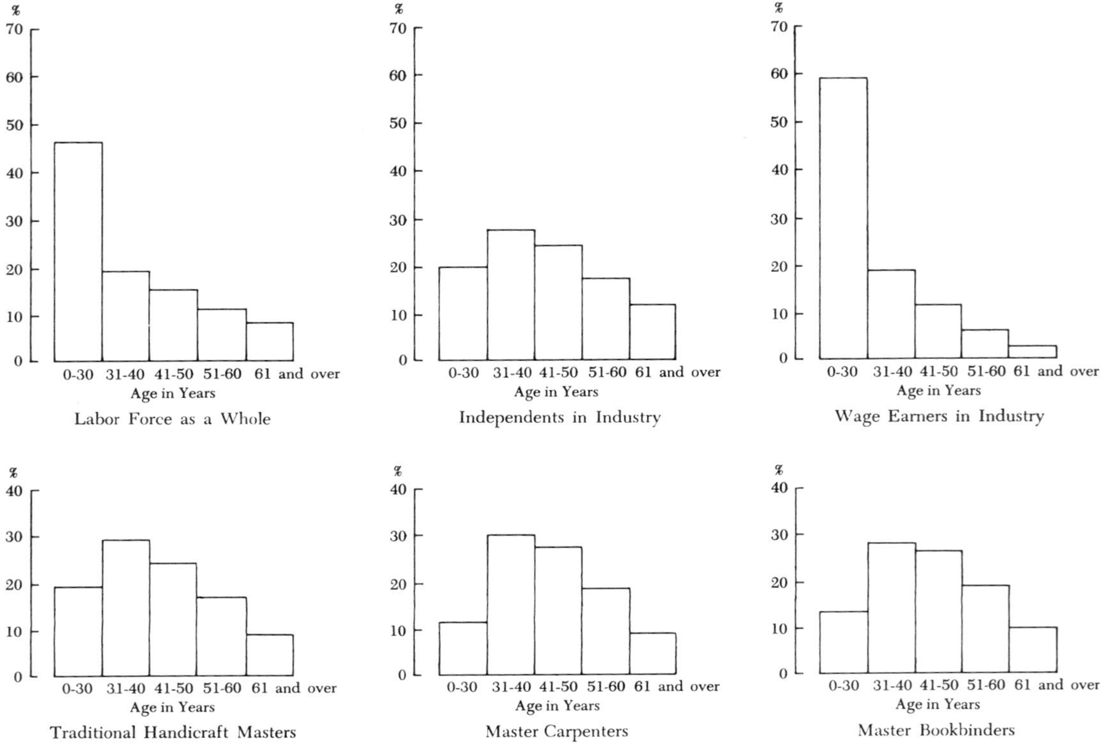

number of dependents for every master within a sample of sixteen traditional handicrafts was 2.6. A single master or a childless married one was indeed a rarity. The family unit was a necessary complement to the traditional craft workshop, and the masters attached ideological and cultural values to it.[41] All the components of this social framework were deemed essential for the proper functioning of workshop and home alike, and indispensable for the preservation of the masters' cherished values.

The literature of the late nineteenth century describing the archetypical master's home naturally tends to obliterate the diversity and complexity of real conditions.[42] Nevertheless, certain traits appear in this literature with unfailing consistency, thereby gaining a measure of credibility. The master-artisan's home is invariably described as modest but impeccably clean and orderly. Within this environment devoutness, obedience, self-discipline, honesty, and frugality appeared to have been strictly observed. These virtues were probably as rare among small masters as among other men, but if literary descriptions do not depict the reality of the masters' life, they at least suggest the qualities most highly esteemed by them.

As late as the turn of the nineteenth century the masters

[41] *Protokoll über die Verhandlungen des Handwerkertages, 1892, Berlin,* p. 148. See also Peter Laslett, *The World We Have Lost,* chap. 1.

[42] For plays and novels dealing with master artisans see e.g., Max Kretzer, *Meister Timpe* (1888), describing three generations of artisans and the tragic disintegration of their family; Ernst von Wildenbruch, *Meister Balzer* (1893), a play about an honest watchmaker in competition with a new local factory; Ernst Eckstein, *Familie Hartwig*; Wolfgang Kirschbaum, *Auf der Walze*; Karl Schieffer, *Der Junge Tobias*; and the autobiography by Fritz Rhode, *Vom Lehrling zum Obermeister.* See also the stories in the *Gartenlaube*, and in the literary supplements of the *DHZ*, 1894-97. Some details and appreciation of this literature can be found in Cecil E. Roberts, "Handwerk und Handwerker in der deutschen Erzählung" and Ernest K. Bramsted, *Aristocracy and the Middle-Classes in Germany*, pp. 200-209.

continued to emphasize their old ethical code, anachronistic as it was. No major article in the masters' journals, and no speech at their national and regional meetings failed to mention the significance of Ehrbarkeit and Tüchtigkeit, Standesehre, Zucht, Ruhe and Ordnung (respectability and solidity, the honor of the estate, discipline, peace and order). To these were occasionally added other qualities, all essential for the healthy development of the individual as well as for the orderly and beneficial evolution of human society in general. They were all endowed by the masters with a significance transcending their strict meaning and were made to appear highly interrelated. An article in the masters' Berlin journal for instance, dwelt at length on the role of punctuality in the development of normal, peaceful, and independent men, and hastened to stress its relationship to conscientiousness and a sense of responsibility, and its significance for a life of order and freedom.[43] Another article, devoted to the virtues of skilled labor, made the master-artisans' finer workmanship a basis for their claim to a position of social and spiritual superiority.[44] Handicraft as such was identified by the masters as their loftiest value: "Handwerk is freedom, morality, and justice," exclaimed their newspaper. "Those who stand against Handwerk are in fact standing against freedom, against morality, and against justice."[45]

The masters thus characterized their vocation and their particular life style as the guarantee of an honest and free existence. Their rhetorical style and the exaggeration associated with it must be understood as their reaction to increasing social pressure, which threatened their cherished values, and to the growing difficulty of protecting a unique cultural environment against the forces of modernization. Indeed, as these values ceased to be shared by society as a whole, they became increasingly more significant as a cohesive factor among the masters, who saw themselves as the last protec-

[43] *DHZ*, February 10, 1894. [44] Ibid., April 28, 1894.
[45] Ibid., March 17, 1894.

tors of those universal ethical truths. They attempted to preserve them against the growing secularization, the declining influence of the old, the continual attacks on the family structure, and the growing demands for more freedom and greater equality.

ONE

THE IMPACT OF INDUSTRIALIZATION

Demarcating the Task

It is important to bear in mind that the economic position of the small independent master artisans in Germany was often unsatisfactory, even before the onset of industrialization. Recent historical work has shown conclusively that the celebrated prosperity of craftsmen during the late medieval period came to an end as early as the sixteenth century.[1] Thereafter members of the guilds and other artisans, both masters and wage-earning craftsmen, experienced a continuous, though uneven decline in material well-being. A rough estimate of the real income of artisans in various regions of Germany over a long period has shown that the average income of a skilled craftsman declined by about two-thirds between the late fifteenth and the early nineteenth centuries.[2] Naturally, the figures vary from craft to craft and from one region to another. Moreover, the overall decline in income, and its various social consequences, no doubt affected master artisans and hired hands unequally, although often the available data make it impossible to distinguish between the two categories. Local studies invariably confirm the general statistical impression: segments of the master-artisan population were among the poorest ele-

[1] See Wilhelm Abel, "Zur Ortsbestimmung des Handwerks," pp. 48-81. See also his "Der Pauperismus in Deutschland," pp. 284-298, and his *Massenarmut und Hungerkrisen*. Also see the collection of essays by members of the Seminar für Handwerkswesen at the University of Göttingen: Wilhelm Abel et al., *Handwerksgeschichte in neuer Sicht*, and the following monographs: Karl Heinrich Kaufhold, *Das Handwerk der Stadt Hildesheim im 18. Jahrhundert*; Klaus Assmann and Gerhard Stavenhagen, *Handwerkereinkommen am Vorabend der Industriellen Revolution*.

[2] Wilhelm Abel, "Neue Wege der Handwerksgeschichtlichen Forschung," in Abel et al., *Handwerksgeschichte*, p. 22.

ments in Germany many decades before the beginning of effective industrialization. In the first half of the nineteenth century a great number of masters were hardly better off than their impoverished wage-earning assistants, and were frequently recipients of poor relief and charity[3]

The poverty of artisans during the pre-March years was correctly identified by contemporaries as one of the many distressing aspects of the much-discussed problem of "pauperism."[4] Indeed, the prosperity of the craft economy was then still directly dependent on the fluctuations of agricultural prices. It was the crisis of the preindustrial, and primarily agricultural, economy that caused the impoverishment of so many master craftsmen during the first half of the nineteenth century. The large-scale unemployment, underemployment, and unprofitable employment throughout the country had little to do with the slow and as yet mostly localized changes in the industrial sector. But even at that early period the prevalent economic hardships were not entirely unrelated to the approaching industrial revolution. They clearly showed the inability of the economy to cope with at least one aspect of modern economic growth—the rapid and continuous increase of population.[5] Within

[3] See Kaufhold, *Das Handwerk*, and Assmann and Stavenhagen *Handwerkereinkommen*, as well as articles by Arno Steinkamp and Martha Scale in Abel et al., *Handwerksgeschichte*, pp. 116-141 and 173-201.

[4] On pauperism and the condition of the various segments of the working population in the pre-March period see Carl Jantke and Dietrich Hilger, eds., *Die Eigentumslosen*, especially pp. 7-48; 223-313; Werner Conze, "Vom 'Pöbel' zum 'Proletariat' "; Wolfram Fischer, "Soziale Unterschichten im Zeitalter der Frühindustrialisierung"; see also Fischer's "Innerbetrieblicher und sozialer Status der frühen Fabrikarbeiterschaft," and directly related to our topic, Fischer's "Das deutsche Handwerk in den Frühphasen der Industrialisierung." On the preindustrial causes of pauperism in the early nineteenth century, see especially Abel's *Massenarmut und Hungerkrisen*, pp. 54-76.

[5] See Walther G. Hoffmann, *Das Wachstum der deutschen Wirtschaft*, pp. 172-173. Some aspects of the problem are dealt with in

the area of the future Reich the population grew from 25 million to over 34 million between 1817 and 1845. The annual increase between 1818 and 1825 was more then 1.3 percent, a rate achieved again only in 1890. This rate of growth in turn gave rise to an increased movement of population and to a steady, though at first slow migration into the towns. Free migration, made possible by new liberal legislation, was almost invariably accompanied by new trade laws, which were experimented with in most of the German states at the time, and which provided for free entrance into the various crafts and professions. As a result, the entire urban economy underwent far-reaching structural changes, which naturally also affected the traditional crafts.[6]

During the first half of the century, the increase in the number of handicraftsmen kept pace with, or surpassed, that of the general population. But while the number of

---

Donald G. Rohr, *The Origins of Social Liberalism in Germany*, chaps. I and II; Conze, "Vom 'Pöbel' zum 'Proletariat'"; Wolfgang Köllmann, "Industrialisierung, Binnenwanderung und 'Soziale Frage'"; see also Köllmann's "Grundzüge der Bevölkerungsgeschichte Deutschlands," and "Bevölkerung und Arbeitskräftepotential in Deutschland."

[6] See especially Karl Abrams, *Der Strukturwandel im Handwerk*, pp. 51-53. There is a long historiographical debate on the question of the changing number of handicraft masters following the introduction of industrial freedom. It is complicated by the different definitions of the term "Handwerker" and by different means of measuring the density of the artisan population. It is summarized in Friedrich Wilhelm Henning, "Die Einführung der Gewerbefreiheit und ihre Auswirkungen auf das Handwerk in Deutschland," in Abel et al., *Handwerksgeschichte*. Henning's conclusion is that in most areas there was an increase in the number of master artisans immediately following the introduction of industrial freedom, but that the major structural change in the handicrafts during the first half of the century, namely the rapid increase in the number of journeymen, was basically independent of economic policy. See also Stadelmann and Fischer, *Die Bildungswelt*, p. 110, and Reinhart Koselleck, *Preussen zwischen Reform und Revolution*, pp. 589-609. On the transformation of the old artisan estate see especially Jürgen Bergmann, "Das 'Alte Handwerk' im Übergang"; also comments in Karl Heinrich Kaufhold, "Das preussische Handwerk in der Zeit der Frühindustrialisierung."

master artisans grew by 58 percent between 1816 and 1843, the number of wage-earning handicraftsmen grew by 140 percent. The ratio between masters and men was rapidly changing, most clearly after 1830 and especially during the 1840s.[7] The easy availability of labor was particularly advantageous to prosperous, enterprising master artisans, who were thus put in a favorable position vis-à-vis their workers and did not hesitate to exploit it. But for the majority of small and individual self-employed master artisans, the growing number of workers merely meant sharper competition under increasingly harsh economic conditions.[8]

The 1840s were particularly bleak for the handicraftsmen. At a time of crop failures and trade crises, overcrowding in the crafts appears to have been truly catastrophic. The liberalized industrial regulations were repeatedly accused of generating and aggravating the crisis, while in fact the changing rate of population growth, the ongoing process of urbanization, and the slow development of a new market economy were probably responsible. With economic conditions improving after mid-century and with spreading industrialization, the material well-being of a growing segment of the population slowly improved. Poverty among artisans remained common, but their difficulties no longer aroused the same public concern. The "social question" in Germany acquired a new meaning. People were now increasingly preoccupied with what seemed the blatant consequences of industrialization, leaving relatively unheeded the more familiar difficulties of the traditional sector.

Friedrich Engels' treatise on *The Conditions of the Working Classes in England* (1844) most powerfully established the connection between industrial development and grow-

[7] Abrams, *Strukturwandel im Handwerk*, p. 55, and Henning, "Die Einführung der Gewerbefreiheit," in Abel et al., *Handwerksgeschichte*, p. 170.

[8] For the case of Berlin see Frederick D. Marquardt's "The Manual Worker in the Social Order in Berlin under the Old Regime," and his "Sozialer Aufstieg, Sozialer Abstieg und die Entstehung der Berliner Arbeiterklasse," pp. 62-77.

ing urban poverty. Whether he had indeed correctly assessed the causes of poverty and social deprivation in England is still a matter of scholarly dispute.[9] In any event, the unmistakable signs of a changing economy and society in England profoundly influenced views on the social question in Germany, even before the actual signs of industrialization were detectable there. In England, the most tangible and impressive aspect of the process of change was undoubtedly the emergence of mechanized factories. In both countries, the general public tended to see these as the fundamental cause of the entire observable spectrum of social change. The greatest public attention was focused on the evolution of a new stratum of industrial workers, employed in the new factories, and driven into scarcely habitable urban dwellings located around them. The consequent development of a powerful economic and political working-class movement captured the interest of scholars and journalists, and forced governments and bureaucracies to concern themselves with it.

Eventually, the growth of big industry came also to be blamed for the hardship of small independent artisans. Through much of the nineteenth century, economists of different schools predicted the disappearance of handicraft production under the pressure of competition from capital-intensive, rationalized, and mechanized industrial enterprises.[10] In the last decade of the century a large-scale study conducted by the Verein für Sozialpolitik was titled "An

[9] See the discussion in Abel, *Massenarmut und Hungerkrisen*, pp. 69 ff.

[10] Marx and Engels expressed this view as early as 1848 in their *Communist Manifesto*. In his pioneering economic and statistical study of small masters, *Zur Geschichte der deutschen Kleingewerbe im 19. Jahrhundert*, Schmoller also conceived of the situation of the handicrafts in terms of a severe crisis, although he gradually came to take a more optimistic view toward the end of the century. For his later view see "Was verstehen wir unter dem Mittelstande?" For further details concerning this discussion see the historiographical note in chap. 2 below.

Investigation of the Conditions of the Handicraft Trades in Germany, with Special Reference to their Competitiveness vis-à-vis Big Industry,"[11] and the debate on the fate of the master artisans was carried on in these terms well into the twentieth century.

Even in the early stages of industrialization, however, some perceptive observers, most notably Gustav Schmoller, recognized that the causes of the alleged decline of the handicrafts were not limited to, and indeed often not closely connected with, the growth of big industry. In his *Zur Geschichte der deutschen Kleingewerbe*, Schmoller set the groundwork for every future investigation of small industrial business in Germany, and specifically for the study of the handicraft economy under the impact of industrialization. He put forward a view of economic growth that is admirably close to that of modern economists. Demographic, institutional, and social factors, he believed, had combined to produce a new market economy and launch a new kind of general economic development.[12] All these factors together, and not the growth of large-scale industry alone, affected the handicraft economy, exercising a profound influence upon the material, as well as the cultural, social, and psychological development of small master craftsmen as individuals and as a group. Industrialization thus conceived was the most important and the most lasting aspect of change experienced by the small masters in Germany during the nineteenth century. It is the purpose of this chapter to examine its effect upon them in some detail.

The task is greatly complicated by the dissimilar impact industrialization made on the various crafts. No two branches were equally affected. All showed one or another

[11] Published in *Schriften*, 62-70 (Leipzig, 1895-97). A summary of the method and overall results of this voluminous study is given in Hans Grandke, "Die vom 'Verein für Sozialpolitik' Veranstalteten Untersuchungen über die Lage des Handwerks in Deutschland."

[12] This view is implicit throughout the book, but it is explicitly expressed in a brilliant paragraph on pp. 660-661.

idiosyncrasy, and none was entirely typical or representative. Any general statement about the economy of the handicrafts in the course of industrialization is bound to be disproven by counterexamples. Moreover, industrialization started at different times in the various regions of Germany, which often made for significant variations in the nature and consequences of the process.[13]

The inherent difficulties are further exacerbated by the quality of the available data. By the late nineteenth century the German statistical bureau was the best of its kind in Europe. The economic information compiled, however, dealt almost exclusively with the input side of production. Employment figures were meticulously collected, categorized, and subdivided, but data on the volume or value of production or on the movement of national, sectoral, or personal income remained scanty and inaccurate. Most discouraging for our purposes is the systematic merging of data for industry and handicrafts, an indication of the ambiguity and fluidity of these concepts at the time. It is also one of the reasons for the peculiar character of research in this area. Studies of the handicraft economy have traditionally been either too general or too specific to contribute to research in social history. Treatments of the matter have either taken the form of sweeping generalizations or concentrated on minute local details of limited historical relevance. The following discussion will attempt to avoid both extremes, endeavoring to analyze the impact of industrialization upon the economy of the crafts and the well-being of craftsmen, keeping the diversity of the situation in mind without denying its overall unity.

Changes in the Volume and Nature of Demand

Initially, the most powerful pressure upon the handicraft economy came from a growing and changing consumer de-

[13] For a case of such regional variations see Noll, *Sozio-ökonomischer Strukturwandel.*

mand. During the economic boom, which in spite of periodic setbacks lasted from 1849 to 1873, the entire German economy expanded at an accelerating rate. Perhaps the most fundamental and lasting aspect of this change was the emergence of mass consumption or what may be conceived of as the "democratization of demand."[14]

Between 1850 and 1873 the German population grew by more than 6 million. A large segment of the population that had previously been too poor to participate in the market economy was now drawn into it. With prosperity in agriculture, rural inhabitants, still constituting two-thirds of the total population, increased their expenditures beyond the minimum required to satisfy basic human needs. The lower urban strata too, under conditions of fuller and occasionally also better employment, joined the ranks of the new consumers. Individual households reduced their own productive activities, and bread baking as well as the making of clothes, leather, and wood articles at home ceased almost entirely. Households gradually became pure consumption units, and shared more fully and more actively in the market economy.

The growing demand posed a special challenge for the small producers. Liberal politicians and social reformers repeatedly urged the small masters to refrain from entering the new market and to continue engaging in so-called "quality production."[15] Although there was an absolute increase in the demand for quality goods with population growth

[14] This point was made very convincingly by Karl Bücher in his summing up of the project of the VSP on the condition of the handicrafts. See *Schriften* 76 (1898): 21 ff. Also H. Rosenberg, *Grosse Depression*, pp. 119-120.

[15] In the background of this liberal demand lay the emphasis on the education of artisans and their transformation from artisans to artists. The *Neues ABC-Buch für freisinnige Wähler*, p. 152, declared openly: "The progress of the handicrafts lies in their development into Kunstgewerbe." It was a theme repeated in speeches of Progressive candidates throughout the country. See the report in the *AHZ* (1888), and a reprint of a letter from the Progressive-party candidate in Dortmund dated March 10, 1893.

and with an improved standard of living, this was an impractical and illusionary solution. During the years of prosperity after 1850 the number of handicraftsmen grew faster than the general population. While in 1855 masters and men constituted 5.85 percent of the total population, they made up 5.95 percent of the total population in 1858 and 6.11 percent in 1861.[16] All of them could not possibly make a living from quality and artistic production. Only a fraction of the 190,000 men who in 1895 worked in small carpentry shops, or of the 320,000 small shoemakers, for example, could have been gainfully employed in producing made-to-order furniture or custom-made shoes, when half the population of 52 million still lived in rural areas, the great majority subsisting on very modest incomes.[17] In practice, for most of the handicraft trades, the expansion of the market meant an increase in the demand for cheap, low quality goods.

The craftsmen's first instinct was to fill this new demand through minimal adjustments in their workshops and the least unsettling changes in their life styles. Shoemakers, for instance, prepared cheap, standardized shoes which took the place of much of their made-to-order quality production. It was only in the late 1860s, with the introduction of a variety of new machines and the penetration of large-scale industry into this trade, that considerable structural changes had to be made.[18] But even in the early stages of industrialization, the pressure to produce quickly and cheaply must have forced greater division of labor, and changed much of

[16] Schmoller, *Zur Geschichte*, p. 94.

[17] See *St.d.R.* 119, pp. 16* ff.; W. Hoffmann, *Das Wachstum*, pp. 173, 178.

[18] On the changes in shoemaking see Friedrich Behr, *Die Volkswirtschaftliche Bedeutung der technischen Entwicklung in der Schuhindustrie* and Ernst Francke, *Die Schuhmacherei in Bayern*. Also Werner Sombart, "Verlagssystem (Hausindustrie)," *HBS*, 3rd ed.; and the monographs on the conditions of the shoemaking industry in *Schriften* 63 (1895); 65 (1895); 70 (1897); for the condition of the craft in the mid-1870s see *St.d.R.* (First Series) 34, part 5. See also Noll, *Sozio-ökonomischer Strukturwandel*, pp. 108-111.

the traditional atmosphere in the small shoemaking shops in ways that are difficult to characterize and impossible to measure.

In carpentry, to take another example, masters often preferred to restrict the range of articles produced, so as to increase productivity with a minimal shuffling of roles within their shops.[19] Thus by 1895 big-city carpenters had developed twenty-two different specializations. Their shops often produced only one item of furniture and occasionally only one model of that item. Little vocational training was needed for this type of production, and no time was spent on giving and receiving special orders, or on designing particular features of the products. While the shops seemed to operate in the traditional manner, the drastically diminished need for ingenuity and skill and the monotony of the new production process must have changed their character in many subtle ways.

To an ever growing extent restrictions on the scope of production were dictated by the market itself. The introduction of new materials, technical innovations, and new patterns of consumption severely reduced the range of handicraft activities. Thus, for example, tin plates quickly went out of fashion, and their replacement by porcelain led to a sharp contraction of the tinsmiths' market. Cartwrights and saddlers lost a substantial number of urban customers as a result of the introduction and expansion of railroads. Coopers' products ceased to be purchased for individual household use, as patterns of food consumption changed, and smaller containers, easier to handle and clean, became available.

[19] On carpentry see especially Voigt, in *Schriften* 65 (1895): 325-498, and other monographs included in the project of the VSP in *Schriften* 62 (1895); 63 (1895); 64 (1895); 69 (1897); 70 (1897). Voigt's study is by far the most ambitious and the most illuminating of the numerous investigations of local carpentry trades included in the project. Additional information on carpentry is in *St.d.R.* (First Series) 34, part 6; and the *Erhebung über Verhältnisse im Handwerk.*

Still, several trades prospered under the changing structure of the market. The sheer size of the demand for new buildings, particularly in the rapidly growing towns, could only have been a blessing for the various building crafts. Between 1886 and 1894 a spectacular construction boom caused many masters from related crafts to move from shop to building site.[20] During these years cabinetmakers often shifted to building carpentry, and urban locksmiths entered the construction business. Many small building masters enlarged their enterprises to include a variety of related crafts, thus moving away from vocational specialization and substituting for it a concentration upon supervision and management. Occasionally, a master craftsman became a building entrepreneur, engaging in a variety of subcontracting schemes and profiting from land speculation and soaring housing costs. A more lasting though less spectacular advantage accrued to town butchers from the overall prosperity and expansion of the market, as meat consumption in Germany rose rapidly during the years of the Great Depression. Between 1873 and 1896 consumption of beef, veal, and pork in Germany increased from 969,000 to 2,056,000 tons, more than doubling while the population grew by only 27 percent.[21] Since a growing segment of the population moved from rural to urban areas, a correspond-

[20] Hoffmann's production index (1913=100) shows a rise for the building industry from the low point of 29.2 in 1886 to 39.0 in 1889 and 50.3 in 1894. See *Das Wachstum*, pp. 390-394. It was especially noticeable in the large cities, such as Cologne, Leipzig, and Berlin. Between 1882 and 1895 the average number of men employed in all building trade enterprises rose from 3.3 to 5.3. With the exception of the woodworking industry, the most spectacular rise in the number of medium-sized businesses and the number of their employees, as well as in the number of large-scale enterprises occurred in the building sector. Medium-sized enterprises grew by 98.1 percent and their labor force by 114 percent, while large-sized businesses grew by 254 percent and their labor force by 264 percent; *St.d.R.* 119, pp. 9* ff. and 16* ff.

[21] W. Hoffmann, *Das Wachstum*, pp. 629 ff.

ingly larger number of people came to rely exclusively on the neighborhood butcher for their fresh meat supply.[22] Electric refrigeration, which eventually changed the patterns of the international meat market, had as yet only a limited effect on the domestic retail trade. Competition from big business in the area of meat preparation and distribution was insignificant, and the entire benefit from the growth of the market was absorbed by small, independent butchers.[23]

Only a few general statements can be ventured on the basis of these examples. Changes in demand and the democratization of consumption affected the handicraft trades in a variety of ways and cannot be labeled either an unmitigated danger, nor an undisputed blessing for the handicraft economy as a whole. They brought about a number of structural transformations in some trades and posed a new challenge to all of them. Furthermore, the consequences of the changes in demand cannot be isolated from the effects of other economic pressures the master-artisan economy had to endure, and it is to the analysis of some of these that we now turn.

The Extent and the Role of Domestic Industries

During the years of prosperity, which comprised the greater part of the third quarter of the nineteenth century, the German market expanded not only its volume but also its geographical boundaries. As early as 1834 the Zollverein had established the beginning of an internal unification of the German market. With the great expansion of railroads

22 In Leipzig, for example, there was 1 butcher for 846 men in 1875, for 1,030 men in 1882, and for 1,266 men in 1895. See Rind, "Die Fleischerei in Leipzig," *Schriften* 68 (1897): 1-2.

23 On the economic position of butchers see *Schriften* 62 (1896); 70 (1897). The percentage of small butchers with less than five employees was 99.4 in 1875, 98.2 in 1882, and 95.3 in 1895. *St.d.R.* 119, pp. 16* ff.

and the establishment of political unity, the prospect of a national economy gradually became a reality. In the main, articles ceased to be produced for a limited local demand and were seldom made with an individual customer in mind. The consumer of handicraft products became increasingly anonymous. More and more articles produced for export were made to satisfy foreign needs, and to suit unfamiliar tastes and habits. The traditional link between craftsman and customer was rapidly dissolving.

Moreover, marketing now required special skills, detailed information on the state of the market, and considerable quantities of capital. The small master was gradually forced to abandon his role as independent tradesman and to rely on middlemen and professional merchants. The pressure of having to produce greater quantities required the master's constant presence on the shop floor as a craftsman and a work supervisor, and he was often relieved to have the marketing side of his little business taken over by more experienced and better-trained men.

In some cases, master artisans who were unable to produce profitably under the new conditions transferred the focus of their activity from production to the retail shop. For many shoemakers and bookbinders, for example, the sale of factory-produced shoes or stationery articles gradually became a more important source of income than the practice of their crafts.[24] It is impossible to estimate precisely the number of small handicraft masters who became small retailers during the last quarter of the nineteenth century.

[24] For the changes in the bookbinding trade, see especially Bernhard Harms, *Zur Entwicklung der deutschen Buchbinderei.* Harms believed that the one-man bookbinding business was an entirely unviable enterprise without an adjacent stationery shop, p. 92. In Gellately's *The Politics of Economic Despair*, only the diverging interests of artisans and retailers are stressed, e.g., pp. 22-27. The line of division between the two groups, however, was always fluid and did not become more distinct even under the effects of industrialization. On this coalescence see especially John R. Hicks, *A Theory of Economic History*, pp. 28-29; 142-145.

Undoubtedly many of them continued to view themselves as master artisans even when they did not in fact practice their crafts any longer. In the majority of cases, however, if they had the choice, skilled craftsmen preferred to abandon the marketing of their wares and to concentrate on the execution and supervision of production.

The abandonment of independent marketing was made possible by, and often constituted the initial step in the evolution of the "putting-out" system.[25] This was a centuries-old form of production in certain parts of Germany, which had initially developed almost exclusively in rural areas. The land-tenure system there—in the East Elban regions for instance—created a surplus of labor on the land, and provided the merchant-entrepreneur with a docile and easily controlled labor force. During the seventeenth and eighteenth centuries, many towns were still the preserve of the guild masters, and unaffiliated merchants had to obtain special royal permits before they could operate their businesses there. It is important to remember that before the middle of the nineteenth century, the German putting-out system (Verlagssystem) was numerically significant only in a few major textile trades, such as the spinning and weav-

[25] The putting-out system, being so complex in nature and so rich in variations, presents extreme difficulties for economic historians. Indeed, there is still no comprehensive study of the development of home industry for any of the western European countries, or for the continent as a whole. Still useful, but far from sufficient are Sombart's "Verlagssystem," *HBS*, 3rd ed., and Paul Mantoux, *The Industrial Revolution in the Eighteenth Century.* Also David Landes, "Technological Change and Development in Western Europe," especially pp. 277 ff. and 348-349; and F. Mendels, "Proto-Industrialization." For specific regions in Germany see Rudolf Forberger, *Die Manufaktur in Sachsen*; Horst Krüger, *Zur Geschichte der Manufakturen und der Manufakturarbeiter in Preussen*; Eckart Schremmer, *Die Wirtschaft Bayerns*, pp. 482-501; J. Kermann, *Die Manufaktur im Rhineland*; Herbert Kisch, "The Textile Industries in Silesia and the Rhineland"; and F.W. Henning, *Die Industrialisierung in Deutschland.* See also Rolf Engelsing, *Sozial- und Wirtschaftsgeschichte Deutschlands*, pp. 152 ff.

ing of cotton, wool, and silk, in several of the clothing trades, such as hat and glovemaking, and in a few other trades in which a relatively homogeneous demand encouraged its development.

In the third quarter of the nineteenth century, the increased demand and the further enlargement of the market, the growing availability of capital, and the greater prospects for industrial profits gave an impetus to the further expansion of the putting-out system. But as the system spread and the merchant-entrepreneur became increasingly involved in production, it became more difficult to establish a precise line of division between independent and dependent master artisans.[26] In the rapidly industrializing Saxonian town of Chemnitz, for instance, master artisans in the textile trades often managed to preserve their independence during good years, but were forced to compromise during bad ones. Thus in the best years between 1800 and 1850 only a quarter of the master weavers in town were dependent, while in depression years dependent master weavers made up over one-half and up to two-thirds of the weaver population.[27]

Statistics on the development of the so-called Hausindustrie (domestic industry) are sparse and inaccurate. The term was used collectively for numerous variations on the basic form of production in which small artisans, working in their own shops, produced for commercial entrepreneurs, on whom they were dependent in various ways and degrees. Data supplied by entrepreneurs as a rule failed to match those provided by the small masters themselves. The definition of home industry remained vague, and the extent and precise nature of it virtually unknown even as late as the last quarter of the nineteenth century. At that time the putting-out system was still gaining ground, especially in some of the

[26] See the analysis in Schremmer, *Die Wirtschaft Bayerns*, pp. 472-479 and in Jürgen Kocka, *Unternehmer in der deutschen Industrialisierung*, pp. 19-34.

[27] See Rudolf Strauss, *Die Lage und die Bewegung der Chemnitzer Arbeiter*, pp. 355-356.

glassblowing and pottery crafts, in tinsmithery, blacksmithery, wagon building, various leather crafts, and barrel and basket making. Particularly susceptible to this organizational form were shoemaking, carpentry, and tailoring. The home-production workers in these three crafts increased between 1882 and 1895 by about 75 percent. In the long run, however, this form of production proved suitable only for tailoring. In carpentry and shoemaking 1895 was the peak year, and from then on domestic industry rapidly declined. Even at that time, only 4.3 percent of all carpentry shops, employing 4.4 percent of the labor in carpentry, were listed as home-industry shops, and in shoemaking only 8.3 percent of the workshops with 6.8 percent of the total labor force in the trade were classified in that category.[28]

By the last quarter of the nineteenth century the domestic system grew mainly in large urban centers, exploiting the masses of job-seeking laborers. But as late as 1895, even in Berlin, the undisputed center of the domestic system in Prussia, only 8.8 percent of the labor force was listed as engaged in home industry. Larger percentages were registered only in Krefeld (12.4) and Elberfeld (11.6), where the textile trades obstinately retained their by then traditional form.[29] On the whole, the domestic system remained strikingly undeveloped during the formative phase of German industrialization. By the end of the nineteenth century it was still common in some of the textile trades, especially in weaving, and relatively important only in the production of musical instruments, toys, some paper and straw articles, and in a variety of clothing trades.[30]

[28] *St.d.R.* 119, pp. 206* ff. For the expansion of home industries in the last decade of the nineteenth century see also Heinrich Rauchberg, "Die Berufs- und Gewerbezählung," and the various articles in *Hausindustrie und Heimarbeit in Deutschland und Oesterreich, Schriften* 87 (1899).

[29] *St.d.R.* 119, p. 271*.

[30] See table 1.1. It is important to note the varying reasons for the low percentage of home industry workers in categories A. and C. In the cotton-spinning industry, for example, over 92 percent of the

TABLE 1.1

DOMESTIC INDUSTRY IN GERMANY—1895

Trade	*No. of shops*	*No. of workers*	*% of all shops*	*% of all workers*
All industry	342,487	457,746	14.1	5.7
a. Silk spinning	1,242	1,858	85.2	28.2
Wool spinning	705	931	27.0	1.7
Cotton spinning	1,432	1,296	58.5	1.7
Silk weaving	15,349	18,656	86.9	33.3
Wool weaving	19,755	27,790	75.9	18.2
Cotton weaving	27,533	33,208	84.1	22.6
b. Glove making	3,891	3,905	64.2	23.3
Basket making	5,598	8,394	20.7	22.3
Straw-hat making	2,530	1,099	83.2	17.8
Production of musical instruments	702	1,234	33.5	16.0
Tailoring	42,942	70,316	15.2	15.8
c. Shoemaking	21,692	26,553	8.3	6.8
Bookbinding	956	2,336	7.4	4.7
Cabinet making	5,514	13,248	4.3	4.4
Gold and silver smithery	557	1,195	9.1	3.5
Watchmaking	878	1,067	5.1	3.2
Barrel making	729	1,185	2.4	2.8
Locksmithery	1,148	3,010	4.3	2.9
Blacksmithery	1,400	2,651	1.7	1.9

SOURCE: *St.d.R.* 119, pp. 206* ff.

In its urban form, home industry in Germany became significant only when it was already becoming obsolete. The factory system followed shortly on its heels. The two forms

labor force was employed in shops with over fifty workers, one of the highest percentages in German industry. On the other hand, only 1.1 percent of the blacksmiths in the country were employed in large-scale industry. Thus, for some of the textile trades home industry was losing ground to the factory system proper, while for the typical handicraft trades, home industry was competing, albeit unsuccessfully, with the traditional craft shops.

coexisted for a while until a wave of new technological innovations in the second half of the century made the factory system the more profitable of the two.

A large-scale domestic shoemaking industry, for example, developed in Germany during the third quarter of the nineteenth century. But at the same time, with the introduction of machinery and an increasing division of labor, shoemaking factories were also being built. In many cases, therefore, the domestic system merely provided a short transition period in the transfer of the craft from the artisan's workshop to the factory. In large towns such as Leipzig and Erfurt, for instance, home industry was directly attached to the shoe factories. Some of the production operations were performed by small artisans in their own shops, and the shoes were then collected and finished on the factory floor. Thus, between 1882 and 1895, the number of small independent shoemaking shops in Germany fell by 4.5 percent and the men employed in them by just over 10 percent. The number of home-industry shops in this trade grew by 50 percent and the men employed in them by about 45 percent. At the same time, big shoemaking enterprises, with over fifty employees, increased by 260 percent (from 71 to 258), and the number of their workers almost tripled (from 7,000 to over 20,000).[31] Large-scale industry was clearly on the ascent, while domestic industry had reached its peak and from then on declined rapidly.

The relatively limited role played by home industry in the industrialization of Germany is of prime importance for understanding the particular effects this process had on the small master artisans. A quick look at the British case will help to clarify this matter.

The putting-out system in England appears to have originated more or less simultaneously in two different environments.[32] In the West Country and in East Anglia the textile

[31] *St.d.R.* 119, pp. 27*, 208*.

[32] The information on the putting-out system in England has been collected from a variety of secondary sources. In addition to those

trades were gradually transformed by the intrusion of large merchant-entrepreneurs, who handled the distribution of raw materials and the marketing of the craftsmen's products. The system evolved here in much the same way as it did, for instance, in the Prussian province of Silesia. At the same time, however, numerous urban handicrafts were also transformed under the pressure of growing foreign trade. In London, as well as in Bristol, Liverpool, and Newcastle, the export merchants gradually gained control of the production process in the export crafts. The production of watches and several light metal articles was increasingly carried on by home industries, and by the end of the eighteenth century many other urban crafts were similarly organized. By the turn of the eighteenth century, the shoemaking, carpentry, and goldsmithing trades in London were all dominated by one form or another of the putting-out system.[33]

In the Black Country the development of light metal trades followed a similar course. Gradually, and almost unnoticeably at first, the merchants and industrial entrepreneurs penetrated these trades. In the absence of major technological innovations, the light metal crafts offered only limited economies of scale.[34] Thus the small shops remained predominant until the end of the nineteenth century, and large firms were distinctly the exception and not the rule.

---

cited in n. 24 above, the following were of great help: J.H. Clapham, *An Economic History of Modern Britain*; T.S. Ashton, *An Economic History of England: The Eighteenth Century*; E.P. Thompson, *The Making of the English Working Class*; G.C. Allen, *The Industrial Development of Birmingham*; Sidney Pollard, *A History of Labour in Sheffield*. Some additional information is given in David Landes, *Prometheus Unbound*. Particularly useful were the little-known works by Adolf Held, *Zwei Bücher zur sozialen Geschichte Englands* and George Brodnitz, "Betriebskonzentration und Kleinbetrieb in der englischen Industrie."

[33] See Ashton, *An Economic History of England*, pp. 91-97, and Dorothy George, *London Life in the Eighteenth Century*, pp. 158-212.

[34] See Allen, *The Industrial Development of Birmingham*, p. 114, as well as Pollard, *Labour in Sheffield*, p. 54.

Nevertheless, the organization of the small shops was radically transformed. The capitalist entrepreneurs in Sheffield or in Birmingham occasionally owned "public wheels," where part of the production process could be performed on their own machines. But in most cases, they concentrated on handling the financial and commercial aspects of the business and left production itself entirely in the hands of the small shop owners. All investigations of the history of the small metal trades have asserted that throughout the nineteenth century "the boundaries of the firms were ill-defined" and that "a continuous scale" was created between master manufacturers and hired workers as early as the beginning of the century.[35]

The system and its variations transformed the small independent masters of traditional urban crafts in England into a range of semidependent artisans. The small masters were almost invariably, though in different degrees, dependent on the capitalist entrepreneur for their livelihood. Some only purchased their raw material from him; others produced to his order and sold him their products. Their payment was only slowly adjusted to the market price of the article, and was normally calculated on the basis of fixed piece rates. Some small masters depended on the factor's weekly credit, repaid at the end of each week in the form of their products; others managed to produce without advance payment. Some were "outworkers," hiring out their skill to various entrepreneurs; others worked consistently for the same man. With the development of the system the merchant-entrepreneur occasionally introduced a division of labor among the artisans and thus made them all dependent upon his organizational capacity in a more intricate system of production.

Among the advantages the domestic system offered the large entrepreneurs was its flexibility in periods of economic slump. The factors then tended to reduce the size of their

[35] Ashton, *An Economic History of England*, p. 102; Pollard, *Labour in Sheffield*, pp. 55-56; Clapham, *Economic History*, p. 174.

overall enterprise and could do so with little or no pressure from their employees. The small masters were simply left in a state of under- or unemployment. In such times they attempted to seek employment on their own, and thus often reverted to a position of relative independence. In better periods, the masters were rewarded for giving up this independence by a more secure income. Thus, there was frequent alternation between economic independence and dependence on the part of many small masters. Normally, economic independence came to be associated in their minds with more difficult times, with lower income and greater poverty.

Increasingly, however, the domestic system became more exploitative, and working conditions in the small domestic shops fell far below the level enforced in the large factories. The worker in domestic industry often had a higher income and standard of living than the small independent master. But compared to the permanent factory hand he was not well off at all. Thus, while in the early nineteenth century, weavers, for instance, fiercely fought for the preservation of their economic independence, by the late part of the century they often joined the trade-union movement in fighting against the domestic system. The union campaign against home industry started in the 1890s. By then, numerous "little masters" in the traditional crafts were union members, fighting against the system that granted them only partial and illusory independence.[36]

The small master artisans in England had a whole century in which to adjust to the gradual loss of their economic independence. By the era of the large industrial factory, many had already assimilated working-class attitudes and ideologies and ceased to place so high a value on their independent position. By contrast, in Germany the domestic system was late to arrive, especially in the towns, and the

[36] Pollard, *Labour in Sheffield*, pp. 125 ff. This development is also hinted at in Hobsbawm, "Trends in the British Labour Movement since 1850," in *Labouring Men*, pp. 377-381.

important social distinction there long remained that between the economically dependent laborers and the independent craftsmen.[37] The German masters were confronted far more abruptly with the effective competition of large industry than were their English counterparts. The new factories developed rapidly in virtually all branches of industry in Germany during the last quarter of the nineteenth century. They were an awesome sight for the traditional small master artisan. They seemed to grow before his eyes, and he did not have a sufficiently long transition period in which to formulate his attitudes toward them, to weigh the advantages and disadvantages of his own position, and to plan an effective and rational course of action.

Economic and Social Effects of the Rise of Large-Scale Mechanized Industry

The various handicrafts were differently affected by the development of large industry. They can be roughly divided into three categories:[38]

1. Trades in which big business competition was negligible
2. Trades in which big business gradually came to dominate the market

[37] It has been argued that Marx's view of industrialization was based entirely on the English case, and that this was one reason for the inadequacy of some of his social predictions. See, for instance, the discussion in Reinhard Bendix, "Tradition and Modernity Reconsidered." It is interesting to note, however, that Marx's model of social stratification appears to have been more closely based on his knowledge and personal experience of the German situation.

[38] For similar categorizations see the addresses by Karl Bücher and V. Philippovich before the VSP on September 23, 1897, in *Schriften* 76 (1896); 21-30 and 76-79; and the summary in Paul Voigt, "Das deutsche Handwerk nach dem Berufszählungen," *Schriften* 70 (1897); 665-670. These, as well as Wilhelm Stieda, *Die Lebensfähigkeit des Handwerks*, have all been extensively used for the following discussion.

3. Trades in which big industry and handicraft shops coexisted, often in symbiosis

The first category included above all the food-producing trades, mainly baking and butchering. Technical innovations in these trades, such as new baking ovens and practicable refrigeration for meat, affected patterns of consumption at that early stage only marginally.[39] Both bread and meat were still only consumed fresh, and the small neighborhood shops remained most suitable for fulfilling the consumers' daily requirements. With the exception of a few cooperative baking establishments, big business hardly intruded into these trades. By 1895, there were only forty-three bakeries in Germany that employed over fifty workers; they constituted 0.1 percent of all baking enterprises, employing only 1.7 percent of the labor force. In butchering, there were by 1895 only nine large-scale shops with 735 employees. The onslaught of big business in baking and butchering was still to come.[40] Also relatively immune to big business competition were the service-oriented crafts, such as those of barbers, hairdressers, and pharmacists; in rural areas blacksmiths and saddlers were to remain indispensable for many years to come.

The second category included the crafts in which big business virtually took over entirely, leaving little or no room for the small handicraft shop. First among these were

[39] On the development of the baking craft see Philipp Arnold, *Das Münchener Bäckergewerbe.* See also the monographs on baking in Leipzig, Breslau, and Jena in *Schriften* 63 (1896); 68 (1896); and 70 (1897). Arnold endeavors to show that the increase in the use of motor power in bakeries was independent of the increase in the number of employees. Bakeries with modern ovens often continued to operate on the same scale and with the same methods as the more old-fashioned ones, but could then afford to shorten the working day and improve working conditions. Eventually, of course, modern machines did transform the bakeries, but the major changes did not take place until the twentieth century. See also Hans J. Teuteberg and Günter Wiegelmann, *Der Wandel der Nahrungsgewohnheiten.*

[40] *St.d.R.* 119, pp. 16* ff.

the various textile industries, in which by 1895, 60 percent of the labor force was employed in enterprises with more than fifty workers. Printing, needle making, tanning, soap making, and several of the pottery crafts were also overrun by big business. In these trades large enterprises produced practically the same articles that had previously been made in small workshops. Through the introduction of more efficient methods of organization and a variety of modern machines, they managed to reduce costs and were thus able to undersell the handicraft masters. Although small independent masters rarely disappeared entirely even from these trades, their number was greatly reduced. It is important to note that the fate of these masters was later to be shared by others as the available industrial machines were made to perform more elaborate and delicate tasks. In the late nineteenth century, however, modern mechanical tools normally performed only rough operations, and were thus able to replace accurate handicraft production in only a limited number of cases.

Most of the traditional urban crafts fell into the third category. Each was differently affected by big industry and devised its own form of adaptation. The overall tendency was a gradual evolution of a division of functions between small handicraft shops and large factories, based on a variety of principles. In the light metal trades, for instance, quality production was performed by master smiths, while simpler articles were made in factories. In the clothing trades, factories produced for mass demand, while master artisans catered to invidual needs. In the building trades, the masters gradually abandoned the production of specific items and concentrated on jobs performed on the building site, installing parts made by large industry. In shoemaking, in watchmaking, and in a variety of other crafts, masters were increasingly pushed into repair work.

In some cases, handicrafts were taken over by big industries as a result of a restructuring of the entire production process. Thus, barrels were now made at the brewer's yard, and books bound by the big printing houses. Basket makers, who in the past took part in the production of baby carriages were deprived of this aspect of their vocation by the creation of new factories, in which the entire production of these articles was performed centrally, using a variety of handicraft skills within the same industrial establishment.

Despite the growing encroachment of the factories into the traditional forms of artisan activities, however, it had become increasingly evident by the end of the nineteenth century that the small handicraft shop was not likely to disappear entirely. The master craftsmen were forced to adjust their modes of operation and to adapt to new market conditions, but only rarely did they go under completely. In spite of big-business competition, small business and the majority of the handicrafts continued to function and even occasionally to thrive.

Nevertheless, as a result of industrialization, the small masters of traditional crafts suffered a drastic decline in their status as an economic group. For centuries they had a virtual, though not an absolute, monopoly over the entire range of production. Then, the exclusive value of their skills was gradually reduced, and their particular services ceased to be indispensable. Moreover, the peculiarities of German social conditions and German industrialization tended increasingly to block the channels of upward mobility for small master artisans. Vocational training and technical knowledge indisputably played a role in the formation of successful entrepreneurs in Germany as elsewhere. For the machine-tool industry, for instance, the particular importance of former artisans as pioneering industrial entrepreneurs in various parts of Germany has been documented.[41]

[41] On the social origins of German industrial entrepreneurs, and the specific role of the handicraft masters during the first half of the nineteenth century, see Fritz Redlich, *Der Unternehmer*, pp. 299-349; Wolfgang Zorn, "Typen und Entwicklungskräfte deutschen Unternehmertums"; Friedrich Zunkel, *Der Rheinisch-Westfälische Un-*

But a close look at the biographies of these men reveals that very few had worked their way up gradually from the traditional handicraft shop to the modern factory. They were usually young men, with limited capital resources but with faith in their vocational and organizational abilities, who took the risk of starting new businesses based on modern technology and a relatively high level of specialization.

The degree to which master artisans participated in the formation of a new entrepreneurial class differed from country to country. The determining factors were apparently the character of the leading sector and the tempo of industrialization. Thus, in England technical skills were of prime importance in the early stage of industrialization. Vocational competence could be applied to the development of light industry with the investment of very small capital resources. The slow process of industrialization provided artisans, as well as other groups in British society, with better opportunities for upward mobility.[42] In Germany, however, large-scale industry grew more rapidly, and the initial

---

ternehmer, pp. 24-26; Hartmut Kaelble, *Berliner Unternehmer während der frühen Industrialisierung*, and "Sozialer Aufstieg in Deutschland 1850-1914." Also the local case study by Klaus Assmann, "Verlag-Manufactur-Fabrik," in Abel et al., *Handwerksgeschichte*, pp. 202-229; Kocka, *Unternehmer in der deutschen Industrialisierung*, pp. 42-54; and "Entrepreneurship in a Late-comer Country."

[42] The flexibility of the English system of social stratification is mentioned in all studies of the industrial revolution. The diverse origins of men recruited into the ranks of the industrial entreprenuers is stressed with much attention to personal and social details and to the emergence of their common consciousness in Mantoux, *The Industrial Revolution*, pp. 365-477. See also Landes, "Technological Changes," pp. 304-306; Sidney Pollard, *The Genesis of Modern Management*, chaps. 2 and 4; François Crouzet, "England and France in the Eighteenth Century," especially pp. 156 ff.; A.H. John, "Aspects of English Economic Growth"; and C. Wilson, "The Entrepreneur in the Industrial Revolution." On the emergence of entrepreneurial ideology in England see Reinhard Bendix, *Work and Authority in Industry*, pp. 1-119; and Harold Perkin, *The Origins of Modern English Society 1780-1880*, pp. 221-230; 271-339.

emphasis on heavy industry made availability of large amounts of capital much more important for admission to the ranks of the new stratum of industrial entrepreneurs. In addition, the growing tendency among new industrialists to emulate the standards and the style of living of the old landed aristocracy made upward mobility all the more difficult for men of low social origin.[43] Upward mobility was virtually impossible for traditional master artisans during the second half of the nineteenth century, since as a rule they suffered from an acute shortage of capital, were poorly educated, and were not sufficiently familiar with technological innovations. Such men managed occasionally to become medium-sized industrialists, but only rarely were they able to join the social ranks of the German big-business elite. While intergenerational upward mobility provided new blood for the entrepreneurial group in Germany throughout the nineteenth century, intragenerational social advancement increasingly became a rarity.

Within their limited means, small master artisans occasionally attempted to join the new age of industrialization by introducing modern machinery. The very act had a meaning beyond its strictly economic implications. It symbolized a public acceptance of new and changing times. But only a few modern inventions proved to be useful in the small craft workshop. Among them the various sewing machines for clothes, leather, fur, and other materials were the most important, and led to far-reaching structural transformations in the relevant crafts. The introduction of power machinery, however, affected the small craft shops in very few cases. Steam-, gas-, or water-powered machinery was designed primarily for use in large-scale industrial enterprises. Such machines overtaxed the resources of the small master artisans and normally proved inefficient and un-

[43] See Zunkel, *Der Rheinisch-Westfälische Unternehmer*, pp. 25-26, 128-132; and Wolfgang Köllmann, *Sozialgeschichte der Stadt Barmen*, chap. IV.

profitable. The small master had to borrow large sums of money, often under extremely unfavorable conditions, in order to purchase one of these machines. More often than not he soon discovered that the machine could not be employed at full capacity in his small workshop, even when he instituted a certain division of labor, and that it was likely to produce more debts for him, and little, if any, additional profit. Later in the century electric motors turned out to be far more suitable for small industrial workshops, and did eventually transform many small handicraft shops into efficient industrial enterprises. But electrical power was applied to the design and construction of machine tools only at the turn of the nineteenth century, and its effects became noticeable only during the twentieth. In 1895, 65 percent of all the motors in Germany were used in small industrial enterprises, but their share in the total horsepower in industry was only 13 percent. The only handicrafts that utilized power machinery to any significant extent were tanneries, machine-making, and carpentry shops. In other crafts the use of motor power remained negligible.[44]

For the majority of the small handicraft masters in Germany, industrialization remained an external force, affecting the entire economy, transforming their overall social and political environment, but only slowly penetrating their traditional workshops. Their lives were changed as a result of the new economy, in the creation of which they had participated only marginally and in spite of themselves, and toward which they increasingly tended to harbor suspicion and resentment. With the advent of a prolonged period of economic instability and deflation following the "foundation boom" of the early 1870s the difficulties the small masters had to deal with as a result of industrialization were accentuated. The process of adaptation to new economic and social roles then had to take place under the additional

[44] See *St.d.R.* 6, p. 68*, I.38ff. and 119, pp. 186* ff. and the section on prices, machinery, and employment in chap. 2.

stress of depressed prices, a decelerated rate of economic growth, and considerable material hardship. The pain of structural change was thus sharpened, and the handicraft masters' capacity to respond calmly and rationally to the new circumstances was severely curtailed.

TWO

THE EFFECTS OF THE GREAT DEPRESSION

A Historiographical Note

As has been shown in the preceding chapter, the effects of industrialization upon the handicrafts were by no means uniformly adverse. Craftsmen were forced to adjust their methods of operation and to adapt to new market conditions, but very few traditional trades completely disappeared in the process.[1] As early as 1848 Marx and Engels predicted the polarization of modern society, of which the most outstanding feature was to be the gradual disappearance of the lower-middle class "partially because their diminutive capital does not suffice for the scale on which modern industry is carried on, and is swamped in the competition with the large capitalists, partially because their specialized skill is rendered worthless by new methods of production."[2] In all the capitalist countries of the West, however, a powerful lower-middle class, as defined by Marx and Engels themselves, survived, and among the various components of that class, the small independent handicraft masters continue to be an important element. In the Federal Republic of Germany a special census in 1956 counted 750,000 artisan shops employing over 3.5 million men.[3] In many trades the personnel increased between 1861

[1] An earlier and somewhat different version of the first three sections of this chapter appeared in the *VSWG* 61(1974). For the revision and for the correction of some mistaken figures I am particularly indebted to Jürgen Kocka.

[2] Karl Marx and Friedrich Engels, "Manifest der Kommunistischen Partei," *Werke*, vol. 4, pp. 469-470.

[3] For the 1956 statistics see Hermann Wellmanns, *Das deutsche Handwerk*, and the data quoted in Fischer, "Das deutsche Handwerk," p. 687; for more recent figures see Wolfram Fischer and Peter Czada, "Wandlungen in der deutschen Industriestruktur," in

and 1961 faster than the general population.[4] Small industrial shops in general, and many traditional handicrafts, have shown great vitality and resourcefulness in withstanding the pressure of modernization. Nevertheless, throughout the nineteenth century and well into the twentieth, a barrage of pessimistic predictions concerning the fate of handicrafts and craftsmen continued to be voiced by scholars of various schools and politicians of different personal convictions. By the late 1890s the situation of small industrial workshops in general and of the handicrafts in particular, became a bone of contention among orthodox Marxists and revisionists.[5] But pessimism with regard to the fate of small handicraftsmen was not confined to "true believers." Karl Bücher, who was to conduct the research project of the Verein für Sozialpolitik on the conditions of the handicraft economy, was an expert on the matter. In a collection of essays first published in 1893, he too expressed the "decline of the handicrafts" thesis, although in a milder form than it had been previously formulated by Marx. Even when the VSP's comprehensive investigation of the handicrafts was completed, several years later, Bücher was still of the opinion that the small master artisans had fertile ground for development only in the rural parts of the country, and that "everywhere in the towns broad strata of small independent persons, who formed the heart of the early town population, disappear and yield place to a disconnected mass of dependent laborers."[6]

Entstehung und Wandel der modernen Gesellschaft, ed. Gerhard A. Ritter.

4 These relationships have been analyzed in some detail in Abel, "Zur Ortsbestimmung," pp. 74-79.

5 See e.g., Karl Kautsky, "Der Untergang des Kleinbetriebs"; Eduard Bernstein *Die Voraussetzungen des Sozialismus*; also, from a more limited point of view, Richard Calwer, "Zur Entwicklung des Handwerks."

6 Karl Bücher, "The Decline of the Handicraft," in his *Industrial Evolution*, p. 214; see also his comments in *Schriften* 76 (1897); 30.

In 1903, the "decline of the handicrafts" was even more pessimistically described by Werner Sombart, who in the *History of the German Economy in the 19th Century* considered the process to be characteristic of nineteenth century economic development as a whole. Hastening to stress that there was no question of a complete disappearance of the handicrafts, he nevertheless asserted his belief that a "comprehensive retreat" was taking place, even in branches in which the handicraft form of production was still predominant, and he believed this retreat to be far more severe than the statistical data at the turn of the century seemed to have indicated. Sombart reasserted this position throughout the numerous editions of his book. In the seventh edition, published in 1927, the thesis was expressed virtually unchanged in spite of ample evidence showing the expansion of many handicrafts and some early scholarly objections to the decline thesis.[7]

As late as 1932 Emil Grünberg, a Marxist social economist, set out once again to prove in statistical terms the progressive deterioration of handicraft industry and the continuing proletarianization of small master artisans.[8] During the Nazi period, research into this issue had a characteristic political bias and is of little value for us. After the second World War, however, it became increasingly popular among economic historians in Germany to regard the decline thesis as misleading and untrue. In Wilhelm Abel's analysis of the position of handicraftsmen within the general

[7] *Die deutsche Volkswirtschaft im neunzehnten Jahrhundert* (7th ed., Berlin, 1927), especially pp. 279-280; 297. For a different view on this issue expressed at about the same time see L.D. Pesl, "Mittelstandsfragen," pp. 118 ff.; and J. Dethloff "Das Handwerk in der Kapitalistischen Wirtschaft," in *Strukturwandlungen der Deutschen Volkswirtschaft*, ed. B. Harms, vol. 2, pp. 3-41. For a social, rather than an economic viewpoint see Joseph Schumpeter's "Das soziale Antlitz des deutschen Reiches," and Theodor Geiger, *Die Soziale Schichtung des deutschen Volkes.*

[8] Emil Grünberg, *Der Mittelstand in der Kapitalistischen Gesellschaft*, pp. 35 ff.

population and their material well-being during the industrial era, and especially in Wolfram Fischer's estimation of the role of small business in the overall growth of the German economy between 1850 and 1914, the decline thesis is dismissed as a gross miscalculation.[9]

A long-term approach to economic history and an emphasis on economics to the exclusion of all other historical factors characterize the modern studies. These perspectives in turn dictate the selection of sources and the use of historical material. They often lead to a complete reliance upon macroeconomic data, and consequently to the casual treatment of vocational and regional differentiation and of periodic short-term fluctuations of the economy.[10] Furthermore, the

[9] Abel, "Zur Ortsbestimmung," pp. 74-79; Wolfram Fischer, "Die Rollc des Kleingewerbes," especially pp. 141-142. A useful summary of the entire controversy is to be found in Noll, *Sozio-ökonomischer Strukturwandel*, pp. 13-22.

[10] Fischer's pioneering studies on the handicraft economy are now collected in *Wirtschaft und Gesellschaft im Zeitalter der Industrialisierung*, part 4. Fischer's focus however, is on small business as a whole, rather than on the traditional handicrafts in particular. His examples of economic growth in the small-business sector are therefore of only limited relevance here. Thus, restaurants and barbershops are typical of the service sector of small business, and their indisputable growth during the six decades between 1850 and 1914 reflects the expansion of this sector of the economy during the advanced stages of industrialization. Proponents of the decline thesis normally relied upon data for small independent *industrial producers*, although admittedly the line of demarcation between them and the service sector may occasionally be very unclear. The building industry, which also plays an important role in Fischer's argument, normally falls within the category of industrial producers. It is, however, singularly unsuitable for long-term analysis. The building sector is notoriously sensitive to fluctuations of the economy. While its index of production (1913=100) increased from 12.4 in 1855 to 49.0 in 1875, it indicates stagnation for the two-decade span between 1875 and 1895. From a high point of 49.0 in 1875 this index fell to 33.8 in 1879 and further to 27.4 in 1882. It then started to rise again and showed a continuous and sustained increase only after 1897. See W. Hoffmann, *Das Wachstum*, pp. 390-393. Alfred Noll essentially fol-

rejection of the decline thesis not only substitutes one over-simplified interpretation of the development of the handicraft economy for another, but also fails to account for the unceasing moaning of small handicraftsmen throughout this development, and for the widespread, although admittedly never unanimous, support of the decline thesis among contemporary economists and historians. Strictly speaking, the reliance upon statistical data to the exclusion of all other types of evidence makes an explanation of these facts irrelevant. From a historical point of view, however, the discrepancy between statistical results and so much of what was said and written at the time must be dealt with. The obvious way out of this dilemma is to suggest that the source of the master-artisans' complaints is to be found in other than economic difficulties; that it was more often than not some unidentified social malaise translated into economic terms. As a result of social and cultural strains, runs the argument, men complained of economic decline and proletarianization in spite of an actual and steady improvement of their economic position. Now, it can indeed be demonstrated that small master artisans in Germany had cause for discontent other than economic hardship. But before we hasten to discredit their own repeated evidence we are at least obliged to reevaluate the nature of our statistical investigation. It is just possible that the root of the discrepancy lies at least in part in limitations in the analysis and not exclusively in the misconceptions of contemporaries.

The transformation of the handicraft economy can and

---

lows Fischer's definition, but introduces a number of significant qualifications. His study is a detailed *regional* investigation, which nowhere presumes to present a national view of the handicrafts. Noll divides the period into two sections: 1875-1895 and 1895-1907, and carefully refrains from imposing the situation of the later period on the earlier one, or deducing trends characteristic of the 1875-1895 period alone from the overall view of the entire period. See his *Sozioökonomischer Strukturwandel*, pp. 23-36, 118-120.

should be discussed not only with reference to the ultimate effects of industrialization upon this economic sector as a whole, and the fate of the small master artisans can and should be perceived not merely between the poles of a preindustrial economy on the one hand, and the final stages of industrialization on the other. It is equally important, and may be equally fruitful, to dwell on an analysis of the stages of industrial growth, and upon its fluctuations and uncertainties, and to study its various social and economic implications for the handicrafts and craftsmen within this context.

Concentrating on the years of the Great Depression, between 1873 and 1896, and dealing only with the traditional urban handicrafts, it appears that, due to the combined effects of industrialization and a prolonged period of economic fluctuations the handicrafts did suffer a limited decline. It was expressed, as Marx had indeed anticipated, in a process of internal group polarization, which significantly changed the structure of the handicrafts and the character of the Handwerkerstand. It did not necessarily entail a decline in the relative material well-being of *all* who were involved in the process. Polarization was not carried to its final logical conclusion, but it was clearly detectable. Master artisans either enlarged their workshops and managed to prosper even under adverse economic circumstances, or were increasingly impoverished, and often proletarianized. The process continued throughout the years of the depression, although its scale varied as the economy swung up and down during these years. In the subsequent period of general prosperity between 1896 and 1914, it decelerated and moderated, and thus failed to reach the logical final stage in which all small masters might be expected to join either the industrial middle class or the propertyless proletariat. What had occurred was a continuous, but uneven and unfinished process of polarization among master artisans, powerful enough to cause a severe structural transformation of the group, but not radical or lasting enough to bring about its disappearance.

Prices, Machinery, and Employment

Industrialization as such forced the small handicraft masters to adjust to changes, to adapt to new methods of production and technique, and to adopt new attitudes toward the commercial side of their business. The structural effects of this process, however, became evident in Germany only under the additional pressure of the Great Depression. This rather unusual depression, did not halt the advent of industrialization. The annual rate of economic growth was reduced from 4-5 percent between 1850 and 1873 to 2.6-3 percent during the years of the Great Depression, but industrialization continued unabated. Old industries expanded, and new ones were built. Between 1882 and 1895 the percentage of the population dependent on industrial employment rose from 33.7 to 36.1. The labor force in industry, mining, and building grew to 29.4 percent. The number of industrial enterprises employing more than fifty men rose by 8,400 or nearly 90 percent, and the share of industrial labor in the big-business sector grew from 26.3 percent to 36.3 percent. In industry as a whole the applied horsepower increased between 1875 and 1895 from 947,000 HP to an impressive 3,350,000 HP.[11]

At the same time, following the crash of the Viennese stock exchange in 1873, investment in the private economy slowed down, interest rates and shareholders' profits declined, and prices, especially of producers' goods and most noticeably of coal and iron, spiraled downward. None of the economic trends that characterized the Great Depression was constant between 1873 and 1896. All reflected with greater or lesser sensitivity alternate periods of slump and of relative recovery.[12] Indeed, the years be-

[11] For a discussion of the economic characteristics of the Great Depression in Germany see H. Rosenberg, *Grosse Depression*, pp. 32-51; Wehler, *Bismarck und der Imperialismus*, pp. 61-99, and *Das Deutsche Kaiserreich*, pp. 41-48. Data are cited from W. Hoffmann, *Das Wachstum*, pp. 264; 391 ff.

[12] See the first section of the introduction.

tween 1873 and 1896 were experienced by the master artisans and their contemporaries not as a continuous period of economic depression, but as a series of crises, varying in severity and differing in their implications.

The most striking manifestation of the Great Depression was the decline of prices in the first phase, and the continuing general low level of prices throughout. Between 1873 and 1896 the wholesale price index of all industrial products in Germany declined from 136 to 77 (1913 = 100).[13] Retail prices also declined, though less rapidly and not as far. The decline of prices was not evenly distributed among the various economic sectors. To begin with, it was the larger producers of consumer goods, and not the small handicraft masters, who were in a position to take advantage of the reduction in the price of basic raw materials. Small producers continued to purchase raw materials in small quantities, taking into account the limited volume of their production, the high cost of storage, and the generally precarious situation of the market. Thus, small producers paid higher prices for raw materials, usually under more difficult credit terms. In the wood industry, for instance, it was reported that big industrialists were often able to pay 10 percent and occasionally as much as 20 percent less for their raw material.[14]

Similarly, the small producers had to spend considerably more on rent than the large producers. The small handicraft masters in particular, who often used their shops for sales as well as production, required good commercial locations and were forced to pay higher rents. Although they could economize on transportation, their costs were still relatively higher than those of large industrialists whose workshops were normally located on the outskirts of town. The market

[13] W. Hoffmann, *Das Wachstum*, pp. 544 ff., and H. Rosenberg, *Grosse Depression*, pp. 43-45.

[14] Stieda, *Die Lebensfähigkeit*, p. 18. For the differential impact of economic fluctuations on handicrafts and on large-scale industry see Theodor Beckermann, "Konjunktur und Konjunkturbeobachtung," pp. 82-91.

for the latter's products extended beyond the borders of their own town, and their transportation expenses did not rise substantially as a result of their less central location. In Düsseldorf, one of the fastest-growing industrial towns during the last quarter of the nineteenth century, small businessmen sometimes spent as much as 40-50 percent of their income on rent, while big businessmen managed to spend only about 15-20 percent.[15]

As prices spiraled downward, the money wages of industrial workers as a whole at first declined and then slowly rose throughout the Great Depression. The early decline of wages was clearly the employers' response to depressed market prices. Master artisans, however, were in a particularly awkward position in trying to reduce journeymen's wages. These were often lower in small workshops than in big industry, so that skilled workers were tempted to seek better-paid jobs in the factories. Handicraft-masters' complaints about the shortage of properly trained men were chronic throughout the depression. Under these circumstances, a master attempting to reduce wages took the risk of losing his workers. In addition, trade-union organizations in these early years concentrated the efforts on the handicraft trades. In Germany, as in other countries, skilled laborers were the first to be organized effectively. The carpenters', tailors', shoemakers', and bookbinders' unions were second in size only to that of the printers.[16] The small entrepreneurs themselves had developed little solidarity and inadequate organization. In their precarious economic position they, as individuals, could not afford the risks and the expense of a common-front resistance to the demands of their workers. Their bargaining position was weak, and their wage bills remained relatively high.[17]

[15] Wilhelm Westhaus, "Das Düsseldorfer Schlächtergewerbe," *Schriften* 62 (1896): 238.

[16] *Correspondenzblatt der Generalkommission der Gewerkschaften Deutschlands*, September 26, 1891; and Karl Zwing, *Geschichte der deutschen freien Gewerkschaften*, pp. 25 ff.

[17] See the section on masters and journeymen in chap. 3.

The decline of the cost of living in Germany during the first phase of the Great Depression between 1873 and 1879 was of prime importance in preventing the contraction of workers' real wages. For many of the small master artisans, however, the meaning of this decline was rather less encouraging. A number of the main commodities composing the cost-of-living index were then produced almost exclusively by small handicraft masters. Thus, the price index of furniture for household consumption declined between 1874 and 1879 from 119.3 to 62.4 (1913 = 100).[18] The decline was then halted, and the index rose again after numerous fluctuations to 78.5 in 1889, to climb sharply through several boom years to 87.7 in 1890, only to plunge to 76.7 again by the end of the Great Depression in 1896. A less dramatic, but nonetheless continuous decline was shown by the price index of clothing and leather articles. These, too, were mainly produced for private consumption and often still in small handicraft workshops. The index for clothing and leather products started, like that for wood articles, at the level of 119.9 in 1874, then gradually declined to reach 79.1 in 1896, and took an upward direction only after the turn of the century.

The master artisans as a whole of course shared the benefit of the falling prices of bread, sugar, and other foodstuffs, the drop in rent, and the decline in the purchase price of housing. The indexes of these prices, however, show more limited declines and more gentle fluctuations. Thus, the price index of food products dropped from 89.0 in 1874 to 76.5 in 1879, reached a low point at 72.9 in 1888, and then climbed slowly, reaching the level of 76.3 by the end of the depression years. The rent index declined between 1874 and 1888 from 87.4 to 81.5 and reached the low point of 80.0 in 1895.

The figures suggest that the overall decline in the cost-of-living index, especially during the slump periods of the

[18] These and all other figures in this paragraph are taken from W. Hoffmann, *Das Wachstum*, pp. 598 ff.

Great Depression, could hardly have compensated the small master artisans for the catastrophic decline in the prices of their own products. Not only were they continuously affected by the structural changes caused by industrialization, but after 1873 they were forced to make their adjustments under the severe strain the prolonged deflation put upon their material well-being.

It has recently been demonstrated that economic growth in the small-business sector of the economy did not lag behind the aggregate growth of the German economy.[19] This appears to be true even for the depression years between 1873 and 1896. While the overall production index for industry and handicrafts (1913 = 100) rose from 26.2 to 49.9 between 1873 and 1896, some typical small-business sectors showed a considerably faster growth rate. In the clothing and leather trades for instance, the production index rose from 43.4 to 76.4; and in the woodworking industry from 35.0 to 60.2.[20] In a period of continuous mechanization and rationalization of production, this growth can be taken as evidence that small business participated in the overall process of industrialization. Increased investment in capital goods by small producers was natural enough at a time of falling interest rates and is in fact suggested by Hoffmann's index of installed horsepower per unit of production in the various sectors of the economy.[21]

However, our relatively detailed information on the use of motor power in small handicraft shops indicates that qualification of these suppositions is required. The figures suggest that the great increase in the use of motor power in the typical handicraft trades, such as light metal work, clothing, and building, could not have been due to significant changes in the small craft shops but only to the disproportionate increase in the use of motor power in the

19 Fischer, "Die Rolle des Kleingewerbes," pp. 136-139.

20 W. Hoffmann, *Das Wachstum*, pp. 391 ff.

21 Fischer, "Die Rolle des Kleingewerbes," pp. 137-138. See also the full table in W. Hoffmann, *Das Wachstum*, p. 212.

medium- and large-sized enterprises, and to the application of modern machinery to new and specialized branches within the last two categories. Thus in the light metal working trades by 1895, 77.6 percent of the large shops used power machinery, while only 2.8 percent of the small ones did so. In the woodworking trades, 75.2 percent of the large shops used power machinery, as against 4.7 percent of the small ones. In the clothing trades the figures show 37.0 percent for the large-scale enterprises and 0.1 percent for the small ones. In no case was more than 1 percent of the small-business labor force employed in workshops using power machinery.[22]

These figures are not surprising. The small master craftsmen had only limited capital resources. While big business could obtain loans from the Reichsbank, at interest rates of 2-3 percent, the cooperative banks, which normally supplied funds for small entrepreneurs, charged 8-9 percent, and often refused credit to master artisans because of insufficient guarantees. The masters were then forced to turn to investment banks, where short-term loans were extended at rates as high as 15 percent.[23] Consequently a small master could hardly expect to make a new motor-powered tool into a profitable economic proposition. If there was any increase in the volume of production of the small handicraft workshops, it should be ascribed not to a significant rise in capital investment but to an intensified and more efficient use of existing resources, labor and capital alike.

Data for a limited number of regions in Germany suggest some growth in both capital stock and capital intensity for many of the handicrafts. But while the evidence for the entire period between 1875 and 1907 is unmistakable, it remains unconvincing for the years between 1875 and 1895. It

[22] For data on motor power in German industry and handicrafts in 1895 see *St.d.R.* 119, pp. 186* ff.

[23] See Voigt, "Das Tischlergewerbe," *Schriften* 65 (1895), and his comments on the declining participation of the handicraftsmen in credit cooperatives between 1870 and 1895 in an appendix to *Schriften* 68 (1896).

is difficult to ascertain the extent to which small master artisans improved their existing tools and introduced small-sized new ones. One can only speculate about their probable efforts to use available space and raw materials more efficiently.[24] It is somewhat easier to gain a view of their increasing exploitation of labor resources.

The poorest among the masters worked themselves and the members of their families long hours, seven days a week. The employment of wife and children in the handicraft shop had been among the traditional features of artisan production, but in periods of economic hardship it was greatly intensified as a way of obtaining additional free labor. While in industry as a whole family members of independent producers constituted only 2.1 percent of the labor force in 1895, their share in small workshops was as high as 8.3 percent. By far the highest employment of family members prevailed in the food-producing trades, in which over one-third of the total number of employees were the employers' relations. A high percentage was also registered in the textile and the clothing trades. Family members employed in these crafts were often female, the wives and daughters of the small shop owners.[25]

Frequently, small masters who wished to increase their output were unable to pay higher wages. They then sought to solve the problem by dismissing their adult workers and taking on a greater number of apprentices and young workers who were poorly paid, if at all. Over half of all the apprentices in German industry were employed in workshops with less than five employees. They constituted over 30 percent of the entire small-business labor force, but only 3 percent of the workers in shops with over twenty employees.[26]

[24] See Fischer, "Die Rolle des Kleingewerbes," p. 140. Also Karl-Heinz Schmidt, "Kleingewerbe in regionalen Wachstumsprozessen," pp. 733-736; and Noll, *Sozio-ökonomischer Strukturwandel*, pp. 46-66.

[25] See *St.d.R.* 119, pp. 102* ff. [26] Ibid., pp. 70 ff.

TABLE 2.1

EMPLOYMENT OF FAMILY MEMBERS IN SMALL INDUSTRY, 1895

Trades	*Family Members as % Employees*	*Women Family Members as % Women Employees*
Bakers	22.3	78.0
Butchers	20.8	74.6
Basket makers	16.8	54.3
Goldsmiths	5.3	28.5
Tailors	5.3	15.3
Tinsmiths	5.3	41.9
Bookbinders	4.6	39.2
Shoemakers	2.4	51.7
Watchmakers	2.2	52.2
Coopers	2.0	39.2
Glaziers	2.0	38.7

SOURCE: *St.d.R.* 119, pp. 102* ff.

Workers under the age of 16 constituted 9.3 percent of the industrial labor force in Germany in 1895, while the percentage for all small industrial shops was 17.4. In the typical craft industries young workers were employed in particularly large numbers. In some of the old crafts, such as baking, tailoring, and blacksmithing they constituted roughly one-fifth of the labor force.[27] In a commentary on the Erfurt

TABLE 2.2

PERCENTAGE OF WORKERS UNDER 16, 1895

	All Shops	*Small Shops*
Industry as a whole	9.3	17.4
Metalworking	15.0	22.8
Woodworking	12.1	17.8
Clothing	16.1	20.0
Food trades	9.7	14.5
Building	6.8	14.2

SOURCE: *St.d.R.* 119, pp. 102* ff.

[27] Ibid., pp. 102* ff.

Program of the Social-Democratic party, Karl Kautsky wrote in 1892: "The small man is impoverished. In order to fight his impoverishment he must be even more industrious. The working day is extended into the late hours of the night; wife and children are made into laborers; instead of the mature journeymen cheaper apprentices are employed in excessive numbers."[28] This may have been an exaggerated view of the overall conditions of independent craftsmen, inspired by Kautsky's orthodox Marxism and the political objectives of his party. But there was enough truth in this picture to make it plausible. This was, indeed, the fate of many small masters by the last decade of the nineteenth century. The fact that their social group as such did not sink into the predicted complete proletarianization did little to comfort the impoverished individuals within it.

Structural Changes in the Handicrafts

Almost without exception the average number of workers per shop in the traditional handicraft trades rose considerably between 1882 and 1895. Thus, for example, the average employment in bookbinding rose within these thirteen years from 3.3 to 4.9—an increase of almost 50 percent. In carpentry the growth was from 1.9 in 1882 to 2.6 in 1896; in locksmithery from 2.6 to 4.1; in tanning from 4.4 to 7.4.[29] These figures, however, should be treated with extreme caution. They represent the growth in the size of shops in an entire trade, but tend to obscure the fact that the increase within the small-shop sector was considerably lower. Master artisans who managed to employ more than five workers were consequently counted in the medium-sized shop category of the industrial census, and thus could not affect the statistical picture of development in the small-sized category. Nonetheless, the rate of growth within the

[28] Kautsky, "Der Untergang des Kleinbetriebs," p. 25.

[29] *St.d.R.* 119, pp. 9* ff.

small-business sector was strikingly low. In the small bookbinding shops, for instance, average employment rose from 1.8 men per shop in 1882 to 1.9 in 1895. In carpentry the growth was from 1.7 to 1.8; in locksmithery from 2.1 to 2.4, and in tanning from 2.1 to 2.2.[30] On the whole, the average size of the *small shops* in the urban traditional crafts remained virtually unchanged.

TABLE 2.3

CHANGES IN THE NUMBER OF MEN PER SHOP, 1882-1895

Trade	*Men per Shop All Shops*		*Men per Shop Small Shops*	
	1882	*1895*	*1882*	*1895*
Potters	3.1	5.2	1.9	2.0
Silver- and goldsmiths	4.2	6.0	1.7	1.7
Blacksmiths	1.9	2.0	1.8	1.9
Locksmiths	2.6	4.1	2.1	2.4
Cartwrights	1.5	1.7	1.5	1.6
Bookbinders	3.3	4.9	1.8	1.9
Tanners	4.4	7.4	2.1	2.2
Saddlers	1.9	2.2	1.7	1.8
Carpenters	1.9	2.6	1.7	1.8
Coopers	1.6	1.8	1.4	1.5
Basket makers	1.5	1.7	1.3	1.4
Bakers	2.2	2.7	2.0	2.3
Butchers	2.0	2.4	1.8	2.1
Tailors	1.5	1.7	1.4	1.5
Shoemakers	1.6	1.6	1.5	1.4
Masons	3.5	4.8	1.6	1.5
Glaziers	1.5	1.9	1.5	1.7
Metalworkers	2.8	4.0	1.8	2.0
Leather workers	2.7	3.4	1.8	1.9
Woodworkers	2.0	2.7	1.5	1.7
Food workers	3.0	3.8	1.9	2.2
Clothing workers	1.4	1.6	1.3	1.3
Building workers	3.3	5.3	1.7	1.7
All industry	2.6	3.7	1.5	1.8

SOURCE: *St.d.R.* 119, pp. 9* ff.; 16* ff.

[30] Ibid., pp. 9* ff. and 16* ff.

Moreover, the computation of changes in the average number of employees per small workshop leaves untouched a whole range of related, and historically significant questions. Above all, it says nothing about the many thousands of masters who were forced out of business altogether, or about those single self-employed artisans who struggled continuously to preserve their economic independence, often fighting a lost battle. In order to obtain a more accurate picture of the structural changes in the handicraft economy, the number of individual self-employed artisans should be taken into account together with the number of those who appear to have been pushed out of their trades. These additional indicators are necessary for a balanced evaluation of the changes in the condition of the handicrafts during the period under consideration. Taken together they reveal three patterns of development:

1. Concentration coupled with impoverishment
2. Expansion coupled with impoverishment
3. Concentration *and* expansion coupled with an increase in material well-being

The first pattern shows most distinctly the ongoing process of polarization within the handicrafts. Characteristic of it is an increase in the average number of workingmen per shop in the entire trade occurring simultaneously with an overall decrease in the number of *small* shop owners and an even sharper decline in the number of the single self-employed masters. For our period this is in fact the pattern revealed by the industrial sector of the German economy as a whole. The average number of employees per industrial enterprise grew between 1882 and 1895 from 2.6 to 3.7. At the same time the number of small shops was reduced by 186,265 or 8.6 percent, and the number of individual self-employed masters by as much as 13.5 percent. The number of medium- and large-scale enterprises grew by only 55,000, and many of these were set up by young men, or by tradesmen coming from other occupations. Thus only a small portion of the men dropped from the statistical category of small industrial shop owners could have been absorbed into that of the medium- and large-scale entrepreneurs. Least likely to have moved up this socioeconomic ladder were, of course, the individual self-employed men. The great reduction in their number suggests that many of these men had to close their independent shops and seek employment elsewhere. A decline in the number of individual self-employed men that is proportionally larger than the overall decline in the number of small shop owners as a whole seems to indicate the fate of these men. Their disappearance from the statistical category of small business *usually* meant a deterioration in their social status, if not always in their actual material circumstances.

The most disastrous decline in the number of small independent masters was registered in the textile trades. However, since the 1895 census was more accurate on the question of domestic industry than the one taken in 1882, it is likely that this apparent decline was at least in part due to the varying degrees of accuracy and completeness in the census data for the two years. The same applies to the decline in the small-shop section of the clothing trades, for which the numbers should also be viewed with a degree of skepticism. Between 1882 and 1895 the number of small shops in the clothing trades declined by over 38,000. Medium- and large-scale shops in these trades grew by only 7,800. Thus, some 30,000 small masters seem to have been forced out of their position to seek employment with other masters or in altogether different occupations. Not infrequently, these men joined the ranks of the unemployed. The nature of the transformation becomes clearer when we observe that while the number of small shops in the clothing trades was reduced by 4.4 percent, the number of individual self-employed men in these crafts declined by 6.5 percent.[31]

[31] An examination of the absolute figures given for the change in the number of single self-employed masters reveals that the single-man shops included numerous domestic industry shops. Only thus can one explain the fact that the decrease in the number of single-

Apparently the decline in the number of small independent masters was particularly pronounced among the poorest of them all. Concentration in the various clothing crafts occurred simultaneously with a decline in the social and economic status of many previously independent craftsmen, and depended in part on their impoverishment.

This pattern of development appears especially distinct in the woodworking industry. The average number of employees per shop in this sector as a whole grew between 1882 and 1895 from 2.0 to 2.7, an increase of just over one-third, and a degree of concentration was also achieved among small businesses in this sector. These figures ostensibly show signs of prosperity, but at the same time the number of small independent masters in the woodworking industry was reduced by 27,000, or 11 percent. During the same period only some 8,000 men joined the ranks of the medium- or large-scale entrepreneurs in this sector of the economy, so that no more than a quarter of the displaced small masters could have been absorbed into the more prosperous section of the woodworking industry. The decline in the number of the individual self-employed in this sector is also particularly dramatic. No less than 20 percent of these men disappeared from the category between 1882 and 1895. It is safe to assume that the majority of them became dependent laborers, in the same branch of industry or in another.

In all the trades that followed the first pattern of develop-

---

man shops was larger, in absolute terms, than the decrease in the number of all small shops. For our purpose, however, this is of relatively little significance. In fact, the line of division between the independent and dependent masters was fluid and extremely vague in theory as well as in practice. In trades in which domestic industry was highly developed, such as the clothing trades, the distinction was particularly difficult to make. This confusion, however, can serve to remind us that all figures in the industrial statistics of the nineteenth century are far from accurate. What they give us is no more than an impression of the scale of some major structural changes.

ment industrial concentration was thus coupled with impoverishment. Some of the master carpenters, for instance, particularly those with four workers or more, weathered the economic hardships of the Great Depression to become modern, small-scale industrialists. Others, however, who could not or, occasionally, would not take part in the concentration process, were pushed into an increasingly precarious economic position.[32] In most cases, it was only extreme poverty that finally forced these men to abandon their own workshops and seek other employment.

The building industry will serve as an example of the second pattern of development, in which expansion rather than concentration was the main feature of development, especially in the small-business sector. Yet, despite the overall expansion of the building trades, many masters lost their businesses and became members of the proletariat. Between 1875 and 1882 almost 150,000 small building enterprises ceased to exist. This was a decline of nearly 30 percent and reflects the sensitivity of the building sector to changing economic climates. In the late 1880s recovery had begun, and between the industrial censuses of 1882 and 1895, the number of small building enterprises in the various crafts grew by over 13 percent, and the number of the individual self-employed building masters increased by 16.3 percent, and constituted over half the total number of independent building masters in 1895. Certain specific building crafts, such as those of the masons and the joiners, showed the same pattern of development, characteristic of areas of production that had undergone only limited technical change, and in which there had therefore been no overriding reason to alter traditional modes of operation. The advantages of industrial concentration in the building crafts were only marginal. These trades were thus able to sustain a large number of independent single masters, but many of them had only a precarious economic existence and were likely

[32] See Voigt, "Das Tischlergewerbe," *Schriften* 65 (1895): 367.

to become unemployed with any downward movement of the economy.[33]

Several industrial sectors, some with a high percentage of small businesses and including some typical handicraft trades, showed a marked tendency toward industrial concentration as well as industrial expansion between 1882 and 1895, and appear to have maintained or increased the well-being of the men independently occupied in them. In the food industry, for example, the average number of employed men per shop increased between 1882 and 1895 from 3.0 to 3.8. At the same time, the number of small industrial shop owners in this sector grew by 6.5 percent and their labor force by 18.0 percent. While just over 8,000 individual self-employed men in this sector counted in the 1882 census were dropped from the 1895 one, as many as 15,000 were added to the overall number of small shop owners. It is of course quite possible that a few small bakers and butchers were unable to carry on profitable businesses and abandoned their shops, but in these trades this was the exception rather than the rule. The growth in the average size of the small shops in baking and butchering was considerably higher than in other trades and far exceeded the average growth for all German industry.[34] Thus, small baking enterprises employed an average of 2.0 workers in 1882 and 2.3 in 1895, and the small butcher shops employed 1.8

[33] This type of development is similar to the trend that has been diagnosed for the handicrafts during the years following the crash of 1929. See the discussion about the "flight into independence" in Wilhelm Wernet, *Handwerkspolitik*, p. 21, and in the last section of the epilogue. Then, too, the increase in the number of independent, self-employed men did not indicate prosperity but growing impoverishment. Thus the rise or decline in the number of self-employed masters can only be interpreted when looked at in conjunction with changes in the size of all small businesses and with other indicators of changes in prosperity.

[34] See table 2.3. On the development in baking see Arnold, *Das Münchner Bäckergewerbe*; the monographs on baking in Leipzig, Breslau, and Jena, in *Schriften* 63 (1896); 70 (1897); and chap. 1.

men in 1882 and 2.1 in 1895—a growth of 15 and 17 percent respectively. The number of individual self-employed bakers decreased between 1882 and 1895 by no less than 27 percent, while the number of all baker-employers rose by 42 percent and of small bakers by over 15 percent. Adding to these figures contemporary reports on the conditions of the small bakers and butchers in the various urban centers in Germany, the unmistakable impression is one of general and increased prosperity.

So far our analysis seems to suggest that in the crafts worst hit by the combined effects of industrialization and economic fluctuations a large number of independent artisans were impoverished and often proletarianized, while in the best-situated crafts some masters actually improved their economic standing, and many managed to retain a relatively secure position. A process of polarization can thus be detected both within some of the major crafts and between them.

Local studies seem to confirm these conclusions, particularly with regard to the small independent handicraft masters in urban centers. As a rule urban masters lacked the security enjoyed by rural craftsmen who were often engaged in agricultural as well as in handicraft production. Moreover, the transition from an independent to a dependent economic position was more likely to occur in an urban setting, where employment opportunities for skilled craftsmen in large-scale industry were available and more accessible.

During the years of general, though mild and fluctuating, slowdown of economic growth in Germany, independent small craftsmen often did experience a polarization within their ranks. It was not a figment of their imagination, nor was its description by social observers merely an outgrowth of some ideological construct. The actual economic position of the masters was not always acute. Indeed, many of them prospered. But at the same time the sight of the impoverished master was common enough, and the precarious posi-

TABLE 2.4

STRUCTURAL CHANGE IN SELECTED HANDICRAFTS, 1882-1895

Trade	% Change in No. of Small Shops 1882-1895	% Change in No. of Single Self-Employed Masters 1882-1895	Industrial Concentration: Men per Shop		Industrial Concentration: Men per Small Shop	
			1882	*1895*	*1882*	*1895*
All Industry	−8.6	−13.5	2.6	3.7	1.5	1.8
Metal workers	−7.6	−14.5	2.8	4.0	1.8	2.0
Wood-workers	−11.7	−20.1	2.0	2.7	1.5	1.7
Clothing workers	−4.4	−6.5	1.4	1.6	1.3	1.3
Building workers	13.8	16.3	3.3	5.3	1.7	1.7
Food workers	6.5	−12.0	3.0	3.8	1.9	2.2
Group 1						
Potters	−47.7	−52.8	3.1	5.2	1.9	2.0
Copper-smiths	−10.5	−14.5	2.6	3.2	2.0	2.1
Black-smiths	−5.9	−18.1	1.9	2.0	1.8	1.9
Lock-smiths	−8.1	−21.9	2.6	4.1	2.1	2.4
Carpenters	−5.5	−14.7	1.9	2.6	1.7	1.8
Lathe workers	−12.5	−17.8	2.3	2.8	1.6	1.7
Glaziers	−12.4	−22.8	1.5	1.9	1.5	1.7
Group 2						
Watch makers	17.4	20.9	1.9	2.1	1.5	1.5
Uphol-sterers	47.3	52.1	2.3	2.5	1.8	1.9
Masons	15.7	28.8	3.5	4.8	1.6	1.5
Building carpenters	8.9	20.8	3.0	3.5	1.7	1.7
Group 3						
Bakers	15.1	−27.0	2.2	2.7	2.0	2.3
Butchers	14.8	−9.6	2.0	2.4	1.8	2.1

SOURCE: *St.d.R.* 119, pp. 9* ff., 16* ff.

tion of others obvious and disturbing even to their more fortunate colleagues. The ability of the economy to overcome periods of depression eventually put a stop to economic polarization among traditional craftsmen, but for many master craftsmen in Germany the prospect of impoverishment remained a real and recurrent threat.

Income and Standard of Living

To measure real income or changes in the standard of living of any one segment of the population during a period of industrialization is difficult in any case. But to do so for the urban master artisans in Germany during the last quarter of the nineteenth century is virtually impossible, partly because of the polarization detectable among them. The fact that both impoverished men and successful entrepreneurs tend to be excluded from the relevant statistical tables presents a particularly intricate problem. The first element is usually absorbed by the dependent working population, while the other disappears into the category of medium- or large-scale businessmen. Furthermore, any attempt to evaluate changes in the economic well-being of those who remained small independent masters immediately encounters numerous additional difficulties. Foremost among them is the enormous variation in incomes, not only among the various crafts but also among the individual masters within one trade. An investigation of conditions among small handicraft masters in Mannheim in the mid-1880s found, for example, one carpenter who employed eleven journeymen and was prospering in spite of the general economic slump, and another who headed a family of ten, and was forced to overwork himself and the employable members of his family seven days a week in his debt-ridden workshop.[35] A study of artisans' income in Leipzig for the year 1893, conducted by Karl Bücher for the VSP, showed the differences in in-

[35] See *Mannheim Erhebung*, Questionnaires 31, 32.

come among master artisans in seventeen selected crafts.[36] The masters were represented in all income categories in town, from the lowest to the highest, but almost one-half of them showed a modest annual income ranging between 700 and 1,250 RM. Table 2.5 is reproduced with slight alterations from Bücher's study. It provides a general impression of the overall diversity of the handicraft masters' income level, and indicates the range within which the master-artisans' annual income was most likely to fall.

The various handicrafts can be ranked in order of average income, giving a sense of the differentiation among the crafts, as well as an indication of the position of each relative to the others. Bücher himself arrived at the list presented in table 2.6, starting with the wealthiest masters. Other methods of ordering the crafts according to the level of prosperity enjoyed by the masters practicing them produce similar results. A recent study of two Westphalian regions found the average income of small master artisans in 1895 to be higher than that calculated by Bücher, ranging from 1,000M to 2,650M. However, the study confirms the existence of considerable variation in the incomes of masters in the various crafts. Here, too, bakers and butchers appear at the head of the list, and tailors, shoemakers, basket makers, and wheelwrights at the bottom.[37] Bücher himself employed an additional index in his study of the master artisans in Leipzig based on the percentage of home owners among the masters in the various crafts. According to this index, butchers and bakers again appeared at the top of the

[36] Karl Bücher, "Einkommenverhältnisse der Leipziger Handwerker," *Schriften* 67 (1896): 699-705.

[37] Noll, *Sozio-ökonomischer Strukturwandel*, pp. 68-69. Noll's study includes a large sample of crafts. Using his data for the Arnsberg district in 1895, the crafts can be listed according to the size of their average yearly income in the following order: bakers, butchers, carpenters, book printers, roofers, turners, goldsmiths, glaziers, masons, bookbinders, coopers, locksmiths, plumbers, saddlers, tailors, shoemakers, brush makers; the list exhibits some regional peculiarities, but in its broad outline confirms previous conclusions.

TABLE 2.5

ANNUAL INCOME IN 17 SELECTED HANDICRAFTS, LEIPZIG, 1893

Income in Marks	*Bakers*	*Confectioners*	*Coopers*	*Bookbinders*	*Brushmakers*	*Turners*	*Butchers*	*Slaughterers*	*Glaziers*	*Plumbers*	*Furriers*	*Saddlers and cartwrights*	*Tailors*	*Locksmiths*	*Shoemakers*	*Carpenters*	*Watchmakers*	*All*
300- 399	–	–	–	1	1	2	–	–	1	–	1	–	40	1	13	3	1	64
400- 499	1	–	2	1	–	–	–	–	1	2	3	3	316	–	41	6	–	376
500- 599	2	1	–	1	–	–	1	1	7	–	–	1	189	1	74	7	1	286
600- 699	1	1	1	2	–	–	2	1	1	5	–	1	189	2	108	7	1	322
700- 799	–	1	1	4	5	5	1	5	4	4	3	8	171	5	221	21	5	464
800- 949	3	4	11	7	4	3	4	24	12	11	8	9	294	15	375	32	13	829
950- 1,099	11	5	10	15	2	8	11	32	12	21	8	21	143	27	133	62	18	539
1,100- 1,249	24	2	7	33	5	11	7	14	20	41	14	24	121	39	102	58	13	535
1,250- 1,399	4	2	5	11	1	4	3	2	5	11	10	9	23	21	28	21	6	166
1,400- 1,599	43	6	6	26	4	7	17	7	20	34	17	15	83	43	49	46	15	438
1,600- 1,899	29	1	4	14	–	4	9	2	16	25	6	10	47	35	37	33	5	277
1,900- 2,199	61	5	5	13	2	4	26	–	14	18	7	11	35	28	21	32	12	294
2,200- 2,499	44	9	1	4	–	1	27	2	12	14	9	9	29	21	12	20	5	219
2,500- 2,799	23	–	1	4	–	–	6	–	3	6	3	1	3	5	1	5	1	62
2,800- 3,299	59	2	2	6	–	2	40	–	3	4	8	7	8	19	11	15	2	188

3,300- 3,799	39	3	1	2	1	1	29	–	2	7	3	2	7	2	6	9	2	116
3,800- 4,299	28	1	–	1	–	–	31	–	–	4	6	2	11	9	2	10	3	108
4,300- 4,799	16	2	–	8	–	–	21	–	–	–	–	–	2	–	1	1	1	52
4,800- 5,399	20	–	1	4	–	–	21	–	1	1	4	3	6	4	1	3	3	72
5,400- 6,299	16	2	–	2	–	1	17	–	1	3	1	1	5	2	–	7	–	58
6,300- 7,199	7	2	1	–	–	–	7	–	1	1	–	–	1	–	–	–	1	21
7,200- 8,399	9	–	–	3	–	–	17	–	–	2	4	2	3	1	1	–	1	43
8,400- 9,599	2	–	–	1	–	–	6	–	–	–	–	–	–	–	1	–	–	10
9,600-10,799	4	2	–	1	–	–	11	–	–	–	–	2	1	1	1	–	1	24
10,800-11,999	1	–	–	–	–	–	5	1	–	–	1	–	–	–	–	–	–	7
12,000-13,999	–	–	–	1	–	1	3	–	–	2	–	–	–	–	1	1	–	9
14,000-15,999	–	1	–	1	–	–	5	–	–	–	2	–	3	–	1	1	–	14
16,000-17,999	1	–	–	–	–	–	2	–	–	1	–	–	1	–	–	–	–	5
18,000-19,999	1	–	–	1	–	–	1	–	–	1	–	–	–	–	–	–	–	4
20,000-21,999	–	–	–	1	–	–	–	–	–	–	2	–	–	–	–	–	–	3
22,000-23,999	–	–	–	–	–	–	3	–	–	–	1	–	1	–	–	–	–	5
24,000-25,999	–	–	–	–	–	–	–	–	–	–	1	–	–	–	–	–	–	1
26,000-27,999	–	–	–	1	–	–	–	–	–	–	–	–	–	–	–	–	–	1
28,000-29,999	–	–	–	2	–	–	–	–	–	–	–	–	–	–	–	–	–	2
Totals	449	52	59	171	24	55	333	90	136	218	122	141	1,732	281	1,241	400	110	5,614

SOURCE: Bücher, "Einkommenverhältnisse," p. 701.

TABLE 2.6

INCOME DISTRIBUTION OF MASTER ARTISANS
LEIPZIG, 1893

Craft	*Percentage Earning Annual Income of*				
	300-1,250M	*1,251-3,300M*	*3,301-5,400M*	*5,401-12,000M*	*Over 12,000M*
Butchers	7.8	38.4	30.6	18.9	4.2
Bakers	9.3	58.6	22.9	8.7	0.5
Confectioners	27.0	48.1	11.5	11.7	1.9
Furriers	30.3	49.2	10.7	4.9	4.9
Locksmiths	32.0	61.2	5.3	1.4	–
Bookbinders	37.4	45.6	8.8	4.1	4.1
Plumbers	38.5	51.4	5.5	2.8	1.8
Glaziers	42.6	53.7	2.2	1.5	–
Saddlers and cartwrights	46.8	43.4	4.9	3.5	1.4
Watchmakers	47.3	41.7	8.2	2.7	–
Carpenters	49.0	43.0	5.7	1.7	0.5
Turners	52.7	40.0	1.8	1.8	3.7
Coopers	54.2	40.7	3.4	1.7	–
Brush makers	68.0	28.0	4.0	–	–
Tailors	84.4	13.2	1.5	0.6	0.3
Slaughterers	85.6	14.4	–	–	–
Shoemakers	86.0	12.8	0.8	0.2	0.1

SOURCE: Bücher, "Einkommenverhältnisse," p. 703.

list, with some 40 percent of the masters owning their own homes, while the smiths and the shoemakers reappeared at the very bottom. In between, several building crafts were placed higher on the home-owning list than on the income list, perhaps because of their occupational affinity with land purchasing and home construction.[38] In a study of population changes and of the occupational and living conditions in Berlin, based on the census of 1871, the hierarchy of handicraft trades according to home ownership appears to have been very similar. Among the small butchers and bakers 30 percent owned their homes; among masons and

[38] Bücher, "Einkommenverhältnisse," pp. 704-705.

joiners the percentage was around 20, while far down on the list were the carpenters with 5 percent, the plumbers with 4 percent, and the tailors and shoemakers with 1.8 percent and 1.3 percent respectively.[39]

A rent investigation in Berlin two decades later, among independent industrial shop owners whose private residences also served as a location for their handicraft workshops, revealed the picture presented in table 2.7.

TABLE 2.7

HANDICRAFTSMEN'S RENTS, BERLIN, 1890

Trade	*Percentage Paying Rents of*				
	0-450M	*451-900M*	*901-1,800M*	*1,801-3,000M*	*Over 3,000M*
Bookbinders	5.81	31.95	40.25	15.35	6.64
Woodworkers	12.42	39.60	31.27	10.75	5.96
Upholsterers	16.86	34.30	34.60	8.72	5.52
Masons	17.88	36.23	23.19	14.49	8.21
Saddlers and cartwrights	14.34	40.07	27.04	11.40	7.15
Glaziers	15.75	42.43	27.88	10.91	3.03
Painters	13.04	56.21	25.78	4.35	0.62
Tailors	28.46	29.47	28.85	8.94	4.28
Shoemakers	35.12	41.96	17.62	3.77	1.53
All industrial and commercial occupations	12.22	31.45	32.59	14.42	9.32
All independently-occupied men working at home	12.64	31.57	32.00	14.33	9.64

SOURCE: *Die Bevölkerungs- und Wohnungsaufnahme*, part 4, p. 82.

Table 2.7 provides a view of the conditions of small masters in several crafts with relation to other independent producers and to all men working independently in Berlin. With the possible exception of the bookbinders, the rent paid by masters in all handicrafts in this sample falls well

[39] See Hermann Schwabe, *Die Königliche Haupt- und Residenzstadt Berlin*, p. 128.

below the average for all industrial shop owners. Once more, tailors and shoemakers appear to constitute the poorest segment of the master population. It should be noted, however, that this table tends to overestimate the poverty of the small masters, because it reflects only the situation of the masters who used their residences as industrial workshops, and these were presumably among the less prosperous ones. The figures, nevertheless, confirm that in Berlin, too, the great majority of the small masters managed to earn only low or lower-middle incomes.

The distribution of the employment of domestic servants among the master artisans in the different crafts gives another index for ordering the trades on a scale of prosperity among themselves and with relation to others.[40] The overall picture supplied by these figures is fundamentally the same. Thus, 46.7 percent of all master bakers and 40.8 percent of all butchers in 1882 employed domestic servants and once again occupied the top position among the master artisans of the traditional urban crafts. Far below trail the bookbinders, with 21.7 percent, the locksmiths with 12.6 percent, and at the very bottom the tailors with 3.6 percent and the shoemakers with 3.2 percent. The changes in these rates between 1882 and 1895 were only marginal.[41]

A quick look at the percentage of those who stood directly above or below the masters in the industrial stratification and employed domestic servants gives some indication of the masters' position in the general socioeconomic hierarchy. In 1882, 87 percent of the owners of breweries, 86 percent of the owners of weaving mills, and 81 percent of the owners of spinning establishments employed domestic servants. Closest to the master bakers on this list were the building entrepreneurs, themselves also often master artisans: 45 per-

[40] For the employment of domestic servants in 1882 see *St.d.R.* 4, pp. 12* ff.

[41] For the domestic servants employed in 1895 see *St.d.R.* 115, pp. 82 ff. See also the discussion in Voigt, "Das deutsche Handwerk," *Schriften* 70 (1897): 659-662.

cent of them could afford to employ domestic help. On the other side of the social spectrum, dependent tailors and shoemakers in home industry appear in about the same position as their independent colleagues with regard to the employment of domestic servants. Journeymen of all crafts, however, fell into a different category altogether. Only between 0.5 percent and 0.2 percent of them employed servants. Thus, the master artisans of the different crafts spanned the gap between the truly capitalist entrepreneurs and the skilled laborers on the income as well as on the social ladder. Some stood quite close to the former, others were indistinguishable from the latter.

A traditional way of measuring the masters' economic position has been to relate it directly to the number of helpers employed in their shops. Although this index, like all others, is far from precise, it does provide some indication of the level and range of masters' incomes.[42] It has been shown, for instance, that among the butchers in Leipzig, masters with up to two employees earned about 1,400M per year, while those with three to five employees managed to secure an income of 4,000M and more.[43] At the other end of the income spectrum, individual self-employed shoemakers in Bavaria, for instance, earned only about 935M a year, while

[42] This measurement was used originally by Schmoller in his *Zur Geschichte des Kleingewerbes*, and has been applied in most studies of the small masters' economic situation since then. The disadvantage of this method is that it obscures the possible increase in the income of those masters who managed to dispense with expensive labor and purchased instead some modern machines. This could have been the case with some tailors and shoemakers, whose productivity rose considerably with the introduction of sewing machines. Labor-saving tools were introduced into other trades also, such as bookbinding. They were not counted in the statistics on the use of motor power, but could have meant a sizeable productivity increase for the small master artisans, and a rise in their income that was not reflected at all in employment figures. See a fuller discussion of the limitations of this indicator in Stadelmann and Fischer, *Die Bildungswelt*, p. 112, and Noll, *Sozio-ökonomischer Strukturwandel*, pp. 51-52.

[43] Rind, "Die Fleischerei in Leipzig," *Schriften* 68 (1897): 123.

with the help of two additional men they often managed to earn about 1,100M, and with five employees, an apprentice, and two sewing machines, the small shoemaker might make about 1,800M per year.[44] All other available local and vocational information supports the assumption that the average number of employees in the master-artisans' shops was highly correlated with the masters' level of income, and can therefore serve as an approximate index of their relative prosperity.

At this point, however, it is important to remember that individual self-employed masters constituted over 50 percent of all the men employed in industry in the German Reich even as late as 1895.[45] While in large cities such self-employed men constituted on the average only 31 percent of all craft masters, this percentage rose to 41 in smaller towns and was as high as 61 in the countryside. Although in Germany as a whole about 13 percent less individual self-employed men were engaged in industry in 1895 than in 1882, in 1895 they still numbered over 1,250,000. Similarly, in spite of a marked decline in the number of such small Alleinmeister in many of the crafts, they still composed over half of the independently employed men in the machine-tool industry, in woodworking, in the clothing trades, and in construction. The 1895 census for Berlin recorded close to 60 percent of independent industrial personnel as working alone, and a local survey in 1890 classified almost 40 percent of all the small masters in the metal trades as Alleinmeister, 50 percent in the machine-tool industry, 41 percent in the woodworking crafts, and up to 87 percent in the clothing industry. Thus, although the group was diminishing, at the end of the nineteenth century it still constituted a formidable part of the small artisan estate.

[44] Francke, *Die Schuhmacherei in Bayern*, pp. 131 ff.

[45] For these and the following data see *St.d.R.* 119, pp. 227* ff.; pp. 9* ff.; *Erhebung über die Verhältnisse im Handwerk*, part 2; the data for Berlin are in *Die Bevölkerungs- und Wohnungsaufnahme in der Stadt Berlin, 1895*, pp. 83-84.

In small shops with one to five employees the slight rise in the increase of men per shop suggests some improvement in the standard of living for the 1875-95 period, and this is supported by sporadic local findings.[46] Occupational statistics, however, may still be misleading, and national data pertaining directly to changes in real income appear to be unobtainable.

In view of the limitations of all these calculations, the discussion at this point must transcend economic criteria and move into an evaluation of social and sociopsychological factors. It is, after all, often not the changes in material well-being that are responsible for the mood among the members of a social group, but these changes measured against the progress of other groups within its immediate social environment. A slight improvement of real income may look unsatisfactory when compared with the showing of a "reference group."[47] And indeed the small master artisans in Imperial Germany seem to have been constantly engaged in comparing their position with that of others, above all the large-scale industrial producers on the one hand, and the journeymen and industrial laborers on the other.

It is easy to imagine that even at times of obvious economic difficulties, the personal standard of living of the well-established industrial entrepreneurs suffered little if any decline. The small masters were often reminded of their need to compete with the new and growing industrial sector and were gradually made aware of their own disadvantages under the pressure of mechanization, a growing market, and a fluctuating economy. Similarly, the improvement in the standard of living of dependent workers during this period was far more consistent and impressive than anything the small masters could boast of. Recent calculations suggest that the index of workers' wages rose between 1880 and 1895

[46] See Noll, *Sozio-ökonomischer Strukturwandel*, pp. 68-74; 233-273.

[47] For the concepts used here see W.G. Runciman, *Relative Deprivation and Social Justice*.

from 88 to 120.[48] There is also evidence to suggest that in most crafts during these years journeymen's wages grew faster than masters' incomes.[49]

The available information does not allow us to calculate with precision the income earned by small masters in the various crafts. It only enables us to assert with a measure of certainty that between 1873 and 1896 a majority of them earned low, or at best lower-middle, incomes. Some were paupers; others managed to retain a comfortable standard of living or even to improve it. But all felt that their material gains did not adequately represent the true value of their work and did not match their expectations. Relative to their immediate reference groups—the larger industrialists and the dependent workers—they constantly felt at a disadvantage. It is to their changing social position, therefore, that we shall now turn in the following two chapters.

[48] See Ashok V. Desai, *Real Wages in Germany 1871-1913*, p. 36. Other calculations give more conservative estimates for the rise in the real wages of workers. See the estimates in E.H. Phelps-Brown and Sheila V. Hopkins, "The Course of Wage Rates in Five Countries," p. 274. They suggest a rise from 93 to 100 between 1885 and 1895. See also Gerhard Bry, *Wages in Germany*, p. 329; and Jürgen Kuczynski, *Die Geschichte der Lage der Arbeiter*, vol. 2, p. 176.

[49] Noll, *Sozio-ökonomischer Strukturwandel*, pp. 74-81.

THREE

THE BREAK BETWEEN MASTERS AND MEN

A Comparison with England

In the course of the nineteenth century it was not only the economic position of the small urban master artisans in Germany that was radically transformed, but also their social standing. The transformation had started long before the onset of industrialization.[1] It picked up momentum from the impact of the rapid changes in the character of the market and the mode of industrial production, and from the economic depression of the last quarter of the century. A new set of relationships then evolved between the small master artisans and other social groups, both inside and outside the handicraft estate. Perhaps the most painful of these changes was the long process of separation between master artisans and their trained journeymen.

An ambivalent relationship between these two segments of the artisan population had always existed, but the ambivalence became increasingly apparent from the early eighteenth century on.[2] By that time the handicraft guilds began to feel continuous pressure from the mercantilist, absolutist states in Germany. The state mercantilism of the bureaucracies in Prussia, Saxony, Bavaria, and elsewhere among the smaller German states supported and encouraged capitalist producers and putting-out entrepreneurs, and

[1] For a stimulating discussion of these early changes within the context of the small German urban communities, see Walker, *German Home Towns.*

[2] For the development of these relationships during the eighteenth century see Stadelmann and Fischer, *Die Bildungswelt*, pp. 97-104; Wolfgang Zorn, "Zünfte" in the *Handwörterbuch der sozialwissenschaften*; Friedrich Lütge, *Deutsche Sozial- und Wirtschaftsgeschichte*, pp. 219-220; and the earlier work by H.A. Mascher, *Das deutsche Gewerbewesen*, part 6. All of these only mention the problem. See also Walker, *German Home Towns*, pp. 73-103; 329-353.

tended to disregard existing guild regulations. This made possible the introduction of handicraft production on a large scale into the countryside and a slow encroachment on guild monopolies in the towns. In addition, the absolutist states repeatedly attempted to restrict the self-governing autonomy of small towns and the self-administration of the corporations within them. But in the course of the battle between townsmen and state governments, guildmasters often joined forces with state authorities in an effort to control the independent activities of journeymen and journeymen's associations. The masters found themselves in a strangely ambiguous position, which became more pronounced with the passage of time, and which eventually came to characterize the nature of their political position within the emerging unified bureaucratic state.

The journeymen's "tramping system" gave a peculiarly transient nature to their grouping. Nevertheless, it also offered them a unique opportunity to operate beyond local limits. Growing solidarity among them caused much alarm in government circles and among the established guildmasters. The Gesellenbrüderschaften (journeymen's brotherhoods) threatened to become special interest organizations representing wage-earning journeymen in open opposition to their master employers and in defiance of town and state authorities alike. The early eighteenth century saw a relatively widespread strike movement among journeymen, and the Imperial government reacted by passing a new industrial bill, which included Draconian measures against any combined action by journeymen's associations. At the same time, however, the 1731 edict also attempted to cure some of the more obvious abuses in the constitutions and the practices of the guilds themselves, and to bring them under more effective supervision by the central civil authorities and the police.[3]

[3] See Hermann Aubin and Wolfgang Zorn, eds., *Handbuch der deutschen Wirtschafts- und Sozialgeschichte*, vol. 1, pp. 536-540; 592-598; and Mascher, *Das deutsche Gewerbewesen*, part 6, pp. 340

The master artisans for their part became increasingly adamant about protecting their traditional privileges. In the first half of the eighteenth century many craft guilds became "closed," practically prohibiting the admission of all but master-artisans' sons.[4] These restrictive measures, combined with the relaxation of state supervision over the traditional economic monopolies of the guilds, and the gradual development of new types of industrial production, encouraged the growth of a nonguild artisan population in the countryside and in towns. In large areas of the Reich, guildmasters gradually lost their economic privileges together with their social prerogatives. But while growing competition and the slow deterioration of the power and prestige of the guilds sharpened the rivalry and ill will between masters and journeymen, the encroachment of the state on the privileges of the handicraft estate as a whole often drew them together. The masters were occasionally forced to accept the independent activities of journeymen's associations in order to enlist them in a common battle against the centralized state bureaucracy. Journeymen were often the most ardent defenders of guild monopolies and of customary guild standards of production and morality. During much of the eighteenth century masters and men often managed to preserve a united front against the state, while the friction and hostility between them were rapidly growing.

A look at Britain may serve to illuminate this peculiar German situation. In England, guild restrictions lost their effectiveness earlier than on the continent.[5] By the eight-

ff. See also Jürgen Bergmann, "Das 'Alte Handwerk' im Übergang," especially pp. 252-261. An English version of the 1731 edict is to be found in Walker, *German Home Towns*, pp. 435-451.

[4] The growing exclusiveness of the guilds is mentioned in all standard economic histories, for example, Lütge, *Deutsche Sozial- und Wirtschaftsgeschichte*, pp. 308 ff. For a local study of the problem see, e.g., Victor Böhmert, *Beiträge zur Geschichte des Zunftwesens*, p. 52.

[5] See Sylvia L. Thrupp, "The Guilds" and the bibliography there; also Held, *Zwei Bücher*, pp. 387 ff.

eenth century, capitalist entrepreneurs were unhampered by legal restrictions, and the surviving handicraft companies were often hardly more than a source of royal income. Membership included both masters and journeymen, and the social gap between them was losing significance in the face of growing competition from large-scale merchants and industrial producers. In 1563 the Elizabethan Code had legally established the medieval "seven years' servitude" of handicraft apprentices in a large number of trades. Clearly, the assigned period far exceeded the requirements of vocational training, and the law was in practice frequently ignored. Originally designed as a means of controlling the admission of new men into the crafts, it had served to underline the social distinction between the young and the mature workman, the skilled and the unskilled. No similar legal distinction was made in England between masters and their journeymen. The latter were above all considered as skilled craftsmen, and were employed either independently or in small workshops. They could usually even train and employ their own apprentices.[6]

Under these circumstances all skilled workers had a common interest in preventing the entrance of insufficiently trained labor into the trades and in maintaining standards of workmanship and production. Their solidarity was demonstrated in 1812-13 when they cooperated to prevent the repeal of the antiquated apprenticeship regulations.[7] Both masters and men attended public meetings and formed a joint action committee. They eventually succeeded in submitting to Parliament a petition with 300,000 signatures protesting the government policy of opening trades to the unskilled. The distinction between them and common laborers

[6] See the short but delightful description of internal relationships within the handicrafts in England at the end of the eighteenth and during the early nineteenth centuries in Dorothy George, *England in Transition*, pp. 119-133.

[7] For the story of the campaign against the repeal of the Elizabethan apprenticeship regulations see T.K. Derry, "The Repeal of Apprenticeship Clauses."

was stubbornly defended, and with the beginning of industrialization it had to be maintained against the prevailing opinion in government circles, in the legislature, and among other social groups.[8] In the early nineteenth century Francis Place complained that "the most skilled and the most prudent workmen" are considered together with "the most ignorant and imprudent laborers and paupers." The differences between them, he argued, "in many cases scarce admit of comparison."[9]

The line of distinction between master artisans and their journeymen, both skilled workingmen, was further blurred in England, as we have earlier seen, by the nature of industrial development.[10] It was this peculiar affinity between masters and men that gave rise to a long historiographical debate concerning the link between the old guilds and the modern British trade-union movement.[11] The traditional corporations in England, in contrast to the continent, were

[8] By far the best treatment of this issue is to be found in Hobsbawm, "The Labour Aristocracy in Nineteenth Century Britain," reprinted in his *Labouring Men*, especially pp. 322-325.

[9] Quoted in Asa Briggs, "The Language of 'Class' in Early Nineteenth Century England," in A. Briggs and J. Saville, eds., *Essays in Labour History*, p. 44.

[10] See the section on domestic industry in chap. 1; also Hobsbawm, "The Labour Aristocracy," pp. 349-350. This blurring of the line between small masters and journeymen is taken for granted by most historians of nineteenth-century Britain. It is almost impossible to find any statement in which the two are distinguished or in which their mingling appears to require an explanation. See, for example, G.D.H. Cole, *Chartist Portraits*, p. 8: "Between these small masters and the skilled artisans who worked *with them* or for bigger employers, there was no sharp division of classes." (Italics added.)

[11] Lujo Brentano sought to establish a direct historical link between the guilds and the trade unions in England. See his *Die Arbeitergilden der Gegenwart*, pp. 89-132. The Webbs vehemently rejected this thesis; see Sidney and Beatrice Webb, *History of Trade Unionism*, pp. 13-21. In his article "The Tramping Artisans," reprinted in *Labouring Men*, Hobsbawm attempted a reevaluation of the role of tradition in labor customs of the nineteenth century, pp. 41-47.

institutions in which masters and men cooperated, although indubitably under the leadership of the former. The trade unions, on the other hand, developed as organizations of wage earners alone and often acted in open opposition to the master employers. Nevertheless, the historical link between these institutions cannot be disregarded.

The spring-knife cutlers in Sheffield in 1820 urged all "corporate trades" to form combinations of masters and men in order to fix prices, maintain standards of workmanship, and enforce the apprenticeship regulations. As late as 1844 they named their new trade union an "Operative Company of Spring-Knife Cutlers, being part of the Commonalty of the Incorporated Cutlers' Company." They were governed by a master, a treasurer, a correspondence secretary, and an executive committee—"a mixture of guild and trade-union functions," as the historian of the labor movement in Sheffield has commented.[12] The balance of power between masters and journeymen within the early trade societies and trade unions gradually shifted in the direction of the wage-earning element. The independent producers and small masters, however, did not hesitate to join these bodies; in some crafts they constituted a significant portion of their membership until well into the nineteenth century. The early trade-union movement was indeed a movement of skilled workmen, reflecting the prevailing social alliances in England. In it skilled workers were joining forces against the intrusion of the unskilled on the one hand, and the encroachment of the large industrial entrepreneurs, on the other.[13]

1848-49: Widening the Gap

The evolution of social stratification in Germany took an entirely different course. The guild tradition in that country centered around the division of the so-called Handwerkerstand into three elements: masters, journeymen, and appren-

[12] Pollard, *Labour in Sheffield*, pp. 66-67.

[13] See Hobsbawm, "The Labour Aristocracy," p. 349.

tices. The distinction between a Meister, who passed his qualifying examination, presented his masterwork to the satisfaction of his future colleagues, and was accepted as a full member into their community, and a Gesell who, though a skilled craftsman, was still outside this community, did not diminish with the weakening of effective guild authority during the eighteenth century, but rather became even more pronounced. Throughout the period guildmasters sought by various means to maintain a position of authority over their journeymen. They consciously avoided any excessive familiarity with their men, and as the guilds became more exclusive and the journeymen's chances of achieving full membership in them slimmer, the traditional comradely relationships between masters and men became increasingly rare.

Since the institution of the guild was an expression of the superiority of master artisans over journeymen on both the economic and the sociopolitical plane, the growing separation between them was alternately and intricately influenced by both economic and sociopolitical changes in Germany. By the early decades of the nineteenth century, as the population grew and with it the pressure from skilled and unskilled craftsmen outside the guilds, estrangement between masters and journeymen was everywhere felt as a constant danger to the very existence of the old handicraft estate and to the social and moral norms it had sought to represent. The severity of the situation varied from state to state and from region to region. The differences were dictated primarily by the local level of industrial development, by the prevailing economic legislation, and by the multitude of ways in which laws and regulations had been implemented by local town authorities.[14] Such diversity characterized the social and economic development of Germany throughout the

[14] On the diversity within Prussia see Koselleck, *Preussen zwischen Reform und Revolution*, pp. 596-597. On the conditions in Upper Bavaria and the Palatinate see Walker, *German Home Towns*, pp. 372-374.

eighteenth and much of the nineteenth centuries. But while it had still been pronounced in the pre-March years, a degree of uniformity began to emerge after the revolution of 1848. The long social and economic conflict was given open political expression during the summer months of that eventful year, and as a result, confrontation virtually replaced cooperation in the relations between masters and men.[15]

Only a fraction of the handicraft population in Germany took part in what was later known as the first Handwerkerbewegung (artisans' movement) in 1848. A few participated in the sporadic demonstrations throughout the country; a somewhat larger group signed one or more of the numerous petitions then circulated among the craftsmen; and a small minority was actively engaged in the organization of local, regional, or national assemblies. In the June 1848 artisans' pre-Parliament in Hamburg, the north was clearly overrepresented. In Frankfurt a.M., several weeks later, the south predominated. East and West Prussia were hardly represented at all, and the master artisans from the Palatinate seem to have opposed the spirit and the practical intentions of the movement altogether.

A detailed study of the economic position and political activity of small masters in Germany during the revolution of 1848 is still lacking. It will be made possible only through a considerable number of local and regional investigations. From what is now known, however, it is difficult to avoid the impression that the majority of the masters throughout Germany were in agreement with the general tendency and the overall mood of the activists.[16] In Magdeburg, a meeting

[15] The importance of the revolution of 1848 in the formation of the German social-stratification system still awaits full investigation. See Stadelmann and Fischer, *Die Bildungswelt*, p. 61.

[16] See Hamerow, *Restoration, Revolution, Reaction*, chap. 8. For some additional comments on regional differentiation see Mascher, *Das deutsche Gewerbewesen*, pp. 514 ff. His analysis, unlike Hamerow's, emphasizes the areas in which agitation against industrial freedom was not popular, but Mascher too admits that "the greater section

of artisans drew representatives from 150 Saxonian towns. In Hamburg, 200 delegates of regional and local ad hoc artisan organizations convened and attempted to unify the movement and give it national dimensions. Finally, 116 masters representing twenty-four German states came together in an assembly known as the Frankfurt Arstisans' Parliament.[17] It was only then that the gulf that had already separated master artisans from their journeymen was given full political and institutional expression. Differences were aired in public, and in the general atmosphere of tension and political excitement the last bridge between the two segments of the old handicraft estate was demolished.

About one-fifth of the delegates to the Hamburg pre-Parliament appeared in the congress list of participants as printers, smiths, etc. It can be assumed that some of them were in fact journeymen and not established master artisans. Indeed, the desired unity of all social elements within the handicraft estate played an important role in this gathering and was repeatedly urged upon the delegates.[18] Karl Georg Winkelblech, an economist from Kassel who in 1848 unexpectedly emerged as the intellectual spokesman of the artisan movement, was deeply committed to the idea of a unified handicraft estate.[19] His detailed plan for the organi-

---

of the handicraft estate" opposed industrial freedom, and thus basically supported the organized Handwerkerbewegung. For Bavaria in particular see Shorter, "Middle-Class Anxiety"; for fuller treatment of the southwestern states see Walker, *German Home Towns*, especially pp. pp. 354-404; for Saxony, see R. Weber, "Die Beziehungen zwichen sozialer Struktur und politischer Ideologie."

17 See Hans Meusch, *Die Handwerkerbewegung von 1848/49*, pp. 35-68; and for the two major congresses, *Verhandlungen der ersten Abgeordneten Versammlung* and *Verhandlungen des ersten Handwerker- und Gewerbekongresses.*

18 The term "Arbeiterstand" was used throughout this congress to indicate masters and men alike, as opposed to other social elements, for example, the "educated." See *Verhandlungen der erstern Abgeordneten Versammlung*, pp. 2-16.

19 Winkelblech's writings appeared under his pseudonym Karl Marlo. He remained relatively unknown, although he was among

zation of industrial labor emphasized the need for cooperation, indeed for parity, between masters and men. It was designed above all to prevent what he saw as the further disintegration of German society, namely the breakdown of solidarity among the segments of the skilled crafts population. In Hamburg he urged the delegates to declare that "only a comprehensive guild constitution including all the industrial sectors is in a position to protect Germany from the fate of France and England and from the danger of communism."[20] Another speaker noted at the opening of the congress that "journeymen, apprentices, and masters together build the united handicraft estate," and continued by lamenting the tendency of some journeymen to call themselves "workers" and thus place themselves not on an equal basis with their masters but "one level lower."[21]

Both the spirit of the Hamburg meeting and its stated aim demonstrated an effort to gloss over the growing discord between masters and journeymen. In the Frankfurt congress, however, where representatives from the Rhine area had the upper hand, the picture was radically different. The traditionalism of the Hansa cities gave way to a more critical realism. The conflict between masters and men was immediately brought to the surface, and at the fourth session of the congress the battle was openly joined. A majority of the masters refused to admit journeymen as lawful delegates, and some even threatened to leave if journeymen were allowed to participate. The journeymen were in no position to appreciate the scope of the evils that had to be resisted, the masters argued, and could not be expected to show a serious attitude toward the goals ahead. Some conciliatory spirits

---

the first modern corporatist thinkers, and his writings had an influence on later corporatist social planners. See W.E. Biermann, *Karl Georg Winkelblech*, and Ralph H. Bowen, *German Theories of the Corporative State*, pp. 53 ff.

[20] *Verhandlungen der ersten Abgeordneten Versammlung*, p. 16; pp. 23-24.

[21] Ibid., pp. 16 ff.

simply urged the journeymen delegates to return to their homes, trusting their masters to represent their interests as their true fathers would and should have done,[22] but the journeymen naturally remained unsatisfied by these promises. Expelled from the masters' assembly, they hastily organized their own separate congress in Frankfurt, and deliberated, like the masters, throughout the rest of the summer.[23] Even this radical step, however, could not obscure the ambivalence of their attitude. The resolutions they finally endorsed disclosed a curious mixture of angry defiance and pleas for cooperation. Journeymen joined masters in demanding the restoration of self-administering bodies for the crafts, and stood with them in opposition to the hated central bureaucracies and the police. At the same time they demanded complete parity with the masters within these bodies and reasserted their right and duty to defend only "their own goals."[24] They were willing to include in the proposed Arbeitervereine (workers' associations) all who made it their duty to work for both the "advancement of the working classes and the reinstitution of the Mittelstand."[25] They made it their avowed purpose to save the Mittelstand from becoming a prey to industrial anarchy, and the entire nation from being divided into "millionaires and beggars."[26] The journeymen's congress rejected the masters' claim to social superiority, characterizing their behavior as unbecoming, egotistic, and irrational, but repeatedly asserted a belief in the unity of spirit and purpose within the handicraft estate. The very existence of the congress was in itself, however, proof of the extent of the estate's corrosion.

The Frankfurt journeymen's congress was only one in a series of revolutionary assemblies in Germany claiming to

22 *Verhandlungen des ersten Handwerkerkongresses*, pp. 19-40.

23 On the journeymen assembly, see Hartwig P. Bopp, *Die Entwicklung des deutschen Handwerkergesellentums*, pp. 231-256; Meusch, *Die Handwerkerbewegung*, pp. 80-91; Noyes, *Organization and Revolution*, pp. 190-220.

24 Bopp, *Die Entwicklung*, p. 242.

25 Ibid., p. 243.

26 Ibid., p. 236.

represent the wage-earning population. Other assemblies also gave expression to the ambivalent attitude of journeymen toward masters and of the hired laborers toward the corporations. In Berlin, Stephan Born presided over the first workers' congress. In spite of his early flirtation with socialism, Born too was caught in the prevailing confusion.[27] In his journal, *Das Volk*, he urged the workers to cooperate with the Kleinbürgertum (lower middle class) against the dangers of free competition and the power of capital. On June 10, 1848, his journal published a list of demands, some of them directly concerned with the common interests of "small masters and Handwerker."[28] Originally favoring a common corporate organization of all handicraftsmen, Born was brought only later in the year to see the depth of the mistrust and hatred between small masters and their men. A last effort by printers to form a joint association of masters and workmen quickly came to naught, and as the year drew to an end, it became increasingly obvious that cooperation between master artisans and journeymen was feared and rejected by both groups. Little beyond resounding phrases remained of their avowed unity. The workers' movement then took its independent course, and the masters were left on their own.

It is important to note that the separation between masters and men, which was so painful for both to accept, appears to have seemed quite natural to men outside the trades. When suffrage was discussed in the Frankfurt National Assembly, the constitutional committee suggested the exclusion of criminal elements and the bankrupt, men on poor relief, domestic servants, handicraft helpers, factory workers, and daily wage earners.[29] It thus disclosed the

[27] See also Dieter Bergmann, "Die Berliner Arbeiterschaft," especially pp. 479-499.

[28] Meusch, *Die Handwerkerbewegung*, p. 42. On Born's program see Stadelmann, *Soziale und politische Geschichte*, pp. 156-160.

[29] *Stenographische Berichte über die Verhandlungen der Nationalversammlung*, vol. 7, p. 5,218. See also Ludwig Oelsner, "Die wirt-

manner in which it conceived of the various gradations within the lower strata of German society. As pauperism spread in the pre-March period, the distinction between those within and those outside "respectable society" became more easily observable and acquired greater significance. It was perhaps the master artisans themselves, as citizens of the small German towns, who most emphatically stressed this distinction. Within the confines of local traditional society the distinction had economic as well as social and political implications.[30] From the social distance of the typical delegate to the Paulskirche, hired workingmen, skilled and unskilled alike, were even more easily conceived of as one social group. Journeymen were classified together with factory hands in contradistinction to the respectable, property-owning part of the population. The liberals in the Frankfurt Parliament, trying to avert the threat presented by their democratic wing had a vested interest in putting special emphasis on the dividing line between property owners and the propertyless, and this tendency was naturally supported by the forces of reaction, who could ultimately only benefit from the estrangement between moderate and radical revolutionaries. In fact, the Prussian bureaucracy had long wished to see the small masters form a bulwark against workers' organizations and their radical demands. State legislation since the reform era had worked toward obliterating the barriers between guild and nonguild masters, while increasingly binding handicraft journeymen and factory workers together, in opposition to their employers.[31] Both the state and the German liberals wished to enlist the handicraft masters for the coming battle against democracy.

When the state governments once again attempted to take matters into their own hands, a conscious effort was made to

schafts- und sozialpolitischen Verhandlungen des Frankfurter Parlaments," p. 95.

[30] See Walker, *German Home Towns*, pp. 283-353.

[31] Koselleck, *Preussen zwischen Reform und Revolution*, pp. 398-399.

conciliate the master artisans. Even in the decade prior to the revolution, the governments had only rarely interfered with the operations of the guilds, and they were now revising their antiguild laws and working to restore a measure of autonomy to the towns and the corporations.[32] Early in 1849, the Prussian government, in an effort to draw support from the disillusioned handicraftsmen, convened a meeting with representatives of "artisans and journeymen" under the auspices of the minister of commerce, industry, and public works.[33] At this point, obviously too late, a last effort was made to attract as many workers as possible away from the emerging Social-Democratic alternative into an alliance with their employers and the government. A bill providing for qualifying master examinations, state licensing for future independent craftsmen, a minimum of three apprenticeship years and three additional years as journeymen in the majority of the crafts was brought before the Prussian Diet. It proposed a minimum age for all those applying for permission to operate independent craft shops, recommended that masters' and journeymen's examinations be conducted by the newly created guilds, and suggested the establishment of special arbitration courts composed of two masters, two journeymen, and one government official. The Prussian bureaucracy thus went a long way toward reintroducing legal restrictions upon the economic freedom that had been so much heralded during the pre-March years and was still vehemently supported by the Frankfurt liberals. At the same time, however, the bill continued a century-old legislative trend, placing both masters and journeymen under the watchful eye of the central bureaucracy and the police.

When the bill came before the Landtag, it seemed to antagonize virtually everybody. It was returned to the government, and when it was debated anew on May 15, 1849, its character had been fundamentally altered. Dependent work-

[32] Walker, *German Home Towns*, pp. 385-394.

[33] See Paul Giessen, "Die preussische Handwerkerpolitik," pp. 28 ff.

ers were excluded from all the proposed new institutions, and the bill became a purely "master-artisans bill."[34] The government apparently decided to make concessions where they would matter the least, and preferred to retain the good will of the masters rather than forfeit the support of masters and men alike. Not surprisingly, the bill was rejected outright by journeymen, and was received with mixed feelings by masters. Eventually, local authorities applied it with the same laxity that had previously characterized their handling of guild regulations. The bill remained essentially ineffective. Nevertheless, the government continued to adhere to the principles that had dictated it. Any organization including proletarian elements was considered a potential danger, and repeated efforts were made to separate the subversive from the loyal elements within the handicraft population. After 1848 the government was consistently careful to distinguish between masters and journeymen, and thus gave official support to a social process that had been in progress for a long time.

But while the separation between masters and men was increasingly accepted by a growing segment of German society, it was still often resisted by men within the handicraft estate. For them, the events of 1848 did not bring to an end the process of attraction and repulsion between master artisans and skilled journeymen, but only marked the widening of the gap between the two groups. The process continued and was greatly accelerated during the third quarter of the nineteenth century. It was encouraged by prevailing social attitudes and by the actions of local and central governments, but above all it moved on inexorably because of the effects of industrialization and rapid economic growth.

The Decline of the Traditional Apprenticeship

The change in the relationship between master artisans and their hired workers began with the transformation of

[34] Ibid., pp. 41 ff.

the structure of the traditional handicraft shop. The master-artisan's shop was more than his place of employment and source of income. It was the focal point of his entire life, the crowning achievement of his years of training, the place where his moral and social values were formulated, the meeting point of his private and professional life. The shop, whether or not it was located in or near his home, constituted an extension of his family living quarters. The team working in it was an extension of the family itself. Apprentices were expected to receive moral and religious education from their master in addition to vocational training, and journeymen were supervised by him in matters of morality and social behavior. The master and his wife were expected to attend to the education of the young men in their shop as much as to that of their own children, and apprenticeship was consciously designed to prepare the youngster for a respectable life within the local community no less than for the successful practice of his acquired trade. If the master craftsman family shop never really measured up to its nineteenth-century idealized image, it was, nevertheless, in its heyday a well-defined and self-sustaining social unit—patriarchal, religious, and authoritarian in character.

The collapse of this social institution started under the pressure of economic change and material decline. Industrialization, accompanied by the need for adaptation on the shop floor, and the emergence of workers' class consciousness increased the strains within the craft workshop; the long years of depression and declining prices gave the final, fatal blow to the old patterns of interaction within it. The transformation of the handicraft shop was slow enough to preserve the illusion of stability but real enough to cause a large measure of anxiety to those involved in it.

The changes that will be described here started at different times in the different parts of what was later to become the new German Reich. They proceeded at a varying pace and took many different routes. While toward the end of the nineteenth century a measure of unity could be detected in the social climate of the handicraft shops throughout the country, some differentiation has persisted well into our own. On the whole, the old customs of the handicraft estate showed a remarkable tenacity. The 1895 industrial census surprisingly indicated that over 80 percent of all apprentices counted as employed in small enterprises were still living with their masters.[35] In Berlin, however, one of the most rapidly industrializing, and perhaps the most modern city in Germany at the time, only about 10 percent of all male workers and 45 percent of all female workers resided with their employers even as early as the mid-1870s. But in typical artisan trades, the numbers were considerably higher. In baking and butchering 67 percent of the hired laborers, 28 percent of the basket-makers' helpers, and almost 20 percent of the glazier journeymen lived with their masters.[36]

During the last third of the nineteenth century, education of the young throughout the German Reich was gradually brought under the supervision of the state. Volksschulen were available in most areas of the country, and vocational schools were established in growing numbers. These were mostly Sunday or evening schools, with a basic curriculum in German, arithmetic, and drafting, and occasional instruction in bookkeeping. Schools in larger cities also offered some vocational training in a number of major crafts.[37] The traditional master artisans made the schools the object of special abuse. Suspicious of the institutional framework as a whole, they were particularly opposed to the theoretical training that was a part of the curriculum in these schools. The only relevant training for future craftsmen, they argued, was the one they themselves had received as apprentices

[35] *St.d.R.* 119, p. 71.

[36] Schwabe, *Die Stadt Berlin*, pp. 104-105.

[37] See Eugene N. Anderson, "The Prussian Volksschule," in *Entstehung und Wandel der modernen Gesellschaft*, ed. Gerhard A. Ritter, pp. 260-279. For the number of vocational schools and for their aims, see Oskar Simon, *Das Gewerbliche Fortbildungs- und Fachschulwesen*, pp. 28 ff. Also Noll, *Sozio-ökonomischer Strukturwandel*, pp. 124-166; 381-386.

and journeymen. Only practical experience at a master-craftsman's shop, they believed, was necessary or useful in preparing a man for a handicraft occupation. Rhetoric aside, it was evident that the masters dreaded above all the loss of control over apprenticeship education, which would be the inevitable result of a well-developed network of vocational schools, combined with the proposed state training centers. Relinquishing their role as educators, the masters feared, would mean a loss of control over the supply of skilled workers and a severe decline in their own social status.[38]

During the 1870s much public attention was given to the Lehrlingsfrage (Apprenticeship question). Since improved education was the liberals' general answer to social oppression and inequality, they naturally also placed a great deal of emphasis on the proper training of apprentices. Improved technical and commercial education was their panacea for all the social and economic ills of the artisans. The next generation of artisans, they argued, should be educated so as to create a cadre of well-equipped masters with entrepreneurial spirit and a positive approach to technological progress. What these reformers did not seem to have noticed was that the master artisans were interested not only in defending their material position, but also and perhaps above all in perpetuating their special occupational status group, with its traditional style of life and its long-cherished set of values. To achieve these ends master artisans staged a long battle to regain control over apprentice education. In a spirit of protest they often refused to allow their apprentices time off to attend the local vocational schools, and they demanded supervisory power over all apprentices, to be administered by the newly established corporate masters' organizations.

Motions for the better regulation of apprentices were submitted to the Reichstag by both liberal delegates and con-

[38] See Karl Bücher, *Die gewerbliche Bildungsfrage*, pp. 13 ff. and his comments in *Schriften* 11(1875); 157-159.

servatives of all shades. In July 1878, the legislature passed a bill for the supervision of child labor which included several measures for ameliorating the conditions of artisans' apprentices. These, however, were regarded by the master artisans and their supporters in the Reichstag as entirely inadequate. In 1884, another amendment to the general Industrial Law sought to give local authorities the option of granting to the new guilds the sole right to supervise apprentice education.[39] This amendment, known as article 100e, was accepted by the Reichstag after a long debate and was received with great hostility almost everywhere in Germany. A full decade later, only 10 percent of the existing guilds, most of them in Prussia, did in fact acquire this privilege.[40] In any event, young workers undoubtedly continued to be trained both by nonguild artisans and at the factories, not always as formal apprentices but under the same conditions and with similar results. As was so often the case, legal measures could not reverse the process of institutional change. Apprentices as well as young employees, increasingly resented even the last vestige of control exercised by their masters.

The decline of the masters' authority over apprentices, and the deterioration of the moral influence of the master's home, was observed with alarm not only by the master artisans themselves, but also by the representatives of other traditional elements in Germany, notably the Church.[41] During

[39] For a general survey of the federal artisan legislation see G. Mayer and E. Loening, "Gewerbegesetzgebung," in the *HBS*, 3rd ed., and Wilhelm Wernet, *Soziale Handwerksordnung*, pp. 292 ff. A short but accurate survey was given by Franz Hitze in the Reichstag; see *Steno. Berichte*, November 24, 1895. Article 100e was debated in the Reichstag on a number of occasions; see e.g., *Steno. Berichte*, March 26, 1881.

[40] Stieda, "Die Innungsenquete," p. 12.

[41] The details of the Center-party position on the handicraft question will be dealt with later. See the section on social Catholicism in chap. 7. For the Catholic position see the articles on the handicraft question in the *Christlich-soziale Blätter*, in particular "Handwerk und Christentum," 1885, pp. 179-190.

the 1887 National Congress of Artisans, a Catholic priest from Aachen introduced a resolution urging upon the masters the importance of their spiritual and religious duties.[42] Eventually accepted at the General Congress of Master Artisans in Munich a year later, the resolution read as follows: "The German General Congress of Master Artisans recognizes the Christian religion as the only tool available for resisting the subversive principles of individualism and socialism. It declares that the conduct of religious education as an obligatory aspect of the education of future artisans is highly desirable."[43]

It was the Roman Catholic church that took the lead in the campaign to improve religious instruction for young artisans. Its representatives urged the masters to lead an exemplary life themselves and thus be worthy of their position as moral and religious guides. Primarily concerned with its own diminishing influence, the Church helped perpetuate the image of the religious and moral superiority of the master artisans. This might have been important for the masters' diminishing self-esteem, but it was at the time no more than an illusion. Religious or moral education of craft apprentices by their masters may have been desirable, as the resolution put it, but it was certainly no longer a practical proposition.

Masters and Journeymen

The authority of masters over their journeymen deteriorated more rapidly and more completely than their control over apprentices. Under the pressure of modern economic developments and the changes in the composition of the labor force, the handicraft workshop gradually became simply a more or less permanent place of employment for journeymen. The sense of community within it disappeared.[44]

[42] *AHZ*, August 26, 1886; August 18, 1888. Also *KZ*, August 16 and September 12, 1888.

[43] *KZ*, August 18, 1888.

[44] For the change in the relationship between masters and men

In most cases journeymen who still resided with their masters ceased to be treated as family members. They were given attic or cellar rooms and had to suffer constant supervision without the benefits of participation in stable family life. Their chances of becoming independently established diminished, and they consequently had to remain hired hands, sometimes even for life. Under these circumstances, the custom of postponing marriage until independently established became untenable, and mature skilled workers began marrying and moving into their own quarters. Occasionally, masters resisted this trend so stubbornly that journeymen were compelled to lodge in their masters' homes and could visit their families only once or twice a week. Normally, however, journeymen moved into the cheap residential areas on the outskirts of the towns, mingling there with migrating and unskilled workers in bars and on street corners, in the local shops, and at newsstands.

In Berlin the number of workers classified as Gesellen increased by over 10 percent between 1890 and 1895. In the new working-class sections of town, however, Moabit and Wedding, their number grew by as much as 40 and 23 percent respectively. During the same years, the number of journeymen resident in typical master neighborhoods either increased slightly, as in Luisenstadt-inside-the-canal, or declined slightly as in Luisenstadt-outside-the-canal.[45] Clearly,

---

see Schmoller, *Zur Geschichte der deutschen Kleingewerbe*, pp. 326-362; Stadelmann and Fischer, *Die Bildungswelt*, pp. 57-59, 72-80; Abrams, *Der Strukturwandel im Handwerk*, pp. 25-43; 86-94; Voigt, "Das Tischlergewerbe," *Schriften* 65 (1895): 347, 499 ff. As late as the end of the nineteenth century some writers still believed in the viability of the old relationship between masters and journeymen. See e.g., Franz Hitze's address to the VSP at its 1897 meeting in *Schriften* 76 (1898): 35-36.

[45] *Die Bevölkerungs- und Wohnungsaufnahme, 1890*, part 1, p. 116, and 1895, part 1, p. 92. On the rough character of the various sections of town, see the data in the same collection, 1885, part 1, pp. 60-62; 84.

the working population of the capital was rapidly concentrating in its own special districts.

The change in the residence pattern of journeymen was only one indication of their growing self-consciousness as a segment of the working class. Union organization was most successful among the skilled artisans, and provided them with a renewed sense of power and self-importance. Socialism, vague as it often was during those early years, helped to make the cleavage between masters and men comprehensible within a larger context. It served to turn the journeymen's intuitive resentment into ideological channels and offered them a well thought-out program of action.

For large numbers of journeymen the prospects of economic independence were still inviting, even at the end of the nineteenth century. The masters' campaign to restrict admission into their trades was not easy to justify when the masters themselves attached such great significance to economic independence. Their weekly journal inadvertently expressed this dilemma: "Although we recognize the longing for better conditions of life and for economic independence as legitimate, we find it necessary in the present business situation to warn the young and the ambitious against 'independence fever.' "[46] Thus while not relinquishing the ideal of independence, the masters had to admit the unrealistic nature of the desire to preserve a sense of common destiny between masters and men, and the disservice done to both by dangling the promise of a common life experience.

The master-artisans' gradual loss of authority over their hired hands was matched by a corresponding loss of social superiority. During the years of economic depression, the dependence of small masters on their skilled laborers became apparent. Big industry and putting-out establishments often successfully competed for this segment of the labor force. As journeymen resigned themselves to the fate of becoming permanent wage earners, the attraction of the small

[46] *AHZ*, March 4, 1887.

shop had to be weighed against the advantages of the factory, in terms of the level of earnings, the conditions of work, and the security of employment. The small shops no doubt lost the more ambitious and often better-trained workers. Those who stayed in their old places of employment gradually became aware of their power over the small masters and began to apply pressure. While in big industry a new type of relationship was evolving between employers and employees, the small master artisans attempted to preserve the appearance of the old structure. Once again, there was little content behind this appearance. The journeymen refused to abide by the rules of paternalism and insisted on being treated as mature, independent men, in full control of their own destinies.

During the eighteenth century journeymen were known to have demanded that masters address them with the title "Gesellen" and avoid the condescending attitude implied by the term "Knechte."[47] In the late nineteenth century, the Gesellen asked to be addressed in the polite plural, "Sie."[48] They regarded the master-artisans' pretensions to social superiority as yet another form of exploitation. The small master artisans now had to face a socially heterogeneous labor force, including many workers' sons, inspired by a new self-respect and a growing sense of internal solidarity and comradeship.

To add to their difficulties, the masters frequently found themselves in worse material circumstances than their own workers. In the small carpentry shops in Berlin, masters had a net income of some twenty-six marks per week. Their helpers, who in most cases did not have families to support or workshops to keep running, earned about twenty.[49] In many trades the masters' income was substantially lower than the earnings of workers in other branches of industry.[50] It was

[47] See Stadelmann and Fischer, *Die Bildungswelt*, pp. 76-78.

[48] O. Allmann, *Geschichte der deutschen Bäcker- und Konditorenbewegung*, vol. 1, pp. 203 ff.

[49] Voigt, "Das Tischlergewerbe," *Schriften* 65 (1895): 414-415.

[50] Compare the estimates of the money earnings of workers in the

extremely difficult to maintain the appearance of greater prosperity and comfort and uphold a higher social status in the face of shrinking income differentiation. The privilege of city and state citizenship, once a source of pride for the town handicraft masters, also ceased to be a sign of their distinction. In small German towns, where artisans comprised a considerable part of the population, local authorities gradually lost their power to grant settlement and citizenship rights.[51] Political rights, too, ceased to be a distinguishing mark of the master artisans. After the creation of the Bismarckian Reich and the introduction of universal male suffrage, local authorities followed suit by gradually reforming their own electoral laws. Many small masters benefited from the extension of suffrage, but by then the right to take an active part in the political life of the community was no longer considered a sign of special status. Moreover, the growing political effectiveness of the workers was often a source of much anxiety for the small masters. In 1882, the General Congress of Master Artisans protested bitterly against the change of the legal age of majority from 24 to 21 years, and the shoemakers' guilds succeeded in pushing through an almost unanimous resolution asserting the right to retain the age of 24 as the minimum age for the independent practice of their trade.[52] The lowering of the age of majority was considered an attack on the customary superiority of elders, both in the shop and in society at large. It was a superiority, the masters believed, that justly reflected the elders' greater sense of civic responsibility and their greater contribution to social stability.

---

chemical industry, in printing, and even in mining in Desai, *Real Wages in Germany*, pp. 109-111, to the incomes of master artisans reported by Bücher; see also Noll, *Sozio-ökonomischer Strukturwandel*, pp. 74-81; and the section on income and standard of living in chap. 2 above.

[51] See Heinrich Heffter, *Die deutsche Selbstverwaltung im 19. Jahrhundert*, pp. 217-220; 407-414. See also Walker, *German Home Towns*, pp. 406-408.

[52] *KZ*, June 6, 1882.

As they lost the symbols of their superiority over the workers, the small master artisans sought to stress their greater moral excellence. The small handicraft shop, they argued, was the supreme expression of the values of frugality and honest workmanship.[53] Moreover, it was a reliable center of religious observance and moral purity, and served to propagate these values among the young. The breakdown of the customary bonds within the handicraft shop was the root of the general religious and moral deterioration of the present age, they believed. In the eyes of many small masters, the workers' new social environment, with its rampant atheism, unorthodox moral code, and revolutionary rhetoric was nothing but a breeding ground for "fraud, frivolity, and licentiousness."[54]

To regain a measure of control over their workers, the various master-artisan organizations joined in a campaign for the reintroduction of compulsory labor books for workers of all ages. Such a written record of the worker's training, experience, and behavior, the masters argued, would be the only effective tool for resisting what they considered to be "workers' terrorism."[55] Several large guilds instituted such labor books independently. Particularly effective were the butchers' and bakers' leagues which, in the manner typical of employers' organizations, refused to hire workers with unsatisfactory records. Indeed, under the pressure of these tactics the first association of butcher-shop workers was

[53] For this sense of moral excellence see the discussion in Stadelmann and Fischer, "Das Ethos des Handwerksstandes," pp. 72-97 in *Die Bildungswelt.* The theme was reiterated at every masters' congress and was cited endlessly in the master-artisan journals. See e.g., *AHZ*, November 8, 1889; April 12, 1890.

[54] *KZ*, March 10, 1878.

[55] See the report on an artisans' meeting in Berlin in *KZ*, March 8, 1878, and on the eighth conference of the Verein Selbstständiger Handwerker und Fabrikanten Deutschlands in Bremen, *KZ*, August 12, 1879. The strongest statement to this effect was made in the Magdeburger Beschlüsse formulated by the artisans' national conference in Magdeburg, 1882. See the *Verhandlungen zu Magdeburg*, pp. 2-5.

forced to disband, and was unable to reorganize until well into the 1890s.[56] During the 1880s, several legal amendments, ostensibly designed to support the masters' efforts, were accepted by the Reichstag.[57] These, however, were mainly intended as devices to aid the political police in the enforcement of the antisocialist laws. The government was only too delighted to exploit the demands of the master artisans for its own repressive purposes.

The emergence of the Social-Democratic party and its trade-union movement had a particularly unsettling effect upon the master artisans in the large cities. In May 1874, the industrial chamber in Hamburg drafted a proposal for a joint corporate organization based on parity between journeymen and handicraft masters. The recommendations immediately aroused much public debate.[58] Significantly, however, the small master artisans in the industrial chamber gradually retreated from their original position, and found themselves entirely isolated in the All-German Congress of the Chambers of Industry, where in 1878 their proposal was finally presented. The tendency of the congress was to press for the introduction of labor books, and to demand greater control over journeymen's hostels and more severe discipline on the shop floor.[59] After early industrial strikes in Ham-

[56] Rind, "Die Fleischerei in Leipzig," *Schriften* 68 (1897): 53 ff. Also Horst Hoffmann, "Das Bäckergewerbe in Jena," *Schriften* 70 (1897); 219 ff.; and Eduard Lehwitz, "Das Bäckergewerbe in Berlin," *Schriften* 69 (1897); 166-172; 176 ff.

[57] See Mayer and Loening, "Gewerbegesetzgebung," *HBS*, 3rd ed.

[58] See the *Jahresbericht der Hamburgerischen Gewerbekammer für 1873/74*, pp. 109 ff., for the recommendation of a special committee of the Hamburg Industrial Chamber. It is interesting that the industrial chambers of Bremen and Lübeck, which basically accepted the report, nevertheless refused to cosponsor it before the national Gewerbekammertag. See *Jahresbericht 1875/79*, pp. 55 ff. See also the totally negative reaction to the proposal in the *Protokolle über die Verhandlungen zu Quedlinburg 1874*, pp. 3-4.

[59] *Jahresbericht 1878/79*, pp. 57; 60-61. See also the "Gutachten über den Gesetzentwurf," in *Jahresbericht 1880/81*, p. 12.

burg, in an atmosphere of general social and political intransigence in the country, and possibly also under the influence of the economic hardship caused by the serious symptoms of depression at that time, the masters in Hamburg did a complete about-face. From 1882 on, no mention was made of parity between masters and men, and the workers were increasingly denied even the right to representation in the vocational trade societies. Thus, during the 1880s masters as well as workers gave up the idea of cooperation. They chose, instead, to face each other in open rivalry.

This attitude gradually spread from the big cities to other parts of Germany. By the end of the depression the line between master artisans and handicraft helpers was clearly drawn. It represented a social, cultural, and political cleavage, which was to become characteristic of industrial society in Germany.

Only one group continued to occupy an ambiguous position in this new rigid social hierarchy: the individual self-employed artisans.[60] The gap between them and the wage-earning journeymen was naturally much narrower than between the latter and the master employers. The easy movement between the positions of dependent and independent craftsmen characteristic of England in the early stages of industrialization could now be detected in Germany too and brought these men closer together. In many cases, the masters were forced to work for larger producers, or to be somehow connected with big industrial shops. In better times they attempted to reassert their economic independence, but the chances to do so during the long years of the Great Depression were few indeed. In the building trades, for instance, there was little to distinguish a skilled journeyman from a self-employed master. Both worked as subcontractors, performed the same jobs, and received the same wages. Many of the individual self-employed shoemakers, to give another example, joined the trade unions

60 See the sections on structural change and on income in chap. 2.

and were often lifelong members of the Social-Democratic party.[61] By the end of the Great Depression nothing remained of their supposedly higher social staus—not even the will to preserve it. Often their independence was no more than a source of additional anxiety, and meant in effect only a smaller income and diminishing security. A growing number of this group identified with the workers, and severed their social ties with other master artisans. For a long time, however, they remained a transitional zone between two hostile camps.

[61] There are no precise figures on the extent of the industrial self-employed masters' participation in the trade-union movement. But see, e.g., the comments in the various articles in *Schriften* 62 (1895), especially those on the shoemaking trade in Altona and Breslau. See also comments in Behr, *Entwicklung in der Schuhindustrie*, p. 92; and the section on social democracy and the small masters in chap. 8.

FOUR

MITTELSTAND AND MASTER ARTISANS

MITTELSTAND: DIVERSITY AND UNITY

BY the time of the Great Depression the masters of traditional crafts in Germany were invariably considered, by themselves and by others, to be members of the Mittelstand. Much of what characterized them as a group, especially in the realm of values and ideals, was shared by other elements of this heterogeneous social stratum. But the Mittelstand itself underwent several transformations during the nineteenth century. Both the term and the social reality it denotes require some clarification.[1]

The traditional estate system did not include a Mittelstand. By the late eighteenth century the word "Stand" was commonly applied not only to the three main orders of society, but also to a variety of occupational groups, each defined by a special set of duties and privileges. A Mittelstand, however, was never among these legally defined estates, although during the first half of the nineteenth century the term was frequently used. It most commonly denoted the equivalent of the English "middle ranks," "middle classes," or "middle class," and occasionally, as if to confuse matters

[1] For some of the attempts to define the Mittelstand as a sociological category see Grünberg, *Der Mittelstand in der kapitalistischen Gesellschaft*, pp. 120-215; Fritz Marbach, *Theorie des Mittelstandes*, pp. 102 ff.; Schmoller, "Was verstehen wir unter dem Mittelstande?" pp. 2-12; and for more recent contributions especially H.A. Winkler, "Bürgertum," and *Mittelstand*, pp. 21-26; also Jürgen Kocka, "Vorindustrielle Faktoren in der deutschen Industrialisierung," pp. 265-286. For a good survey of the history of the term see Puhle, *Agrarische Interessenpolitik*, pp. 98-102, and the bibliography cited there. See also Annette Leppert-Fögen, *Die deklassierte Klasse*, pp. 8-37; and Arno Mayer, "The Lower Middle Class as Historical Problem." The following discussion attempts an operational rather than a comprehensive definition of the term and the social group it was supposed to denote.

further, of the French "bourgeoisie." This ill-defined term was applied, for analytical or for political purposes, to all or to parts of the "middle ranks," including such diverse elements as industrial entrepreneurs, financiers, public officials, professional men, handicraft masters, and small retailers.[2]

The confusion was not merely terminological. The stratification system of Prussia and the other German states during the pre-March years was indeed chaotic. The old social hierarchy, complex and dynamic in itself, was preserved and perpetuated by a system of legal privileges, while new social groups were forming, preparing to demand their share of wealth, respectability, and power.[3] Social stratification in the early nineteenth century was a mesh of partly distinct, partly overlapping hierarchies, and ambiguity in the use of social terms was only one manifestation of this reality.

Later in the century, Wilhelm Riehl, a conservative but usually perceptive social observer, used the terms Bürgertum, Bürgerstand, and Mittelstand interchangeably.[4] For Riehl, the Bürgertum-Mittelstand consisted of all social groups and subgroups located in the social hierarchy between the nobility and the peasantry. The Mittelstand was for him a descriptive term, literally rendered by the English "middle ranks." By joining it to Bürgertum he had apparently hoped to reduce the ambiguity of that term, which from the late eighteenth century on had at least three distinct meanings in Germany. A Bürger could mean an owner of town citizenship, a member of civil society regardless of estate, and a state resident who was neither a nobleman nor

[2] See Winkler, *Mittelstand*, p. 22.

[3] For the fluid social situation during the first half of the nineteenth century, see Koselleck, *Preussen zwischen Reform und Revolution*, pp. 52 ff.; and Werner Conze, "Das Spannungsfeld von Staat und Gesellschaft im Vormärz," in his *Staat und Gesellschaft im deutschen Vormärz*, pp. 207-269.

[4] Wilhelm H. Riehl, *Die bürgerliche Gesellschaft*, pp. 195-217.

a peasant.[5] Riehl wished to apply the word to the last category only, and the term Mittelstand was added in order to clarify this point. Instead it only served to underline the inadequacy of his categories.

In the 1850s, the term Mittelstand came increasingly to be applied to only one segment of the Bürgertum—its lower layer. By that time Bürgertum and Mittelstand could no longer be equated. The one was then applied with growing consistency to the upper level of the "middle ranks," while the other came to denote the lower. When the important social distinction in Germany was considered that between nobles and Bürger, the Bürgertum as a whole or in its upper layer, that closest to the nobility, indeed constituted the "middle." When later in the century the distinction between proletarians and Bürger gained in significance, the lower layer of the Bürgertum just above the proletariat became a meaningful "middle." The term Mittelstand was coined within a conceptual framework that conceived of society as basically divided into three. Its meaning changed as a result of the overall transformation of the system of social stratification. It was by nature dependent on the composition of the strata above and below it.

The division of the German middle ranks into two distinct groups was not new. The Prussian code of 1791-92 distinguished between "exempted" and "actual" Bürger.[6] By creating the category of "Eximiertes Bürgertum" the Prussian Allgemeine Landsrecht (general code) gave a legal expression to the existing social rift within the Bürgertum, while in turn sanctioning and deepening it. The upper Bürgertum, defined by a series of legal privileges, was then primarily a service class. It included all military and civil servants, priests and scholars, some professional groups, the rich nonnoble landowners, and a sprinkling of commercial and in-

[5] See Koselleck, *Preussen zwischen Reform und Revolution*, pp. 87-88.

[6] Ibid., pp. 89-115.

dustrial entrepreneurs. Together they were considered "an estate of the state" (Staatsstand), serving the state and dependent upon it. This legal category corresponded to what Hegel later defined for Germany as a whole as the "Stand des Allgemeinheit," a phrase that can best be translated as "a universal estate," in contradistinction to the particular, regional, and local ones.[7] In a recent study the men included in this category were succinctly described as "movers and doers."[8] Most of their legal privileges survived the Prussian reforms, and many of them remained in force even after 1848. During these years the gulf between the upper Bürgertum and the "actual" Bürger, citizens of the towns, members of corporations, subject to local and corporate law, was growing continuously. Early economic development in the pre-March period, while slowly changing the composition of the upper Bürgertum by increasing the share of Besitzbürger within it, did not reverse this trend. Wealth became gradually more important in defining the upper Bürgertum, but that only worked to deepen the gulf between it and the lower Bürgertum, the newly defined Mittelstand. Members of the Bürgertum were defined as nonnoble possessors of either Bildung or Besitz (education or property), or some combination of the two. In a long process of "feudalization" they drew nearer to the nobility, and the distinction between them was often blurred. At the same time, members of the Mittelstand, socially located now in the "middle" between the combined upper class and the proletariat, were defined as nonproletarian possessors of some Bildung and Besitz, though of considerably less than those above them. "Considerably less" is admittedly a vague measure for distinguishing between two social groups, but unfortunately an absolute line of division can never be drawn. Even when the upper Bürgertum was defined by law a certain degree of ambiguity

[7] On Hegel's concept see Walker, *German Home Towns*, pp. 195-198, and Rolf K. Hočevar, *Stände und Repräsentation beim jungen Hegel.*

[8] See Walker, *German Home Towns*, pp. 119-133.

remained inevitable, and judges in the early nineteenth century frequently had to decide the legal status of a person on the basis of subjective impressions and prevalent public opinion.[9] By the second half of the century it became reasonably clear that men of nonnoble origins who were state bureaucrats or large industrial enterpreneurs were members of the Bürgertum, while the lower-echelon local magistrates and small industrial producers were Mittelständler. Nonnoble large merchants, highly skilled professionals, and the top managerial personnel were members of the Bürgertum, while small retailers and the low-ranking white-collar employees belonged to the Mittelstand.

That a quantitative difference in possession of social goods eventually acquired a qualitative meaning is not surprising. Even Marx and Engels, setting out to define the bourgeoisie by making the ownership of the means of production its one essential characteristic had to acknowledge this fact. They hesitated to include "small manufacturers, shopkeepers, artisans and peasants" within the bourgeoisie, and were forced to admit into their scheme an additional class, socially and politically unique, the petite bourgeoisie.[10]

In discussing the various differentiations within and among the propertied and the propertyless, Max Weber, too, stressed the possibility of "a quantitative difference with possible qualitative consequences" for the identification of social groups, and mentioned as an example the social gulf separating large and small landowners in Germany.[11] The large estate owners of Prussia east of the Elbe, Weber argued, could not possibly be grouped together

[9] Koselleck, *Preussen zwischen Reform und Revolution*, pp. 99-100.

[10] Karl Marx and Friedrich Engels, *Werke*, vol. 4, pp. 469-470. Marx's best treatment of the petite bourgeoisie as a separate social class and an independent political force is to be found in his two essays on France, "The Class Struggle in France 1849-50," and "18th Brumaire of Louis Bonaparte."

[11] See his *Wirtschaft und Gesellschaft*, part 3, 9, pp. 631-640.

with peasants in southern and southwestern Germany. Similarly, it had become increasingly obvious to late nineteenth-century observers that large commercial entrepreneurs, operating in the modern national and international markets, could not be ranked with small retail shopkeepers; nor could large modern industrial entrepreneurs be grouped with traditional small craft masters. The quantitative differences in their income and wealth was fundamental. It entailed significant differences in modes of production, in the overall approach to economic activity, in all forms of business behavior, in human values, and in life style.

Dividing the Bürgertum into two main social strata, however, does not solve the problem of heterogeneity. In fact, it merely substitutes two heterogeneous social strata for one. Throughout its history the Mittelstand included groups that were economically independent and dependent, rural and urban, traditional and modern, prosperous and impoverished. The diversity has led some social analysts to deny the very existence of a single Mittelstand and to question the usefulness of the term.[12] But while social terms used by contemporaries do not bind future historians, they are often useful and occasionally indispensable. Social terms that have been in daily use for over a century and acquired crucial social and political significance cannot be simply shoved aside. Bürgertum and Mittelstand were more than descriptive terms in nineteenth-century Germany. Both acquired unique socioeconomic, ideological, and political connotations, while indicating distinguishable social strata.

Until the end of the nineteenth century, the Mittelstand included primarily small independent industrial producers and retailers. Small home renters and home owners, low-ranking state and municipal clerks, and even small independent peasants were also occasionally included within

[12] Even Emil Grünberg comes close to this conclusion in his *Der Mittelstand in der kapitalistischen Gesellschaft*, pp. 165-167. See also Fritz Croner, *Die Angestellten in der modernen Gesellschaft*, pp. 41 ff. and 184 ff.

it.[13] This "old Mittelstand," as it was later to be known, was chiefly but not exclusively composed of people in independent occupations. The later inclusion of white-collar employees and junior industrial and commercial managerial staff as a "new Mittelstand," however, did not necessarily represent a drastic departure from the common self-image of the Mittelstand as a group. In fact, the low-ranking state and municipal employees always occupied a special place of honor among Mittelständler, since they carried the added prestige conferred upon all civil servants in Germany. The white-collar employees themselves attached a special significance to their real or imagined affinity with the bureaucracy, and for decades expressly preferred to consider themselves Mittelständler and not members of the wage-earning working class.[14] Significantly, this preference developed despite the fact that the new industrial employees occupied an ambiguous position within the traditional Mittelstand. The new Mittelstand was after all a child of the new economy. It grew as a result of the bureaucratization and rationalization of large-scale commercial and industrial firms. Not only its interests but also its entire world outlook was often in conflict with the interests and attitudes of the old Mittelstand, whose economic, social, psychological, and ideological links were with the old order.

The application of the term Mittelstand to industrial employees in Germany indicates the political significance of this term. Bureaucrats and the ruling elite in Germany, fearing the growing power of the revolutionary working-class movement, and still attempting to control the onslaught of industrial capitalism, had a special interest in strengthening and enlarging the so-called Mittelstand. They emphasized the demarcation between small masters and their journeymen, or between white-collar employees and indus-

[13] See Schmoller, "Was verstehen wir unter dem Mittelstande?" p. 157 and the other literature cited in n. 1 above.

[14] See Kocka, *Unternehmensverwaltung und Angestelltenschaft*, pp. 171-198; 523-535.

trial workers. Using their influence on public opinion and acting in their legislative and administrative capacities, they perpetuated the concept of a "healthy Mittelstand" as an indispensable loyal social element, stressing the unity and uniqueness of this group.[15]

In considering the peculiar composition of the Mittelstand, it would be well to remember that other social groups were, and are, likewise no more than a combination of diverse social elements. The German Bürgertum was as heterogenous as the German Mittelstand. Even the working class, eventually so conscious of its unity, was initially a conglomeration of diverse elements drawn together on the basis of similar, but not identical, socioeconomic positions, and similar, but not identical, interests and ideals.[16] It is the conspicuous lack of practical cooperation among the various Mittelstand elements that obscures this point. Schematically speaking, the German Bürgertum was the major force behind the liberal movement in Germany and was responsible for both its successes and its eventual failure. The German working class expressed itself collectively in the support of socialism and the Social-Democratic party, in trade unionism, and in a peculiar working-class subculture.[17] In contrast, the German Mittelstand rarely managed to present a common front on any public issue. Its diverse social elements never successfully merged into unity of action or faith.

Common action by itself may not be a sine qua non of a definable social group.[18] However, the inability of the German Mittelstand to transcend its internal differences and emerge united in any joint social action was one of its most important characteristics. The differences among the

[15] Ibid., pp. 534-540; and Winkler, *Mittelstand*, pp. 57-64.

[16] This has brilliantly been shown for England by E.P. Thompson in *The Making of the English Working Class*, especially chaps. 7-9.

[17] For the working-class subculture, see Gunther Roth, *Social Democrats in Imperial Germany*, and Dieter Groh, *Negative Integration und revolutionärer Attentismus*.

[18] For Weber's opinion on this matter see *Wirtschaft und Gesellschaft*, p. 635.

various Mittelstand elements were not unbridgeable. They were hardly more fundamental than the differences prevailing within other social coalitions. This was particularly true in the context of German society, in which political lines often cut across social divisions. By the end of the century the "feudalization" of the German Bürgertum gave a social dimension to a long-standing political alliance between itself and the old landowning nobility. By that time aristocratic landowners and small independent peasants, despite the social gulf separating them, had developed a cooperative relationship culminating in the establishment of a peculiar, but nonetheless effective, common political front.[19]

At the end of the nineteenth century all the major social groups in Germany were complex entities, held together by a variety of social ties, economic interests, and political goals. Members of the Mittelstand themselves tended to conceive of it as a group distinguished above all by a unique life style and a common set of personal and social values. In spite of the occupational heterogeneity of the group, its members had a similar, if not always identical, status within German society, and in spite of the great variation in income levels and property holdings, they could be roughly classified as a single economic stratum.[20] The Mittelstand was a social as well as a cultural and political reality in the second Reich, within which the traditional handicraft masters, as individuals and as a group, occupied a unique place.

Master Artisans and Other Mittelständler

By the beginning of the Great Depression the master-artisans' previous community—the community of the traditional Handwerkerstand—had practically lost its social

[19] See Max Weber in *Verhandlungen des 8. evangelisch-sozialen Kongresses*, pp. 205 ff.; Sombart, *Die deutsche Volkswirtschaft*, p. 463; Kehr, *Der Primat der Innenpolitik*, pp. 53-86; and Puhle, *Agrarische Interessenpolitik*, especially pp. 57-59; 64-71.

[20] The most convincing attempt to divide German society on a strict income-property scale is still Schmoller's "Was verstehen wir unter dem Mittelstande?" pp. 157-158.

meaning. It continued to exist only as a memory. The institutional framework associated with it deteriorated, and the masters appeared to be incapable of finding a replacement. Their relations with their journeymen and with other paid assistants became formal and increasingly tense. The internal ties among them were not only ineffective but also socially and culturally unsatisfactory. Even within the Mittelstand the masters found themselves in a peculiar situation. By the last quarter of the century the small independent handicraftsmen's inclusion in the Mittelstand was rarely disputed, but within it their position was ambiguous and uneasy. As manual workers, the masters were outsiders in a social group whose members were normally employed in nonmanual occupations and proud to be thus differentiated from ordinary workers. In this respect the masters were unique among shopkeepers, public officials, school teachers, and white-collar employees. Their dissimilarity to common laborers had to be established by other means. Moreover, as small producers in a social group whose members were essentially consumers, the masters' economic interests often clashed with those of other Mittelstand elements, and their relations with them all were unstable and strained.

Most complex of all were the relations that developed between master artisans and small retail shopkeepers. Neither group was homogeneous or unified, and indeed often the two were practically undistinguishable. Many artisans who engaged in trades that proved susceptible to radical technical innovations, but that still required personal attendance upon customers, enlarged their shops and sold factory-made products in addition to, or even in place of, their own. Thus, shoemakers frequently became small retailers, using their skills for mending and fitting shoes; bookbinders, losing business to large publishing houses and printers, often developed their own stationery shops and became, in effect, small retailers.[21] But the more the distinction between the

[21] See the section on domestic industry in chap. 1 and n. 23 there. Also Gellately, *The Politics of Economic Despair*, pp. 22-27 and chaps. 2-3.

two occupational groups lost its actual significance, the more vehemently it was defended.

It is difficult to assess objectively the relative status of the various occupational groups within the Mittelstand. Some of the prosperous handicraft masters undoubtedly enjoyed higher social prestige than ordinary small retailers. Shopkeeping, however, as a nonmanual occupation, usually requiring a certain level of education, was frequently considered a more respectable occupation than craftsmanship.[22] An examination of publications by master artisans suggest that they, at least, believed themselves to have been too often unjustly allocated a social position inferior to that of small retailers. This may have not been the case in fact, but the belief itself was a significant factor in forming their self-consciousness, in determining their relationship to their social environment, and eventually in aggravating their sense of resentment and anxiety.

Thus, in spite of widespread poverty and unemployment among young commercial assistants, a master's son who took an apprenticeship in a small retail shop was often viewed as having taken a step upward. While individual masters were pleased to see their sons achieving what they believed to be a social advance, as a group they continued to object vehemently to the criteria that so defined it. In January 1894 a series of letters published in the Berlin *Deutsche Handwerkerzeitung* (*DHZ*) proclaimed the superiority of craftsmanship over shopkeeping and other commercial activities.[23] A caricature portrayed a short, thin, and somewhat hungry-looking shopkeeper ceremoniously taking his hat off before a tall, muscular, bearded artisan,

[22] See Karl Bücher, *Die Arbeiterfrage im Kaufmannsstande*, pp. 23-24. Also Wilhelm Kimbel, *Unser Handwerk in Not*, a reprint from the *Gartenlaube*. The theme often appears in articles in the master-artisans' newspapers. See, e.g., *AHZ*, February 22, 1889; August 18, 1893. For a general review of the situation of the small retail trader, and the history of the retail shopkeepers' movement, see A. Lampe, "Einzelhandel," in *HBS*, 4th ed.

[23] *DHZ*, January 13, 20, 27, 1894.

wearing a stained working suit, and holding a disproportionately large wooden hammer. In the caption, the shopkeeper addresses this archetypical artisan with the pronoun Sie. The same symbol of social equality and respectability that was often demanded by journeymen from their masters, was here sought by the masters themselves.

Small master artisans occasionally found themselves unable to withstand the competition of tradesmen for whom commerce was a primary occupation and who frequently possessed more adequate education and more useful social and economic ties. As industrial producers, they were only too often forced to rely on small middlemen, who, they believed, exploited them by unjustly appropriating a large portion of the market price of the handicrafted products. The Church's traditional aversion to commerce was maintained by the masters, and served even in the late nineteenth century to legitimize their contempt and their open enmity. By virtue of their honest labor and indispensable productive function, the masters argued, they were in fact the social superiors of shopkeepers. Their peculiar ability to combine the use of both capital and labor within one institution, the handicraft workshop, should confer greater respectability than the one-sided and often morally suspect activity of shopkeepers.

As wealth and material well-being became increasingly important in the allocation of social prominence, the small masters sought even more vehemently to protect their status. To begin with, they criticized the entire system of assigning social prestige. Wealth, they claimed, was a distorted criterion for measuring respectability and eminence. It was the ownership of property, especially solid and immovable property, that counted, but also the capacity to add to the material and cultural resources of the nation.[24] In this respect too, the masters believed, they were in fact the social superiors of shopkeepers and should be so

[24] Ibid., September 8, 1894. Also January 6, September 15 and 22, 1894.

recognized regardless of economic standing. Thus, close as the shopkeepers were to the masters in social status and economic well-being, they were nevertheless often the latter's direct competitors economically, socially, and culturally. The insecurity of the two groups under the pressure of industrialization made reconciliation and cooperation between them all the more unlikely.

Occasionally the small masters also clashed with other elements of the Mittelstand with whom they had little direct contact and who could hardly have presented a real challenge to their position. As primary producers, the masters found themselves repeatedly in conflict with the essentially service-oriented elements of the Mittelstand. It was a clash between producers' and consumers' interests. The clearest expression of this conflict was the controversy over the establishment of consumers' cooperatives, which were particularly favored by government officials during the late nineteenth century. Despite the fact that as representatives of authority government officials tended to inspire a certain degree of awe among the small handicraft masters, the masters felt compelled to confront them on this issue. To be sure, the masters put the major blame upon the state itself, which according to them had left its employees greatly underpaid and thus virtually forced them to adopt such improper measures as the establishment of consumers' cooperatives. Purchasing at wholesale prices, and selling at a discount in cooperative shops to members only, appeared to the masters to be a flirtation with communism, carried out "over the bodies of the medium- and small-sized industrial producers."[25] Karl Metzner, himself a master artisan and a Catholic Reichstag member, described the consumers' associations to an enthusiastic audience of masters as a danger to the entire Mittelstand. "It is a revolting sight to observe even high state officials engaging in business competition with shopkeepers and artisans," he ex-

[25] *AHZ*, December 8, 1893.

claimed.[26] Metzner voiced one of the central articles of faith in the philosophy of the masters. The various economic functions, they believed, should be strictly apportioned among the different social and occupational groups. "Handicrafts to the handicraftsmen" was a popular slogan of the small masters' movement throughout the nineteenth century. It embodied their general fear of competition and their rigid view of the function of the separate estates in society. The continuous fusion and redifferentiation of social functions in modern society seemed to them a danger to both Stände and Staat. Government officials engaged in production and commerce were more than competitors: they were helping to undermine the entire social order. As respected and responsible men, argued the masters' spokesmen, officials could have been expected to know better. Consumers' cooperatives, some of the handicraft masters believed, were only a part of a comprehensive plot to destroy the social order, to bring about debilitating social equality and erode the Christian monarchical state. A master who supported these "subversive" organizations was but "a murderer of his fellow men, and would finally be driven to ruin by destroying those on whose existence he himself depended."[27]

Not all the masters were equally opposed to consumers' cooperatives. Some stood to benefit from them, and with the exception of the bakers and the tailors, were rarely affected by the few existing ones. As in the case of the conflict between masters and shopkeepers, however, the issue had broader cultural connotations. The cooperatives were correctly seen by the masters as an expression of an overall sociopolitical attitude. They signified the acceptance of the liberal modern economic order, which meant that "self-help" was the only route open to the less prosperous. The basis for cooperative organizations was in communal

[26] *Protokoll über die Verhandlungen zu Halle 1895*, p. 125. See also the illuminating debate on consumers' organizations at the same congress, pp. 117-137.

[27] Ibid., p. 127.

action, rather than in the rugged individualism and economic independence that the masters strove to promote. The hostility of the masters was a protective gesture of small producers against the power of organized consumer associations. But more generally it was directed against the establishment of new social and economic institutions, and against the acceptance of and the adjustment to the new values they implied.

The master artisans felt the greatest affinity for the small independent peasants, who they believed to be their counterparts in agriculture. Together the two groups represented the traditional "productive" estates, the "practical masters" of the nation.[28] In the 1890s, the organizers of the Bund der Landwirte (BdL, The Agrarians' League) were quick to exploit this strong fellow feeling. The Bund's ideological scheme was designed specifically to attract the small rural master artisans, many of whom were in fact part-time peasants or agricultural employees, and it was rather successful in drawing some elements of the handicraft population into its agrarian interest-group organization.[29]

At first, the urban masters, who were not expected to join the Bund der Landwirte, were nevertheless among its most staunch supporters. In 1894 the masters' newspaper in Berlin characterized the BdL as the "stonewall of protection against Manchesterism," and the masters' organizations hoped to be able to cooperate with the BdL in order to fight their common enemies.[30] However, when the Bund

[28] *DHZ*, January 6 and September 22, 1894.

[29] The Mittelstandspolitik of the Bund der Landwirte (BdL) was intended to appeal above all to the handicraft masters. There are no statistics on the number of master artisans in the BdL prior to 1899. At that time it included 14,000 Handwerker. The number rose to 18,000 in 1900, to 40,000 in 1901, and reached 49,000 by 1906. Almost half of these were partly engaged in agriculture in addition to their permanent handicraft occupation. Puhle, *Agrarische Interessenpolitik*, pp. 39; 98 ff.

[30] *DHZ*, January 6, 1894. See also September 22, November 3, February 24, 1894, and November 23, 1895.

began to advocate peasants' cooperatives, the urban masters lost some of their original enthusiasm. This attack on their estate by those who professed to be their closest allies was a particularly bitter experience.[31] It soon became evident that the BdL intended to pursue an independent policy and that competition between it and the various master-artisans' organizations was unavoidable.

In any case, the urban masters' cooperation with the peasantry could not have lasted long without disclosing the ambiguity of the relationship. Urban centers, so detested and scorned by peasant politicians, were after all the home of many masters. Although masters often expressed concern over the moral deterioration of the town, growing insubordination and widespread religious indifference, they were in no position to reject city life as a whole.[32] Individual masters could and, indeed, occasionally did leave the towns, although primarily for economic reasons, but for those who remained, a total rejection of town life hardly offered a satisfactory ideological position. In their everyday life they observed what they considered the city's depravity, as well as its glamour. They were forced to deal from within with its new social atmosphere and relationships. Peasant life could provide them with a distant ideal, but not a realistic alternative.

[31] The first attacks on the BdL came toward the end of 1894 (see *DHZ*, November 17 and 24, 1894), but the real disappointment came only later. The *DHZ*, which was in 1894 on the whole sympathetic to the BdL, was vehemently and bitterly antagonistic to it by 1897; see *DHZ*, September 11, 1897. In 1894 a master tailor from Erfurt, Johannes Wilhelm Jacobskötter, who was active in the local anti-Semitic Reformverein, was elected to the Reichstag on the BdL ticket. He then became the conservative spokesman on matters of handicraft legislation, but was never more than a marginal figure in the organized masters' movement. The masters complained that the BdL ran artisans as candidates only in districts most unlikely to elect them. *DHZ*, November 24, 1894.

[32] See *DHZ*, January 27, 1894.

STATUS INCONSISTENCY AND SOCIAL ISOLATION

By the late nineteenth century the material circumstances of small master artisans in Germany had been deteriorating for a long time. The effectiveness and prestige of the guilds had declined, and the disintegration of the traditional handicraft community was alarmingly advanced. Nevertheless, the masters often managed to preserve a relatively respectable social standing until the very end of the nineteenth century. Their social prestige was usually far above the level suggested by their material condition, and the discrepancy between the masters' place on the income and wealth scales and their position in the status hierarchy created a social situation that was loaded with tension.[33] In fact, the social history of the master artisans through much of the nineteenth century can be perceived as a prolonged struggle to prevent their status and prestige from sinking to match their actual material condition. With the advent of industrialization, the masters no longer appeared to be economically indispensable, and their social status was continuously threatened. When the Great Depression gave another blow to their economic position, it became increas-

[33] The meaning and relevance of status inconsistency have been debated in the sociological literature for the last fifteen years. The concept has thereby been greatly refined, and in spite of some severe attacks upon it, appears to be still useful and illuminating. See Gerhard E. Lenski, "Status Crystallization"; William F. Kenkel, "The Relationship between Status Consistency and Political Attitudes"; K. Dennis Kelly and William J. Chambliss, "Status Consistency and Political Attitudes"; Andrzej Malewsky, "The Degree of Status Incongruence and its Effects," in *Class, Status and Power*, ed. R. Bendix and S.M. Lipset, pp. 303-308. The most original contribution to this debate is W.G. Runciman's in *Relative Deprivation and Social Justice*, pp. 30 ff. and 41 ff. and in "Status Consistency, Relative Deprivation and Attitudes to Immigrants," in *Sociology in its Place*. See also Gary B. Rush, "Status Consistency and Right-Wing Extremism," and Steven Box and Julienne M. Ford, "Some Questionable Assumptions in the Theory of Status Inconsistency."

ingly improbable that they could continue to preserve a social standing based on long-vanished conditions. In a society in which wealth was coming more and more to determine an individual's social standing, the gap between the masters' economic position and their social prestige became increasingly difficult to maintain.

Initially, the masters struggled to close this gap by improving their economic standing, and when efforts in this direction failed, they attempted to preserve at least their unique social position. Soon the futility of this effort too became clear, as their social status fell relentlessly to match their economic standing.

As the century drew to a close, however, the inconsistency in the master-artisans' social position acquired a new dimension. While the gap between their economic position and their social standing was diminishing, a new one developed between the general public appreciation of their social standing and their own self-esteem. Thus an inconsistency between social consciousness and social reality replaced the one between the various components of that reality.[34]

Since the small master artisans were involved in manual labor, and since their property was often retained only through great personal effort and conferred only limited material advantages, they remained as a group at the bottom of the internal social hierarchy of the Mittelstand. They constituted a kind of transition zone at its lower boundary, a position the masters refused to accept. They wished to be distinguished from their employees by their ownership of capital, small as it often was. They claimed superiority over other segments of the Mittelstand be-

[34] For the various aspects of this problem see Stanislaw Ossowski, *Class Structure in the Social Consciousness*; also F.M. Martin, "Some Subjective Aspects of Social Stratification," in *Social Mobility in Britain*, ed. D.V. Glass; John H. Goldthorpe and David Lockwood, "Affluence and the British Class Structure"; W.G. Runciman, "'Embourgeoisment,' Self-Rated Class and Party Preference," and "False Consciousness," both in *Sociology in its Place*.

cause they were skilled laborers. They demanded special respect because they believed the handicrafts represented a unique combination of capital ownership and skilled workmanship.

In their 1882 national congress the masters openly claimed preeminence within the Mittelstand: "The German handicraft estate is, and was for centuries, the elite of the Mittelstand, and as such should be protected from undesirable elements and preserved for the benefit of the entire nation."[35] The masters made special efforts to represent themselves as economically, culturally, and politically indispensable in the life of the German Reich. The following quotations give not only the content of their claim but also some of its special flavor:

> If one excludes from the body of the economy the many-sided activity of the master artisans, the entire culture would instantly collapse.[36]

> With the handicrafts a higher form of culture was brought into the world. This is proven historically and is so commonly accepted that it requires no further proof.[37]

> One should not forget that the strength of our Christian monarchical state depends, in effect, on the existence of an independent handicraft estate.[38]

Fighting to assert a social superiority they did not possess, the masters were forced to stress the distinction between themselves and their immediate social inferiors. Not only did they break with the journeymen, they were also eager to be kept socially apart from the untraditional and often poorly-trained small industrial producers, whom they

[35] Quoted from a report on the national artisans' conference in Magdeburg in the *KZ*, June 3, 1882.

[36] *DHZ*, April 7, 1894.

[37] Ibid. See also the eloquent article in the *DHZ*, February 24, 1894.

[38] Quoted in the *KZ*, July 22, 1884.

derogatorily called Pfuscher (bunglers). In reality, the masters in their small shops hardly differed from their less fully-trained or nonguild colleagues. Again, as the actual social distance lost its significance, the masters became more and more vehement in demanding its restoration. It was as a result of this diminishing distinctness that the issue of the qualifying examination (Befähigungsnachweis) gained such prominence among the reform demands of the masters' interest organizations. It was to be a legal instrument for the preservation of the purity of their social status group, to serve as a formal line of demarcation in a society that paid increasingly little attention to their claim to moral and vocational superiority. It would preserve the handicrafts, so they believed, for the true handicraftsmen.[39]

The debate over the masters' qualifying examination was also indicative of their position in relation to their direct social and economic superiors outside the Mittelstand, namely the medium- and large-scale industrial producers. The handicraft masters, fighting to preserve their small workshops and traditional style of life, developed an ambivalent attitude toward these social climbers. On the one hand, they envied the industrialists' economic success and higher social rank, but on the other they could not help despising the new standards of production and professional manners associated with the new industry. From the early years of the Great Depression on, the issue of competition with the large industrial entrepreneurs was uppermost in the minds of the small masters. They then demanded the masters' examination as a protective device. It was to be applied only to small masters to help them safeguard their own area of economic activity. In a memorandum sent to the German chancellor by the Central Guild Committee in Berlin on January 22, 1886, the masters explained that they did not

[39] On the Befähigungsnachweis, see especially Thilo Hampke, *Der Befähigungsnachweis im Handwerk* and the section on the masters' League, chap. 9.

oppose large-scale industry.[40] In fact, they rejected the theory that mass poverty had to accompany the advent of modern machinery; they wished to exploit this cultural progress for their own benefit. They only wanted to impress upon the government, they stated, the necessity of prescribing for each element its own sphere of activity. It was imperative that the particular sphere of the handicrafts be defined on the basis of skill and proper training and be protected against all intervention from the outside. Unable to stop the spread of industrialization, the masters hoped at least to protect themselves against its invasion into their living space.

Toward the end of the century, however, it became clear that the coexistence of factories and handicraft shops was economically beneficial for many handicraft branches, and indispensable for some. The demand for the masters' examination took on a different connotation. By the last decade of the nineteenth century, the masters demanded that an examination be required of all industrial producers, small and large alike. They not only wished now to protect themselves but also to force their own standards and values on others. Factories and handicraft shops, explained the masters' journal, could easily coexist in harmony since the factories were actually created to serve handicraft producers, and this hierarchical relationship between them was both natural and just.[41] The principle of vocational competence should be applied in all spheres of activity, so as to establish a clear social boundary between the trained and the untrained, the qualified and the unqualified, the true masters and the Pfuscher.[42] In fact there was little chance that the Befähigungsnachweis would be legally established. It was repeatedly rejected by the Reichstag as an impractical, bureaucratic, and ineffective solution to the problem of or-

[40] See *Denkschrift an seine Durchlaucht den Herrn Reichkanzler* (Berlin, 1886), in Bayerisches Hauptstaatsarchiv, MH-14636.

[41] *DHZ*, July 21, 1894. [42] Ibid., March 31, 1894.

ganizing or protecting handicraft production. Big industry would not hear of such arrangements. It hoped to absorb the more prosperous masters into its own ranks and had little desire to cooperate with others. Its interests were continually in conflict with those of the small traditional craft masters on matters of apprentices' education, the role of the guilds, and the jurisdiction of industrial chambers.[43] Naturally the masters' claim to superiority could not be taken seriously by large industrialists, and the masters' insistence on the importance of vocational examinations only served to underline the social distance between them and those both above and below them on the social ladder. Eventually it only enhanced their sense of isolation.

In an effort to overcome this isolation, the masters emphasized the identity between their interests and those of the nation as a whole.[44] Indeed, in a society that was continuously torn by internal struggle, such an attitude appears to have been vital for the preservation of a minimal sense of social belonging. It was not uncommon even among the groups who openly solicited state protection in ways that clearly threatened to jeopardize wider social interests. Failing to achieve a lasting alliance with other social groups the masters also faced objective difficulties in attempting to secure a proper social standing. In German society of the late nineteenth century, an aristocratic origin, a special position within the bureaucracy, a high level of education, or a conspicuous "closeness to the throne" were the most important factors in the determination of social prestige.[45]

[43] See Winkler, *Mittelstand*, pp. 57-64; also Johannes Wernicke, *Kapitalismus und Mittelstandspolitik*, pp. 326 ff.; Hartmut Kaelble, *Industrielle Interessenpolitik*, pp. 164-168; Emil Lederer, *Die wirtschaftlichen Organisationen*, pp. 56 ff.

[44] On this as a general tendency characteristic of interest groups in Imperial Germany see especially Wolfram Fischer, "Staatsverwaltung und Interessenverbände," now in his *Wirtschaft und Gesellschaft*, pp. 206-209; for a comparative perspective see Ernst Fraenkel, *Deutschland und die westlichen Demokratien*, pp. 32-47.

[45] See Fritz K. Ringer, "Higher Education in Germany in the 19th Century."

The masters did not share any of these qualifications. They were as a rule of low social origin and had normally only the most rudimentary education. They were losing their authority in the community and workshops and appeared incapable of replacing it with some other kind of social influence. They were politically unorganized and ideologically disoriented. Their opinions were often considered anachronistic, and their attitudes old fashioned. By the end of the nineteenth century, their claims to social superiority were treated at best with indifference and at worst with outright mockery.

The masters found themselves particularly infuriated by the attitude of the educated elite. An 1889 article in the masters' newspaper expressed their indignation with the condescending attitude characteristic of a large part of the "so-called—and often wrongly so—educated estate."[46] It accused the educated of empty talk concerning human equality, accompanied by a pretentious and arrogant attitude toward the common, working man. Even more than this disparagement the masters resented the paternalism associated with it. The publication of scholarly works concerning the situation of master artisans was repeatedly exploited by the masters' newspapers as occasions for attacks on "scientific bungling."[47] The organized masters often refused to cooperate with officials or private investigators, and when the government decided to sponsor a study of their economic conditions, their interest organizations reacted with exasperation. They rightly believed it to be primarily a delaying device and argued that the masters alone were in a position to judge the severity of their own situation and suggest the proper remedies.[48] They considered an investigation conducted by experts to be an overt insult. Under-

[46] *AHZ*, February 22, 1889.

[47] *DHZ*, July 21, 1894. See also April 20, 1895.

[48] See the report in the *Statistische Jahrbücher deutscher Städte*, 5 (1896); 278, and the article in the *DHZ*, July 21, 1894, as well as the opening speech in *Protokoll über die Verhandlungen zu Halle 1895*, p. 5.

standably they felt particularly bitter toward the men who were directly responsible for much of the shift in the social norms and values that made the masters' claims to social superiority entirely unacceptable to a growing segment of German society.

By the end of the Great Depression the social isolation of the master artisans was virtually complete. They were considered employers by workers and potential employees by other industrial entrepreneurs. As producers they were treated with suspicion by other elements of the urban Mittelstand, and the interests of both peasants and larger industrial businessmen collided with their own. Even while various groups within the Mittelstand were attempting to organize politically, and drawing closer together socially and ideologically, it was a long time before the Mittelstand as such could provide the masters with a feeling of belonging even remotely reminiscent of the old community of the handicraft estate.[49] The sense of isolation they suffered as a result of industrial change was greatly exacerbated by the simultaneous modernization of German society and its sharp division into increasingly more distinct classes.[50] The masters felt left out of these classes, and observed with a sense of helplessness and a growing hostility the social environment forming around them.

[49] On Mittelstand organizations mainly after the turn of the century see Leo Müffelmann, *Die politische Mittelstandsbewegung*; and Wernicke, *Kapitalismus und Mittelstandspolitik*. The best general discussion of this issue is to be found in Winkler, *Mittelstand*, pp. 49-57. See also Gellately, *The Politics of Economic Despair*, pp. 148-196.

[50] See the opening section of chap. 11.

FIVE

APATHY, FRAGMENTATION, DISORIENTATION

The Breakdown of Traditional Associations

Sensing the deterioration in their social status and their growing isolation within German society, the small master artisans turned inward. They made repeated efforts to mold themselves into a unified group, capable of protecting their social and economic interests and of presenting a common ideological and political front. This was not an easy task. They first had to overcome their by then almost traditional public apathy and battle against political indifference, ideological disorientation, and notorious organizational fragmentation. A brief description of this general condition is necessary in order to understand the peculiar nature of the organizational and political efforts they eventually made at the time of the Great Depression.

The master artisans never entirely overcame either their disposition to remain politically inactive or their inefficiency in dealing with public matters. Apathy, disorientation, and the inability to cooperate or sustain coordinated action, however, were particularly typical of their public behavior during the quarter century that preceded the economic slowdown of the 1870s and the establishment of the Bismarckian Reich. During the last quarter of the century these tendencies gradually subsided, but they nevertheless continued to coexist along with a new tendency toward more directed and purposeful common action.

As late as April 1890, a leading article in the *Allgemeine Handwerkerzeitung* (*AHZ*) claimed that some 70 percent of all masters in the country showed no interest at all in the affairs of their Stand.[1] They were all well aware, argued the

[1] *AHZ*, April 7, 1890. For earlier complaints about masters' apathy see *Protokolle über die Verhandlungen zu Darmstadt 1877*, p. 22;

article, of the social maladies that had to be combatted if their fortunes, economic as well as social, were to revive. But their inertia and apathy prevented them from forming a united front to fight these evils. The percentage cited cannot of course be accurate, but it does suggest the extent of the problem and the difficulty it presented for the activists.

Apathy was frequently explained by the masters themselves and by their contemporaries as arising from their debilitating poverty. The poor independent master could hardly afford to neglect his workshop in order to attend social gatherings or political meetings. He was frequently unable to pay even the smallest of fees, and was far too preoccupied with earning his daily bread to be able to spare the time for debates, campaigns, and elections.[2] It may be assumed with relative confidence that many of the small masters, in the rural areas especially, but also in the smaller towns and perhaps even in large urban centers, were among the chronic nonvoters in Germany, and that many of them never joined any of the masters' clubs or their numerous interest organizations.

Apathy toward public issues, however, was not limited to the poor masters. In Hamburg, over 6,000 small artisans were eligible to vote in the 1873 election for the city chamber of industry, but only 1,800 of them exercised their right.[3] The percentage of masters voting in these elections, in Hamburg as elsewhere, remained low throughout the years of the Great Depression, in spite of the growing prestige and influence of the chambers. The participation of masters in elections for the local Gewerbegerichte (indus-

---

and Arthur Löbner, *Wie das deutsche Kleingewerbe über die Innungsfrage denkt*, p. 11.

[2] The average guild entrance fee was 4 marks in 1895. It ranged, however, from 24.5 M in Dortmund to 1.8 M in Danzig. *Bayerische Handelszeitung*, September 14, 1895.

[3] *Jahresbericht der Hamburgerischen Gewerbekammer für 1873/74*, p. 2.

trial arbitration courts) was equally poor: in 1892 only 600 small employers participated in the election in Frankfurt a.M., and a year later in elections in Munich, only 750 bothered to vote. This was such a low turnout that a second election was held, in which some 2,800 of the 35,000 small master employers cast their ballots.[4] Even the strained relationship between small employers and their workers, which the courts of arbitration sought to relieve, was not sufficient to rouse the small master artisans out of their indifference.

In this connection it may be useful to recall Marx's description of the social conditions responsible for the peculiar character of French peasant society: "The small-holding peasants," he wrote in the *18th Brumaire of Louis Bonaparte*, "form a vast mass, the members of which live in similar conditions but without entering into manifold relations with one another. Their mode of production isolates them from one another instead of bringing them into mutual intercourse. . . . Each individual peasant family is almost self-sufficient. . . and the identity of their interests begets no community, no national bond and no political organization among them."[5] With some obvious modifications this analysis can easily be applied to the small master artisans, in the rural as well as the urban areas of Germany. In their case, too, a consideration of their characteristic mode of production and peculiar life style may help to explain the prevalent public apathy and chronic inability to cooperate.

Traditionally, the focus of the master's life was his family. It provided the foundation for both his economic and his moral existence. It utilized so much of his time and energy

[4] *Sozialpolitisches Zentralblatt* 1(1892); 123 ff.; 2(1893); 265. The industrial arbitration courts varied in character from one region to another. On this complicated system see Karl-Erich Born, *Staat und Sozialpolitik seit Bismarcks Sturz*, pp. 92 ff.; Adelheid von Saldern, "Gewerbegerichte im wilhelminischen Deutschland," pp. 189-203.

[5] Quoted from the 1963 International Publishers edition, pp. 123-124.

that he rarely felt the need to be associated with larger social institutions. The attraction of the old guilds lay in providing just the kind of institutional framework that could coexist with and supplement the functions of the individual artisan's household. The old guild absorbed the entire artisan family, and was, in effect, an organization of families rather than individuals. It participated in the education of apprentices and in the supervision of journeymen; it celebrated the young master's newly achieved independence, his marriage, the birth of his sons. It supported him in times of poverty or illness and protected his widow at the time of his death. It was also the channel through which he could wield political influence in the local community. The guild was designed to encompass the master artisan in the multiplicity of his social roles: as a father and educator, a skilled craftsman, a husband, the head of a family, and a citizen. That was the source of its vitality and of its peculiar popularity among the masters even when it was, economically and socially, an institutional anachronism.

By the early years of the Great Depression, however, little remained of the old guilds. Without the active support of the law, and in a period of rapid industrialization, they gradually ceased to exist. In the mid-seventies approximately 6,000 guilds still operated throughout the entire German Reich. In several of the eastern provinces of Prussia where industrialization was late to penetrate, the guilds managed to survive in relatively large numbers. In the industrial provinces of the western and southwestern German states, however, they were almost entirely extinct. By 1878 even in the relatively developed Silesian province, some 1,500 guilds claiming close to 23,000 members still seemed to function, but in the Rhine province only 34 guilds still operated at that date and in Westphalia only 6, claiming 1,700 and 500 members respectively. Of the 1,370 guilds that had operated in Baden during the 1850s, fewer than 50 were reported in existence in the late 1870s. Moreover, throughout the country, where guilds did exist, they were all too often nothing but empty shells.[6]

The small master artisans, stripped of their former sociocultural environment, at odds with their journeymen, and only rarely truly allied with other social groups, became increasingly aware of the need to replace their old institutional framework and to form new types of associations. The new structures, they hoped, would help to revive their lost sense of community, and provide them with a new and more adequate base from which to work together in the face of material hardship and the enormous social transformation then in progress.

Organizational Fragmentation

In the early 1830s the governments of the southwestern German states, generally liberal in their approach to economic issues and hostile toward the old guilds, encouraged the formation of new industrial associations. In Baden, in Hesse, and later also in Hanover and Prussia, such groups had active government support. They were normally called Gewerbevereine (industrial associations), a name that must be used cautiously, since in different parts of the country various organizational forms, varying in function, in purpose, and in the character of their membership were so designated.[7]

In Baden the industrial associations were originally no more than social clubs for men who shared a common interest in technical matters and in the practical sciences. They served as meeting places for industrialists, large and small, for commercial and financial businessmen, vocational teachers, university professors, and others. The number of

[6] See Eugen Jäger, *Die Handwerkerfrage*, p. 136, and von Hertling's report to the Reichstag, *Steno. Berichte*, May 5, 1880.

[7] W. Noack, "Gewerbevereine," in *HBS*, 3rd ed. See also Alexander Lang, "Die Badischen Gewerbevereine."

small traditional master artisans among them was small and diminishing. The Sponsoring Committee of the Industrial Associations in Baden, a central organization set up in 1877 and attached to the Ministry of Commerce, included seven representatives of the industrial associations themselves, six appointed members, and an additional five representing the ministry. The first two categories included four professors and teachers, two factory owners, one bank director, two government officials, and four men of whom two were listed as printers, one as a mechanic, and one as an engineer. Not one small master artisan of a typical traditional craft figured among them.[8] Within the local associations too, the number of small handicraft masters varied greatly. In the Mannheim local Gewerbeverein, for example, their number declined continuously between 1877 and 1894, although their proportion of the total membership remained roughly constant at about one half. In Karlsruhe, 264 of the 318 members in 1888 were listed as "engaged in industry or industrialists," but of the twelve-man executive committee only two were handicraft masters. In fact, many industrial associations did not include anyone who was actively engaged in industry or handicrafts.[9]

The industrial associations in Hesse and in the Rhine province were similar in composition and structure to those set up in Baden. In Bavaria, however, many so-called Gewerbevereine were in fact the direct heirs of the extinct guilds. Characteristically, they often included handicraftsmen from a single trade only. But while this was the common character of the Gewerbevereine in the capital, many industrial associations elsewhere in the Bavarian state were more like the organizational model prevailing in Baden. In parts of Saxony, and in the Hanseatic towns, the industrial associations functioned as grass-roots organizations, centralized at the top by the semiofficial chambers of

[8] See the report on the meetings of the committee in the Badisches Generallandesarchiv, 236/9612.

[9] Ibid.; also Lang, "Die Badischen Gewerbevereine," p. 30.

industry. Everywhere the associations were primarily concerned with technical and educational matters and geared to serve the special needs of their local communities. Thus, efforts to provide them with a central national organization failed repeatedly, and the Verband der deutschen Gewerbevereine (League of German Industrial Associations), which was finally established in Cologne in 1892, always remained a weak and ineffective body.

Gewerbeverein members naturally held a variety of political views, but tended to be men of liberal convictions who had an interest in the technical and organizational revolution in industry and in the overall changes in the market economy. It is difficult today to assess with precision the occupation or the economic standing of the master craftsmen who *did* belong to these associations. Most likely they were recruited from among the practitioners of the more prosperous, modern, and technologically advanced trades. Few masters of traditional crafts ever joined them.

A similar group of progressive and relatively well-to-do masters participated in the activities of the industrial chambers in Germany. Like the Gewerbevereine, these differed in character and composition from state to state, and from one city to another.[10] They were elected by a variety of methods based on voting qualifications in accordance with the local system of municipal election and tax collection.

In the Hanseatic towns the chambers of industry were separate from the more powerful chambers of commerce, while in Saxony (with the exception of Leipzig), in Bavaria, and in Württemberg they constituted a section of the comprehensive Handel- und Gewerbekammern (chambers of commerce and industry). The number of delegates representing the various economic sectors within these bodies varied from chamber to chamber, but none of them was

[10] See Thilo Hampke, *Handwerker- oder Gewerbekammern?* and Rudolf Graetzer, *Organisation der Berufsinteressen*, pp. 90 ff.; also Hampke's "Gewerbekammern" in the *HBS*, 4th ed.

primarily concerned with the affairs of small industry, and even less with the special needs of the handicrafts. The status and the function of the industrial chambers also varied in different localities. While they had a semiofficial position with advisory powers and some self-administrative functions in Saxony and in the Hanseatic cities, they were legally private institutions, only occasionally subsidized by government funds, in the small Thuringian states. During the 1880s the centrally organized Gewerbevereine in Baden achieved a semiofficial position and thereafter substituted for industrial chambers in this state.

On the whole, the industrial chambers were mixed institutions with varying degrees of local influence, having a limited impact on national policies. The Hanseatic chambers instituted annual meetings to coordinate their efforts, and an All-German Congress of Commercial and Industrial Chambers (Handel- und Gewerbekammertag) gradually evolved, in which matters of common interest were discussed, and joint resolutions on matters of national importance were formulated. The chambers failed, however, as effective interest organizations because of their heterogeneous composition and their varied and insufficiently defined ties with the authorities. In most cases the chambers were operating legally as public bodies and served primarily to inform the bureaucracy about various economic issues. They constituted a strange and unique hybrid between public corporations and interest organizations.[11] In any event, with the possible exception of the three northern Hanseatic cities, they played only a very limited role in representing the economic, social, or political interests of the small traditional master artisans.

Undoubtedly, the most successful attempt to organize small master artisans during the third quarter of the nineteenth century was made by the various wings of the German cooperative movement.[12] In the early 1850s the out-

[11] See H.A. Winkler, *Pluralismus oder Protektionismus?*

[12] See Helmut Faust, *Geschichte der Genossenschaftsbewegung*,

standing liberal social reformer Schulze-Delitzsch began to agitate for the so-called "Innungen der Zukunft," the guilds of the future. At the same time, a conservative social reformer, the then little-known Victor Aimé Huber, was propagating his own version of the cooperative ideal and his own cooperative scheme. Both were influenced by the British cooperative movement, and both wished to emphasize the role of free cooperative associations and creative self-help in the overall task of solving the "social question." Despite the superficial similarity of their social programs, the two men were inspired by very different social ideologies. Schulze's cooperatives were designed to turn as many workingmen as possible into small independent producers, and to make their cooperative and individual enterprises economically viable within the context of an industrial, liberal economy. Huber's associations, on the other hand, were conceived as weapons with which to fight the onslaught of this new economy. The cooperative movement gained much publicity in Germany during the 1850s and 1860s, when popular political activity was virtually at a standstill, and when a growing general prosperity and new economic opportunities provided the necessary conditions and atmosphere for social experimentation.

Schulze's cooperative movement was the more successful and renowned of the two.[13] Originally intended to appeal to all workingmen in Germany, independent and dependent laborers, Arbeiter and Handwerker alike, the cooperatives were supposed to give expression to the ideal of workers' solidarity and brotherhood, and provide for the individual worker's material needs. Schulze actually succeeded in establishing a network of cooperatives throughout the country. They were mostly credit cooperatives, or cooperative associations for the purchase and supply of raw materials,

---

pp. 248 ff. See also the critical review by Rudolf Meyer in *Der Emancipationskampf des Vierten Standes*, vol. 2, pp. 178 ff.

[13] For his efforts and ideas see Werner Conze, *Möglichkeiten und Grenzen der liberalen Arbeiterbewegung*.

while producers' or consumers' cooperatives were rare. The credit and raw-material cooperatives readily attracted small independent craftsmen, but the majority of wage earners showed little interest or enthusiasm for them. Thus, Schulze's cooperatives won a considerable following among Mittelständler. By 1864 he reported the existence of 455 cooperatives, with a total membership of 135,000. Ten years later the number of cooperatives had doubled and the membership quadrupled.[14]

The cooperative movement, however, never grew to be a force for change among the German handicraft population. Stories of cooperatives suffering from a chronic lack of capital and eventually taken over by one or several prosperous members were only too common.[15] Reported mismanagement and bankruptcies led to widespread mistrust of the entire organizational form.[16] In the late 1870s, the movement rapidly lost its appeal and its practical significance. Schulze's cooperative movement was emphatically apolitical. It was not meant to give voice to its members as a collectivity. It certainly did not intend to represent the small handicraftsmen as a separate, conscious social group. The tone of the movement was outspokenly liberal, and master artisans were conceived within it as members of the large working population, as at most an avant-garde section of it. It could not serve as an organizational basis for promoting the interests of small master artisans, and its popularity among them was a marginal and passing phase of their group history.

14 Ibid., p. 17.

15 Such incidents are reported by Karl Hampke, "Tischlergewerbe in Posen," *Schriften* 62 (1895): 89-90; Voigt, "Das Tischlergewerbe," *Schriften* 65 (1895): 469-470; Arthur Cohen, "Das Schreinergewerbe in Augsburg," *Schriften* 64 (1895): 559; Behr, *Entwicklung in der Schuhindustrie*, p. 94. On some successful producers' cooperatives, see Reinhardt, "Bäckergewerbe in Breslau," *Schriften* 68 (1896): 103.

16 See the section on master artisans and other Mittelständler in chap. 4 above.

Thus, after the dissolution of the old guilds, trade organizations of various types mushroomed everywhere in Germany. They were usually established locally and formed a confused mosaic of fragmented groups, with various and occasionally contradictory purposes. In Hamburg, for example, the building crafts alone had at least four different trade organizations: the Corporation of Masons, the Association of the Building Trades, the large Bauhütte (Builders' Club) incorporating a number of smaller groups, and a Corporation of Building Joiners. In the metal trades more than ten different organizations partly cooperated and partly competed with each other.[17] Disunity was the hallmark of the masters' trade associations everywhere.

By the 1870s, in spite of a multitude of masters' clubs and trade societies, there was no organization capable of representing them as a social group and voicing their collective demands. The various groups had little effect even within their local communities, and the total lack of coordination among them made any combined public action by small master artisans virtually impossible.

Prepolitical Group Action: 1848

It was extremely difficult to sustain any kind of association of small master artisans in Germany even for purely social or cultural purposes, and particularly difficult to unite them for consciously directed political action. As individuals and through their guilds, small masters had long participated in and exercised a great deal of influence on local and municipal government.[18] The unique kind of political experience acquired in their small home towns, however, did not facilitate their adjustment to the new demands of political action on a state and national scale. Following the Napoleonic wars and throughout the nineteenth century

[17] *Jahresbericht der Hamburgerischen Gewerbekammer, 1873/4*, pp. 74 ff.

[18] Walker, *German Home Towns*, especially pp. 73-107.

effective political activity in Germany had to be organized across local boundaries, as state officials gradually took over most of the significant functions of government. For the small urban master artisans this transfer of power required the reformulation of earlier political concepts and the adoption of new tactics. The old channels of influence were partially blocked, and new ones had to be created.

The small master artisans first appeared as a loosely organized political group on the national scene during the revolution of 1848. In order to appreciate their political and ideological searching during the Great Depression, it is necessary to turn back and briefly examine their group activity at this early stage. Fortunately, we have a number of scattered reports on various artisans' meetings, especially some held during the summer of 1848. But while the story of the masters' public action during these critical months has often been told, their precise role in the overall revolutionary situation and the exact nature of their involvement remains unclear. Were they revolutionaries or counterrevolutionaries? liberals or conservatives, social democrats or social conservatives, progressives or reactionaries? This lack of clarity is not peculiar to the historiography of artisans in the German revolution of 1848. The task of categorizing in clear-cut political terms the revolutionary activities of the masses in Europe after the French Revolution has proved to be exceedingly complex. After 1789 and throughout the nineteenth century the "crowd" made the revolutions, manned the barricades, and generally supported the activities of revolutionary assemblies and constitutional conventions. At the same time, however, it almost invariably made demands alien to the central revolutionary ideology, justifying them in terms that made little sense in the context of this ideology. The Parisian sans-culottes of 1793-94 provide the best-known example.[19] Like the het-

[19] See especially Soboul, *The Parisian Sans-Culottes*, pp. 117 ff.; 249-261. On Robespierre and the popular movement, pp. 250-254. Also, G. Rudé, *The Crowd in the French Revolution*, chap. 13.

erogeneous revolutionaries of earlier years, they sought to control the rising price of bread and were roused to action primarily for the betterment of their material conditions. Their direct political interest was limited to the fight for self-government of the various city sections, and their economic demands were often considered outright reactionary by the bourgeois National Assembly. Robespierre himself became increasingly uneasy at the measures for control and protection that his Committee of Public Safety had felt compelled to introduce under pressure of the Paris sections. At the same time, the political demands of the French revolutionary leadership aroused little enthusiasm among the small master artisans, retailers, and journeymen of Paris. The leadership and its popular following had different conceptions of all three revolutionary ideals: liberty, equality, and fraternity.[20]

In part this divergence was the consequence of an unequal level of politicization. This is particularly important to remember in the case of the 1848 revolution in Germany. The master-artisans' involvement in the events of 1848 can best be described as prepolitical. If politics is defined as the process and practice of government, these men had little or no idea of its nature, complexity, or even of their capacity to affect it.[21] The specific demands of their group were limited, and they were as yet incapable of integrating them into a coherent ideology, or into the general, national political struggle. Thus, the master artisans in 1848 were in most cases neither revolutionary nor counterrevolutionary, neither progressive nor reactionary. Throughout the first half of the nineteenth century, together with other low strata of German society, they were in effect outside national politics, which until then had been a matter for monarchs and bu-

[20] See especially the discussion in Leppert-Fögen, *Die deklassierte Klasse*, pp. 134-161.

[21] For the various definitions of politics, and an excellent bibliography, see Michael Freund, "Politik," in *Handwörterbuch der Sozialwissenschaften.*

reaucrats. Government affairs were conducted far above the heads of common German subjects. In the absence of effective representative bodies, with very few free associations and an almost total lack of public communication, only the ruling aristocratic-bureaucratic elite could effectively influence the government. Even in the southern German states, the incipient parliamentary system, which began to function during the first half of the nineteenth century, provided the more prosperous and politically conscious elements of the middle class with a chance to express themselves, while small masters, retailers, and other Mittelstand groups remained within the confines of their provincial and occupational spheres.[22] By 1848, the small master artisans in most areas of Germany were concerned about their material needs and the threatening change in their social environment, but were still unable to couch their anxiety in the language of politics. They rarely understood the possibility of carrying out a social and economic struggle as part of a political process in which they were equal participants, and this remained true for large segments of the German population for many decades to come.[23]

By contrast the connection between political and economic reform in England was generally recognized and accepted even by the newly politicized workingmen. The House of Commons, unlike the continental estate Diets, was an assembly of representatives from counties and boroughs.[24] It openly buttressed not only the political power

[22] See Rolf Weber, "Zur Geschichte der kleinbürgerlichen Demokraten"; Shorter, "Middle-Class Anxiety"; and Mack Walker, "Home Towns and State Administrators: South German Politics, 1815-30."

[23] Recently Dieter Bergmann in "Die Berliner Arbeiterschaft," described the highly political approach and commitment to democracy of a leading elite among the Berlin workers. How prevalent these attitudes were among the common workers even in Berlin is difficult to ascertain. In any event such clear political consciousness cannot be detected among small master artisans during the 1848 revolution.

[24] On the uniqueness of the British constitutional system see Otto Hintze, "Typologie der ständischen Verfassungen des Abendlandes,"

position of a gentry-aristocracy, but also its economic interests. When the middle class of entrepreneurs and merchants wished to strengthen its social and economic position, it concentrated above all on achieving a stronger influence on government through parliamentary reform. The workers' tactics were similar. Under the common law they possessed a degree of legal and civil equality. Realizing their growing significance in the state, they proceeded to demand equal political rights.[25] As early as 1826, a speaker in an assembly of workers in Manchester explained that "the purpose of Parliamentary reform is to secure to the labourer the fruits of his own labour. . . and to every British subject a full participation in all the privileges and advantages of British citizens."[26] William Cobbett conceived of parliamentary reform as a solution to the social problems of craftsmen, and the Chartist movement as a whole managed effectively to channel economic and social grievances into political demands and action.[27] This was the pattern characteristic of the labor movement in Englnad throughout the nineteenth century. It was only after full political rights were gradually achieved during the last quarter of the century that the working-class movement in England began to concentrate more directly on social issues and particularly on economic ones.

Developments were far more complex in Germany. There the struggle of the masses for their rights did not follow this path, with demands moving from civil rights to political

in his *Staat und Verfassung*, pp. 120-139; and Fraenkel, *Deutschland und die westlichen Demokratien*.

25 For the gradual changes in the concept of equality, especially as seen from the British perspective, see T.H. Marshall, "Citizenship and Social Class," in his *Class, Citizenship and Social Development*, pp. 78 ff.

26 Briggs, "The Language of Class," p. 66.

27 See the comments in Smelser, *Social Change in the Industrial Revolution*, pp. 250; 261 ff. Also Asa Briggs, "The Local Background of Chartism," in *Chartist Studies*, pp. 1-32; and an older account, F.F. Rosenblatt, *The Chartist Movement in its Social and Economic Aspects*, pp. 50-69.

and then social rights. The struggle for all three was carried out in Germany simultaneously, and the emphasis shifted according to circumstances from one to the other. Demands for reform always had to be channeled through the bureaucracy, and the absence of popular institutions mediating between society and government made direct intervention by both old and new social elements in the political decision-making process virtually impossible. Such intervention was the secure monopoly of a small elite, while other groups could only operate outside the existing political order, in a revolutionary fashion.

Indeed, the pre-March years saw a growing revolutionary potential among various social elements in Germany including the small masters. The latter had fought for years for a revision of the liberal economic legislation against unyielding state bureaucracies. During the early months of the revolution, they assembled in various towns throughout the country and organized in an effort to find more effective ways of putting pressure on the new authorities. In fact, they only continued to ask for measures they had been advocating in vain for years. They sought to achieve what they believed would be more equitable treatment at the hands of the bureaucracy, and consequently an improvement in their material circumstances. But for the most part they did not realize the political nature of their own action. They were in fact organizing in order to bring pressure upon the authorities to act on their behalf and were therefore deeply involved in the revolutionary political process. But many of them still hoped to conduct their affairs in traditional ways, disclaiming any demand for power or influence, wishing to stay outside the political arena.

In the Hamburg Vorparlament (pre-Parliament), the master artisans proposed to add a social parliament to the political one that had already been deliberating for several months in the Frankfurt Paulskirche. This body was to control all matters of industrial, commercial, and social legislation and to be based on a substructure of local and vocational organizations, thus securing representation for the lower strata of society in matters that directly concerned them. The masters did not intend to interfere with the work of the National Assembly, but wished to be heard on matters of economic and social policy through a separate institution, designed neither to control nor to restrict a more responsive bureaucracy, but to cooperate with it.[28]

As the North German Artisans' Congress in Hamburg planned a national conference in Frankfurt a.M., one of the delegates suggested in all seriousness that the delegates there should be free to discuss politics among themselves in the lobbies, but strictly forbidden to touch upon it in the meeting hall.[29] This may have been suggested as a precaution against illegal activity under the existing combination law, but was in any case characteristic of the way in which the masters conceived of themselves and of their own action. They fought, above all, to gain new economic guarantees in order to replace guild monopolies and privileges and to terminate the long period of what had appeared to them to be industrial chaos. For the purpose of improving their social and material standing, they demanded that far-reaching economic and organizational measures be taken. They acted politically and made plans for reforms that had political implications, but they shied away from admitting even to themselves the nature of their involvement.

The Masters' Ambivalent Liberalism

The demands for reform that the master artisans formulated in their nationwide assemblies during 1848 were

[28] For the master-artisans' proposals for constitutional reform see *Verhandlungen der ersten Abgeordneten Versammlung*, pp. 22-23; and the *Entwurf einer allgemeinen Handwerker- und Gewerbeordnung für Deutschland*; also the additional details given in Bierman, *Karl Georg Winkelblech*, vol. 1, pp. 110-152.

[29] *Verhandlungen der ersten abgeordneten Versammlung*, p. 57.

considered to be outright reactionary and totally unacceptable by the majority of the delegates in the Paulskirche.[30] In their wake, generations of historians have also deemed them indicative of the masters' entrenched conservatism and basic reactionary tendencies.[31] Surprisingly, however, during the next two decades the small masters proved to be among the most persistent supporters of the various liberal parties and associations.[32] How can this phenomenon be explained? Did they revise their position en bloc under the renewed bureaucratic absolutism during the period of reaction? Were there always two distinct groups, a liberal and a conservative one, inexplicably undiscerned by both contemporaries and historians? Or is it perhaps our mistaken interpretation of their stand in 1848 that leads us to perceive a drastic shift in their position during the postrevolutionary years? Undoubtedly, disillusioned by the government's reactionary policies and continuous neglect of their affairs, some masters changed their views during the third quarter of the nineteenth century. Some of them were always liberal and remained so throughout the period. But the apparent change in the position of others requires taking a fresh look at the master-artisans' public stand during the revolution itself.

[30] See *Verhandlungen der Nationalversammlung*, vol. 2, p. 856; vol. 4, p. 2,404; vol. 7, pp. 5,101, 5,114, 5,222 ff.; vol. 9, pp. 6,362 ff. Also Hamerow, *Restoration, Revolution, Reaction*, pp. 152-153.

[31] See, e.g., A. Sartorius von Walterhausen, *Deutsche Wirtschaftsgeschichte 1815-1914*, pp. 138 ff.; Valentin, *Geschichte der deutschen Revolution 1848/49*, vol. 2, pp. 101-103; Hamerow, *Restoration, Revolution, Reaction*, pp. 155 ff.

[32] Eugene N. Anderson, *The Social and Political Conflict in Prussia*, p. 35; also Theodore S. Hamerow, *The Social Foundations of German Unification*, pp. 368-371. Hamerow, however, gives more weight to the growing conservatism of small masters even at that early stage. On the role of small artisans in the left-liberal and early Social-Democratic movement, see Gustav Mayer, *Die Trennung der Proletarischen von der Bürgerlichen Demokratie*; Gustav Seeber, *Zwischen Bebel und Bismarck*; and Rolf Weber, *Die Kleinbürgerliche Demokraten.*

Significantly, the master artisans at the time did not consider themselves antiliberal, nor did they initially intend to oppose the liberals in the Frankfurt Parliament. In their own view their program was neither conservative nor reactionary, and its incompatibility with the mainstream of nineteenth-century liberalism did not seem self-evident to them. A number of factors must be taken into account if this is to be understood. To begin with it is well to remember that pre-March liberalism, particularly in Prussia, was above all antibureaucratic and antiabsolutist. Its essential content was negative: opposition to an oppressive, interventionist state and to the political domination of unproductive, privileged social groups. Thus, it was heir to both the economic and the political liberalism of eighteenth-century England and France.[33] Adam Smith's economic theory was not initially designed to support the claims of a rising industrial capitalism, but to serve as a tool in the battle of a society of small producers against the restrictions of mercantilist state economic policies. It aimed to encourage prudence and diligence, which were characteristic of the social and economic behavior of small, honest, enterprising, and community-minded masters. Political liberalism, too, especially in prerevolutionary France, aimed at satisfying the demands for liberty, equality, and fraternity of the small burgher, not just those of the new capitalist or the educated professional man. In the postrevolutionary years, however, both in England and in France, liberal theory was increasingly adapted to the interests, economic and political, of the capitalist middle class. The gap between its conception of freedom and that of the lower-middle class widened rapidly and became increasingly evident. Only in Germany and particularly in Prussia, under the continuous rule of an absolutist autocratic state, could the conflicting interests of the two groups and their

[33] See Leppert-Fögen, *Die deklassierte Klasse*, pp. 114-134. Also Jürgen Habermas, *Strukturwandel der Öffentlichkeit*, pp. 71-103.

ideological differences continue to be ignored or glossed over.

The master-aristans' 1848 program for reform in no way differed from that advocated by them during the pre-March period. It was based on an assertion of their right to administer their own affairs, a call for legislation to insure the civil rights of assembly and association, and a plan for a revision of existing trade laws, virtually amounting to a repeal of the hated industrial freedom. It was this last item that eventually gained the masters their notoriety as reactionaries and caused the break between them and the Frankfurt liberals. In the context of pre-March politics, however, this development could hardly be expected. Indeed, when in the autumn of 1810 the Prussian liberal administrators introduced the so-called Gewerbefreiheit edict, allowing free entry into the trades, and a year later ordered an end to the Zunftzwang (compulsory guild membership), abolishing compulsory membership in the guilds, they met with sharp opposition and not only from conservative landed interests or the traditional guilds.[34] The major objections were voiced by the social element that was meant to be the main benefactor of the new reforms, the city Bürgertum. The city council in Königsberg, for instance, known for its stubborn battle for constitutionalism, came out strongly against the new industrial legislation. It stressed the inherent conflict between those liberal economic measures and the existing political structure of Prussia, and warned that the two could not possibly coexist. It objected above all to the disparagement of urban self-government which would be a direct consequence of unlimited occupational freedom. The city councilors in Königsberg and later also in Berlin opposed the Gewerbefreiheit because it came into conflict with their newly-won city autonomy, in itself an important liberal achievement.

[34] See Ernst Klein, *Von der Reform zur Restauration*, pp. 110 ff.; see also Walker, *German Home Towns*, pp. 260-275.

Furthermore, many of the liberal thinkers of the day did not identify unlimited free competition with liberalism, and often placed a greater emphasis on the demand for the free association of citizens for the protection of their common interests. In southwestern Germany, for instance, where liberalism took on particularly strong political connotations, it was never thought of as antithetical to a degree of economic protectionism.[35] Selbstverwaltung (self-administration) was a demand directed against the oppressive intervention of the police state in all aspects of civil life in pre-March Germany. Advocating it expressed a drive for independence and represented a truly liberal trend.

As late as 1848, the opposition of the small master artisans to Gewerbefreiheit was strongly linked to the liberal struggle for free local institutions and self-government. The guilds were often represented as a model for such self-administrating bodies, designed to protect the interests of their members without becoming a tool for government and police control. The demand to reestablish the guilds, however, lent itself to various interpretations even at that time. The masters themselves failed to agree upon the precise character the new guilds should have. Some supported the old guild system, and others advocated a new corporate structure, although even on this issue the battle was not between reactionaries and progressives.[36] Both groups acknowledged the irreversibility of overall liberal economic legislation, and rather than replace it, wished to supplement it by reinvigorating the guilds in one way or another. They all saw that the main difficulty was achieving a compromise between the principle of industrial freedom and a degree of Zunftzwang. The argument was about ways of establishing effective guildlike institutions within a liberal

[35] On the various attitudes among liberals with regard to economic issues see Donald G. Rohr, *The Origins of Social Liberalism in Germany*, pp. 102-157, and J.J. Sheehan, "Liberalism and Society."

[36] *Verhandlungen der ersten Abgeordneten Versammlung*, pp. 8-11; 18-24.

state. In practial terms the masters differed among themselves only in the degree to which they emphasized the need to introduce an obligatory membership clause into the proposed legislation, and it was this obligatory membership that gradually acquired symbolic significance for both the master artisans and the bourgeois liberals in the Paulskirche. On this point the sacred concept of liberal individual freedom and its practical implications for the development of capitalism contrasted sharply with the small masters' ideal of freedom.

During the 1840s the Prussian bureaucracy had succeeded in separating municipal citizenship rights from state trade laws, and thereby helped to bring out into the open the conflict of interest between the artisans and the industrial and commercial bourgeoisie.[37] In the revolutionary situation this contradiction came to the fore. The Frankfurt liberals, confident in their victory over absolutism, no longer thought it necessary to seek support from the small masters. Setting themselves apart from all the radical-democratic elements led by their social inferiors, they disregarded the masters' demands.[38] They were as yet unable to perceive or appreciate the significance of the growing split between masters and journeymen, and only later in the century did they realize the need to gain the support of the former in their own battle, not against the bureaucracy this time but against the proletariat.

The growing split between the liberal bourgeoisie and the small masters did not escape the attention of the Prussian conservatives. The bureaucracy immediately attempted to enlist the masters in its own fight. Failing to come to terms with the liberals in Frankfurt, the masters wrested

[37] See Werner Conze, "Das Spannungsfeld von Staat und Gesellschaft," in his *Staat und Gesellschaft*, pp. 207 ff. Also Koselleck, *Preussen zwischen Reform und Revolution*, pp. 597 ff.; Ilja Mieck, *Preussische Gewerbepolitik in Berlin*, pp. 207 ff.; Walker, *German Home Towns*, pp. 329-353.

[38] See especially the conclusions in Shorter's article, "Middle-Class Anxiety," pp. 312-315.

some concessions from the now more cooperative bureaucracy, but did not rally as a group to its support. As reaction in post-1848 Germany increased, the majority of small masters once again supported the liberal opposition. By this time, however, it was evident to them as well as to their bourgeois allies, that their economic ideal was incompatible with the central liberal ideology, which was increasingly being adapted to the needs of industrial capitalism. Nevertheless, the two groups continued to cooperate for a number of years. It was the separation of political from economic liberalism, by then a common state of affairs in German politics, that made possible the perpetuation of this strange alliance.

The economic liberalism of the Prussian and other state bureaucracies during the pre-March years forced many bourgeois liberals to take a stand in opposition to a government whose economic policy they had to support.[39] After 1850, a number of years of agricultural prosperity led the conservative landed elite in Germany to support free trade enthusiastically, though it was at the same time fighting against political liberalism. These developments forced the liberals to recognize the double nature of their ideology and convinced them that their struggle against the state had to be fought on the political plane alone. In that atmosphere it is not very surprising that the combination of radical political liberalism and reactionary economic policy then characteristic of the stand of the small masters could be tolerated or conveniently ignored.[40] From 1848 until well into the 1870s this mixture of ideas apparently did not provide masters with a sufficient motive for deserting liberalism as such, or for joining the conservative camp.

In 1860, at a time of a renewed campaign for the reintroduction of industrial freedom in Germany, the master artisans attempted to revive their organized movement. At

[39] See Koselleck, *Preussen zwischen Reform und Revolution*, pp. 560-637.

[40] See Winkler, *Mittelstand*, pp. 40-43.

the same time the Conservatives, beginning to realize their need for popular support, tried to encourage the masters' organization and to turn them into their allies. But the masters' new Bund failed to recruit members and disintegrated completely by 1864. This was a bitter disappointment for the Conservative leadership, especially those of the *Kreuzzeitung* circle who had early perceived the potential affinity between themselves and the small masters.[41] The masters' demand for corporate self-administration, the Conservatives believed, was bound to clash with the increasingly individualistic conception of German liberalism, and could be easily channeled to fit in with the efforts to recreate the traditional Ständestaat in its preabsolutist form. In fact, there were always masters who conceived of their position within this context and shared the nostalgic social concepts of Prussian Junker conservatism. But this was not the universally accepted version of the masters' collective demands until well into the 1870s.

In an 1853 letter from Frankfurt a.M., Bismarck provided a characteristic assessment of the master-artisans' political position: "Here one can hardly find even one artisans' organization with other than decisively democratic direction, and even the masters, with the exception of a few who are under the influence of the Catholic priesthood, and who do not present a tight conservative phalanx for their own self-interest, all belong to the Bewegungspartei, and practice this nonsense so far as to read to their journeymen during working time, when they themselves are not busy, the writings of Red Democracy."[42] Bismarck also volunteered his opinion as to the reason for the masters' position: It was a "burning desire for equality," he claimed, that inspired them to

[41] Hugo Müller, "Der Preussische Volksverein," pp. 28 ff. On the conflicting views among masters, see *Der zweite Handwerkertag zu Frankfurt a.M. September 1863*, pp. 50 ff. See also Hermann Wagener, *Die kleine aber mächtige Partei*, pp. 42-44.

[42] Otto von Bismarck, *Die Gesammelten Werke*, vol. 14/1, p. 302, letter of April 27, 1853.

compete with the life style of commercial magnates and bankers, and with the influence of the proponents of the Republic. Bismarck's description, however, did not correspond to conditions everywhere in Germany, and was in any event much exaggerated. It appears that during the third quarter of the nineteenth century, following the open confrontation with the bourgeois liberals in 1848, and during a period of relative economic prosperity, many small masters remained essentially indifferent to political and ideological issues. At that time even their interest in changing existing economic legislation was limited. When they did take a stand, however, the small master artisans were still most likely to be liberals. This was true for the more prosperous and progressive masters in the industrial associations, as well as for the more traditional masters in the short-lived Masters' League. The ambiguous nature of their liberal ideology was by then clear enough but did not as yet force them out of the liberal camp. Under the unique political and economic conditions prevailing in Germany, and in spite of the experience of 1848, the loose alliance between bourgeois and Mittelstand liberals continued until the onset of the Great Depression. Only then did a change in the overall mood in Germany and a reshuffling of the political and ideological fronts bring about the masters' gradual desertion of liberalism and launch a new period in their group history.

SIX

THE DESERTION OF LIBERALISM

Liberalism on the Defensive

The years immediately following the stock-market crash in European capitals and the beginning of the so-called Great Depression witnessed a crucial struggle by liberalism for respectability and influence in the German Reich. Under the boots of the Iron Chancellor, political liberalism, impressed by and grateful for his achievements, looked meek indeed. At the same time, during the first few years of the new Reich, in a period of prosperity, speculation, and rapid economic growth, the prestige of Rudolf Delbrück's liberal economic policies was still at its peak. After the disgraceful years of the Prussian constitutional conflict, economic liberalism remained the major ground for the liberals' claim to success. With the onset of the Great Depression, however, economic liberalism also lost its attraction. Unification had been accomplished by war under the authoritarian leadership of Bismarck, and continuous profitable economic growth began to seem a dangerous illusion. While the weakness of political liberalism under the system designed by Bismarck was not immediately apparent, the economic depression was there for everyone to observe and experience.[1]

The *Gartenlaube* was a Mittelstand journal with known liberal leanings. Beginning in December 1874, Otto Glagau, one of its editors, published a series of articles bitterly at-

[1] On the discrediting of liberalism after 1873 see H. Rosenberg, *Grosse Depression* pp. 62-78, and Wehler, *Das Deutsche Kaiserreich,* pp. 79-93. For the liberal parties at the time see F.C. Sell, *Die Tragödie des deutschen Liberalismus*; Seeber, *Zwischen Bebel und Bismarck*; and Ludwig Elm, *Zwischen Fortschritt und Reaktion.*

tacking liberalism as a doctrine and as a political force.[2] At the same time, *Germania*, the major Catholic newspaper, came out with some strongly antiliberal and anti-Semitic articles, and in June and July of 1875 the *Kreuzzeitung* hastened to take the lead in the antiliberal campaign with its famous "Era Articles."[3] The Gründerzeit (the foundation era) was now called the Schwindelperiode (the swindle period). Liberalism, which had earlier appeared triumphant, was now denounced as the main villain. Bismarck himself became increasingly impatient with his liberal allies. His growing disregard for them encouraged men who had previously checked their antiliberalism purely out of loyalty to the government to join the antiliberal chorus. At the same time Social Democracy was making great headway in the major industrial cities of Germany, and among its followers too no love was wasted on the liberals. Within a couple of years the social and the political environment of the Reich had in the main become suspicious and unfriendly toward the liberals.[4] The liberal parties were now forced to operate in the face of open hostility while they themselves were torn by internal friction. Both the left-wing Progressive party, and the mixed National-Liberal party experienced a considerable decline in public support. Men from various walks of life left them, but perhaps the most disastrous desertion was that of their Mittelstand voters.

Otto Glagau, who first published the antiliberal articles in the *Gartenlaube*, had previously been an economic correspondent of the *National Zeitung*, one of the leading liberal dailies of Berlin. His desertion of liberalism, although perhaps motivated by his own personal failure, presaged the behavior of many of his readers.[5] He articulated the

[2] These appeared in *Die Gartenlaube* between December 1874 and December 1875. See H. Zang, "*Die Gartenlaube.*"

[3] *KZ*, June 29 and 30 and July 1 and 2, 1875.

[4] See especially H. Rosenberg, *Grosse Depression*, pp. 51-57; 62-78.

[5] On Glagau see the brief, but illuminating comments in Hellmut

shift that was taking place in their attitudes, and in turn had an effect on their thinking and political choices. Glagau's book, *The Bankruptcy of the National-Liberals and the "Reaction"*, was frequently reprinted during the seventies.[6] It contained a peculiar mixture of elements, characteristic of a new type of popular political writing, combining vehement antiliberalism with militant anti-Semitism and a kind of nostalgic, apolitical conservatism.

It was indicative of the mood among master artisans that Glagau, who was a shrewd if not an original political observer, should devote his second book to their fate.[7] As a matter of fact, his peculiar ideology readily appealed to them. His antiliberalism was based on opposition to the economic measures introduced by the Liberals at the time of the creation of the Reich. He repeatedly blamed these measures for the collapse of the economy and for the consequent misery and impoverishment among his Mittelstand readers. His anti-Semitism helped explain the degeneration of German liberalism, which he himself and many of his readers had once fully supported. His nostalgic conservatism easily fitted in with the masters' vision of their medieval glory and their attachment to the guild idea.

For those many small masters who had always wavered in their support of liberal economic policies, the antiliberal trend was a relief. Now at last their economic demands were consistent with their overall political orientation. But the particular ambivalence toward liberalism that had characterized the masters' position from the pre-March days to 1873 continued to dictate the pattern for their political behavior during the first phase of the economic depression

---

von Gerlach, *Von Rechts nach Links*, p. 110. Also Peter G.J. Pulzer, *The Rise of Political Anti-Semitism*, pp. 88-90; Paul W. Massing, *Rehearsal for Destruction*, pp. 10-14; and Richard S. Levy, *The Downfall of the Anti-Semitic Political Parties*, pp. 16 ff.

[6] Otto Glagau, *Der Bankerott des Nationalliberalismus und die "Reaktion."*

[7] *Deutsches Handwerk und historisches Bürgertum.*

as well.[8] This peculiar mixture of political liberalism and economic demands with strong conservative overtones was once referred to by a member of the *Kreuzzeitung* circle as "reactionary hocus-pocus."[9] By the 1870s the masters' political stand was rarely understood, as it could not possibly be by anyone seeking to find a consistent ideology in the vacillating search of a social group subject to a multitude of material and spiritual pressures. During the seventies, in a changing economic and political environment, the masters' political stand became increasingly untenable. What had been acceptable in pre-March Germany and even during the time of reaction, became impossible to maintain in the atmosphere of the new Reich.

By the late 1860s, German liberalism was unequivocally attached to a policy of free trade. A series of liberal economic measures was enacted by the parliament of the North German Confederation, dominated by the Liberals. Complete industrial freedom on all internal matters was gradually adopted by the states joining the Reich, and a policy of free trade was maintained, still supported by the conservative grain-growing landowners east of the Elbe. Political conservatism did not yet exclude support for specific liberal economic measures, just as political liberalism could still be combined with opposition to such measures. At the start of the agricultural depression in Germany in 1875-76, however, the separation between liberals and antiliberals became sharper. The agrarians quickly withdrew their support of free trade, and in the face of unfavorable market conditions began to clamor for state protection.[10] Losing interest in free trade, the conservative forces in the Reich could

[8] See the section on the masters' ambivalent liberalism in chap. 5.

[9] Wagener, *Die kleine aber mächtige Partei*, p. 43.

[10] H. Rosenberg, *Grosse Depression*, pp. 169-191; Wehler, *Das Deutsche Kaiserreich*, pp. 100-105. See also Alexander Gerschenkron, *Bread and Democracy in Germany*; Nikolai Ivo Lambi, *Free Trade and Protection*; and Karl W. Hardach, *Die Bedeutung wirtschaftlicher Faktoren.*

now launch a more comprehensive attack on liberalism, condemning both its political and its economic doctrines.

From an ideological standpoint the changing market situation could have enabled the liberals to present a more clearly integrated program, more fully combining political and economic liberal demands in an effort to fight Bismarck's sham parliamentarianism and his increasingly anti-liberal measures. In practice, however, this fuller integration of political and economic liberalism turned out to be a source of weakness rather than strength for the liberal parties in the Reich. As the conservatives deserted the ideal of free trade, the liberals remained to shoulder the sole responsibility for the economic crisis. Under the conditions prevailing in the 1870s, ideological consistency was an asset for the conservatives and a liability for the liberals.

At the same time economic issues became the focus of public attention in the Reich, and played an increasingly significant role in German politics. The constitution of the Reich, and Bismarck's masterful manipulation of its various provisions, operated to weaken the existing political parties. Continuously compromising its ideology, each of them gradually came to be associated with a specific economic interest, and had to adjust its policy accordingly. A number of independent interest-group organizations grew alongside the political parties, seeking to pressure the government to protect and advance their economic interests. Unlike the earlier chambers of agriculture, commerce, and industry, these were free associations seeking to influence governmental decision making directly through pressure on the bureaucracy and indirectly through influence over the major political parties.[11]

[11] See H. Rosenberg, *Grosse Depression*, pp. 118-168; Thomas Nipperdey, "Interessenverbände und Parteien," pp. 262-268; Gerhard Schulz, "Über Entstehung und Formen von Interessengruppen in Deutschland"; Wolfram Fischer, "Staatsverwaltung und Interessenverbände," in *Wirtschaft und Gesellschaft*; H.J. Puhle, "Parlament, Parteien und Interessenverbände 1890-1914," pp. 340-377. Also Fraenkel, *Deutschland und die westlichen Demokratien*, pp.

The need to deal with economic matters together with the gradual weakening of the parties and the growing importance of interest-group organizations helped to transform the character of the German state. It now interfered directly in social and economic processes through a policy of protectionism, ostensibly designed to assist the weaker groups but operating in practice to favor the better organized and the more influential social elements.

While international free trade became the major target for the organized attacks of heavy industry and large landowners, internal industrial freedom came increasingly to represent all that the Mittelstand disliked in the existing socioeconomic order. The term Gewerbefreiheit, which had originally denoted only legislation concerning freedom to engage in any trade or occupation anywhere in town or country, gradually took on a wider meaning and came to be associated with the end of all forms of state, city, or guild protectionism. With the opening of Germany to international free competition, Gewerbefreiheit came to stand for the new liberal economic system operating in an enlarged, national market. It is perhaps illuminating to remember that in late eighteenth- and early nineteenth-century England, "free trade," as the most outstanding feature of the emerging liberal economy, was a term applied to the system as a whole. Similarly, French "laissez faire," originally associated exclusively with the freedom of domestic commerce, also eventually acquired a wider meaning.[12] In the same way, Gewerbefreiheit in Germany gradually came to be identified with the entire complex of liberal economic policies, and became a catchword for the emerging modern economy and its various manifestations. This naturally

---

32-48, and Dirk Stegmann, *Die Erben Bismarcks*, pp. 113-128; 131-159.

[12] On the meaning of free trade and laissez faire see the *International Encyclopedia of the Social Sciences*, vol. 9, pp. 15-21; and the *Handwörterbuch für Sozialwissenschaften*, vol. 4, and the bibliography cited there.

caused a great deal of confusion. The term Gewerbefreiheit acquired different meanings for different people, and frequently meant either more or less than the word itself denoted. In the 1870s with the growing demand for state protection, the attack on Gewerbefreiheit was renewed. The small masters who had previously opposed it in spite of its link with liberalism were gradually moving to a new position. Openly joining the protectionist forces, they were now opposing Gewerbefreiheit precisely because it was a central tenet of liberalism. The changing economic and political atmosphere in Germany opened the way for the masters' massive abandonment of liberalism, but the process was slow and painful. It took many years to accomplish and was never entirely completed.

Holding on to Liberalism

In September 1872, 262 delegates from 145 cities, claiming to represent over 60,000 master artisans, convened in Dresden for the First German Artisans' Congress.[13] This might have been just another abortive attempt at organizing the small masters but its timing was, by sheer coincidence, particularly fortunate. The meeting was intended as a preliminary organizational step and was given the task of preparing for the next national congress, which was to announce the creation of a new master-artisans' organization. The second congress convened only a few weeks after the collapse of the Vienna stock exchange, in an already radically different economic climate. Thus the efforts of the organizers acquired special urgency, and the new Verein Selbständiger Handwerker und Fabrikanten Deutschlands (Association of Independent Artisans and Manufacturers) was immediately saddled with the

[13] See Heinrich Schulthess, ed., *Europäischer Geschichtskalender* (1872), September 25-27, pp. 193 ff.; and Wilhelm Stieda, "Handwerk," in the *HBS* 3rd ed.

task of formulating a common position in response to new circumstances.

In spite of the feeling of urgency at the time of its inception, the Verein was short lived and never succeeded in enlisting more than 12,000 members. It flourished for a year or two but gradually deteriorated as the decade drew to a close. Its actual life span coincided with the first stage in the political development of the master artisans during the depression years. It therefore provides a focal point for this part of our investigation. The minutes of the yearly Verein meetings, with newspaper reports filling in where these are unavailable, offer invaluable source material through which to follow the changing mood and political attitudes of the masters.[14]

The history of the poorly educated is always hampered by a lack of sources. Master-artisans' opinions must, too, often be indirectly deduced. But at meetings of their oganization, representatives of the masters delivered speeches, recording some of the prevailing opinions in their communities year by year. They enable us to reconstruct the master-artisans' views on matters related to their condition, on issues of general public interest, and on their changing social allegiances and political sympathies. The history of the master-artisans' interest organizations themselves is only of secondary importance in this context, and organizational problems will therefore be dealt with only when they reflect more general ideological or political issues.

The reconstruction of the history of the masters' organizations is in itself an important and difficult task. Characteristic of these bodies throughout the later part of the nineteenth century was their fragmentation and decentralization. In a period in which even the most powerful

[14] For the 1873-1881 period *Protokolle über die Verhandlungen zu Quedlinburg 1874*; *Cologne 1876*; *Darmstadt 1877*; for the best available reports on other congresses see the reviews in the *Kreuzzeitung*.

political parties had only weak, if any, central organization this was hardly surprising. Only toward the end of the century did the master artisans, together with the major political parties and interest groups, manage to unite their local branches into more or less effective national organizations. Decentralization, however, was not merely the result of an absence of organizational talent, but also an expression of the reality of regional division within Germany and the fluidity of the German social and political structure. A tradition of local organizations, concerned only with immediate occupational and municipal issues, was particularly strong among master artisans, and their local guilds and associations tended to preserve their independent positions throughout most of the depression years. The chronic disagreement among the masters was based to a large measure on the fact that within the different regions of Germany, there was variation both in the socioeconomic conditions of the handicraft trades and in the available political alternatives. Local variation was also typical of the new Verein, but it did not obscure the general political trend discernible throughout its history: the masters' gradual desertion of liberalism.

A contemporary study of master-artisans' opinions in Saxony conducted by the local chamber of industry found that as late as 1879 a great majority of the masters supported the establishment of a new form of guild organization. The author presenting the results was quick to place their stand in the context of the government's general economic policy: "Industrial freedom and the freedom of movement present no obstacle to the creation of these corporations," he explained, "nor are those freedoms endangered by them."[15] The same view was repeatedly expressed by members of the master-artisans' Verein. They asserted their faith in, and desire for "freedom," including economic freedom, but wished to place it within explicit limits. "One should not

[15] Löbner, *Wie das deutsche Kleingewerbe über die Innungsfrage denkt*, p. 12.

confuse industrial freedom with industrial lawlessness," explained one of the leading Bavarian masters.[16]

Throughout the 1870s a large number of masters continued to believe that corporate self-administering bodies were compatible with the liberal industrial legislation then in force. The great majority of the masters did not wish to reintroduce the old Zunftzwang, which had in the past meant compulsory membership in the guilds for all masters, as well as exclusive control of handicraft production by the corporate bodies. During 1879, one of the worst years of the depression, the Berlin Bureau of Handicraft Corporations, a body with considerable national influence among master artisans, sent a memorandum to the Prussian minister of commerce, industry, and public works making this point with particular firmness: "We must explicitly protest against the assumption that we wish to make the license for the operation of a workshop conditional upon membership in the guilds and violate the principles of industrial freedom. We deny the notion that we strive for compulsory guilds. According to our goals, the entry of individuals into the guilds must not be obligatory but should remain entirely optional."[17] In their new organization the master artisans placed their emphasis not on the demand for compulsory guilds, but on that for self-administration. "Handicrafts for the handicraftsmen" was then the most popular slogan of the masters' movement. Reform, they argued, had to come from within their own ranks and not through "patronization by the authorities."[18] On the face of it the masters merely demanded changes in industrial legislation that would make it possible for them to establish effective self-administration. They strove for legislative rather than administrative reform within the existing con-

[16] From a report on the eighth congress of the Verein in Köppen, August 7-9, 1879, *Christlich-soziale Blätter* 1879, p. 570.

[17] *Denkschrift des Büreaus der Innungsvorstände Berlins*, March 31, 1879 (Stadtsarchiv Köln, III/4, no. 1).

[18] Löbner, *Wie das deutsche Kleingewerbe über die Innungsfrage denkt*, p. 20.

ception of the Reich trade law. In the 1878 Verein congress, the masters made their demands explicit. They wished to see the Reichstag enact a special handicraft law, whereby the new guilds were to receive extensive supervisory power over the education of apprentices, and thus in effect control over the future composition and size of an entire range of handicraft occupations. They wished these new bodies to be entirely free of all "police and legal" regulations. Thus, and only thus, they believed, could a self-administering network of powerful masters' organizations be established.[19]

A compromise between the masters' specific demands and their liberalism, such as it was, seemed particularly crucial for the continued existence of the new Verein. The organization's main support came from the masters in big cities, and from men of more or less conscious liberal ideology. The largest delegations to the Verein congress in 1874 came from seven large towns—Berlin and Breslau, Hamburg and Bremen, Magdeburg, Dresden, and Hanover—all of them important liberal strongholds, each with its unique character. In all of them, with the obvious exception of the two Prussian cities, liberalism had a strong tinge of local patriotism, occasionally even a particularist tendency, along with a stress on self-administration.

The master artisans in the Verein came primarily from towns in which a strong liberal tradition was associated with an emphasis on *political* liberalism and on liberal economic provisions concerned with commercial and financial matters. None of these places was known in the 1870s for its unqualified support of domestic industrial freedom. In Berlin and Breslau a strong Progressive majority was maintained throughout the 1870s.[20] Only once during the decade was the Progressive candidate in the eastern sec-

[19] *Christlich-soziale Blätter*, 1878, pp. 723 ff. See also Jäger, *Die Handwerkerfrage*, pp. 127 ff.

[20] On the particular voting history of the various regions in Germany see the *Statistisches Jahrbuch für das deutsche Reich*, 22 (1901); also Fritz Specht's useful volume, *Die Reichstagswahlen von 1867 bis 1897.*

tion of Breslau defeated by his National-Liberal opponent. Significantly, however, the latter was Eduard Lasker, among the most outstanding political liberals of his party, and a man of left-liberal convictions. In Berlin, particularly in the third and fourth election districts where small industrial shops were most numerous, the Progressives had an unrivaled majority until 1878. Up to this date no more than 500 votes were ever cast for a Conservative candidate in these districts. Here, undoubtedly, the small master artisans voted for the Progressive party together with journeymen and other Mittelständler. Naturally, it was not the liberal economy of the left-wing liberals that had attracted these small employers and skilled employees. It was their emphasis on political liberalism, their adherence to the ideal of equality, and their faith in a democratic system of government.

In Magdeburg and Dresden the situation was similar. Left-wing liberals, although not always members of the Progressive party, won the Magdeburg mandates throughout the 1870s, and numerous master artisans in town undoubtedly supported them. In Dresden, too, the urban election district west of the Elbe had sent Progressive candidates to the Reichstag up to 1877. Then, following a battle between the Socialists and the right-wing Liberals, an all-out contest between Socialist and Conservatives became the characteristic feature of Dresden political life. That city became one of the first in Germany to register the transfer of the popular vote from the left-Liberals to the Conservatives. Presumably its large artisan population had contributed a good deal to this transformation.[21]

In Hamburg and Bremen the political picture was somewhat different. Throughout the seventies these cities were

[21] On Saxony, see Rudolf Kötzschke and Hellmut Kretzschmar, eds., *Sächsische Geschichte*, vol. 2, pp. 212 ff.; Hans Gabler, "Die Entwicklung der deutschen Parteien," pp. 28 ff. For the regional variations in attitudes and political position on one particular issue, see Hardach, *Die Bedeutung wirtschaftlicher Faktoren*, pp. 86 ff.

strongholds of the National-Liberal rather than the Progressive party. But the National-Liberal party, even more than other political parties at that time, was strongly decentralized, and its local branches were allowed to retain their unique political character. In the Hanseatic cities, National Liberalism was supported primarily by the commercial contingent, and was conceived of as the most appropriate heir to the tradition of political freedom and independence of the Imperial free cities. Economically, National Liberalism was above all concerned with matters of commercial policy. It was strong on the demand for free trade, but rather indifferent to issues of domestic industrial freedom. Big industry in these two Hanseatic towns was concentrated mainly in shipbuilding, while the majority of other industries remained in the hands of small entrepreneurs and traditional small master craftsmen. The strong position of the small masters in the local chambers of industry was only one of the results of this development. During the 1870s, before the Social-Democratic party had become strong, the small master artisans there gave their votes to the powerful National-Liberal party, and they did so without having to sacrifice their persistent demand for reform of handicraft legislation.[22]

Another center of recruitment for the Verein was the city of Hanover, where during the seventies a continuous battle raged between local particularists and National Liberals. Throughout the decade Hanover's Reichstag seats were held by Guelph candidates, mainly supported by the small peasantry. It is most likely that the small master artisans in both urban and rural areas of Hanover also gave their votes to this party. The hated Gewerbefreiheit was

[22] On the politics of master artisans in Hamburg, see the speech by their leader Johann Friedrich Ludwig Voss in the *Protokolle über die Verhandlungen Berlin 1892*, pp. 118-119. On general political and economic developments in Hamburg, see Ernst Baasch, *Geschichte Hamburgs*; Heinrich Laufenberg, *Geschichte der Arbeiterbewegung Hamburgs*; and R. Comfort, *Revolutionary Hamburg*, especially pp. 9 ff.

associated in their minds with Prussian dominance. They felt that within the larger structure of the Reich, they could no longer have any influence on the course of industrial legislation, and they resented Prussian influence not only as Hanoverian patriots, but also as traditional master craftsmen.

Particularism was also a strong force in Dresden and in Hamburg. Thus, a strong anti-Prussian element was already detectable in the Verein at the time of its establishment. It was this non-Prussian contingent that eventually led the anti-Berlin and antiliberal opposition faction within the organization.

In spite of the general liberalism of the main body of the Verein, a conservative segment always existed within it. As early as 1874 a debate on the title for the proposed new artisans' journal brought out the heterogeneous political composition of the Verein. Suggestions for a title included both The Liberal Industrial Journal and *The Conservative Industrial Journal*, and only with some effort did the Berlin leadership succeed in passing a conciliatory resolution naming the new publication simply *The Industrial Journal* (*Die Gewerbezeitung*).[23] The Verein was created prior to the wave of interest-group formation in Germany around 1876, and toward the end of the decade it was increasingly pressured by its members to join the campaign for economic protection started by the newer bodies. The leaders of the organization, however, remained overwhelmingly liberal, at least up to 1879, and it was indicative of the changing mood within the Verein that their liberalism gradually became a source of embarrassment. The fact that two of the Berlin activists, members of the central executive body of the Verein, simultaneously served on a local election committee of the Progressive party became a subject for repeated accusations and denials.[24]

[23] *Protokolle über die Verhandlungen zu Quedlinburg 1874*, pp. 9-10.

[24] *KZ*, June 5, 1882.

It was easy enough for the masters to agree on a great number of other issues. Throughout its existence, the Verein supported the introduction of a compulsory workbook to be carried by all dependent workers and resented the Reichstag decision to limit this obligation to workers under twenty-one.[25] The organization clearly drew its membership mainly from master employers, who deemed the workbook their one remaining measure of control over increasingly insubordinate helpers. The Verein also demanded such measures as a restriction of handicraft production in state prisons, a reorganization of tender regulations to allow greater artisan participation in government contracts, and a reform of the patent law. On all these matters agreement was achieved with a minimum of controversy. The tension within the Verein between the liberal majority and the growing conservative minority was exposed when discussion turned, again and again, to the guild issue, which had become a question of general political interest. In the new atmosphere created by the economic depression, the liberal interpretation of the demand for the constitution of the guilds became increasingly less plausible and more difficult to uphold. The guild issue gradually became the focus of the masters' fight for social protection, waged in alliance with the conservative forces in the Reich.[26]

Breaking the Ties

In the early seventies, the masters' organizations deliberately tried to remain apolitical. In their recorded public meetings partisan political issues were only rarely discussed, and the occasional opinions offered could not be viewed as representative of the larger body of artisans in the Reich. Initially, while the Verein took a moderate liberal tone, the desirability of a united master-artisans' vote was frequently

[25] See the section on masters and journeymen in chap. 3.

[26] See the discussion in Winkler, *Mittelstand*, pp. 44-64; and his "Der rückversicherte Mittelstand." See also chap. 9 below.

reiterated although usually in rather abstract terms. In 1876, the annual national meeting of the Verein in Cologne formulated a resolution which was accepted in almost all later masters' meetings although its political meaning changed with the times. It read as follows: "The industrial and handicraft estate declares it to be most desirable that [its members] should elect their own candidates from within their estate and that whenever this is not possible they should work, with full energy, for candidates who are willing to be active in the spirit of the following principles."[27] Following were the demands for revision of industrial legislation "as so often formulated by . . . artisans' meetings," the creation of obligatory vocational schools, a new patent law, and the creation of handicraft and industrial chambers.[28] By means of this vaguely worded resolution the leadership of the Verein managed to maintain an ostensible internal unity on matters of political choice in the face of a growing conservative challenge.

In local meetings of the Verein and other master-artisans' organizations, however, a militant, antiliberal stand became increasingly common. The changing attitude toward the issue of reintroducing the guild system was symptomatic. In June 1879, a shoemakers' congress convened in Paderborn, a medium-sized Westphalian town, openly denounced the halfhearted attitude of liberal master artisans toward efforts to rebuild the guilds. It demanded the introduction of compulsory membership in the guilds, thus closing the trades to nonguild members, and called for official examinations for all journeymen and masters.[29] A year later representatives of masters from twenty-seven Upper Silesian towns voiced the same sentiments and proclaimed the same demands.[30] In these and other local meetings, the liberals were vehemently attacked for their supposedly heartless disregard for

[27] *Protokolle über die Verhandlungen zu Köln 1876*, p. 26.
[28] Ibid.
[29] Jäger, *Die Handwerkerfrage*, pp. 142 ff.
[30] Ibid., p. 164. See also Hampke, *Der Befähigungsnachweis*, p. 44.

the plight of the masters. The liberal façade which had so long accompanied masters' demand for the new guilds was gradually dropped, and for the first time liberalism was rejected as a whole and on principle.

The national Verein, too, was soon affected by this new conservative wave. As early as 1876, a master artisan from Hanover urged the masters' representatives at the national congress to "sacrifice their political principles" to their urgent economic needs.[31] In effect he demanded a desertion of liberalism in favor of the political forces that declared their unqualified support for the masters' economic and organizational reform program. At the time his plea passed virtually unnoticed. Four years later, however, the liberal leaders of the Verein were forced to use the threat of resignation to prevent the congress, this time meeting on the liberals' home ground in Berlin, from passing a resolution in favor of the obligatory guild system. And at the Magdeburg congress in 1882, the motion was finally carried by a vote of 254 to 54 despite the pleas of the leadership and its use of extensive procedural maneuvers.[32] The drive to abandon the cautious liberal position of the Verein came from various parts of Germany. Above all it was supported by a new element within the organization—the Catholic masters from the Rhine province, from Westphalia, Bavaria, and the eastern regions of Upper Silesia. All over Germany it was the Catholics who first openly broke with liberalism; among the masters, too, it was the Catholics who initiated the master artisans' change of heart.[33] The gradual desertion of liberalism, however, was by no means limited to Catholic master artisans. Voices of protest and loud demands for new social

[31] *Protokolle über die Verhandlungen zu Köln 1876*, pp. 26-27.

[32] For the 1880 Verein congress in Berlin see *KZ*, October 13, 1880; *Christlich-soziale Blätter*, 1880, p. 750. For the Magdeburg congress, see *Verhandlungen des allgemeinen deutschen Handwerkertages zu Magdeburg 1882*. See also the full report in the *KZ*, June 3 and 6, 1882.

[33] See the section on social Catholicism in chap. 7.

legislation came also from the Protestant North. In Berlin, Hamburg, and Hanover, the changing political position among master artisans was slowly becoming evident.

The openly antiliberal stand of the Verein at its final meeting in Magdeburg in the summer of 1882 was due to the decision of some traditionally liberal delegations to support the masters from Westphalia in their conservative political campaign. The delegates from the kingdom of Saxony as well as from the Prussian province were openly divided. Even the delegates from Berlin, who had previously led the liberal front within the organization, now appeared to be disunited. The local Association of Independent Artisans proposed a resolution in which a new antiliberal position was clearly formulated: "The false industrial freedom in Germany caused the full destruction of the handicraft estate; sharpened the economic antagonism between capital and labor; increased the exploitation of the latter by the former and is therefore responsible for the rapid development of Social Democracy to the detriment of German national well-being."[34] Liberalism was more deeply rooted among master artisans in the urban centers of the Protestant North, such as Berlin, Dresden, and Magdeburg, than in the Catholic areas of Bavaria or the Polish centers of Silesia. The opposition to it was slower to emerge, and the available political alternatives were more difficult to perceive. Nevertheless, by the late 1870s, a move away from liberalism was easily detectable among small masters everywhere in the country. If it was not motivated by conservative nostalgia, it was emerging out of the masters' growing apprehension in the face of the new socialist working-class movement. The rationale for the desertion of liberalism varied from place to place, but the basic political phenomenon was the same everywhere.

The period between 1877 and 1884 witnessed a general restructuring of political forces in Germany. Under new

[34] *Verhandlungen zu Magdeburg 1882*, p. 4.

circumstances men transferred political allegiances, and parties changed their commitments. A quick look at the results of the Reichstag elections during these years reveals some of the consequences of these shifts.[35] In 1877, 40 Conservative delegates were elected to the Reichstag, 38 members of the Reichspartei, 128 National Liberals, and 48 Progressives from the various left-liberal factions. Only eighteen months later, following the election of July 1878, the Reichstag included 59 Conservatives and 57 delegates of the Reichspartei, but only 99 National Liberals and 36 left-liberals. By 1881, the Conservatives were reduced again to 50 seats, the Reichspartei to a mere 28, the National Liberals to 47. In 1884, a great increase in the Conservative vote swelled their Reichstag contingent to 78, while the National Liberals regained 4 seats, and the Progressives suffered a decline from 106 seats in 1881 to 67 in 1884.

Similar erratic fluctuations can also be observed in typical Mittelstand electoral districts. The third and fifth districts of Berlin, encompassing the southern and northern inner city respectively, included many Mittelstand voters with a sprinkling of better-situated bourgeois elements. In both these districts the established liberal parties were fast losing their supporters to small independent liberal splinter groups, as well as to the Social Democrats. Gradually, however, voters in these districts shifted their support from the extreme left to the extreme right. The Social-Democratic vote in the fifth Berlin election district declined between 1878 and 1881 from 3,600 to 160 votes. On the other hand, the Conservatives who did not poll any votes in this district before, amassed 1,260 votes in 1878 and as many as 5,300 in 1881. By the 1881 election, 27 percent of the voters in the third election district in Berlin, 20 percent of the fourth, and 32 percent of the fifth voted for Conservative candi-

[35] Specht, *Reichstagswahlen*, provides a series of tables covering changes in the relative power of the various parties and shifts in the political allegiances of the various states and provinces within the Reich. See pp. 88-104.

dates. Even in the increasingly Socialist sixth district almost 9,000 votes were given to a candidate of a Conservative master-artisans group. Over 40,000 of the Conservative votes cast in Berlin during this election went to militant and anti-Semitic Social-Conservative candidates such as Liebermann von Sonnenberg, Adolf Stöcker, and Adolf Wagner.

These figures do not of course reflect the precise changes in political opinions and affiliations among the small master craftsmen in Berlin, or elsewhere in Germany. The geographical dispersion of the artisan population makes it virtually impossible to isolate their vote. While the voting habits of workers and peasants are relatively easy to determine with the help of regional studies, in the case of the small master artisans we are forced to rely on indirect and impressionistic evidence. Nevertheless, what clearly emerges from all available information is the prevailing tendency among small handicraft masters to dissolve their traditional though often awkward ties with liberalism and seek political alliances elsewhere.

SEVEN

COMPETITION FOR THE MASTERS' VOTE

The Liberals React: The Administrative Approach

Both the creation of the new German Reich with its new set of political institutions and the economic depression of the 1870s with its various ramifications accelerated the process of politicization in Germany. Between 1871 and 1873 the percentage of eligible voters who exercised their right to vote rose from 51 to 63, and then reached its nineteenth-century peak of 77 in 1887.[1] Among the small handicraft masters, too, many who had never before taken an active interest in public issues on a national scale, began to be drawn into politics. Others who had had a tradition of political allegiance felt increasingly unsure about their former stand. From about 1877 on, the masters as a group began to show signs of political restlessness. In the course of several years they appeared to be experimenting with the available alternatives. None of the political parties in Germany entirely suited their purposes or their mentality, although all sought to gain their votes. The master-artisans' political behavior during these years continued to reveal ideological disorientation and a lack of clear political direction. The parties in the Reich gradually came to understand that the masters constituted a significant reservoir of undecided voters, and all launched campaigns to recruit them.

The Liberals, aware of the gradual defection of the "small man" from their ranks, made special efforts to halt the trend. For the left-wing Progressive party, the loss of the master-artisan votes was at first lumped with the wholesale transfer of working-class political allegiance to the Social-Democratic party and was not in itself deemed particularly serious. In Progressive-party election committees the percentage

[1] *Vierteljahreshefte zu St.d.R.*, 1898, III.

of small shop owners and handicraftsmen sharply declined between 1878 and 1880, but stabilized itself at about 15 percent by the mid-1880s.[2] In some regions, in the northeastern port towns and the Hanseatic cities for example, the Progressives succeeded in attracting the support of anti-tariff liberals who had earlier voted for the more moderate National-Liberal party, and were thus able to maintain their strength. In Saxony too, divided as it was on the issue of the government agricultural tariff policy, much of the support previously accorded to the strong National-Liberal party shifted to the Progressive party and its future allies, the Secessionists. Many master artisans in the Southwestern Industrial Associations remained Liberals, and the chambers of industry in Saxony, Hamburg, Bremen, and Lübeck, which included representatives of small crafts, continued to follow a moderate liberal line on most issues until well into the 1890s. Nevertheless, it was clear that Mittelstand voters as a whole were no longer sure Liberal voters. In areas such as the southwest and the east, where, in the absence of a large industrial and commercial business group, liberalism depended on its Mittelstand supporters, the defection of small shopkeepers, master artisans, and the like threatened to become disastrous and forced local Liberal-party organizations to move with caution on all matters of economic policy.

It was the National-Liberal party, however, that felt most seriously endangered by this development. In March 1878, during the Reichstag debate on a new industrial bill presented by the government, the National-Liberal spokesman had the thankless task of trying to steer a middle road between the rejection of the bill by the Progressive party, and its support by the Conservatives. The draft proposed to regulate labor contracts, provide greater supervision of female and child labor, and improve the education of handicraft and industrial apprentices. Finally accepting the gov-

[2] Seeber, *Zwischen Bebel und Bismarck*, pp. 31, 100, and 102.

ernment proposal, Dr. Julius Gensel, the National-Liberal delegate, vehemently opposed the Conservative amendment calling for the introduction of exclusive guild apprenticeship regulation, and expressed the hope that the effect of the bill as a whole would be "to increase courage and confidence in [artisans'] circles, so that they would be capable of using their own energy for improving the conditions of industrial life."[3] The National Liberals were prepared to work for the amelioration of the craftsman's condition, but were still unwilling to modify their basic economic and social ideology.

During the debate all the parties in the Reichstag were forced to take their stand on the issue of reforming handicraft regulations. But the positions changed soon afterward as political alignments were reshuffled with the introduction of the Socialist Law. The National-Liberal compromise regarding the passage of the antiliberal antisocialist bill was only the first of a series of compromises, the best known of which was their eventual support of the 1879 agricultural tariff bill.[4] The National Liberals first compromised their political and then their economic doctrines. Their position on the handicraft reform program was far less significant in the overall development of the party. It was strongly influenced by their fear of a revolutionary working-class movement and was indicative of their continuous capitulation before the demands of the government. The National Liberals were at first strongly opposed to any legal protection of the master artisans, but they evolved a middle-of-the-road position, insisting that every additional compromise was to be the last.

Within the National-Liberal leadership it was Johannes

[3] *Steno. Berichte*, March 12, 1878.

[4] On the introduction of the tariff see the literature in n. 10, chap. 6. On the position of the Liberals see Ludwig Maenner, *Deutschlands Wirtschaft und Liberalismus*, pp. 42-43, and Hermann Block, *Die parlamentarische Krisis der nationalliberalen Partei 1879-1880*, pp. 1-24.

Miquel who, as on many other issues, preceded his colleagues in accepting a compromise on the question of the guilds and the master-artisans' organization. In the 1869 debate concerning the liberal industrial legislation of the North German Confederation, Miquel had called for special legal provisions to facilitate the preservation of the guilds.[5] At that time his position was of marginal importance, and only assumed significance ten years later. By 1879 Miquel was the mayor of a middle-sized Hanoverian town on the border of Westphalia - Osnabrück. In cooperation with the local leaders of the Verein selbständiger Handwerker und Fabrikanten there, he drafted a proposal for a new statute for the Osnabrück Shoemakers' Guild, and attempted to introduce it as a model for other craft guilds in the town.[6] His proposed statute assigned the guild the central role in reviving the communal spirit among master artisans, improving the general education and the vocational training of apprentices, and establishing industrial arbitration courts to handle labor disputes.[7] His efforts had some local success, but were of little national significance.

In the 1878 Reichstag election the National Liberals lost twenty-nine seats. This was a clear warning of danger, and the party finally felt compelled to act. Under the circumstances, Miquel now believed, a neglect of the master artisans posed a danger not only to the Liberals but to the entire social order. The growing revolutionary agitation in the country made it imperative to uphold and strengthen the loyalty of the Mittelstand.[8] In January of 1879, Miquel was sent to deliver a lecture before an assembly of master artisans in Landsberg, East Prussia.[9] In this barely indus-

[5] *Steno. Berichte*, March 18, 1869.

[6] See Hans Herzfeld, *Johannes von Miquel*, vol. 1, pp. 388 ff.

[7] "Miquel's Statute" is reprinted in full in Jäger, *Die Handwerkerfrage*, pp. 131-133.

[8] Herzfeld, *Johannes von Miquel*, vol. 1, p. 394. See also Winkler, *Mittelstand*, pp. 57-58.

[9] Johannes von Miquel, *Reden*, vol. 3, pp. 36-49.

trialized region the National Liberals were confronted with strong rural conservatism and relied heavily on the vote of the "small men" in urban centers. It was an urgent matter that took the Hanoverian politician all the way to Landsberg, and he was determined to make the most of it. "On the whole," Miquel said, "the time of the great political questions in Germany is over," while social issues, he explained, "were not matters of party politics and should not be made to yield political capital."[10] The free associations of master artisans, which had so far been enthusiastically supported by the Liberals, were, indeed, "useful pioneers," but were proving insufficient. What was needed was a new structure for the "Guilds of the Future."[11] The masters themselves, he continued, must take the initiative, and they would then be fully supported by the Liberals, not merely with "beautiful promises" but with meaningful legislative action.[12] Miquel was telling the masters what they had been eager to hear, but he still placed fundamental responsibility for the improvement of their lot on their own shoulders. His plan was only semiprotectionist in character, and he promised only conditional support.

At the same time, the Prussian minister for commerce, industry, and public works distributed Miquel's new guild statute throughout the country with a circular encouraging local authorities to work for the establishment of new free guilds to represent the interest of the entire artisan estate.[13] The new guilds were intended to strengthen public spirit and vocational pride among masters, to improve their technical skills, and to promote better business management in their workshops. They were to supervise the establishment of appropriate vocational schools, social security organizations, and industrial arbitration courts. Basically, the government followed Miquel's line, promising, as he had, that if the master artisans showed initiative and the desire and

[10] Ibid., p. 37. [11] Ibid., p. 40. [12] Ibid., p. 44.

[13] *Circular an sämmtliche königliche Regierungen* Bayerisches Hauptstaatsarchiv, MH-14638.

power to act, they would find the government willing and ready to cooperate. The Prussian bureaucracy was not yet prepared for a drastic revision of its role in the economy. It was not yet ready to give the masters unconditional protection.

The campaign for the establishment of new free guilds ended in total failure. A number of new guilds were set up, and many old ones revised their statutes according to Miquel's model in an attempt to inject new life into their disintegrating organizations. Actually, however, there was nothing new in either Miquel's or the government's proposals, and there was no reason why the new Liberal-inspired guilds should succeed where the old ones had failed. Economic conditions at the close of the decade were worse than ever, and the mood of the country was increasingly anti-Liberal. Joining the protectionist demands of stronger economic groups, and encouraged by the conservative parties, the master artisans clamored for more government protection. As this was not yet unequivocally supported by the Liberals, nor by the still Liberal-inspired Prussian bureaucracy, the defection of master artisans from the ranks of the liberal parties continued unabated.

The Liberals React: The Legislative Approach

In the summer of 1880 the left wing of the National Liberals led by Heinrich Rickert and Ludwig Bamberger seceded from the party. The immediate cause of the split was the new tariff policy which the majority of the National Liberals in the Reichstag had supported. Twenty-eight delegates then formed the secession group and stood firm on the issue of economic freedom. Naturally enough, as they purported to take an ideological stand, they could not afford to budge even on the minor issue of handicraft legislation.[14] The split weakened the National-Liberal party

[14] On the secession see Maenner, *Deutschlands Wirtschaft und*

but increased its ability to maneuver on matters of economic policy. The first instance of this greater maneuverability was the National-Liberal stand on the new guild law.

Bismarck never showed any particular interest in the demands of the master artisans. The workers constituted a real danger; the masters were merely a nuisance. Nevertheless, his government was forced to take some action in response to the flood of artisans' petitions and the continuing pressure from the Conservatives. Bismarck's extensive social legislation was primarily designed as the corollary to his repressive policy toward the growing workers' movement. But it was also conceived with the intention of providing an institutional alternative to the parliamentary system.[15] For several years Bismarck toyed with the idea of establishing a national economic council (Volkswirtschaftsrat), which would be the central organization for an elaborate structure of local and professional representative bodies. He succeeded in implementing his idea in Prussia, but the Economic Council there was soon shown to be a powerless body, engaged in fruitless and often entirely academic controversies. Bismarck's flirtation with the idea of the corporate state was only a minor episode in the history of his antiparliamentarism, but it was during this short episode that his government finally became more responsive to the demands of the small master artisans. By the late 1870s economic liberalism was no longer a valid principle for the new coalition that ruled Germany. There were at last no political or ideological obstacles to a more conciliatory policy toward the masters. The semiofficial *Nord-*

Liberalismus, pp. 56-57; Block, *Die Parlamentarische Krisis*, pp. 1-36; and Seeber, *Zwischen Bebel und Bismarck*, pp. 110 ff.

[15] See the discussion in H. Rosenberg, *Grosse Depression*, pp. 210-227; also Hans Rothfels, "Bismarck's Social Policy," pp. 301-302; J. Curtius, *Bismarcks Plan eines deutschen Volkswirtschaftsrates*, especially pp. 13-14; 54; Heinrich Herrfahrdt, *Das Problem der Berufsständischen Vertretung*, pp. 65-67; 81; Bowen, *German Theories of the Corporative State*, pp. 148-156.

deutsche Allgemeine Zeitung slowly shifted its position with respect to the establishment of the guilds,[16] and in the winter of 1881 the government presented to the Reichstag a draft bill for the overall reorganization of handicraft corporations in Germany.

The Kaiser's speech on the occasion of the reopening of the Reichstag on February 15, 1881, outlined the purposes of the forthcoming guild legislation. The new law was "to secure the means by which the isolated power of the individual men, who are occupied in the same industrial branch, will be strengthened by bringing them together within co-operative associations, and thus improving their economic ability as well as their moral fitness."[17] It defined the tasks of the guilds as those of creating and preserving a "common spirit" among the members and protecting their occupational interests. It assigned them the regulation of relations between masters and journeymen and gave them the right to establish their own industrial arbitration courts. Above all, it made it possible for the guilds to control the education of apprentices, even those employed by nonmember masters. The bill was still in the spirit of Miquel's proposals, and went one step further by seeking to give legal authority to the previous administrative recommendations of the Prussian ministry. It did not establish compulsory guilds, but it openly expressed a favorable opinion of guilds as such, and was willing to grant them official authority in educational and administrative matters.[18]

When the bill was finally submitted to the Reichstag, in February 1881, the entire liberal press rose up in arms. The Progressive *Berliner Tageblatt* called the project a "hybrid creation," and predicted that it would only cause confusion and internal conflict.[19] In an editorial on February 21, the

16 *Norddeutsche Allgemeine Zeitung*, February 19, 1881; June 15, July 21, 1882.

17 *Steno. Berichte*, February 15, 1881.

18 Ibid., March 26 and June 9, 1881. For the bill itself see the *Reichsgesetzblatt*, 1881, no. 19.

19 February 4, 1881.

Kölnische Zeitung, the mouthpiece of liberalism in the Rhineland, reiterated the classic liberal position. Industrious masters with economic and technical ability, it argued, were flourishing. It was only the untrained and the uninspired who demanded government help so insistently. In Hamburg, the liberal *Hamburgerische Korrespendenz* echoed this theme and added: "The young and active masters show little inclination toward the entire guild issue. They consider it merely the start of a reversal to old conditions."[20] Even the older masters, continued the argument, considered the bill a half-measure, increasing their duties and responsibilities rather than providing them with special rights or additional powers. In spite of this vocal opposition, however, the liberal front collapsed even while it still appeared united and unyielding. From the beginning of the debate, the *Kölnische Zeitung* made sure that its position was flexible.[21] Industrial freedom, it reassured its readers, ought not to be considered sacrosanct, although restrictions upon it could only come from the government itself, acting in the general public interest. A month later the position of the paper was even more outspoken: "Our political friends do not stand against revision of German industrial legislation; indeed, many times they have raised their voices in favor of the improvement and the further development of this legislation."[22]

While the Progressive press remained in open opposition to the new governmental efforts, the National-Liberal press attempted painfully to steer a middle course, and eventually came to regard the new bill as a victory. Thus while in fact the bureaucracy at first followed the Liberal line on this issue, the Liberals now gradually came to support the policy proposed by the government.

The main debate over the 1881 bill centered on the revision of paragraph 100e of the Reich industrial legislation. The government sought to put teeth into the measure by al-

[20] February 20, 1881. [21] February 19, 1881.
[22] March 21, 1881.

lowing local authorities to grant the guilds the right to supervise apprenticeship training by guild members and nonmembers alike.[23] The section was cautiously phrased, but it was immediately considered by all the Liberal factions in the Reichstag as an unacceptable departure from the principle of industrial freedom. Liberal efforts focused almost exclusively on attempts, both in the plenary sessions of the Reichstag and in committee, to eliminate or alter that section. At the last moment the Conservatives added fuel to the fire by presenting yet another amendment depriving nonguild masters of even the right to train apprentices. The Liberals were outraged. Lasker himself took the podium and launched into one of his brilliant speeches against the law as a whole and against the Conservative amendment in particular.[24] Finally, the amendment was rejected by a close vote of 125 to 122. No one on the left voted for it, although many Liberals chose not to take part in the vote at all. The Conservatives voted for their amendment as a bloc, and were generously supported by the Center, while the Reichspartei was almost evenly split on the matter. The final vote was a victory for the Liberals, and made the passage of the bill as first presented by the government more palatable for them. The *Hamburgerische Korrespondenz* characterized the bill in its final form as a "knife without a blade,"[25] and the *Kölnische Zeitung* saw in it an ingenious device for pacifying the irate masters without giving in to their reactionary demands.[26]

In the excitement over article 100e, many Liberals overlooked the danger inherent in the overall conception of the bill. Without a doubt, it made the guild issue a permanent aspect of the problem of state protection in Germany. It ignored the potentially liberal aspect of the guilds as institutions of self-government and emphasized exclusively the privileged position of the masters and their dependence

[23] See chap. 3.
[24] *Steno. Berichte*, June 9, 1881.
[25] June 10, 1881.
[26] March 21, 1881.

on the bureaucracy. The new law placed the guilds securely under the supervision of local administrators, who were to attend all guild meetings and approve every single decision taken by them. During the Reichstag debate, Eduard Lasker was quick to note this point, but his objections were of no avail. The government, he argued, has produced "a creature which is to be entirely dependent upon it. It will be suffered as long as it follows the direction of the government, and when it does not, one has ready at hand the right of dissolving it."[27] The legislative reform sought by the master artisans turned out to be a double-edged tool. Protection was provided, but at a price. The debate over the bill disclosed the final deterioration of the guilds as autonomous self-administrating bodies. It made the issue of their reorganization into a matter of clear-cut conflict between progressive and reactionary forces in Germany. At the same time the bill failed to put an end to the small masters' demands for further government protection. Encouraged by the government's attitude and the position of the Conservative and Center parties, the master artisans continued their campaign for guarantees and privileges. The protectionists among them saw the bill as a half-measure, and the National-Liberal approval of it as a deceptive and halfhearted move.

In the subsequent Reichstag election, in October 1881, the National-Liberal party lost almost half its supporters, and during the next few years they made renewed efforts to regain their Mittelstand voters. When in 1882 the government announced its intention of embarking on an extensive legislation program for the "well-being of the workers," the National-Liberal party was determined not to let the Conservative and Center parties reap all the political benefits of this course of action. It now strove to become the indispensable backbone of government social legislation, and had thus traveled a long way from its original "Manchesterist" posi-

[27] *Steno. Berichte*, June 9, 1881.

tion. Commenting on the new demands on the part of the masters' interest organization, the *Hannoverische Kourier* wrote in April 1882: "When the need for state intervention became clear German Liberals never shrank back from it on theoretical grounds . . . and have always seen it as fully justified."[28] The Liberals, the article continued, saw it as their duty to help the weak, which was well within their tradition. This was the tenor of Miquel's position throughout the 1880s, and it is not surprising that his main backing within the party came from the southwestern German states, where the Liberals depended almost exclusively on the vote of the urban, Protestant Mittelstand in their battle against the rapid growth of the Catholic center and the onslaught of conservatism. Thus while the Progressives incorporated the Secessionists with their rigid position on economic policies into their party and took a hostile stand on matters of handicraft legislation, the National Liberals drew ever closer to the protectionist position of the government, in a desperate attempt to preserve what was left of their Mittelstand support.

Social Catholicism and Social Conservatism

While the Liberals attempted to halt the desertion of their small-master supporters, other parties sensed the opportunity and soon began to compete for the masters' undecided votes. In the drive to recruit new members from among these men, the Catholics had the greatest success, limited only by the exclusive nature of their political organization. For the Catholic masters, and for them alone, the Center party became an obvious and satisfactory alternative. Indeed, it was the Catholic contingent within the masters' Verein that was the first to abandon all Liberal ties and form a new political alliance.

The early desertion of liberalism by Catholic master arti-

[28] April 15, 1882.

sans was not primarily due to any planned campaign on the part of the Center party. The shift became possible when the antiliberal points of view propagated by prominent Catholics for almost a quarter of a century were finally transformed into a real political force as a result of Bismarck's Kulturkampf. In 1864 Bishop von Ketteler, prompted by the debate between Shulze-Delitzsch and Ferdinand Lassalle on the nature and purpose of cooperative organizations, published a book entitled *Christianity and the Labor Problem*,[29] in which he presented Christianity as a social and political doctrine, and advocated the establishment of corporate associations on the model of the medieval guilds. His disciple, Pastor Kolping, devoted his life to organizing Catholic associations of young artisans, journeymen, and apprentices.[30] In the late seventies Franz Hitze, later the leading Catholic social thinker, asserted in *Capital and Labor* the need to reestablish a social order in Germany partly based on the old medieval guilds.[31]

A corporate organization of society, adapted to the needs of the modern world but following the medieval guild system, was and remained for decades the stated aim of Social Catholicism. It had special appeal to the master artisans who so lovingly cherished the memory of the medieval Golden Age. For Catholics who had still not formulated a political position, and for those who had just broken away from liberalism, here was an obvious ally.

During much of the 1870s, however, the support provided

[29] First published in Mainz in 1864. See also Bowen, *German Theories of the Corporative State*, pp. 79 ff.; and Edgar Alexander, "Church and Society in Germany."

[30] See Bowen, *German Theories of the Corporative State*, pp. 85-89; and Paul Behr, *Die Katholischen Gesellenvereine in Deutschland.*

[31] See in addition Emil Ritter, *Die Katholisch-soziale Bewegung*, pp. 58 ff. For Hitze's position see his speeches in the Reichstag: *Steno. Berichte*, November 24, 1891; January 15, 1895; March 30, 1897; also his *Schutz dem Handwerk*; and the address to the VSP in *Schriften* 76 (1898): 35-71.

by this ally was often merely verbal. The Catholic-Center party was then preoccupied with fighting the Kulturkampf. Only around 1877-78 did the party relax somewhat as the chancellor gradually severed his ties with the Liberals and initiated negotiations with the Center party. His willingness to negotiate indicated he might also be willing to change his policies. During an 1877 Reichstag debate on a series of amendments to the industrial law, Graf von Galen, an old and respected member of the Center Reichstag delegation, presented his party's stand on the social question.[32] Even at that late date, however, it was nothing but a general statement, urging the government to act in the economic and spiritual interest of the workingman, and protect him from the devastating conditions of modern industry. Von Galen's speech was eloquent and moving, but it satisfied virtually no one, in or out of his party. It took years before the Center party realized the importance of establishing a coherent policy on social issues. Meanwhile, the majority of Catholics organized in the Center party were still primarily preoccupied with their fear of a powerful secular state. A new compulsory guild system, regulated and controlled by the state, could only have been viewed with suspicion by the victims of the Kulturkampf. As late as 1882, the *Christlich-soziale Blätter* in an article on handicraft organizations categorically rejected compulsory guilds.[33] The Center party in the Reichstag, following the energetic leadership of the young Georg von Hertling on this issue, took the same position. Thus, by the end of the first decade of the Great Depression, the small master artisans who hoped to reinstitute the guilds

32 *Steno. Berichte*, April 16, 1877. See also the *Christlich-soziale Blätter*, 1877, pp. 665 ff.; and Georg von Hertling, *Erinnerungen aus meinem Leben*, vol. 2, pp. 314 ff.

33 *Christlich-soziale Blätter*, 1882, p. 459. On von Hertling's consistent liberal position see his *Erinnerungen*, pp. 322-323; and E. Ritter, *Die Katolisch-soziale Bewegung*, pp. 120 ff.; also von Hertling's speech in the Reichstag presenting a minority position on the government handicraft law in *Steno. Berichte*, July 26, 1897.

in their medieval form, or in what they believed this to have been, found only sporadic support in the Center party. Even so, its ideology combined with its increasing concern for the lower strata of the population in general appeared to offer an alternative to discredited liberalism.

The Protestant Church in Germany was even less sensitive to social issues than the Catholic. For decades it simply chose to ignore the "social question," and failed to evolve any positive social philosophy of its own or any program for social action.[34] This attitude was shared by the one avowedly Protestant political force in Germany, the Prussian conservatives. In the 1850s, Ludwig von Gerlach and his *Kreuzzeitung* circle led what was then known as the "Zünftlerreaktion" (guildsmen's reaction), paying special attention to artisans' and workers' problems. Most Prussian Junkers, however, showed little interest in these matters. During the third quarter of the century, with favorable conditions in the international grain market, they supported a policy of free trade, but opposed Liberalism out of fear of, and contempt for, all liberal political aspirations. This aristocratic sentiment differed fundamentally from the master-artisans' antiliberalism, which was based above all on objections to specific liberal economic measures.

Gradually, however, small groups of conservative intellectuals began to evolve a new critique of liberalism. The most original and outstanding thinker among them was Karl Johann Rodbertus.[35] Hermann Wagener and Rudolf Meyer,

[34] See Meyer, *Der Emancipationskampf*, pp. 348 ff.; Emil von Laveleye, *Die sozialen Parteien der Gegenwart*, pp. 143 ff.; Karl Valerius Herberger, "Die Stellung der preussischen Konservativen zur sozialen Frage"; Erich Stock, *Wirtschafts- und Sozialpolitische Bestrebungen der deutschkonservativen Partei*; William O. Shanahan, *German Protestants Face the Social Question*, pp. 357-387.

[35] On Rodbertus see K. Diehl, "Rodbertus, Johann Karl," in the *HBS*, 3rd ed., and the bibliography there. Very little has been written about Rodbertus within this context. See, e.g., Erich Thier, *Rodbertus, Lassalle, Adolf Wagner*, pp. 15-22; and especially Rudolf Meyer, *Was Heisst Konservativ Sein?*

two of his disciples, propagated his theories and helped spread their influence into journalism and politics. The two attacked von Gerlach's alleged disregard of the modern world and claimed that they alone represented enlightened conservatism. Wagener's point of view was clearly revealed in the title of his famous pamphlet, *The Solution to the Social Question from the Standpoint of Reality and Practicality, by a Practical Politician.* His reformist position was unequivocal. In 1878 he wrote: "It only remains to be seen whether the various classes of our society will have sufficient foresight, energy, and understanding to bring about *a new order.* If they pass their test in these matters, they will be ruled by free institutions and elected officials. If they do not, they will be ruled by the iron hand of Caesarism."[36] Little did he realize the prophetic nature of his pronouncement, or his own paradoxical role in the process. His conservatism was, indeed, of a new and unique type. Perhaps the first theoretician of the "conservative revolution," he eventually became a tool for the preparation of the social and political alternative he had so clearly rejected.[37]

The main objective of the Social-Conservative reform plans was to prevent the polarization of German society according to the model predicted by the Socialists. They were therefore, vitally interested in projects aimed at preserving the Mittelstand as the necessary middle ground between the forces of capital and labor. "The main task," explained Rudolf Meyer in his voluminous history of the fourth estate, "remains the conservation of the Mittelstand."[38] Accordingly, the reestablishment of the handicraft guilds became a major theme in Social-Conservative plans. It is interesting and significant that V. A. Huber's efforts to encourage a cooperative movement among the masters always remained at

[36] Quoted in Laveleye, *Die sozialen Parteien*, p. 152.

[37] For Hermann Wagener see his *Erlebtes*; and Wolfgang Saile, *Hermann Wagener und sein Verhältniss zu Bismarck*; also H.-J. Schoeps, "Hermann Wagener—Ein konservativer Sozialist."

[38] Meyer, *Der Emancipationskampf*, p. 349.

the periphery of Social-Conservatism. A cooperative system was suspect in the eyes of the Social Conservatives no less than in those of traditional conservatives. The job of a successful conservative movement, according to Rudolf Meyer, was to institute a revolution from above, emulating the glorious accomplishment of the Prussian reformers of the beginning of the century. Any popular movement, even if clearly unrevolutionary, was a potential danger. The momentum for reform had to come from the crown and from responsible aristocratic leaders, if a full-scale revolution from below was to be averted.[39] Thus the state played the major role in Social-Conservative reformist ideas; it was above all here that they differed fundamentally from old conservative thinkers like Friedrich Stahl and Ludwig von Gerlach, and from the proponents of Catholic social programs, like Bishop von Ketteler and Peter Reichensperger. On this issue they broke with a long conservative tradition of suspicion of the state, and opened the way for the future, relatively frictionless cooperation between the autocratic German government and the Conservative party.

Yet during the first decade of the Great Depression, Social Conservatism was not popular among the aristocratic Prussian Junkers. Many of them were Prussian patriots, and openly mistrustful of the new Bismarckian Reich. Under the pressure of economic conditions, however, they slowly came to realize how much they needed widespread popular support, and gradually accepted the inevitable alliance with men far beneath them in the social hierarchy.

On the basis of shared objections to liberal economic principles, a group of Prussian conservatives and small master artisans worked together as early as 1862. The election committee of the Preussische Volksverein (Prussian People's Association) cooperated closely with the executive committee of the master-artisans' new Bund, and made its support of the artisans a major issue in the election campaign. Among

[39] Ibid., p. 360; and his *Was Heisst Konservativ Sein?*, p. 14.

seventeen candidates in Berlin, no less than seven were master craftsmen. A master shoemaker, one Herr Panse, campaigned vigorously for the Conservatives among his colleagues, but his success was apparently very limited. The masters' organization as a whole refused to commit itself politically for fear of endangering its fragile internal unity. Moreover, the alliance with the Conservatives was never happy, and the masters repeatedly complained of the condescending attitude of their partners. Soon, both the Conservative Verein and the masters' Bund ceased to exist, putting an end to the incipient alliance.[40]

Political conservatism with a lasting interest in social issues developed only with the establishment of the Deutschkonservative Partei. In its 1876 program the new coalition of conservative forces proclaimed that: "In contrast to the 'limitless freedom' advocated by the liberal theory, we are striving for *organized economic freedom* in industrial and commercial life. We demand proper attention from the legislature to all working people, and a just appreciation of the presently neglected interests of landownership, industry, and handicraft. We further demand the gradual elimination of the privileges of big money capital. We demand the repair of the serious damage which the exaggerated economic concentration and the lack of strict order have inflicted upon agriculture and small business."[41] The *Kreuzzeitung*, establishing itself as the main organ of the new party, began to show a consistent interest in matters related to the small artisans. Conservative associations throughout the country devoted an increasing number of meetings to the past and future of the handicraft guilds.[42] In April 1877, the Conservative Reichstag delegation opened its campaign for gov-

[40] See H. Müller, "Der preussische Volksverein," pp. 24-46; and *Der zweite deutsche Handwerkertag zu Frankfurt a.M. 1863.* See also the section "The Masters' Ambivalent Liberalism" in chap. 5.

[41] Wilhelm Mommsen, ed., *Deutsche Parteiprogramme*, pp. 68-69.

[42] See, e.g., reports in *Die Post,* November 7, 1880; *Norddeutsche Allgemeine Zeitung,* November 11, 1880.

ernment protection of small masters. Their spokesman, Karl Ackermann of Dresden, was most emphatic on this issue: "Take care that the artisans' estate, which is equally distant from wealth and from poverty, and which finds its satisfaction in its own labor, its happiness in the work of its hands, and its honor in its civic virtues, should recover its Golden Age. Take care that order and discipline should be restored wherever they have been destroyed, and that the German towns should preserve their most essential basis—a contented Bürgertum properly divided according to the organization of its labor."[43] In spite of his eloquence, the Conservatives were very cautious in their support of the master-artisans' extreme demands for revising industrial laws. Following the passage of the 1881 new guild law they attempted to persuade the masters to give it a proper chance and to make serious efforts to operate within it. They then played a moderating role, and were therefore often distrusted by the more militant masters.

At the 1883 national congress of artisans, Ackermann explained that: "The Conservatives have joined the master-artisans' efforts not on the grounds of party interests . . . they are indeed pleased with artisan support but whatever they do for them is only done in the interests of the entire fatherland."[44] The amount of electoral support the small master artisans gave the Conservative party during the late seventies and early eighties is difficult to estimate, but the potential affinity between them and the Conservatives became increasingly more evident during these years. Otto Glagau, in his pamphlet on the history of the handicrafts, explicitly defined his view of the link between the small master artisans and the aristocratic Conservatives. It was not a political bond but rather a common nostalgia that could provide the foundation for a meaningful and lasting alliance between them. The Middle Ages, so ran Glagau's argument, were not an era of darkness, but a time of "more severe discipline,

[43] *Steno. Berichte*, April 16, 1877.
[44] *KZ*, February 3, 1883.

wiser order, respectable and happy life." The German nation had then had a richer and more useful existence. The common people had even been in better physical condition then. The crafts were inseparable from the arts, and working men were endowed with rare spiritual integrity.[45] A similar view of the past, sketched by Conservative journalists in the *Kreuzzeitung*, by Conservative authors and party leaders, helped to bring together small masters, who lovingly preserved the memory of their medieval respectability, and the aristocratic Conservatives, who cherished the memory of their past greatness.

On the other hand, the small master artisans had little in common with the Conservatives socially, culturally, or politically. They had no political power, social prestige, or economic stature to protect. For their part, the Conservatives, though eager to gain the masters' votes, were reluctant to share their social or political privileges. Thus, despite their dissatisfaction with liberalism, the masters were slow to go over to the Conservatives. Their Verein was careful to maintain its pressure-group character and avoid any direct political commitment. In spite of growing demands at several national masters' conferences for the adoption of a clearer stand in favor of the Conservative party, the leadership continued to hesitate.[46] The majority of the politically-minded masters needed a period of transition before they could overcome their distaste for the Conservatives and finally find their way into their political camp.

Efforts at Building an Independent Political Party

In the political vacuum that developed, several outstanding master-artisan leaders made a number of attempts to set up a separate political organization and put forward their own candidates in a number of election districts. As

[45] Glagau, *Deutsches Handwerk*, pp. 1-17.

[46] See, e.g., reports on the debates in the master-artisan congresses: *KZ*, October 10, 1880 and August 6, 1881.

early as 1877, several masters known to be active members of the Progressive party formed a liberal splinter group, apparently in order to present their own version of liberalism, which would be less offensive to the artisans. Almost 4,000 votes went to this independent Liberal Artisans' party in Berlin.[47] Following the 1878 election campaign many masters, moved by Bismarck's patriotic arguments, became disenchanted with the Liberal opponents of his anti-Socialist legislation, and having apparently nowhere to turn set out to establish a new political body. On October 28, 1878, members of the industrial chambers in Hamburg and in Zittau, and the chief editor of the Verein's journal, the *Allgemeine Gewerbezeitung* in Berlin, organized a meeting of master artisans from the entire Protestant north. Aware that many masters had abandoned liberalism, they were determined to make use of the large-scale desertion in order to create their own political party—the first Mittelstandspartei. The new party was to be called the Deutsche Handwerker und Gewerbepartei (German Artisans' and Industrial party); its program called for putting an end to the "old-fashioned patronizing of the handicrafts by the police and the bureaucracy" as well as to the existing "economic un-freedom." It proclaimed its support of the workers' efforts to improve their lot, although it explicitly opposed their "latest forms of organization." The party was to remain basically liberal and to concentrate on the specific vocational demands of the small master artisans.[48]

At the next national congress of the Verein, representatives of the new party attempted to gain support for their political efforts. Master-carpenter Brandes, the outstanding leader of the Berlin masters during those years, argued that it had long been an open secret that "independent artisans

[47] This party is referred to by Specht in *Reichstagswahlen*, pp. 123-127 as the "Progressive (Artisans) party."

[48] *KZ*, November 7, 1878; and the reprint of the party program on October 10, 1880. See also Jäger, *Die Handwerkerfrage*, pp. 127-128.

constituted a political party" and that it was time for them to embark on a serious organizational effort to give it a real public existence.[49] The most ardent opposition came from the Catholic masters. The Bavarian masters especially, who were by then mostly supporters of the Catholic-Center party, did not want change, wishing to preserve the interest-group character of the artisan organization. Their argument, however, quickly revealed the confusion in their political thinking, and their ambivalence toward the nature and role of their interest group. As late as 1883, master-shoemaker Billing from Munich still argued that the masters consituted an "economic-political party," and that they wished only to promote economic policy while party politics remained "a matter of indifference" to them.[50] Overriding the Bavarian opposition, however, the 1879 assembly did agree to convert the Verein into a Verband der Selbständigen Handwerker und Gewerbepartei (League of Independent Artisans and the Industrial party).[51] Significantly, the word "Fabrikanten" (manufacturers), was dropped from the name of the organization. It had apparently antagonized many group-conscious small masters. The new name was chosen as a compromise despite its grammatical awkwardness, and was a symptom of the masters' lack of clarity about either the actual or the desirable character of their organization.

In fact, the small master artisans never succeeded in forming an independent political party, although the idea was repeatedly advocated and the project repeatedly attempted. Following another total failure in the late 1870s, the Berlin leadership limited its political involvement and concerned itself primarily with preserving the political neutrality of the master-artisans' interest organization. The political initiative passed to others. In Leipzig almost 5,000 artisans voted for an independent Handwerker candidate in

49 *KZ*, August 10, 1879; also the *Vossische Zeitung*, August 9, 1879.
50 *KZ*, May 25, 1883.
51 *Vossische Zeitung*, August 9, 1879.

the 1881 Reichstag elections. This number constituted over 20 percent of the vote in that city and undoubtedly included many former Liberals.[52] In 1884, the Krefeld delegation to the master-artisans' national congress sought support for a "German Patriotic party." They envisaged a program designed to appeal to all strata of the population, calling for concerted action to provide for the "welfare of the entire people," free and secret elections, freedom of conscience and religion—all these combined with the traditional demands of the masters, the peasants, and the Mittelstand as a whole. The program was warmly applauded by the congress but was not officially endorsed.[53] Throughout the last two decades of the century other experiments of the same kind always ended in failure.[54] In the early part of the Great Depression, other political alternatives were still open, and the masters inaugurated a period of political experimentation seeking an alliance that would fulfill their needs and aspirations. They were then increasingly attracted by the popular extremist parties on the right and on the left, the parties of the political fringe.

52 Specht, *Reichstagswahlen*, p. 293; and the report in the *Schlesische Zeitung*, February 12, 1881.

53 *KZ*, July 24, 1884.

54 See *KZ*, June 3, 1882; August 3, 1886; September 9, 1886. Also the debate on this problem in *Protokolle über die Verhandlungen Berlin 1892*, pp. 162 ff.

EIGHT

THE APPEAL OF THE EXTREMES

ANTI-SEMITISM: BERLIN AND THE PROTESTANT NORTH

As the antiliberal campaign gathered strength in 1874-75, anti-Semitism immediately became popular.[1] A host of newspaper articles, pamphlets, and books proclaimed the connection between the operations of Jewish capitalists and the collapse of the Vienna stock exchange, and blamed Jews and "Jew-like Germans" for the economic catastrophe.[2] It was at best a result of their irresponsible behavior, so ran the argument, and at worst an outcome of their sinister scheming. Attacks on liberalism during the 1870s were almost invariably accompanied by anti-Semitic pronouncements, demonstrating the continuous link between the antiliberal campaign and the development of anti-Semitism in nineteenth-century Germany. Antiliberalism and anti-Semitism often coincided and interacted during the pre-March years and became increasingly intertwined during the revolution of 1848. Men who opposed liberalism on either political or economic grounds often expressed anti-Semitic sentiments. Jewish emancipation, a central tenet of the liberal ideology, was interpreted by antiliberal forces as an attack on the very essence of traditional society as a whole. The final legal emancipation of the Jews granted by a law of the North German Confederation in 1869 did little to

[1] Material from the first two sections of this chapter has been used in the author's "The Social and Political Function of the late 19th Century Anti-Semitism," pp. 418-431.

[2] The anti-Semitism of the "Era Articles," which opened the antiliberal campaign in the *Kreuzzeitung* in July 1875, was strong and overt. See also Constantin Frantz, *Der Nationalliberalismus und die Judenherrschaft*; Glagau, *Der Bankerott des Nationalliberalismus*; Wilhelm Marr, ed., *Die deutsche Wacht*; C. Wilmanns, *Die goldene Internationale*; and Ernst Henrici, *Was ist der Kern der Judenfrage.*

change these attitudes. The association with anti-Semitism continued to be characteristic of German antiliberalism for many years to come.[3]

Although no open anti-Semitic pronouncements were heard in the master-artisans' congresses in Hamburg and in Frankfurt a.M. during the summer of 1848, there is enough evidence to show the prevalence of anti-Semitic sentiment among master artisans at that time.[4] A group of masters from Leipzig, for example, sent out a circular to all guild-members in Germany, closing a tirade of antiliberal rhetoric with an attack on plans for Jewish emancipation. The Jews, they argued, were the most dangerous enemies of the honest German Bürgertum, of all workingmen, and of society at large. They were hated as "strangers who were nowhere at home and who have no heart for the people where [*sic*] they live."[5]

During the following years of rapid industrialization masters often continued to associate their material difficulties with the economic activity of the Jews. In their daily life, however, they could only rarely have encountered direct Jewish competition. In the old territories of the German Reich, Jews were barred from the practice of most handicrafts. In Prussia in 1817 only 4.6 percent of the Jews were engaged in handicrafts, while over 90 percent were employed in various commercial occupations.[6] The number of Jewish craftsmen undoubtedly increased considerably during the nineteenth century, first under the influence of the

[3] For the pre-March period by far the best study of anti-Semitism is Eleonore Sterling, *Judenhass*, especially pp. 115-130. See also Reinhard Rürup, "Kontinuität und Diskontinuität der 'Judenfrage' im 19. Jahrhundert," pp. 385-415.

[4] See the minutes of these meetings: *Verhandlungen der ersten Abgeordneten Versammlung*, and *Verhandlungen des ersten deutschen Handwerker- und Gewerbekongresses.*

[5] *Offener Brief an alle Innungsgenossen Deutschlands.*

[6] See Mark Wischnitzer, *A History of Jewish Crafts and Guilds*, pp.197-205; and H.-M. Klinkenberg, "Zwischen Liberalismus und Nationalismus," p. 366.

French occupation and then through the effects of liberal state legislation. Jews all over Germany entered new professions, a sign of their growing social emancipation.[7] Centuries-old customs, however, among both Jews and Christians, slowed the entry of Jews into the traditional crafts, and most new legislation left a host of trade restrictions untouched. Even by 1895 less than 20 percent of the Jewish labor force in the country was engaged in industry and handicrafts, as compared with over 35 percent of the general population.[8] Significantly, the percentage of independent craftsmen among the Jews was far greater than among Christians. In Berlin, only 1 percent of all the men employed in the various woodworking crafts were Jews, but as many as 35 percent of them were employers, 19 percent self-employed artisans, and 45 percent wage earners.[9] This internal stratification is confirmed by a special study based on the general statistical survey of 1912, in which as many as 17,000 independent Jewish craftsmen were counted among 40,000 Jewish artisans.[10]

The Jews were concentrated in a few trades: they were mostly tailors, shoemakers, bakers, and butchers. Moreover, the great increase in the number of Jewish craftsmen noted toward the end of the nineteenth century was a direct result of the growing immigration of Jews from the newly acquired Polish territories of Prussia, but as late as 1880 these newcomers constituted less than 4 percent of the total Jewish population of the Reich.[11] Thus, Jewish competition in the handicrafts, though not entirely absent, could not have been widespread. Equally unrelated to real economic cir-

[7] See Jacob Toury, *Prolegomena to the Entrance of Jews into German Citizenry* (Hebrew), pp. 94-111.

[8] Klinkenberg, "Zwischen Liberalismus und Nationalismus," p. 368.

[9] Voigt, "Das Tischlergewerbe," *Schriften* 65 (1895): 377.

[10] For these and the following data see J. Segall, *Die beruflichen und sozialen Verhältnisse der Juden.*

[11] Klinkenberg, "Zwischen Liberalismus und Nationalismus," p. 366.

cumstances was the identification of Jews with peddlers, who were considered the competitors of the established small masters. Research has shown here, too, that in 1852 77.5 percent of all peddlers in Germany were non-Jews, and that this percentage rose to over 95 by 1895.[12]

Nevertheless, during the second half of the nineteenth century the emancipated Jews were conspicuous in the growing German towns. Small peasants and agricultural laborers who found their way to these cities usually encountered a far larger proportion of Jews there than they had in their previous communities.[13] Intermingling in gentile society and often showing remarkable energy and resourcefulness in advancing their social and economic position, Jews were an unpleasant novelty for the new townsmen.[14] Furthered by demagogues and rabble-rousers anti-Semitism became increasingly popular in the German urban environment, attracting new immigrants as well as a segment of the old established community.

The unique character of anti-Semitic sentiment and the emerging anti-Semitic movement of the mid-seventies may be summed up in a slogan first coined and publicized in the notorious and endlessly paraphrased *Gartenlaube* articles: "The social question is the Jewish question." Otto Glagau, the author of these articles, is himself an interesting illustration of the role his brand of anti-Semitism played in the decade after 1875.[15] For Glagau Manchesterism was the main enemy. It was the cause of the allegedly confused Ger-

[12] Bernard D. Weinryb, "The Economic and Social Background of Modern Anti-Semitism," in *Essays on Anti-Semitism*, ed. K.S. Pinson, p. 29.

[13] The rate of urbanization was much more rapid among Jews than among non-Jews in Germany. By 1900, 48.5 percent of the Jews lived in cities classified as large, while only 16.2 percent of the non-Jewish population lived in them. See Weinryb, "The Economic and Social Background," p. 25 and passim.

[14] Nowhere is the encounter more vividly described than in Adolf Hitler's *Mein Kampf*.

[15] See the section, "Liberalism on the Defensive," chap. 6.

man legal system, of the corruption of parliament and society, and of the overall moral bewilderment of the people. Judaism, he argued, was the supreme expression of this suicidal doctrine as well as its effective and talented agent. This thesis offered the ex-liberal masters, among others, a way out of their ideological and emotional ambivalence. If it was embarassing for them to attack their previous allies, it became comprehensible as a defense against the progressive Verjudung of the German liberal movement. If it was unpleasant to attack the patriotic German liberals as a whole, it was easy enough to attack the Jews among them. Thus it was not capitalism that was to be blamed, but Jewish capitalism; not liberalism but Jewish Manchesterism; not the national government but its Jewish advisers.

While all parties attempted at the time to appeal to the small handicraftsmen, the most vocal were the various new anti-Semitic organizations, parading their social conservatism, their support for state protection, and above all their ardent opposition to all manifestations of liberal political and economic doctrines. The Soziale Reichspartei (Social-Imperial party) led by the "progressive" ex-liberal Ernst Henrici, the Deutsche Volksverein (German People's Association), organized by the conservative Max Liebermann von Sonnenberg, the Saxonian Deutsche Reformpartei (German Reform party), and the various anti-Semitic leagues and conferences all wished to appear as allies of the small handicraft masters in their economic struggle against liberal economic legislation, and against the competition of big capital and modern industry. Each in its particular style supported the master-artisans' limited demands for compulsory guild membership, the reintroduction of masters' qualifying examinations, a restriction of prison workshop production, a reorganization of the tender system, etc.[16]

In May 1880, the two most prominent leaders of the Berlin master-artisans' movement took part in a public meeting

[16] See Massing, *Rehearsal for Destruction*, pp. 77-89; and for some of these party programs, Specht, *Die Reichstagswahlen*, pp. 66 ff.

organized by Adolf Stöcker's Social-Conservative party. The formerly liberal leaders of the masters' national Verein were ceremoniously seated at the platform. They had traveled a long way since they had been active on behalf of the Progressive party in Berlin and had tried to preserve the basic liberal stand of the artisans' movement.[17]

The story of Adolf Stöcker has often been told.[18] The son of a country blacksmith, he rose to become a Lutheran pastor and was eventually appointed to the post of court chaplain in Berlin. Early in life he was influenced by Rudolf Todt, another Protestant pastor, who in 1877 publicly called upon the Protestant Church to take a clear stand on the social question and make Christianity a "dam against the tide of anarchy and socialism."[19] In December 1877, Stöcker joined the newly created Verein für Sozialpolitik and was there introduced to some of the proponents of Social Conservatism and to some of the conservative Kathedersozialisten (Socialists of the Chair). But the intellectual atmosphere of this organization was not to his liking, and he was determined to create a new party, which would mobilize mass support for his own activist brand of Social Conservatism and divert the workers from the subversive doctrines of Social Democracy. In the early part of 1878, Stöcker cam-

[17] See the report in Marr's anti-Semitic publication, *Die deutsche Wacht*, July 1880.

[18] The only available full-scale biography of Stöcker was written by the official Nazi historian, Walter Frank. See his *Hofprediger Adolf Stöcker*. As to his activities, von Gerlach's comments in his memoirs *Von Rechts nach Links*, pp. 102 ff., are illuminating; see also Wanda Kampmann, "Stöcker und die Berliner Bewegung"; L.L. Snyder, *From Bismarck to Hitler*, pp. 13-24; K. Wawrzinek, *Die Entstehung der deutschen Antisemitenparteien*, pp. 18-29; Massing, *Rehearsal for Destruction*, pp. 21-47; Martin Broszat, "Die antisemitische Bewegung im Wilhelminischen Deutschland," pp. 19-39; Levy, *The Downfall of the Anti-Semitic Political Parties*, pp. 17-19; and Pulzer, *The Rise of Political Anti-Semitism*, pp. 88-101.

[19] Rudolf Todt, *Der Radikale deutsche Sozialismus und die Christliche Gesellschaft*.

paigned vigorously among the Berlin workers,[20] declaring himself not only a better German patriot and a more devout Christian but also a more practical social reformer than the socialists. His goal, stated his first public program, was to close the growing gap between rich and poor by guaranteeing the economic security of the workers. In January 1878, at a meeting at the Handwerkersaal in Berlin, he presented a program that was almost exclusively geared to the needs of the working class.[21] His eloquence, however, apparently fell upon deaf ears: in the following election, the Social Democrats doubled their strength in Berlin, while Stöcker's party secured only 1,422 votes. Clearly the workers were not taken with Stöcker's propaganda. The promise of social reform under the banner of the "old forces"—the monarchy and the Church—held little attraction for the Berlin proletariat.

Although the workers remained indifferent to Stöcker's campaign, he inadvertently achieved great popularity among various elements of the Berlin Mittelstand, especially among small master artisans and retailers.[22] At first these men appeared to be particularly attracted by the growing anti-Semitism of his campaign while their attitudes toward the social reforms he advocated were undefined. Stöcker himself was not originally anti-Semitic, but his own experience in Berlin as well as the experience of other reformers of various political persuasions soon convinced him that anti-Semitism could be most useful in achieving a degree of political support among the diverse Mittelstand groups of the capital.

In March 1880, Stöcker was invited to Breslau to deliver a speech on the Handwerkerfrage.[23] His audience consisted

[20] On this period see Siegfried Kaehler, "Stöckers Versuch eine christlich-soziale Arbeiterpartei in Berlin zu begründen," pp. 227-265.

[21] Adolf Stöcker, *Christlich-Sozial*, pp. 3 ff. See also Felix Salomon, ed., *Die deutschen Parteiprogramme*, pp. 71 ff.

[22] See Kaehler, "Stöckers Versuch," pp. 227-265.

[23] Stöcker, *Christlich-Sozial*, pp. 338-353.

of master artisans, liberals and ex-liberals, as well as a group of hard-core conservatives. The speech was indicative of the role Stöcker played in the political evolution of the master artisans as a social group, and of the function of his political anti-Semitism. Significantly, he found it necessary to begin by encouraging the small masters to finally take a decisive step away from liberalism. They should be able to stand proudly and unequivocally behind their demand for new guilds, he argued, and be able to declare: "This is really what we want. We want the guilds . . . the guilds in the spirit of our own century, with all the means and powers of the present."[24] Reacting to continuous heckling from the floor, Stöcker was forced to explain that he was not, in fact, objecting to liberalism as such, but only to the present subverted and corrupted liberalism. On the other hand, the essence of his own party's efforts was "not reaction, but action," he insisted. Throughout the speech, among the first delivered away from his home base in Berlin, Stöcker was forced to take a defensive attitude, very unlike his usual oratorical style. The Breslau audience was neither a mass of enthusiastic supporters, nor a frankly hostile socialist assembly. Stöcker found himself confronting a crowd of disillusioned and confused men, seeking a substitute for their former political creed.

During his years of political experimentation, primarily but not exclusively in Berlin, Stöcker became aware of the need to provide his potential supporters with an emotional battle cry, stronger than a negative attitude toward liberalism or a nostalgic view of past society. Anti-Semitism, by then already practiced by other Social Conservatives, seemed the obvious choice, and Stöcker enthusiastically took it up. He operated in the spirit of Liebermann von Sonnenberg, the Junker among the anti-Semitic Social Conservatives in the capital during these years, who so shocked the young Hellmut von Gerlach when he casually remarked:

[24] Ibid., pp. 339-340.

"First we want to become a political power; then we shall seek the scientific evidence for anti-Semitism."[25]

An accurate assessment of the extent of master support for anti-Semitic political candidates in national and local elections during the late 1870s and early 1880s requires detailed local and regional studies. Masters undoubtedly accounted for a considerable segment of the 46,000 anti-Semitic votes cast in Berlin during the 1881 election.[26] In Dresden, another center of handicraft production, a building master won the Reichstag seat on the anti-Semitic ticket of the Deutsche Reformpartei. The inadequate sources, however, do suffice to suggest the function that organized anti-Semitism played in the overall political development of the masters: in various parts of Protestant Germany, the masters' desertion of liberalism and their move toward the conservative camp was made through a flirtation with radical Social Conservatism and political anti-Semitism. At the time often no more than a transitory stage, it was significant in forming the masters' political consciousness, and indicative of future developments.

Anti-Semitism: The Mixed Catholic-Protestant West

As in Prussia and Saxony, so too in the mixed Protestant-Catholic areas of western Germany, it took a militant Social-Conservative, anti-Semitic movement to induce the small master artisans to sever their ties with the Liberals. The small master artisans in the Rhineland and Westphalia were the first to renew the demand for the repeal of Gewerbefreiheit and a reconstitution of the guild system in the 1870s: it was they who worked to accentuate the antiliberal tone in the discussions of the Verein selbständigen Handwerker. Conservative spokesmen, such as von Kleist-Retzow of the Deutschkonservative Partei, and the brothers

25 Von Gerlach, *Von Rechts nach Links*, p. 112.
26 Pulzer, *The Rise of Political Anti-Semitism*, p. 99.

Reichensperger of the Catholic Center, attempted to win over the masters in this region by outspokenly supporting revision of the relevant industrial legislation and by endeavoring to accommodate the masters' militant mood. But the master artisans in the west, like their colleagues in the north and east, also needed a transition through Social Conservatism seasoned with a great deal of anti-Semitic verbiage before they could finally join the established Conservative forces.

Freiherr Friedrich Carl von Fechenbach was a Protestant landowner from Hesse who started his political career in the National-Liberal party, joining the Deutschkonservative Partei in 1878.[27] By the next year he had evolved his own political program and for several years was stormily engaged in publicizing it and attempting to give it an organizational backbone. Living in a mixed Catholic-Protestant area, he envisioned a Social-Conservative program capable of uniting Protestants and Catholics into a mighty political force, jointly withstanding the tide of socialism. Von Fechenbach's political objectives were the abolition of the Kulturkampf, far-reaching social legislation particularly for peasants and artisans, and the institution of strong anti-capitalist and anti-Semitic legal measures. Early in 1880 he attempted to reach an agreement with Stöcker, Perrot, and a number of other south-German Protestant Social Conservatives. When these efforts failed, he invited a number of prominent Protestants and Catholics interested in the social question to a meeting in Frankfurt a.M., at which a Verein für konservative Sozialreform (Association for Conservative Social Reform) was established. The program of the new Verein urged an end to the anti-Catholic campaign, restrictions on the power of "money capitalism," a break with the policy of "unrestricted competition," a return to the joint silver and gold standard, a "healthy" colonial policy through an "organic treatment of emigration," an expulsion of all non-Christians from all legislative bodies, and the

[27] H.-J. Schoeps, "CDU vor 75 Jahren."

establishment of a representative system based on the principle of vocational estates.[28]

In a sequence remarkably like that followed by Stöcker, von Fechenbach sought to create a powerful grass-roots movement alongside his organization of conservative notables. Operating after Stöcker, and no doubt attempting to avoid his mistakes, von Fechenbach immediately concentrated on the recruitment of Mittelstand elements, especially master artisans and peasants. For the former his program included a demand for the establishment of compulsory guilds with legal corporative rights, and the replacement of taxation on industrial enterprises with an inheritance tax and taxes on stock profits and luxuries. Like Stöcker in Berlin, von Fechenbach in the Rhine area combined a strong antiliberal campaign with fervent anti-Semitism and a typically conservative longing for the past. In the rapidly industrializing regions of western Germany it was a mixture specifically designed to appeal to the small ex-liberal master artisans, who turned increasingly to the old social-industrial structure as a remedy for all their difficulties.

By 1881, von Fechenbach had established some fifty branches of his Verein zum Schutze des Handwerks (Association for the Protection of Handicrafts); most were in western Germany, but some were as far away as Hamburg and Breslau.[29] In Cologne, he prepared the ground for establishing a new master-artisans' organization, and for several years managed to publish a bimonthly artisans' journal, *Die Innung*, subtitled *An Organ of the Social-Conservative Union for the German Handicrafts.*[30] In May 1881 the So-

28 *Die Post*, November 23, 1880. See also Hugo Böttger, *Das Programm der Handwerker*, pp. 137-138, and Jäger, *Die Handwerkerfrage*.

29 Jäger, *Die Handwerkerfrage*, p. 176; and a propaganda pamphlet entitled *Die Demokratische Partei und die Handwerker*, which describes in detail von Fechenbach's activities among the small handicraft masters.

30 The degree of von Fechenbach's appeal can be judged from the reports on the master-artisans' national congresses. For 1881

cial-Conservative Union met in Berlin for its second general congress. The character of the organization appeared to have changed radically since the first congress. Very few Catholic social reformers were present, and the various Protestant anti-Semitic politicians took the lead in the debates. It became clear immediately that the hopes for Catholic-Protestant cooperation were to be shattered again. Since the Union's first congress, both the Conservative and the Center parties had openly objected to the new organization. Bismarck and his government foresaw only fresh trouble from the new body, and remained hostile to it as they had previously been to Stöcker's Social-Conservative agitation in Berlin. The *Christlich-soziale Blätter*, representing the Catholic reform movement in southwestern Germany, claimed that within a year von Fechenbach's Union had abandoned the Catholic-Protestant dialogue and allowed its meetings to degenerate into a continuous Protestant monologue. It then proceeded to assure its readers that "Catholic master artisans as well as all other estates now find their best representation in the Center party."[31]

In fact, the Center party in western Germany was most uneasy about von Fechenbach's organizational efforts among the small masters. It was particularly in the mixed Catholic-Protestant areas of the Rhineland and the Ruhr that this militant Social Conservatism seems to have had the greatest success. In Dortmund, for instance, a town with a large Catholic minority and a strong tradition of liberalism, situated in the middle of the Ruhr industrial region, von Fechenbach's antiliberal, antiindustrial and interdenominational

---

see the *KZ*, August 5; for 1882 and 1883 the minutes of the meetings: *Verhandlungen zu Magdeburg 1882*, pp. 25-36, and *Verhandlungen zu Hannover 1883*, pp. 23-25. Von Fechenbach's most ardent supporters in the masters' organization during these years were the master tailors Fasshauer from Cologne and Möller from Dortmund. Both remained until well into the 1890s among the most militant anti-Semitic and radical of the master-artisan leaders in Germany.

[31] *Christlich-soziale Blätter*, 1881, pp. 326 ff.

campaign was warmly appreciated by many small handicraft masters. They responded enthusiastically to his call for a joint Catholic-Protestant battle against the power of capital, the intrusion of large-scale industry, and the growing militancy of the socialist workers. During these years, Reichstag delegates from the mixed Catholic-Protestant regions of Westphalia included Protestant Social Conservatives, among them Adolf Stöcker himself, and militant Catholic reformers, such as Freiherr von Schorlemer-Alst. In Bavaria, on the other hand, the Center party had little to fear from Social-Conservative propaganda. There the small master artisans, with other Mittlestand groups, had been supporting Center-party candidates for years. They could see little need for cooperation with the small minority of Protestants in their primarily Catholic region, and were suspicious of von Fechenbach's efforts. Neither his appeal for interdenominational political action nor his strong anti-industrialism seemed particularly relevant to the Catholic masters in this economically underdeveloped area of Germany.

In 1883 a meeting of Catholic social reformers from western Germany formulated a set of principles which were to be later known as the "Haide program." With regard to the artisans' question, the Haide program clearly stated that: "The handicraft estate constitutes the most important and numerous productive estate beside the agricultural one. Its continued existence is a social necessity, and it must be preserved and supported."[32] The Catholic Social Conservatives went on blaming "absolute industrial freedom" and the predominance of materialistic and atheistic attitudes for the plight of the handicraft masters. They demanded separate handicraft legislation that would create a framework for compulsory guilds, state examinations for masters, and improved vocational training. By means of these resolutions

[32] *Frankfurter Zeitung*, July 27, 1883. See also E. Ritter, *Die Katolisch-soziale Bewegung*, pp. 79-86, and Jäger, *Die Handwerkerfrage*, pp. 280 ff.

the local Catholic leadership hoped to regain the confidence of the master artisans. Indeed even the militants among them appeared to be satisfied with the Haide program and considered it a victory for their branch of radical Social Catholicism. Soon afterward, however, the leadership of the Center party dissociated itself from this program. In a general Catholic congress in Düsseldorf, Ludwig Windhorst stated emphatically that the Haide program was not to be construed as official party policy. Taking a more moderate stand he declared: "If everything included in the handicraft section of the Haide [program] could be attained, I would reject none of it. But, whether or not all of this is indeed attainable is still to be investigated."[33] The same year Windhorst himself appeared at the national congress of master artisans in Hanover and attempted to convert it to his more moderate stand by making the same request for greater realism.[34] The catholic conservatives, like the Protestants, were cautious about supporting the militant demands of the master artisans. Gradually, as the memory of the years of economic catastrophe faded, the vehemence of the antiliberal campaign diminished everywhere in the country, and the Social-Conservative, anti-Semitic movement disintegrated into small rival groups.

The master artisans, too, were in a better mood for compromise and moderation. Von Fechenbach's movement was short lived. For a while, the tireless Freiherr toyed with the prospects of a national anti-Semitic movement and helped draft the program for the Deutsche Reformpartei, established in Dresden in September 1881. By 1885, however, he had finally become a member of the Center party. Many of his previous supporters followed the same route. By the middle eighties, both the Protestant Social Conservatives and their Catholic counterparts joined the established conservative parties. Within a larger political perspective, the anti-Semitic interlude had served to smooth the transfer of

[33] *Hamburgerische Korrespondenz,* September 15, 1883.
[34] *Verhandlungen zu Hannover 1883,* p. 16.

allegiance for a segment of the urban population, including many small master artisans, from the liberal to the conservative camp.

Social Democracy and the Small Masters

For thousands of small independent handicraft masters who became involved in national politics for the first time during the 1870s, and for thousands more who were in the process of abandoning their liberal ties, the young Social-Democratic party presented itself as a ready alternative. Although the separation between independent and dependent artisans was slowly proceeding, self-employed individual masters and employers of one or two journeymen often preserved a degree of solidarity and a sense of common destiny with skilled dependent artisans.[35] There is no doubt that many of them joined the working-class movement in Germany throughout the 1860s and the early 1870s. Both the Lassallean Arbeitervereine (workers' associations) and the early Social-Democratic Arbeiterbildungsvereine (workers' educational associations), particularly active in the industrial towns of Saxony were as attractive to small masters as they were to journeymen. Lassallean candidates in the Reichstag and various municipal elections, such as Hasenclever in Berlin and Grillenberger in Nuremberg, appealed to workers, artisans, and Kleinbürger alike. In the early 1880s, Social-Democratic representatives were elected to numerous municipal councils through a voting system that allowed very few wage earners to participate. These men could not have been elected without substantial support from Mittelstand voters, probably including a considerable number of small master artisans.[36]

[35] See the concluding remarks in the section on income and standard of living, in chap. 2.

[36] Eduard Bernstein, *Die Geschichte der Berliner Arbeiterbewegung*, vol. 1, pp. 94-105; pp. 320 ff.; Hugo Eckert, *Liberal- oder Sozialdemokratie*, pp. 57 ff.; Karl-Ernst Moring, *Die Sozialdemokratische*

Prior to the Social-Democratic party congress in Erfurt in 1891 and during the years of antisocialist legislation in Germany, the Social-Democratic ideology was in many ways merely a radical left-wing critique of liberalism. Its socialism was vague and often played only a relatively minor role in the political and organizational activities of the party. It combined the democratic tenets of *political* liberalism, which had previously attracted the small master artisans to the left-liberal movement, with a strong and well-argued opposition to liberal *economic* doctrines. As long as it managed to play down its objections to the private ownership of the means of production and did not harp on the theme of the unavoidable decline of the Mittelstand, it could indeed appear as a potential ally of the small masters.

In the primarily agricultural regions of Germany, where large industrial enterprises were few and scattered, the Social Democrats were forced to appeal primarily to masters and employees in the small handicraft shops. Thus, in Bavaria and in the southwestern German states, the Social Democrats relied heavily on the support of lower-middle-class elements, and constantly appealed to master artisans.[37] The small masters, engaged in manual labor alongside their hired hands were natural recruits for the socialists in areas with a small wage-earning proletariat. Thus for instance, at the end of the century the Social-Democratic candidate in Constance, on the southwestern border of Württemberg, was a small master painter; and in Mannheim, the Socialist candidate in the 1881 election was a small retailer, one Au-

Partei in Bremen 1890-1914, pp. 33 ff.; Vernon L. Lidtke, *The Outlawed Party*, pp. 182-184.

[37] This was the cause of a prolonged ideological and tactical debate between the radicals and moderates in the party. See *Protokolle über die Verhandlungen des Parteitages, Berlin 1892*, pp. 239 ff. On the recruitment of nonworkers to the SPD, especially under the leadership of Georg Heinrich von Vollmar in Bavaria, see Franz Mehring, *Geschichte der deutschen Sozialdemokratie*, vol. II, pp. 603-611.

gust Dresbach. Appealing in his election pamphlets to all "artisans, peasant, and workers," Dresbach maintained that "all of you together constitute the middle and the working estates, the foundation of all production and the source of all value. If you would correctly understand your interests and be united then your victory could not fail to come."[38]

But even this typical Mittelstand socialist could not avoid the real controversy that was keeping the small masters out of the Social-Democratic party. To masters' insistent questions on whether they could obtain any help or were doomed to disappear with the further modernization of the economy Dresbach evasively replied: "Yes and no. The *handicrafts* cannot be helped; but the *handicraftsmen* must and can be helped."[39] Such answers could hardly satisfy masters who still operated their small workshops, often with some success, and hoping to maintain their positions as independent producers, did not wish to exchange them for the promise of workingmen solidarity.

During the 1870s and the early 1880s, many small master artisans, especially in large towns, still voted for the Social-Democratic party. In 1881 a large portion of the 47,000 anti-Semitic voters in Berlin were undoubtedly recruited from among previous Social Democrats, both Mittelständler and workers.[40] But at that time many of them were typical protest voters and not ideological fellow travelers. By voting for the socialists the master artisans above all registered their anxiety and their discontent with existing social and economic trends and policies, and their disgust with the apparent indifference displayed by the established political parties, liberal and conservative alike, toward their fate. Election results in three voting districts in Berlin seem to support this assumption.

[38] From the leaflets collected by the political police in Mannheim (Badisches Generallandesarchiv, 236/17081).

[39] Ibid.

[40] See Lidtke, *The Outlawed Party*, pp. 163-164; also Bernstein, *Die Geschichte der Berliner Arbeiterbewegung*, vol. 2, pp. 58-76.

TABLE 8.1

ELECTION RESULTS, BERLIN 1881
(In Percentages)

	Conservatives	*Progressives*	*Social Democrats*
Third district			
1st ballot	27.0	60.0	12.0
By-election	21.6	59.3	19.0
Fourth district			
1st ballot	19.9	46.9	32.6
2nd ballot	—	50.1	49.9
Sixth district			
1st ballot	23.1	48.8	27.5
2nd ballot	—	50.8	49.7

SOURCE: *Monatshefte zur Statistik des deutschen Reiches*, March 1882.

It appears that in 1881 many voters who cast their first ballots for the conservatives preferred to vote for the socialists on the second. In the third election district in Berlin, known for its large Mittelstand electorate, a by-election was held later in the year. Here too the Conservatives lost a considerable number of votes while the Social Democrats recouped some, though by no means all, of their previous losses. The figures, however, can be interpreted in a number of ways. It must be remembered that by the late 1870s and early 1880s, urban election districts in Germany were all socially heterogeneous, and that election figures as a rule therefore do not reflect all the actual movements of votes from one party to another but provide only the final distribution. Nevertheless, considering the general mood of master artisans during those years, it is reasonable to assume that by 1881, many of them, residents of the populous handicraft areas of Luisenstadt, Stralauer, and the Oranienburger quarters of Berlin, when finally faced with a choice between Socialists and Progressives, voted for the Socialist candidates. They were above all intent on voting against the Liberal candidate by supporting either the extreme right or the extreme left, thus expressing their discontent through a radical negation of their traditional political stand.

A similar situation developed in other major cities. At the national congress of the master-artisans' Verein in Berlin in 1881, a master tailor from Hamburg defiantly announced that he and many of his colleagues in Hamburg, when faced with a choice between the two Liberal parties and the Social Democrats decided to cast their vote for the socialists who, they were convinced, were better equipped to understand the small masters' needs. Although other voices from Hamburg hastened to silence him, he no doubt represented the views of at least some of the small masters in that city.[41] Even the militant master-artisans' leader from Hamburg, the master-painter Voss, who was a radical Social Conservative throughout the 1880s and an active anti-Semite, seems in later years to have become a left-wing city councilor. More significant are the results of elections for the industrial arbitration courts in 1892-93, in which a majority of the votes, even in the employer section, went to the Social-Democratic candidates in two of the election districts in Berlin, in Frankfurt a.M., in Munich, and in Nuremberg.[42]

Conservative master artisans from Breslau, Cologne, Dortmund, and Munich, who repeatedly called upon the government to deal without delay with their needs and demands occasionally used the threat of a mass transfer of master-artisan political allegiance to the Social-Democratic party. The threats all came from places where a segment of the masters' population was already known for its socialist affiliation. It was by no means an unthinkable choice for small masters, and it seemed an imminent danger to the leadership of the master-artisan organizations.[43]

[41] *KZ*, August 5, 1881. See also the report on the 1887 congress in *KZ*, August 16, 1887.

[42] *Sozialpolitisches Centralblatt*, vol. 1 (1892), pp. 123 ff.; vol. 2 (1893), p. 265.

[43] See *Protokoll über die Verhandlungen mit Vertretern, 1891*

Exact figures on the support given to the Social Democrats by the small master artisans are not available.[44] It has been calculated that throughout the 1890s and up to the 1903 election, nonworkers accounted for at least one-quarter of the Social-Democratic voters, and in some large cities up to one-half.[45] It is difficult, however, to estimate how many of these were independent small masters. In Nuremberg, for instance, 8.6 percent of the Social-Democratic party members were independent producers, constituting the third largest group in the party after the metalworkers and the woodworkers.[46] The number of masters who occasionally voted for socialist candidates was certainly much higher than the number of committed party members, and it is therefore safe to conclude that in some regions the number of master artisans supporting the Social Democrats was substantial, and their contribution to the total socialist vote not insignificant.

Artisans in some trades, particularly those most severely hit by industrialization and repeated economic slumps, were more likely than others to join the Social Democrats or to vote for its candidates. Small shoemakers, for example, apparently voted far more often for the Socialists than did master bakers, tanners, or independent building masters.[47] Robert Michels, in a unique study of the social composition of the German Social-Democratic party published in 1906, concluded that the more traditional crafts, where workers

---

(Bayerisches Hauptstaatsarchiv, MH-14661), pp. 4-5; 11; *AHZ*, June 6, 1890. Also the section, "The Government Discredited," chap. 10.

[44] Since the Social-Democratic party claimed to represent primarily the interests of the working class, information on the social composition of the party was not collected in any systematic way. However, R. Blank, "Die soziale Zusammensetzung," and Robert Michels, "Die deutsche Sozialdemokratie," provide some material on this question.

[45] Blank, "Die soziale Zusammensetzung," pp. 513-524.

[46] Michels, "Die deutsche Sozialdemokratie," p. 505.

[47] See Francke, *Die Schuhmacherei in Bayern*, p. 231; Hechscher, "Die Schuhmacherei in Altona," *Schriften* 62 (1895): 19-29.

still tended to live with their masters and where a reasonable chance for economic independence still existed, were as a whole infertile ground for the Social Democrats.[48] It was the individual self-employed master, in particular, chronically on the brink of losing his independence, who most consistently tended to join urban wage earners in supporting the Socialists. Such men, standing economically as well as socially between the small master employer and the hired laborers, were naturally more easily attracted to Social-Democratic ranks. They were most numerous in Berlin, in the urban centers of Saxony, in Hamburg, and in Bremen, and no doubt helped to give the Socialists their early victories in these cities.

Characteristic of the master-artisans' political behavior during the years from 1877 to 1884, then, was their apparently erratic movement between the extremes. Having deserted the liberal camp in great numbers they set out in search of a new political alliance, all the more necessary for them at a time of economic insecurity and social decline. Finding themselves in a state of political isolation, they kept shifting allegiance as they searched for a trustworthy political ally.

Small master artisans, looking for political support, turned in considerable numbers to extremist parties, if at this stage only as a temporary stopgap. The ex-liberal masters, as well as previous nonvoters, showed an initial dislike of the established conservative parties. They sought to ally themselves with parties that expressed in a militant and popular fashion their antiliberalism and their general disgust with the social and economic situation in the Reich, parties that would pledge to support their specific group interests. The militant Social-Conservative and anti-Semitic parties of the late 1870s fulfilled these requirements. These parties claimed they were a popular and spontaneous development, and aimed at attracting protest voters, especially from among the working population. The Social Democrats, sharing their

[48] Michels, "Die deutsche Sozialdemokratie," pp. 509-517.

right-wing opponents' vehement anticapitalism, antiliberalism, and general opposition to the existing order, also appealed to the lower strata of society. In so far as the Socialists managed to allay the immediate fears of small urban proprietors and succeeded in playing down the more militant articles of their platform, they served as a plausible rallying point for some of the small masters. Political attachments at this stage, however, were not lasting. The extremes did indeed attract disaffected Mittelständler, but at the same time they aroused their suspicions and their fears. The masters turned to the extremist parties because they most clearly represented their principal sentiment at the time—antiliberalism. But when in a more positive mood they hoped to find solutions to their difficulties in what they considered a more orderly and more responsible fashion, they sought alliances elsewhere. Meanwhile their energy was directed toward the building of effective interest-group organizations and toward attaining their limited practical demands for economic and social protection.

NINE

THE ISOLATION OF INTEREST-GROUP POLITICS

Social and Political Background

Economic difficulties and social stress were often experienced by small master artisans in Germany prior to, and during, the nineteenth century. Nevertheless, it was only as a result of the combined force of economic pressures, increased political friction, and an acute sense of insecurity, characteristic of the first phase of the Great Depression between 1873 and 1879, that a considerable portion of the small masters was effectively politicized. They then entered the political scene both as individuals, often newly enfranchised, and as an organized social group. While they were cautiously feeling the ground in this new territory, the political environment in Germany was undergoing profound modifications. It was not just the relative power of the various political elements within the Reich that was changing noticeably but also the character of the political process itself. The transformation took place in the concept of politics as well as in its operation, in the consciousness of those who took part in it as well as in their overt actions. Politics became increasingly identified with the battle between the various economic interest groups within the state. While this struggle had previously raged under the cover of ideological and moral controversies, it gradually came to be carried out more openly and its crudity admitted.[1] Recognition of this

[1] The origins and consequences of the ideological character of the German parliamentary system and the strongly held belief in the role of political parties as representatives of a specific Weltanschauung were first analyzed by Max Weber in his "Politik als Beruf," in *Gesammelte politische Schriften*, pp. 529 ff. For more recent literature see especially Fraenkel, *Deutschland und die westliche Demokratie*, and the bibliography cited in chap. 6, n. 11, above.

aspect of politics in Germany was promoted and accelerated by the growth of the socialist working-class movement on the left, and by the development of powerful interest organizations on the right. The Social-Democratic party was the political agency of one particular social class. It never denied its ties with the trade unions, always the major source of its strength. Other socioeconomic elements, despite their vocal criticism of Social Democracy and their self-righteous protests against the operations of the trade-union movement, did not hesitate to develop their own pressure groups.

Under the unfavorable conditions of the market after 1873, the big industrialists, especially in the iron and textile trades, initiated a campaign urging, first, the retention of the protective tariff and then an increase in its rates. Within a few years they were joined by some of the large landowners who felt compelled to seek governmental and bureaucratic aid against the growing competition of American and Russian grain.[2] Unlike previous economic associations, the Central Association of German Industrialists and the agrarian Union of Tax and Economic Reformers were independent interest-group organizations with specific goals and tactics that went beyond mere fraternization and the expression of collective opinion. Without claiming any official status and with no formal ties with the bureaucracy, they succeeded in exerting influence upon the various political parties, the course of public opinion, and the day-to-day decisions of the authorities. What they clamored for was protection against unfavorable economic conditions and state help to preserve their economic privileges.

This open and aggressive solicitation of state protection by specific economic interest groups was a novelty in German politics. Nevertheless, the new style of public activity met with only meager and ineffectual opposition. In the late

[2] See Lambi, *Free Trade and Protection*, pp. 83-150; and Kaelble, *Industrielle Interessenpolitik*, pp. 3-9; also Hardach, *Die Bedeutung wirtschaftlicher Faktoren*, pp. 86-111; 150-179.

1870s it was only one aspect of the overall tendency in the country to substitute collective action for the discredited liberal individualism. The growth of economic interest groups was a manifestation of this trend and in turn operated to strengthen it.[3] A common front of agrarian and industrial interests had managed to bring about the institution and renewal of protective tariffs. On its own initiative, but as a result of indirect pressure from organized workers, the government had introduced comprehensive social security legislation. Now the state was expected to intervene regularly in the economic process, react to pressures from organized groups, take them into account, and fulfill their just demands.

In Germany, the possibility of using political power to achieve economic objectives was first realized by the most powerful economic groups in the country. The master-artisans' awareness of their potential as an organized force was late to develop, and it was not until the 1880s that they tried to exert their power. The Verein was an old-fashioned occupational organization, vacillating between a corporate tradition and a liberal conception of free association. Its tactics were restricted to formulating petitions, sending out circulars, and otherwise seeking to be heard by state officials. It was not yet set up as a modern pressure group, with clear-cut objectives and a professional staff equipped to work for their achievement. Its ineffectiveness was increased by the diversity of opinions and affiliations of its members. The mixture of liberal political convictions and reactionary economic demands practically paralyzed its leadership. The organization was never certain about its political position, nor was it ever united with regard to its specific social and economic goals.

Consequently, the Verein was saved from becoming a tool of the politicians, but it was also prevented from exerting any effective influence on them. The nature, purpose, and practice of interest-group politics were apparently still un-

[3] H. Rosenberg, *Grosse Depression*, pp. 78-82.

clear to the majority of the organized small masters. In the atmosphere of the late 1870s in Germany, however, the political neutrality of their organization became increasingly difficult to maintain. The prevalent tactics of interpellation, in which local groups presented their demands to the various candidates and promised to support the one who backed them most outspokenly, had proven particularly inadequate in the case of the politically split and geographically dispersed small masters.[4] A fully politicized masters' interest organization, capable of acting with and exerting influence upon the various authorities in the Reich, was evidently necessary. During its yearly meetings, the leadership of the Verein was repeatedly asked by members to state its real political loyalties. Vague promises to support only "friends of the handicraft estate" given by the organization gradually became insufficient even as a tactical device and unsatisfactory for a growing number of politically minded masters. As it was, however, the Verein could not be transformed into an effective interest-group organization and had to be replaced. The years between 1877 and 1881 were spent in hectic and uncertain activity, until the need to enter politics as an organized collectivity became apparent. Many of the masters had for several years experimented as individuals with the available political alternatives only to find themselves further isolated. Under pressure from the continued depression, the battle for their economic interests seemed even more significant. Considering the attitude of the government during the late 1870s and the early 1880s and the generally favorable posture of the major political parties in the Reichstag, interest-group politics clearly began to offer new and more promising ways through which the masters could be heard, acknowledged, and assisted. Then, after years of experimentation and repeated failure, when the masters finally succeeded in establishing a relatively unified

[4] For these tactics see Nipperdey, "Interessenverbände und Parteien," pp. 376-377.

pressure group, they realized that despite sporadic victories, such a policy, too, could further intensify their isolation.

The Master-Artisans' League

At the national congress of master artisans in 1882, the old Verein was replaced by a new organization. The congress in Magdeburg declared the establishment of an Allgemeine deutscher Handwerkerbund (General Union of German Artisans), and took the first step toward changing the character of the master-artisan movement. By a vote of 254 to 54 the assembly passed a resolution calling unequivocally for the legal institution of obligatory guilds, for compulsory masters' examinations, for the introduction of workers' labor books, and for the establishment of handicraft chambers to serve the masters as the supreme organs of their self-administration.[5] The assembly responded to the new government guild law with formal graitude, but with unconcealed suspicion and disappointment. Now that the government had finally taken some steps toward the masters, the masters seemed to have become more determined and were expressing their demands with greater decisiveness and clarity. Political liberalism was no longer an obstacle. Instead of the exclusive big-city representation which was the rule in the previous masters' congresses, the Magdeburg assembly included delegates from many small and medium-sized towns, primarily from Saxony but also from the eastern Prussian provinces and western Germany. It brought together delegates from seventy-five towns and was in effect dominated by the outspoken representatives of the west German Bund and the Provincial Association of Westphalian Artisans, which had both previously been under the influence of von Fechenbach's militant Social Conservatism.

[5] *Verhandlungen zu Magdeburg 1882*, p. 35; *KZ*, June 3, 1882; and Schulthess, *Europäischer Geschichtskalender*, May 30 and June 1, 1882.

The "Magdeburg resolutions," as they were later called, opened with a declaration of purpose: "The recently introduced legal regulations of the guild system, and the standard guild statute published thereafter cannot lead the German Artisans' Congress to stop its activity for the revision of the German industrial legislation. It declares that only a total revision of the Reich's industrial law will be of any practical assistance [to its members]."[6] Thus, the master artisans in their new interest organization finally diverged from the conciliatory position of the big-city, liberal leadership of the old Verein. The economic hardships of the first wave of the depression, the virulent antiliberal campaign, and the atmosphere of insecurity and political bitterness had left their mark.

The passage of the Magdeburg resolutions was an important victory for the conservative forces within the master-artisans' movement. It was, however, only a partial one. The Berlin leadership still proved to be powerful and influential, enjoying the support of the large Saxonian delegation, which voted for the conservative resolutions but mistrusted the reactionary, mostly Catholic representatives from western Germany. The Bavarians, suspicious of the west German connections with von Fechenbach, remained loyal to the old leadership for a time. Thus the central office of the new Bund remained in Berlin, and the newly elected executive committee was composed of five master artisans, all residents of the capital. Two of the veteran artisan leaders, however, master-carpenter Brandes and the Obermeister-tailor Koeppen, declined reelection. They apparently realized that their position within the organization, with its new name and a new power alignment, was irrecoverably lost. In order to avoid an open rift they accepted nomination as honorary presidents of the new Bund but did not participate in its activities.[7]

[6] *Verhandlungen zu Magdeburg 1882*, p. 46.
[7] Ibid., pp. 35-36.

At the following congress in Hanover the break between the Bund and the old Verein passed from the ideological to the organizational level. The yearly report of the Verein executive committee revealed its complete ineffectiveness, and the complaints of the Berlin leaders that "the worst enemy of a unified masters' organization is the prevalence of discord, hair splitting, and petty jealousy among them," did not help to endear them to their colleagues.[8] The seat of the executive committee was moved from Berlin to Cologne, and five militant master artisans from Hanover, Dortmund, and Cologne were elected to it. The Saxonian masters were poorly represented at that congress, while the west Germans further increased their strength. The most crucial vote was cast by the Bavarians, who were delighted to observe the declining influence of von Fechenbach on the west German masters, and apparently decided this time to throw their weight to them. The following year the seat of the new Bund was moved once again, this time to Munich, where it stayed until the end of the century. The Bavarian masters openly took upon themselves the leadership of the organization.

The Bund was a loose association of local and provincial organizations, with membership open to individuals as well as to organized groups. Its national executive committee was strengthened by representatives of the various provincial branches, and the federal character of the organization was stressed. In the months between the annual general assemblies there was little or no cooperation among the various regional divisions, which had their own executive committees and their own yearly congresses. Each of them gradually developed its own specific character. The Bund concentrated its efforts on pressing the legislatures to pass additional measures providing social and economic protection for small master artisans. It had none of the fraternity spirit of the old guilds, and its local branches were based on a

[8] *Verhandlungen zu Hannover 1883*, p. 7.

mixed membership of artisans from various trades, working together for common political ends.

During the 1880s the size of the Bund membership ranged between forty and fifty thousand, drawn mainly from Bavaria, the Rhineland, Westphalia, and later also from parts of southwestern Germany.[9] Its official goal was rather awkwardly but aggressively defined as "the protection and the advancement of the social, political, and economic interests of the artisans by legally bringing about compulsory measures, namely the introduction of corporative bodies for the removal of the conditions of indecent subjugation and exploitation of the members of this estate by the privileged ruling classes."[10]

The strongest political power behind the master-artisan Bund was the Catholic-Center party, although no official tie between them was ever acknowledged. The Center party, no longer oppositionist, was gradually evolving its own social-reform program mainly under the influence of its most prominent social thinker, Franz Hitze. In 1877 Georg von Hertling could still argue in the name of the Center-party majority that "it was impossible to hope that one could bring back to life old-fashioned modes of production through legal and police measures."[11] But in 1880, Hitze in his major theoretical work, *Capital and Labor and the Reorganization of Society*, recommended the establishment of "estate socialism," and the organization of the handicraft estate in compulsory guilds absorbing "the entire social life of the craftsmen."[12] Meanwhile the party also changed its electoral orientation. During the 1880s, it concentrated on attracting worker, peasants, and artisans, and played a crucial role in the passage of Bismarck's social insurance legislation. It

[9] The figures were derived from reports made by the Bund at its annual meetings and from various newspaper articles.

[10] From the Provisorisches Statut accepted by the master-artisans' congress in Hanover, 1883: *Verhandlungen zu Hannover 1883*, pp. 1; 20-24.

[11] Von Hertling, *Erinnerungen*, p. 323.

[12] Hitze, *Kapital und Arbeit*, p. 474.

brought into its parliamentary fraction a number of small master artisans, and initiated and supported numerous amendments to the Reich's industrial legislation aimed at strengthening the guilds and fortifying the privileged position of the masters within them.[13]

There are no figures on the ratio of Catholics to Protestants within the Bund, nor is there any precise indication of how much actual support Catholic small masters gave the Center-party candidates. By 1887 the Center parliamentary group included three master artisans, Georg Biehl from Munich, Jacob Euler from Bernsberg, and Carl Metzner from Neustadt in Silesia. All three played a major role in the decisions made by the Bund; Biehl was for many years president of the organization. The 1885 general congress of the Bund passed a resolution calling on master artisans to vote only for candidates who explicitly promised to work for the advancement of the handicraft estate.[14] This was an old formula borrowed from the defunct Verein. In the political context of the years between 1881 and 1890, however, its implications were far clearer than they had been during the preceding four years of political instability. During most of the eighties, the formula meant in effect votes for the Conservative party from the northern Protestant masters, and for the Center party from the Catholics.

The specifically southern and Catholic nature of the Bund made it particularly sensitive to developments in Austria. In March of 1883, the Austrian Reichsrat made the examination of master artisans compulsory in a number of handicraft trades, and instituted legal measures providing for the organization of obligatory corporations of artisans.[15] Official

[13] See the pamphlet first published in 1903 by the Catholic Volksverein entitled *Was hat das Zentrum für die Handwerker getan.*

[14] The resolution adopted at the 1885 Frankfurt congress of the Bund was passed again unchanged at the 1886 conference. See *Verhandlungen zu Kösen 1886*, p. 63.

[15] See the report on guild reform in Austria in the address of V. Philipovich of Vienna at the VSP conference, *Schriften* 76 (1898): 72 ff.; and the summary in "Gewerbegesetzgebung," *HBS*, 4th ed.; also

examinations for master artisans had been the major demand of the Austrian masters' movement for years. In that economically backward country the masters were still primarily preoccupied with preventing the spread of "Pfuschertum," i.e., the practice of handicraft trades by people trained in unconventional ways, newcomers to the towns, and Jews. The introduction of large-scale industry, which eventually became the most pressing problem of the organized masters in Germany, still hardly concerned their Austrian colleagues. It was also of relatively minor significance for the southern German masters.

But the masters' examinations caused immense administrative confusion in Austria. A strict definition of the various handicraft trades was necessary in order to prevent masters in one occupation from infringing on the rights of masters in others, but this was well-nigh impossible, even at Austria's stage of industrial development in the 1880s. The masters themselves, no doubt, realized the difficulties inherent in the operation of the system. Their insistence upon it can be understood only if it is kept in mind that the examinations were conceived of by them not as an economic device but as an instrument for controlling the social composition of their group. It was designed to restrict the overall number of master artisans in the country, and admit into the ranks only those with proper traditional vocational training who had the cultural and moral superiority presumably acquired through such training.

The success of the master-artisan movement in Austria naturally impressed the leaders of its German counterpart, especially in Bavaria. Gradually the demand for obligatory masters' examination as a prerequisite for the practice of all handicraft occupations became the main article of reform in the program of the German Bund. As the interest organization was not based on occupational, but on local and

H. Rosenberg, *Grosse Depression*, pp. 227-252, on the character of Austrian social policy, and Waentig, *Mittelstandspolitik*, on the master-artisan movement.

regional divisions, it was all the more susceptible to plans that applied to the master artisans as a specific sociocultural unit, rather than as an agglomeration of craftsmen from various, distinct handicraft trades. The Bund's emphasis on the issue of the Befähigungsnachweis, and its relative indifference to the issue of the guilds served in the end to deepen the rift between the Catholic masters from the industrially backward southern regions and their colleagues from the more industrialized northern urban centers.

The Reorganization of the Guild Movement

While the leaders of the new Handwerkerbund were busily reconstructing the master-artisan interest organization in the mixed image of social Catholicism and reactionary Protestant social conservatism, the master artisans in Berlin took the lead in building up an artisan movement around the renovated institution of the guild. According to the 1881 revision of the industrial law, the guilds, recognized and encouraged by it, were to foster the artisans' "communal spirit" and protect their "industrial interests."[16] The law conceived of the new guilds as institutions in which masters and journeymen would cooperate, but in practice they were also to serve as bureaucratic instruments of control over masters and men alike. The guilds were not free associations; they were subject to the provisions of federal industrial legislation, and not of the Combination Act. Defined by law, their goals were not a matter for debate among the members. Active involvement in politics was strictly forbidden and remained outside the scope of these organizations. They were structured on an occupational basis, were legally open to all masters regardless of belief or affiliation, and were intended by the law merely to organize the men according to their crafts, and to supervise their vocational education as well as the order and morality of their conduct.

In spite of these legal restrictions, the master-artisans'

[16] *Reichsgesetzblatt*, 1881, no. 19, article 97.

leadership in Berlin immediately perceived the organizational and political potential of the guilds and decided to use them as the basis for a new master-artisan interest organization. They wished to benefit from a corporate legal status, and at the same time transform the guilds into a base for a modern interest group pressing the government for further support and protection. Their first efforts were aimed at enlarging the number and increasing the power of the local guilds themselves. In 1880 there were fifty-seven guilds in Berlin. By 1883 their number had risen to sixty-nine, and they included nearly one-half of all small employers in town. Some of the old guilds revised their statutes to fit in with the new law and the recommendations of the government, and forty-four of them combined into a local guild association.[17] An executive committee laid out a list of principles for the national movement, contacted guild committees in over one hundred towns, and eventually called a national guild congress, claiming to represent some one hundred fifty thousand master artisans from all parts of the country.[18] Taking advantage of new legislation, a Central Ausschuss der Vereinigten Innungsverbände Deutschlands (Central Committee of the United Guild Associations of Germany) was established in Berlin in 1885 as the central institution of a new nationwide master-artisan organization. The declared aim of the Central Committee was to protect the interests of the small master artisans within their corporate organization. But in addition to the traditional prom-

[17] *Statistisches Jahrbuch der Stadt Berlin* 8 (1880): 149; *Die Bevölkerungs- und Wohnungsaufnahme*, 1885, part 1, p. 84. Statistics on this matter, however, were very inaccurate. Reports in the statistical yearbook of the city of Berlin do not correspond exactly with the lists given in the report of the special committee investigating the population and living conditions of the city. Nor do these two reports correspond with the data given by Thilo Hampke in the *Bayerische Handelszeitung*, September 14, 1895.

[18] See *KZ*, June 16, 1885; Böttger, *Das Programm der Handwerker*, pp. 139 ff.; T. Hampke, *Der Befähigungsnachweis*, pp. 59 ff.; and the entry "Handwerk" in *HBS*, 3rd ed.

ises to see to the proper training of apprentices and provide social security for the members, the Central Committee also announced its intention of working for further revisions of industrial legislation. The committee planned to solicit government help in strengthening the power of the guilds and transforming them into effective self-administrating bodies.

Unlike the Bavaria-centered Bund, the Central Committee in the Reich capital, continuously in contact with federal bureaucratic authorities, hoped to become an advisory body regularly participating in the decision-making process of the government in matters of handicraft legislation and administration. In the absence of handicraft chambers, the Central Committee hoped to become an equivalent semiofficial organization. The guilds were to aid in rebuilding a community of interests among the masters, enabling them to cooperate for the preservation of their status and the improvement of their economic conditions. They were designed to assist the small producers in times of rapid and widespread industrialization, strengthen their self-confidence, and increase their ability as individual producers to withstand the growing competition of mechanized big business. For many small master artisans the guilds were to play a role similar to that assigned to cooperative associations in the plans of liberal social reformers. They were not, however, organized as cooperative associations, even though they did occasionally develop similar characteristics. Indeed, they were often promoted as an antidote to the various liberal cooperative schemes. Within the guild the economic independence of the individual small master artisan was usually left intact. The organization was meant only to serve him in indirect ways by raising his spirits and improving his vocational and commercial opportunities. In some cases it also provided social security in times of personal need.

The Central Guild Committee, however, had further plans. As a pressure organization it intended to gain government support for its organizational efforts, but above all it intended to work for the enactment of laws and regulations that would mobilize government authority for the protection of small masters against the competition of modern, capitalist big business. It expressed the masters' growing concern with the ongoing process of economic and social modernization, eventually joining the campaign for state intervention in the economy and for state support for traditional socioeconomic groups.

In the Reichstag it was the Conservative party that worked actively for a reform of the Reich industrial law, striving to strengthen the position of the guilds. In the winter of 1884, the Reichstag finally passed the Conservative amendment to the famous article 100e, giving local authorities the option of restricting to guild members the education and employment of apprentices.[19] The amendment, which with slightly different wording had aroused a storm of protest in the Reichstag only three years earlier, now passed virtually without debate and proved particularly timely for the development of the guild movement. It gave a great momentum to the efforts of the master artisans in Berlin, and appeared to indicate the realism of their approach and justify their plan to maintain continuous pressure on the legislature. Indeed, the affinity between the policies of the Berlin-led masters' movement and the Conservative party became increasingly evident. The two appeared to work for the same goals and to employ the same tactics. Leaving behind the militancy of the transition period between 1879 and 1884, the masters now drew closer to the established conservative forces.

The ties between the Conservatives and the Berlin guild movement were made quite explicit during the 1885 Guilds Congress. Cautious that it remain within the legal restrictions prohibiting the guilds from taking part in politics, and true to the tradition of the masters' movement in Berlin, the congress avoided any open admission of sympathy for the Conservative party as such, but did pass a resolution expressing its gratitude to the Conservative Reichstag mem-

[19] *Reichsgesetzblatt*, 1884, no. 34.

ber Ackermann for his "tireless efforts on behalf of the artisans."[20] During the 1870s the preservation of political neutrality was crucial for the existence of the politically heterogeneous master-artisan movement. In the early eighties, this apparent neutrality had become no more than a tactical device. In order to present a powerful front, the guild movement needed as many followers as it could possibly recruit, and it was careful not to alienate the masters who were usually politically to the right of, but occasionally politically to the left of, the official Conservative party. The guild movement relied on the policies of the Conservatives in the Reichstag, and generally welcomed them with satisfaction. It nevertheless preserved its independence in order to be able to put further pressure on the Conservatives, and if possible on other political parties, to take ideologically more radical positions, and politically more effective measures with respect to the artisans' specific demands.

The Conservative party itself was split on the issue of the guilds, but managed to arrive at a formal consensus. The party was to work indirectly for the eventual institution of obligatory guilds by gradually strengthening the vocational corporations within the framework of existing laws.[21] The *Kreuzzeitung*, representing the extreme Social-Conservative wing among the Conservatives, frequently pointed out the persistence of liberalism among the small masters, reproaching not only the artisans themselves, but also the official leadership of the Conservative party. Here was an impressive bloc of potential voters, the *Kreuzzeitung* believed, which could easily be won over to political conservatism if greater energy were only applied to the problem. In its articles the influential conservative paper attempted to compensate for the occasional faltering of the official Conserva-

[20] *KZ*, June 16, 1885; for the Conservatives' reaction to the first Innungstag see *KZ*, June 20, 1885.

[21] See the detailed discussion in Stock, *Wirtschafts- und sozialpolitische Bestrebungen*, pp. 16-20; 57-75.

tive leadership.[22] Its editorial of June 20, 1885 read as follows: "Let us repeat: the German master artisans are on the right track. If they continue in this direction their efforts will not be in vain. Not only our sympathy, but our full cooperation to the limits of our power, will be given to them because their goals are ours."[23] It is evident that a growing number of Protestant master artisans all over Germany tended to support the Deutschkonservative Partei in national and local elections. They were united by the demand for social protection and state help, and a common enmity toward liberalism.

During the 1880s, the shift in the master-artisans' orientation even reached parts of southwestern Germany, where the artisans' political liberalism was well known for its intensity and consistency. In 1884, several new Handwerkervereine were established in the main cities of Baden. They immediately embarked on a public campaign for the revision of state industrial regulations and of the Reich industrial law, and demanded both the institution of obligatory guilds and the introduction of compulsory masters' examinations. They sought legal help in their competition with the Pfuscher on the one hand and big industry on the other. A memorandum the Heidelberg Masters' Association sent the local Conservative candidate demanded above all the extension of the guilds' legal authority. Apparently greatly disturbed by the growth of trade unionism in their region, the masters sought control over the activity of journeymen and apprentices.[24] The new conservative artisans' association in Heidelberg quickly made up in intensity what it lacked in age and experience. In 1886 it published a pamphlet entitled *Industrial Freedom and the Guilds*, which harped on all the well-known conservative themes, com-

[22] *KZ*, July 26, 1884; June 20, 1885; September 9, 1886; August 18, 1887; and, later, April 21, 1895.

[23] *KZ*, June 20, 1885.

[24] See *Denkschrift zu handen des Herrn Reichstagsabgeordneten Metzner, Januar 1885* (Badisches Generallandesarchiv 236/9652).

bining the master-artisans' vehement anticapitalism, their general antiliberalism, and their desire for the revival of the old hierarchical social system. It revealed the growing anti-Semitism among them and their open hostility toward Social Democracy.[25]

By the mid-1880s, the Catholic masters in southwestern Germany had already been attached to the Catholic-Center party for some time while the Protestants were moving in the direction of the Conservative party. The emerging pattern of allegiance among the small master artisans in the various regions of Germany was similar. Everywhere, in increasing numbers although in various degrees and never totally, they came to support the dominant conservative forces in Germany. This fact was clearly indicated by the character of the new master-artisans' interest organizations. While they attempted to preserve a façade of political neutrality, they came to be more and more dependent on the Center party in the south and on the Conservatives in the north. The situation in the mixed areas was naturally more complex. Catholic masters tended to concentrate in the local units of the Bund, and Protestants preferred to establish local branches of the Guild Association. This apparent division along the lines of religious affiliation and political allegiance was never absolute, but during the 1880s it became increasingly conspicuous in various parts of the country.

The Scope and Composition of the Guilds

In the early 1880s the new guilds became the main organizational units of the master artisans in Germany. They were the object of endless public discussion, the subject of numerous legal provisions and amendments, and the building blocks of the masters' major interest-group organization. They were the focus for the master-artisans' hope for com-

[25] *Gewerbefreiheit und Innungen*, published by the Vorstand des Heidelberger Handwerkervereins.

munal rejuvenation and individual prosperity. In the late 1870s there were about 6,000 guilds in various parts of the country, but most of them were small and of little practical significance. They grew rapidly during the 1880s, and by 1888 the reactivated guild movement could claim to represent as many as 10,000 guilds and over 300,000 members.[26] The numbers for those years are probably somewhat exaggerated. For the following decade, however, relatively precise information on the scope and composition of the guild movement is available. In 1895 there were 10,223 guilds in Germany with a membership of 321,219. Of these, 7,823 guilds operated in Prussia, especially in the eastern provinces, encompassing over two-thirds of the total membership. In proportion to the population, guild membership was greatest in Mecklenburg-Schwering (5,358 members in 173 guilds), in Hamburg (4,558 members in 28 guilds), in Bremen (1,169 members in 23 guilds), and in Saxony (55,574 members in 1,264 guilds). The various Thuringian states were moderately represented, while the guilds in the southern German states were distinctly less successful. By 1895 there were only 156 guilds in Bavaria with 11,144 members, 28 in Württemberg with 1,112 members, 31 in Baden with 1,063 members, and 26 in Hesse with only 996 members.[27]

Following the lead of the Berlin masters, the guild movement gradually developed a double system of centralization. Members of various craft guilds were represented by central guild committees at the local level, while they combined on a separate occupational (Fach) basis nationally. Despite this duplicate organizational structure, or perhaps because of it, many guilds remained unaffiliated either locally or occu-

[26] These figures were given in a report to the second guilds congress in Berlin, by master-carpenter Brandes. See the *Verhandlungen zu Berlin 1888*; also *KZ*, September 12, 1888.

[27] Stieda, "Die Innungsenquete," pp. 12 ff. The findings of the statistical survey of 1895 and of a variety of studies on this problem are summarized in Rudolf Graetzer's article, "Zur Statistik der deutschen Innungen."

pationally. By 1894, only 45 of the 68 craft guilds in Berlin combined to form the local Guild Committee. In Hamburg 7 out of 28 guilds remained outside the local organization, in Munich 10 out of 22, and in Breslau as many as 35 out of 61. In a group of 29 large cities including Leipzig, Dresden, Hanover, Danzig, and Dortmund, only 455 of the 650 guilds were members of the local Guild Committees, representing 44,000 of the total of 60,000 guild members.[28] On the national occupational level as well, the central organizations had managed by 1893 to organize only 40 percent of the guilds with about 40 percent of the total guild membership.[29] Occasionally, rivalries between personalities or among guilds representing the same craft in the same region were the cause of this limited success of the masters' central organizations. More often, however, local guilds remained unaffiliated out of sheer apathy or because their membership did not approve of the general social and political tone of the central bodies.

Although the new guilds in the large urban centers of Germany constituted a mere 6 percent of the total number of guilds in the country, they soon became the center of the entire movement. The urban guilds were on the average much larger than those in rural districts or small towns, and their efforts were generally more persistent and effective. By 1892 as much as 22 percent of the guild membership in Germany resided in 42 of the large cities and less than 10 percent in rural areas. On the whole, therefore, the movement had a distinctly urban character. This was due to a variety of reasons—historical, social, and economic. In the Middle Ages, guilds were restricted by law to the towns. Even when regulations were relaxed during the eighteenth century, the guilds never spread to the rural regions of Germany in large numbers. Thus, the rural master artisans lacked the historical memory and tradition of the guild sys-

28 *Statistisches Jahrbuch deutscher Städte* 4 (1894): 280; 283-284.
29 Ibid. 5 (1896): 282-283.

tem and were consequently far less responsive to the call for its reconstruction. Moreover, the geographical dispersal of masters of the same craft among small agricultural communities made it virtually impossible for them to create unified occupational associations. The guild form had a special attraction for master employers, its main official function being the supervision of vocational training and the regulation of labor relations. Since over two-thirds of the rural masters were individual self-employed men, they had little or no incentive to join the movement.[30]

All centrally organized craft guilds had several characteristics in common. At both the local and national levels they represented above all the urban master artisans engaged primarily in traditional crafts. The Central Guild Committee in Berlin was composed of masters from seventeen different crafts, among them a baker, a cooper, a blacksmith, a chimney sweep, a roofer, a turner, a glazier, a basket maker, a furrier, a painter, a saddler, a locksmith, a paver, a cartwright, a tailor, a shoemaker, and a carpenter—all masters of typical traditional crafts. These were also the trades organized on a vocational basis in the national craft leagues, along with those of the butchers, the plumbers, the dyers, the upholsterers, the wig makers, the barbers, the building masters, and the bookbinders. By the end of 1893 the United Leagues encompassed 4,266 guilds and 136,967 members—all masters of traditional crafts.[31] The central organiza-

[30] The feasibility of extending the guild movement into the rural areas of Germany was one of the major questions the 1895 Innungsenquete was designed to answer. Characteristically, in spite of the fact that the statistical results made it quite evident that vocational guilds in rural areas were bound to be too small to be effective, the government proceeded to impose a guild system on the entire country, allowing for the establishment of mixed guilds, that is, guilds of master artisans from a variety of crafts. See the discussion in P. Voigt, "Die Hauptergebnisse," pp. 1,017 ff.; and the text of the *Handwerkergesetz* in the *Reichsgesetzblatt*, 1897, no. 37, pp. 663-706.

[31] *Statistisches Jahrbuch deutscher Städte* 5 (1896): 283.

tions of these craft leagues were all located in Germany's large cities, eighteen of them in Berlin itself, two in Leipzig, and one each in Hamburg, Breslau, Magdeburg, Bremen, and Lübeck. In the annual national masters' congresses these same crafts were always strongly represented, and undoubtedly the proportion of organized masters in them was higher than in the more modern and more mechanized trades. Thus, in Berlin, where our data for the 1880s are relatively precise, all the copper- and tinsmiths in town were members of their respective guilds. By then, over half the smiths, the lace makers, the bookbinders, the coopers, the basket makers, and the bakers were also members of their respective craft guilds, and in the populous trades of shoemaking and carpentry between a quarter and a third of all the craft masters were guild members.[32]

More questions remain to be answered: what was the socioeconomic composition of the urban guilds, and where can their members be located on the ladder of social position and economic prosperity in comparison with unorganized masters? There are no general answers to these questions. The well-being of the guild masters was naturally dependent on the overall conditions in their particular craft in a specific location. In certain crafts, such as shoemaking for instance, numerous individual self-employed masters were included as members of the local guilds. In others, even large-scale entrepreneurs chose to become guild members. On the whole, however, guild members constituted the middle stratum of the independent master-artisan population, including primarily men who owned small traditional handicraft workshops and worked in them with the help of two or three journeymen.

A survey of guild masters in Berlin in 1885 revealed that each employed on the average 3.0 workers, while the general average among the masters outside the guilds was 1.6. Of the guild members 57 percent were master

[32] *Die Bevölkerungs- und Wohnungsaufnahme*, 1885, part 1, p. 84.

employers, while only 52 percent of the total number of masters in Berlin employed hired hands.[33] The general picture everywhere in Germany was similar. For every guild master carpenter in Posen in 1894 there were 2 workers and 1.3 apprentices, while for every nonguild master there were only 1.6 workers and 0.9 apprentices.[34] In Berlin the number of workers per master mason in the local guild was 26.8. For the masters outside the guild the number was only 11.4. In tailoring, generally a much poorer trade, the number of workers per guild master was 1.8, while for others it was only 0.9. Among the coopers in the guild the number was 1.4 and outside 0.3.[35] It is important to note, however, that a few truly large-scale masters in a guild could greatly affect these calculations. They normally also occupied positions of power within the guilds and influenced their character considerably. In Leipzig, for example, nine of the eleven large-scale master bookbinders in town were members of the local guild. Four of them were members of its executive committee, employing among them some 400 workers.[36]

A more general view of the social composition of the guilds can be obtained from the data collected by the Prussian Bureau of Statistics for 1900.[37] Although the 1897 guild law had by then been in operation for over two years, it had had only a limited effect on the general composition and character of the guilds, and the data for 1900 probably still reflect quite accurately their nature during the previous decade. In 1900, 50 percent of the Prussian handicraft masters were members of local guilds, employing 73 percent of all journeymen in the handicraft trades and 65 percent of

[33] Ibid., pp. 84-85.

[34] K. Hampke, "Tischlergewerbe in Posen," *Schriften* 62 (1895): 90.

[35] Calculated from the data in *Die Bevölkerungs- und Wohnungsaufnahme*, 1885, part 1, p. 84.

[36] Friedrich Goesch and Moritz Hecht, "Die Buchbinderei in Leipzig," *Schriften* 66 (1896): 334-335.

[37] These results were reprinted in the *Erhebung über die Wirkung des Handwerkergesetzes*, p. 27.

the apprentices. Most striking was the situation in rural areas, where the organized masters normally resided in a few provincial urban centers but employed among them most of the hired workers in the crafts. In Hesse-Nassau only 25 percent of the master population were guild members, employing 67 percent of the journeymen. In Schleswig-Holstein, the 47 percent of the masters who were members of guilds employed as many as 94 percent of all workers in the crafts. This pattern was repeated in other Prussian provinces with the exception of Pomerania and Saxony.

The guilds' concern with labor relations made them particularly attractive to master employers, and tended to affect their composition. In the case of master builders and bakers, for instance, the guild leagues operated openly as employers' associations, issuing labor books to their journeymen and carrying on an organized resistance to the Social-Democratic trade-union movement.[38] In Hamburg only two of the guilds, those of the notoriously impoverished tailors and shoemakers, had a considerable number of individual self-employed masters. In 1887, additional workers were employed by all but 1 of the 156 members of the bakers' guild in Hamburg, all but 6 of the 105 members of the blacksmiths' guild, all but 14 of the 346 master butchers.[39] Yet in Hamburg as a whole, over one-half the total number of industrial workshops were owned by individual self-employed men. In 1882 the percentage of individual masters in Hamburg was as high as 11 among the bakers, 15 among the blacksmiths, and 23 among the butchers.[40]

[38] On the master-builders' organizations see Franz Habersbrunner, *Die Lohn- Arbeits- und Organisationsverhältnisse im deutschen Baugewerbe*, pp. 86 ff.; also the various speeches in the *Protokoll über die Verhandlungen Innungsverbandes Baugewerksmeister zu Hannover 1893*. On the character of the bakers' organizations see the remarks in Eduard Lehwetz, "Das Bäckergewerbe in Berlin," *Schriften* 68 (1896): 176 ff.

[39] *Jahresbericht der Hamburgerischen Gewerbekammer für 1887-89*, p. 57.

[40] *St.d.R.* 6, part 2, pp. 30 ff.

The composition of the guilds in Hamburg and Berlin, however, is only characteristic of guilds in the large and highly industrialized urban centers. In the less industrialized areas of Germany, as for example in the eastern Prussian provinces, the small individual masters often played a much greater role in the guilds, giving them a different social and political coloring. At the national level the guilds did not represent the poorest of the master artisans but rather the middle stratum. It was a movement composed of men undergoing a great deal of social and economic stress, who saw themselves as being under constant threat, but were still for the time being holding on to relatively comfortable positions.

Influence and Limitations

All the available information suggests that what was known as the German Handwerkerbewegung during the Great Depression was a movement of urban master artisans from traditional crafts. By 1895 close to three hundred thousand men were organized in occupational guilds. It was estimated at that time by contemporary scholars, politicians, and leaders of the master-artisans' movement themselves, that these constituted no more than 10 percent of the German handicraft masters.[41] This estimate, however, was challenged convincingly by Paul Voigt in the summarizing paper of the VSP project on the conditions of the handicrafts in Germany, and does not stand up to careful scrutiny.[42] According to 1895 industrial statistics, there were 3 million small independent producers in Germany. The number quoted for the guild membership at the same period is in

[41] See Böttger, *Das Programm der Handwerker*, pp. 181 ff.; Stieda, "Die Innungsenquete," p. 9; see also von Boettichers' speech in the *Steno. Berichte*, January 14, 1895; and the polemics against him in the masters' congress: *Protokoll über die Verhandlungen zu Halle 1895*, p. 23.

[42] Voigt, "Das deutsche Handwerk," pp. 663-664.

fact 10 percent of this total. However, not all of these 3 million men were eligible for membership in masters' guilds. Only 2 million were engaged in mining, industry, and building, the categories that guild masters could be drawn from. Of these, 57 percent were individual self-employed masters, and over half resided in rural areas. Thus it appears that from an estimated total of between six and eight hundred thousand urban masters in traditional crafts in Germany at that time guild members constituted between one-third and one-half.[43] Even the central national guild leagues appear to have included closer to 20 than to 10 percent of their potential membership.

Moreover, in attempting to evaluate the significance of the guild movement among the small master artisans, it is crucial to see it in a proper historical context. At the time when the master-artisans' central guild organization could claim a membership of about 300,000 men, the newly created Bund der Landwirte had a membership of just over 160,000. There were then over 5 million owners of farms with less than twenty hectares in Germany, compared with the 2 million small independent industrial workshop owners.[44] The Central Guild Committee in Berlin was no less representative of the small traditional master craftsmen than the Bund der Landwirte leadership was of the German peasantry. Indeed, all indications suggest that the Guild Committee operated with less direct influence from above and from outside, and that it represented a larger fraction of its grass-roots base. It can thus justly be considered the best-organized representative of urban traditional master artisans in Germany during the last two decades of the nineteenth century.

The guild movement, however, was unable to take full advantage of its size; even the occasional government concessions during the 1880s in the area of handicraft legislation were not a direct outcome of its activity. Several fac-

[43] *St.d.R.* 119, pp. 9* ff.; 16* ff.

[44] Puhle, *Agrarische Interessenpolitik*, pp. 37-38; 336. Also *St.d.R.* 119, p. 16*.

tors contributed to the ineffectiveness of the movement at that time, first and foremost the character of the organization itself. Leaning heavily on the corporate tradition of the old guilds, and striving to emulate the semiofficial chambers of industry and commerce, the Central Guild Committee rarely took the initiative in presenting the small masters' demands; when it did, it was always careful to remain within the accepted, traditional mode of operation characteristic of the chambers. Limited by law to nonpolitical activity and committed to an ideology of law and order, it made continual efforts to accommodate itself to the realities of political life in the Reich and to the restrictions imposed by the authorities. Throughout the 1880s it attempted to make the most of the 1881 guild law, and despite pressure from its membership confined itself to matters of detail rather than issues of principle. In fact, it accepted the limitations on any fundamental reform of industrial legislation imposed by the still influential liberal parties and their champions in the central bureaucracy. This conciliatory stand, however, did not make the Central Guild Committee a party to high ranking consultations on matters pertaining to the guilds. It was rarely consulted by bureaucrats and had only marginal influence on the relevant decisions of the various parties. Even the Deutschkonservative Reichstag delegation remained throughout the decade without a single representative of the master-artisans' movement.

The cautious line of the Guild Committee and its efforts to preserve its political independence deprived the movement of a number of potentially powerful devices. At the same time, other interest-group organizations developed new tactics and were able to influence the government by mobilizing public opinion and especially by concluding alliances with the major political parties.[45] Naturally, political support was far more easily obtained by powerful interest organizations, such as those representing the agrarians and

[45] Puhle, *Agrarische Interessenpolitik*, pp. 293-294. See also Puhle's "Parlament, Parteien und Interessenverbände," pp. 344-349.

the big industrialists, than by an organization of relatively poor men, hampered by legal restrictions and the heterogeneity of its membership. For both the semicorporate guild organization and the free masters' Bund a complete identification with one of the central parties in the Reich could mean a loss of influence and the ability to maneuver. Neutrality, however, had no better result, eventually leading to the political isolation of these organizations and to an accentuation of their members' sense of helplessness and impotence.

During the 1880s the Conservatives were little affected by the position of the organized masters and followed their own policy on matters of handicraft legislation. Their efforts to gain the support of the small artisans did not as yet force them to yield to the pressure of the masters' organizations. Equally unaffected were the National Liberals, whose main electoral efforts throughout the period were directed at the individual master. Under these circumstances the leadership of the masters' organizations was often reduced to total inaction, and repeatedly taken by surprise at the turn of events. It failed to influence the bureaucracy directly, and lost the chance to force it to action indirectly.

The existence of two rival organizations of masters further weakened their effectiveness, underlining the internal disagreements among the masters and making it easier for the authorities to ignore their demands. The Bund and the Central Guild Committee were originally hostile bodies. The Berlin leadership of the old artisans' Verein, ousted from the Bund for its moderate position, stood at the center of the guild movement. The incompatibility of the two organizations was further accentuated by their different institutional character. While the Bund was organized on a regional basis, the guild movement was organized on an occupational basis. The conflict between them took on a pattern familiar from the history of the working-class movement, in which regional organizations normally represent the militant position, and vocational organizations the moderate one.

Nevertheless, the two movements managed to coexist peacefully for some time despite their structural and ideological differences. As the memory of the first wave of the depression slowly receded, and as the second downward trend was gradually reversed around 1886, the differences between the master-artisans' organizations lost much of their poignancy.

The artisans' movement enjoyed several years of quiet activity, turning its attention inward and concentrating on the development of its organizations. By the end of the decade, however, the real source of its weakness gradually became evident. The Bund was unable to break out of its regional boundaries, and its growing reliance on the Center party deprived it of national significance. The guild movement, on the other hand, was collapsing from the apathy of its members, their lack of administrative and organizational ability, and inadequate financial resources. The local guilds hardly ever fulfilled their assigned tasks, and members' participation in their activities must have been very limited indeed. In 42 large cities in Germany, studied in 1892, a total of over 650 guilds operated fewer than 150 vocational schools, and only 66 arbitration courts. Even in Berlin, the center of the guild movement, only two-thirds of the guilds in 1892 offered any kind of social insurance to their members. In Cologne, 2 insurance schemes supported 75 masters. Only 45,000 men participated in over 280 separate guild insurance schemes in the large German towns.[46] On the average these social security institutions had 165 members and could be of only marginal economic significance. The "free guilds movement," as it was occasionally called, had little to show in terms of practical results.

Apparently membership in the guilds was often only a formal matter, and regional and national ties among the guilds were normally loose and ineffective. Thus, the activists in the Central Guild Committee in Berlin presided over a nominally large, but practically weak organization, whose

[46] *Statistisches Jahrbuch deutscher Städte* 4 (1894): 283.

members could not even be moved to act on matters clearly pertaining to their personal social security and were all but impossible to mobilize for more general and far-reaching reforms.

Eventually, the master-artisans' interest-group activity during the 1880s only aggravated their political isolation and increased their dependence on the bureaucracy. On the whole this activity exacerbated their sense of futility and frustration. Neither active political involvement nor passive acceptance of government policies seemed to bear fruit. Limited social and educational efforts were no more effective. With the third wave of the Great Depression, beginning in 1890, the inadequacy and inefficacy of the masters' organized activity became more and more obvious. The masters were once again severely hit by falling prices and reduced economic activity, and their political efforts during the preceding decade appeared of little consequence. The movement was forced into a new phase of militancy, reflecting both the anxiety of the small masters and the general social and political mood of the country.

TEN

POLITICAL HOMELESSNESS

Adjustment to Political Change

Toward 1890 the Bismarckian empire entered a period of relative internal peace, and a semblance of cooperation among the hostile elements within it seemed to have developed. In 1887 the two main rivals of the previous decade, the Prussian Conservatives and the National Liberals, reached a temporary political alliance. Bismarck led them with a confident hand, committed to neither and making use of both. At the same time the Kulturkampf finally died out, and German Catholics gradually broke out of their political isolation. In spite of the long-felt bitterness that the anti-Catholic campaign had produced, these so-called "enemies of the Reich" quickly became an integral part of the new state and eventually proved indispensable for the preservation of its political structure. The integration of the southwestern and southern states into the German Federation proceeded more smoothly than had been anticipated by most political observers, and the specter of separatism lost much of its menace. A spirit of reconciliation slowly penetrated public attitudes. Even the hostility toward the socialist working-class movement lessened, and Bismarck's objective of periodically renewing the Socialist Law became increasingly more difficult to achieve. A general and rather spectacular economic recovery between 1887 and 1889 helped to blur temporarily the prevailing social antagonisms within the Reich, and the previous mood of gloom seemed to give place to one of hope and guarded optimism.

It is only against this background that the following stage in the economic, social, and political development of the Reich can be understood. In 1890 the German economy began to register a new slump. It was the third depression within twenty years, and this time it meant a severe and prolonged crisis. The same year, Bismarck was forced to resign. His internal policies developed dynamics of their own that eventually threatened the delicate balance of conflict and cooperation which he himself had established, and which had been so essential for the preservation of the social and political status quo in the Reich. Without Bismarck the government naturally took on a very different character. It underwent a period of vacillation and instability, so that political uncertainty was added to the prevailing sense of economic insecurity.[1] In a satirical essay published in the *Preussisches Jahrbuch* of 1893, Hans Delbrück ridiculed, but accurately grasped, the contemporary public consensus that one was living in "einer bösen Zeit" (a bad time).[2] Renewed public depression often exhibited extreme features, manifested in a variety of exaggerated fears, a tendency to radicalism, and an obstinate adherence to certain ideas and goals.[3]

The master artisans, affected once again by the depression and shaken by the political fluctuations within the Reich, were particularly susceptible to this mood. The year 1890 opened a new phase in their political history, paralleling the last cyclical downward trend of the Great Depression. It was characterized by a heightened sense of political isolation among the small masters, adding to their feeling of economic deprivation and social alienation. Under these combined pressures the masters developed a generalized social hostility, eventually finding a unique ideological and political expression.

The first signs of an approaching turning point in the political development of the master craftsmen could be per-

[1] For a general history of this period see J.C.G. Röhl, *Germany without Bismarck*, especially chaps. 2-4.

[2] *Preussische Jahrbücher* 79 (1893): 1-28.

[3] On the psychological depression accompanying economic slumps see H. Rosenberg, *Grosse Depression*, pp. 51-57; also Wehler, *Imperialismus*, pp. 62-64.

ceived as early as 1887, at a time of growing prosperity and relative internal peace. It was then that the masters began to realize the extent of their political homelessness. The creation of the Conservative-Liberal Cartel came as an unpleasant surprise to a whole segment of German society. The master artisans organized in the southern Handwerkerbund were hit with particular severity. From the time of its establishment, the Bund's antiliberalism constituted its main political tenet. In the economically backward regions of the country, where the Bund had its greatest success, liberalism was still singled out as the main enemy of the small master artisans. The liberal industrial legislation of the Reich, and what were considered its disastrous consequences, were the target of the Bund's most virulent attacks. During the 1887 election campaign the Bund was suddenly faced with a coalition of its worst enemies and its best friends. The National Liberals and the German Conservatives conducted a joint political campaign, excluding the Center party from their alliance. The Bund's official organ lamented that "the two parties which are friendly to the master artisans are standing today against each other in the election campaign, and allying themselves with parties hostile to the artisans—indeed, a sad picture of the present [state] of our parliamentarism."[4]

As the new alignment of power in the Reich was made public, the *Allgemeine Handwerkerzeitung* in Munich, the voice of the Handwerkerbund, was at first stunned almost speechless, and then proceeded to carry on a heated campaign against liberalism in general and the National-Liberal party in particular. The peculiar political situation in Bavaria, where the Bund had its greatest influence and its major source of power, may have intensified the fury. There the Catholic-Center party, the decade-long supporter of the Bund, was in an especially difficult situation. It now had to face a National-Liberal Bavarian government, greatly strengthened by a coalition with the main Conservative forces in the Reich. Within this context the Bavarian Lib-

[4] *AHZ*, January 25, 1887.

erals appeared as the sole spokesmen of true German patriotism, and the artisans' journal opened its attack on them by contesting this claim. Above all, argued the *Allgemeine Handwerkerzeitung*, patriotism meant the protection of Germany from further internal polarization and disintegration. The master artisans, therefore, the representatives of a "healthy Mittelstand," were themselves the true patriots, more dedicated and more consistent than the treacherous forces of liberalism, "the originators of Social Democracy and of anarchy."[5] From its Bavarian base the paper urged its readers to reject the call of the Liberals, and to refrain from supporting them even when they ran on a joint ticket with the Conservatives.

The Bund had indeed cause for alarm. In the primarily Catholic areas in Bavaria and in parts of Silesia the Center party was strongly entrenched among Catholic Mittelstand voters, and the danger of a revived political liberalism seemed remote. The new coalition, however, presented the liberal alternative to voters in the mixed Catholic-Protestant areas, the regions that had only begun to supply new members to the Bund. It was in fact these regions that, in the 1887 elections, helped the Liberals double their seats in the new Reichstag. In Saxony the Liberal vote grew from 64,000 in 1884 to 161,000 in 1887, in Württemberg from 62,000 to 110,000, and in Baden from 93,000 to 122,000. In the Prussian province of Saxony, the Liberal vote almost tripled, rising from 34,000 in 1884 to 97,000 in 1887.[6] All these were regions where the Bund was beginning to make serious headway. By the late 1880s the Bund was entirely committed to a conservative course, and a swing to the Liberals together with a relative improvement of material circumstances gave their efforts to increase membership a severe blow.

Above all, the new Liberal-Conservative alliance made

[5] Ibid., March 4, 1887. See also the barrage of anti-Liberal articles in the *AHZ* throughout 1887.

[6] Specht, *Reichstagswahlen*, pp. 88-101.

clear the growing political isolation of the master artisans. In the same way in which they had felt left behind with the advent of industrialization and the consequent restructuring of German society, they were now left behind by political developments. An alliance between liberalism and conservatism, for them still a veritable heresy, was already quite admissible, and often desirable, for others. What was unthinkable for all in 1877 and unnecessary in the early 1880s was quietly accepted by 1887. The masters were unwilling to swim with the tide. For Bund members an alliance with liberalism was inconceivable, and the public approval of this alliance brought home to them the extent of their ideological and political isolation.

The first consequence of the Bund's embarrassment was a renewed rivalry between it and the Central Guild Committee in Berlin. Once again Catholics and true believers appeared to face a united front of Protestants and suspect moderates. The master artisans in the Bund detested the Liberal-Conservative coalition on principle, fearing that it would force the Conservatives to drop their social reform program, and that what they perceived as their essential interests would then be compromised. For the guild movement, however, the alliance was not altogether unpleasant, and its assessment of future prospects remained more optimistic. Indeed, the Liberals as a whole seemed to be following the master-artisans' own example by moving, hesitantly and slowly to be sure, but continuously and persistently, toward the right. The new guild movement had grown under the auspices of protectionist legislation, made possible by this general political shift. It was not, therefore, inclined to take an oppositionist stand, but continued to seek support and cooperation from the state.

The adjustment of the main segment of the guild movement to the political trend of the time made it a perfect target for the attacks of the uncompromising southern Bund. The "Berlin Spirit," wailed the *Allgemeine Handwerkerzeitung*, was sick, and the master-artisans' movement must take care not to be infected. It was disgraceful, continued the paper, that the center of the guild movement was located in an area so hostile to the master artisans, and so thoroughly riddled with liberalism. The spirit of patriotism and self-sacrificing devotion, characteristic of master artisans throughout the country, was completely lacking in this city of vice, claimed the paper, and it was time for conscientious masters to reject the Berlin leadership and oppose its compromising attitude.[7]

The uneven industrialization of Germany was in fact the basis of the rift within the master-artisan movement. The guild movement generally represented masters in the relatively industrialized regions. By the late 1880s these seemed to have become reconciled to industrial and social change as an inevitable evil, and were willing to fight for their particular interests within the general framework of the new social and political structure. Limited by law to nonpolitical activity, the guild movement placed special emphasis on specific practical demands for social protection, while it was moderating its anticapitalism, moving on to the antisocialist line of defence. At the same time the Bund, under the leadership of masters in the nonindustrial or partially industrialized regions of Germany, still attempted to halt oncoming changes. Its general antimodern stand took precedence over its battle for social and economic privileges.[8]

The movement's internal tension became evident in 1888 during the General Master-Artisans' Congress in Munich.

[7] *AHZ*, March 31, 1887.

[8] "Social Protectionism" is a term introduced by Winkler in his studies of the Mittelstand and is now widely used in the literature on Imperial Germany. The term can apply to government policy on handicraft matters, or to the organized masters' reform demands. It is useful in both cases, and is particularly illuminating for the study of the masters' interest-group organizations. For investigating the overall sociocultural and sociopolitical stand of master artisans in Imperial Germany, however, the term is too narrow. "Antimodernism" is introduced here not in order to replace "Social Protectionism" but to supplement it.

The old Bavarian leader, master-shoemaker Billing, openly confronted the Berliners, and master-tailor Möller, the central figure in the Westphalian movement, managed to pass a resolution stipulating a complete division of labor between the two rival organizations. Relying on the different legal status of the two, representatives of the Bund wished to assign to the Central Guild Committee responsibility only for the internal affairs of the guilds, matters of vocational education and economic advancement, while the Bund was to take action in all political matters. The same resolution was presented a month later to a general congress of the guilds in Berlin and was naturally enough vigorously opposed by the members of the Central Committee, and defeated in a close vote.[9] In spite of its conciliatory tone, the Möller resolution obviously attempted to relegate the central guild organization to a secondary position. There was no reason for the stronger and larger northern guild movement to accept such dictation from the small and weaker Bund.

Immediately after the reconvening of the Reichstag in 1887, however, it became amply clear that the alarm of the Catholic masters had been unjustified. The Conservatives and the Center party continued to cooperate on matters of social policy, and were as ever "united in the labor and in the battle for the reconstitution of the German Handwerkerstand."[10] In fact, the Free Conservatives and eventually the National Liberals as well were gradually coming closer to the joint social-conservative position of their larger partner.[11] The Reichstag passed a series of amendments designed to strengthen the guilds, and the prospects of further

[9] See the report in the *KZ*, August 18 and September 14, 1888; and the *Verhandlungen des Zweiten deutschen Innungstages zu Berlin 1888*, pp. 21 ff.

[10] *Steno. Berichte*, November 24, 1891.

[11] See the debate on the Ackermann amendment for the institution of a compulsory examination for masters in *Steno. Berichte*, March 24, 1887; and the separate amendments of the Free Conservatives, supported by a segment of the National-Liberal party during the following session of the house.

concessions seemed real enough. After a short period of vocal agitation, the Bund and the guild movement both settled down to a quieter period, taking advantage of the short temporary prosperity of the late eighties. They seemed to have overcome the first serious crisis in their relations, and regained some confidence in the good will of their political supporters.

The Government Discredited

The confidence of the guild movement was based above all on the pronouncements and actions of the federal government in Berlin. Without much enthusiasm, but nevertheless in consistent fashion, the government agreed to an increasing number of the master-artisans' reform demands, in principle if not always in practice. Late in 1884, Ackermann's amendment to article 100e of the federal industrial law, which only three years earlier had been so bitterly opposed in the Reichstag, passed the house by 159 to 156.[12] According to its provisions local authorities were to be given the right to restrict the training of apprentices to guild masters only. It thus became possible to make this aspect of the masters' social and economic position contingent upon membership in a guild. In 1886 another amendment, this time to article 104 of the industrial law, empowered the Bundesrat to confer the status of corporation and the rights of a legal entity upon local and regional guild associations (Innungsverbände). In 1887, an amendment to article 100f allowed the respective local authorities to grant guilds the right to tax nonmembers for such services as the guild vocational schools and the guild-supported journeymen's inns.[13]

Characteristic of all these concessions was the transfer of responsibility from the Reich government to state and local

[12] See *Steno.* Berichte, March 26, 1881; *Reichsgesetzblatt*, 1884, pp. 34 ff.

[13] For a summary of these amendments see "Gewerbegesetzgebung," in *HBS*, 4th ed., and chap. 9.

authorities. Thus, the federal government could demonstrate its good will, while the actual extent of the reforms depended on the decisions of local bureaucracies. The federal government's conciliatory position on matters of artisans' legislation was particularly conspicuous in contrast to the open hostility of some of the state governments. In Bavaria, as well as in Baden and in Württemberg, the liberal state governments consistently refused to confer any special privileges on the handicraft masters in the guilds, and invariably objected to all further legislation in this direction. By 1895 few guilds outside Prussia exercised rights under the amended articles 100e and 100f.[14]

In fact, government legislation during the 1880s represented a compromise between the demands of the Conservative forces in the Reich, both Catholics and Protestants, and the continuous objections of the various state bureaucracies. When in 1889 the Reichstag finally passed an amendment providing that the privileges stipulated in articles 100e and 100f of the industrial law were to be granted upon the decision of the majority of local masters, not at the discretion of the administration; and when a year later it even passed a resolution for the introduction of compulsory masters' examinations, the Bundesrat openly refused to go along. The responsible minister did not even present the two resolutions to the federal chamber since even the Prussian bureaucracy refused to support them there.[15] The dualism of the Imperial and the Prussian bureaucracies enabled the Federal Government to appear more responsive to the demands of the Conservatives in the Reichstag than in fact it was. In its federal guise it was agreeable and sympathetic; in its Prussian role it was practical and unyielding. A Reichs-

[14] See Graetzer, "Zur Statistik der deutschen Innungen," and the *Statistisches Jahrbuch deutscher Städte* 4 (1894): 273 ff. and 6 (1896): 278 ff.; see also the masters' complaints in the Bayerisches Hauptstaatsarchiv, MH-14643.

[15] See Franz Hitze's indignant speech and von Boetticher's reply in *Steno. Berichte*, November 24, 1891.

tag majority meant little against the opposition of the Prussian government, all the more so when it was supported, as in this case, by the bureaucracies of several other states. At the same time, the sham parliamentary system enabled the various political parties to make impractical demands without having to shoulder the responsibility for their implementation. It allowed them to carry on a political campaign and attract political support on the basis of half thought-out proposals and irresponsible plans.

Following the first disillusionment with the social policy of the new Caprivi government, it became essential for both the federal government and the Conservative parties to show sympathy and support for the small master artisans. The social-insurance legislation Bismarck had promoted and instituted during the 1880s was intended by him to supplement his oppressive anti-Socialist policy.[16] Neither he nor organized socialist labor ever took this program to be more than an effort at pacifying disgruntled industrial workers. Others, however, attempted to see it as a step in the direction of establishing a true "social monarchy." As the ineffectiveness of anti-Socialist legislation became evident, the social conservatives in the parties and in the state bureaucracies argued for its complete abolition. To absorb the working class into German society, they wished to rely primarily on expanded social legislation. The young Kaiser shared these views, and stressed them clearly in his customary message at the opening session of the 1890 Reichstag. Von Berlepsch, former president of the industrialized Prussian Rhine province, became the new Prussian minister of commerce and industry, and immediately started to prepare a comprehensive new "workers' bill." He was enthusiastically supported in this by a staff headed by Theodor Lohmann, a veteran social planner who resumed his post in the ministry after Bismarck's resignation.[17]

[16] Born, *Staat und Sozialpolitik*, pp. 20-30; and H. Rosenberg, *Grosse Depression*, pp. 210-227.

[17] On the shifts within the administration see Hans Rothfels,

Enthusiasm was rather short lived, however. In the new election, freed from the anti-Socialist law, the Social Democrats made striking progress. Between 1887 and 1890 they increased their constituency from 763,000 to over 1,427,000.[18] The young Kaiser, the Conservatives, and the bureaucracy were all duly impressed, and responded by announcing a temporary pause in social legislation, as they were naturally losing faith in the effectiveness of their own social and political tactics. Contrary to their hopes, the workers showed no sign of gratitude. Instead, they appeared to have become even more radical and antagonistic. Reconciliation was then seen by a growing number of Germany's leading Conservatives as nothing but wishful thinking. Their hopes for Germany's industrial proletariat seemed frustrated. The support of the small independent masters therefore acquired new importance. It became far more crucial to mobilize the masters, together with other Mittelstand elements, for the task of maintaining the status quo. This was especially desirable as the master artisans were showing considerable good will, and clearly did not yet mean to go over to the side of progress and socialism. In fact they were apparently consolidating their position among the Staatserhaltende (state-preserving) forces in the country as true patriots, monarchists, conservatives, and proper antisocialists.

The handicraft legislation of the 1890s must be seen in this context. It was undertaken as a temporary substitute for more comprehensive legislation on behalf of the industrial workers. It was intended to create a legal framework that would maintain the solidarity of the small master artisans and the dominant social and political forces within the Reich. As it became obvious that confrontation with the increasingly self-conscious working class was inevitable, the Conservatives' need to enlist popular support became more

---

Theodor Lohmann, especially pp. 63-115. Also Born, *Staat und Sozialpolitik*, pp. 90-112.

[18] Specht, *Reichstagswahlen*, pp. 100-101.

urgent, and they were forced to consolidate their actual and potential support for the approaching social struggle. The support of the Mittelstand, urban and rural alike, was then considered indispensable to the acceptance of Conservative reactionary policies and plans. The peasantry was organized to fulfill its role within the new Bund der Landwirte. The small masters were to be organized for that purpose within a new and elaborate guild system. The preservation of the Mittelstand had been a major aspect of social conservatism even in the 1870s.[19] But by the early nineties the problem became urgent. The reorganization of the masters, claimed Franz Hitze in the Reichstag, was necessary for "social peace" and for the well being of the fatherland as a whole.[20] Bureaucrats were equally emphatic. State Secretary for the Interior von Boetticher, promising new legislation on the organization of artisans, expressed the government hope that "the handicraft estate will continue to be, as it has been until now, a protection for the crown and the fatherland, and that it will prove wrong the suspicion that it may overwhelmingly turn toward the Social-Democratic position. I wish to express the hope," he continued, "that it will then be capable of preserving the 'Golden Ground' upon which it was previously sustained."[21] The crucial role of the handicraft estate in protecting Church and state alike, in upholding German patriotism and preserving German standards of honesty and devotion was endlessly reiterated in artisans' meetings, and the *Kreuzzeitung* never tired of asserting that "the German handicraft estate constitutes the strongest dam still protecting the middle strata of our nation from being flooded by Social Democracy."[22]

The master artisans themselves, already relatively well organized and sensitive to nuances in the utterances of public figures, were quick to realize their growing social signifi-

[19] See the section on social Catholicism and social conservatism in chap. 7.

[20] *Steno. Berichte*, November 24, 1891.

[21] Ibid.

[22] *KZ*, February 15, 1892.

cance under the new circumstances. They were determined to make the most of it. During the late 1870s and the 1880s the masters followed the lead of the political parties and other interest-group organizations in demanding social protection and state help. Now they quickly responded to the challenge of the government itself. They rapidly organized themselves to pressure the apparently responsive bureaucracy to accept their most extreme protectionist demands. To begin with, the masters looked askance at government reformist efforts. The new government was suspected of liberalism, and nothing could more readily arouse the hostility of the small masters at the time. Nevertheless, the positive attitude of both the government and the major political parties worked to heighten their expectations. They were soon to be disappointed. Though the government was now ready to consult representatives of the master-artisans' movement, it was intent on pursuing a realistic line of social reform, giving concessions to small producers without in any way compromising the interests of big ones. The new administration wished to act on behalf of the small masters. It planned to harness them effectively to the protection of the existing social order in Germany, but could do so only without antagonizing its own major allies. It appeared determined to press through its own reforms in its own way.[23]

As a result of a joint appeal to the Kaiser by the Central Guild Committee and the executive committee of the Handwerkerbund, a conference was arranged between representatives of these bodies and the top bureaucrats in the ministry of the interior and the Prussian ministry of commerce and industry, which took place in Berlin in June of 1891.[24] All the major figures in the master-artisans' organized movement were present at that conference. They included Beutel and Faster from Berlin, Fasshauer and Möller from the Rhine and Westphalian provinces, Biehl and Nagler

[23] See Winkler's *Mittelstand*, pp. 57-64.

[24] *Protokoll über die Verhandlungen mit Vertretern 1891* (Bayerisches Hauptstaatsarchiv, MH-14661).

from Munich, and Dr. Brehmer, the veteran legal adviser of the industrial chamber in Lübeck. The proceedings of the conference were supposed to remain secret, but were soon publicly discussed by both the government and the leadership of the artisans' movement.[25] The accuracy of the protocol published by the government was contested by the participants, and the precise course of the discussion cannot be established today. But while the controversy over the protocol was indicative of the new tension between the government and the master-artisans' movement, it was itself of little significance. What clearly emerged from the meeting was the divergence of opinion between the representatives of the master-artisan movement and the bureaucracy about what the forthcoming handicraft legislation should be. In unambiguous terms Dr. Wilhelmi, von Berlepsch's deputy, asserted the impracticality of compulsory guild membership, and made it plain that no amount of argument or threat would affect the government's position on the matter.[26] Long afterward the masters were still quoting him as a justification for their own intransigence. The government was willing to legislate in support of the organization of the small masters, but it refused to follow the specific demands of their movement.[27]

Gradually the relationship between the federal and the Prussian governments on the one hand and the various master-artisans' organizations on the other degenerated into open hostility. Most militant were the members of the Bund,

[25] See the rather heated debate in the Reichstag between von Boetticher and Biehl, *Steno. Berichte*, November 24, 1891. Also the speeches in the *Protokoll über die Verhandlungen, Berlin 1892*, pp. 12. ff.

[26] *Protokoll über die Verhandlungen mit Vertretern 1891* (Bayerisches Hauptstaatsarchiv, MH-14661) pp. 6; 11.

[27] See also von Boetticher's speech in *Steno. Berichte*, January 14, 1895, stressing even at that late date that "we are not opposing a guild organization on principle . . . but we have been, and I believe still are, opponents of the organizational form demanded by the corporative handicrafts based on the principle of obligatory guilds."

who had little to lose by attacking von Berlepsch and his team. The representatives of the Berlin guild movement, hampered by the legal restrictions, had initially showed greater tolerance and patience but were eventually forced by the militancy of their membership and pressure from the south to join forces with the rest of the movement.

The large Guild and Artisan Congress, which convened in Berlin in February 1892, was unique for the bitterness of its tone and the aggressiveness of its demands. The leaders of the movement mounted the podium in succession to denounce the government and lament its desertion of the master artisans. The handicraft masters were the "pariah of the legislature," explained Biehl; "the stepchild of the nation," added Voss. They constituted "the second largest estate," but were "totally forgotten" by the authorities. The Caprivi government, based on open support by the hated National Liberals, represented all that the small masters feared and detested. "From a ministry whose atmosphere is congenial to Dr. Miquel," explained Voss, "*we* have nothing to hope for."[28] The artisans' journals complained repeatedly of the government's disregard of masters' petitions, of the unjust taxation of small masters, and of the discrepency between the attitude of the Austrian government and that of the Reich toward the small master artisans.[29]

Observing the growing fear of Social Democracy in government circles, the master artisans devised a new strategy. Small, independent masters frequently joined the socialist labor movement and the Social-Democratic party throughout the period. This could have constituted a threat to the small masters' interest organization, but eventually became a weapon it wielded. The socialist small masters were in fact unlikely to be former members of guilds or of other local handicraft groups. They were among the poorest master

[28] *Protokoll über die Verhandlungen, Berlin 1892*, pp. 42, 48, 62, 115.

[29] See, e.g., the articles in the *AHZ*, July 13, 1888; and May 24, 1889.

artisans, and only rarely took any active interest in the master-artisan movement. But as early as 1883 Fasshauer, the militant master-tailor from Cologne, had cautioned that if reforms were not forthcoming, the masters would choose "the road of revolution against the exploitation of productive and creative forces."[30] At the time, he was alone in his warning, since the master-artisan movement was then moving in the opposite direction, becoming more conservative and moderate rather than more radical and revolutionary. The movement was then at the end of its early militant phase. It was at the beginning of a new one by 1890-91 when the warning was repeated by Fasshauer himself at the June Handwerkerkonferenz, by Möller from Dortmund and Biehl from Munich, and then echoed from all sides.[31]

In the next national assembly of master artisans, representatives from Hamburg and Frankfurt moved to have the "free guilds" dissolved.[32] These institutions, they argued, imposed nothing but duties on their members. The radical tactics of the industrial workers, explained master-painter Voss of Hamburg, brought them daily practical improvements. The masters, on the other hand, being loyal Conservatives and avowed supporters of "the party of order" could be, and indeed were, conveniently disregarded. Voss' rhetoric notwithstanding, the resolution was clearly no more than a tactical move, finally rejected by the assembly, as well as by its original proponents. Its purpose was merely to make clear to the government, whose representatives were in the hall, the degree of disaffection among the master artisans. In the same vein, the Catholic Reichstag delegate from Silesia, master-artisan Metzner, claimed that "our present guilds are not fit to live; on the other hand, however, they cannot die either," and assured the government that any new form of organization not responding to the demands of the or-

[30] Quoted by Jäger, *Die Handwerkerfrage*, pp. 274-275.

[31] *Protokoll über die Verhandlungen mit Vertretern 1891* (Bayerisches Hauptstaatsarchiv, MH-14661) pp. 4-5; 11.

[32] *Protokoll über die Verhandlungen, Berlin 1892*, pp. 107-117.

ganized masters themselves, would not be accepted. According to him the proposed new reform plans only served "to rob the masters of their faith in the good will of the government."[33]

Thus, two years after the beginning of the third wave of depression in Germany and shortly after the inauguration of the government's new social policy, the great majority of organized small masters lost much of their earlier faith in the government's intentions. The government's own proposals first worked to encourage the masters' militancy and intransigence in the face of renewed economic hardship. Soon, however, it became clear that the government itself could not go beyond the limits set by the interests of more powerful economic groups. At this point the masters were no longer ready to compromise. The government's previous concessions came to be seen as tactical steps designed to pacify rather than support their movement. A major source of the master-artisans' confidence and optimism during the 1880s was now eliminated.

Alienation from the Parties

By the early 1890s the controversy between the Handwerkerbund and the Central Guild Committee lost much of its significance in the face of serious internal disagreements within each of these organizations. Within the Bund the Bavarian master artisans, once again following the official line of the Catholic-Center party, showed relative restraint in times of crisis. As was the case ten years earlier, it was the masters from the mixed Catholic-Protestant regions, such as the Rhine province, Westphalia, and Silesia, who led the militant faction of the Bund. In Berlin, and in much of the Protestant north, the masters were also divided into two groups: the loyal and open supporters of the Conservative party and the devoted interest-group men, who, attempting

[33] *Steno. Berichte*, November 24, 1891.

to preserve political neutrality, were increasingly swept toward militant anti-Semitism and independent Mittelstand politics.[34]

On November 24, 1891, von Boetticher, the secretary of the interior, in answer to questions by Franz Hitze and other Center-party Reichstag delegates, promised to bring before the house a new guild law, providing for the establishment of handicraft chambers.[35] He made it absolutely clear, however, that the government would not and could not institute obligatory guilds or compulsory masters' examinations. The reaction of the house reflected the position of its members. On the whole, the speakers from the right were satisfied with the ostensibly sympathetic and rather detailed reply of the minister. Biehl, the official speaker of the Center party on matters of handicraft legislation and the Bavarian president of the Handwerkerbund, first engaged in a long verbal battle with von Boetticher, but finally expressed general satisfaction with the government approach. In fact the Center-party delegates in the Reichstag either opposed all compulsory provisions of the handicraft legislation, or were prepared to accept the noncompulsory system as a useful and welcome step forward. The reaction of the Conservatives was similar. In 1891, the Deutschkonservative Partei still had no representative of the master artisans among its Reichstag delegates and, with the exception of several extremists, was generally satisfied with the government's reply. It appeared from the debate that the two most loyal supporters of the master-artisan movement of the 1880s were now prepared to accept less than their full demands, and to settle for a compromise.

The position of the National Liberals was rather less predictable. In the early 1880s the party had been adamant in

[34] The master-artisans' national congress in 1892 was the first to hear open anti-Semitic speeches and resume the discussion about the desirability of an independent artisans' party. See *Protokoll über die Verhandlungen, Berlin 1892*, pp. 61, 163 ff.

[35] *Steno. Berichte*, November 24, 1891.

its opposition to compulsory measures. In 1881, when the Conservatives presented their amendment to article 100e, the entire National-Liberal delegation voted against it.[36] Its unequivocal position, however, had gradually eroded during the decade. Early in 1887, the National Liberals had still voted overwhelmingly against various Conservative amendments on the introduction of compulsory masters' examinations. Several months later, apparently under the influence of the new coalition, the National Liberals supported an amendment to article 100f that extended the potential power of the guilds over nonmember masters. In a speech to the plenary session of the Reichstag, Johannes von Miquel stated his party's latest position: "As a beginning of obligatory guilds and the establishment of state compulsion, we would have had to reject the amendment. As a final step in the efforts to preserve both industrial freedom and the guilds, we are in a position to support it."[37] Keeping in mind the National-Liberal record of gradual capitulation to the government position on other legislative matters, it is hardly surprising that on this issue, too, Miquel's party was eventually prepared to make further concessions.

The ambivalence of the National Liberals was again displayed during the November 1891 debate. The party spokesman, this time a delegate from the Palatinate, asserted his conviction of the importance of self-help, but added: "That, however, should not stop us from legally supporting the entire estate in its efforts, and actively help it to pursue its economic, as well as its general estate interests."[38] The National Liberals refrained from making a clear reply to von Boetticher's statement of intentions, but indicated their probable support for moderate legislation in the spirit of his suggestions. Indeed, three years later, it was the National-Liberal Freiherr Heyl zu Herrnsheim who demanded fuller details

[36] See the discussion in "The Liberals React: The Legislative Approach," chap. 7.

[37] *Steno. Berichte*, May 12, 1887.

[38] Ibid., November 24, 1894.

about the promised new handicraft bill, and by 1896 the party openly accepted the compulsory handicraft chambers and proffered only half-hearted opposition to the final bill introducing the peculiar "voluntary-compulsory guilds."[39] Throughout the 1890s all three major political parties supported the existing order. While they clearly realized the importance of keeping the small master artisans content and strengthening their antirevolutionary stand, they refused to grant them concessions that might have harmed the more powerful interests of the big industrialists. They agreed to compromise only when they were finally convinced that these interests were no longer in jeopardy.

The Progressives and Social Democrats in the Reichstag remained opposed to the introduction of all compulsory measures in handicraft legislation. Both parties voted consistently against government proposals. Their opposition, however, was based on entirely different arguments. The left-wing liberals rejected the government approach on the grounds that the handicraft economy and handicraft producers did not in fact need government help. In the 1891 Reichstag debate the Progressive speaker assured the house that "the 'golden ground' of the handicrafts exists today as much as it has ever existed."[40] The government reform plan was designed to favor a minority of masters, he continued, at the expense of others, and it would only create a maze of legal conflicts and disputes. The ideological position of the left-wing liberals concerning the entire handicraft question was stated unequivocally: "True assistance lies only in that one asks from oneself as much as possible, and from others and from the state as little as possible."[41] Furthermore, the Progressives' negative attitude toward all the proposed handicraft legislation was directly related to their objections to any attempt at reviving the Ständestaat in whatever form or disguise, and therefore to all occupa-

[39] Ibid., January 14, 1895; March 30, 1897.
[40] Ibid., November 24, 1891. [41] Ibid.

tional organizations supported and controlled by the bureaucracy.[42]

During the 1890s the Progressive party did not openly represent an economic interest group or specific social class. It claimed to stand for the active and enterprising independent handicraft masters, and it is likely that some of the masters in the Hanseatic cities and the large port towns on the North Sea, and a certain number in other parts of the country, still voted intermittently for the left-wing liberals. In line with their long-standing opposition to monopoly, the left-wing liberals systematically supported legislation to restrict unfair business practices and the like, and could thus assert themselves as defenders of small industrial entrepreneurs. They were, however, consistently opposed to the protectionist master-artisan movement. During the years of the Great Depression the movement developed open hostility to liberalism, its earlier ties with the Progressive party having long since dissolved.

In contrast to the optimistic stand of the left-wing liberals on the situation of the handicrafts, the Social Democrats took the view that this form of production was doomed and that therefore the handicraft legislation was irrelevant and of no practical importance. Indeed, continuous experimentation with guild laws, which inevitably failed, argued the Nuremberg socialist Grillenberger, was bound to result in a wholesale conversion of master artisans to socialism.[43] The handicraft estate, he explained, resembled a dead body which one could galvanize but no longer bring back to life. It represented an obsolete and antiquated social order, added August Bebel, entirely incapable of surviving under the conditions of modern capitalism.[44] All efforts to ameliorate the condition of small handicraft masters, argued the Social Democrats, must come to nought in the face of the

[42] See Eugen Richter's speech, *Steno. Berichte*, January 14, 1895, and his pamphlet, *Gegen die Zwangsinnung*.

[43] *Steno. Berichte*, November 24, 1891.

[44] Ibid.; see also Kautsky, "Der Untergang des Kleinbetriebs." pp. 1-29.

inexorable progress of large, mechanized industry. The sooner the small masters recognized and accepted this simple truth the easier their readjustment would be.

The 1891 Reichstag debate had no practical result. It merely served to increase the sense of isolation and betrayal among the organized small masters. While the Bavarian spokesman of the movement in the Reichstag, Georg Biehl, expressed his limited satisfaction with the government approach, it was a master artisan from Silesia, the Catholic Karl Metzner, who gave vent to their disappointment and bitterness. "In my opinion," he exclaimed in the course of the debate, "the statement of the state secretary was a death sentence for the independent handicraft estate, decorated with roses."[45] And it was this position that was echoed at the next national congress of master artisans in Berlin, in February of 1892. The moderate views of a number of masters from Berlin were drowned in a wave of militant verbiage. Fasshauer announced that under prevailing conditions, the preservation of the "Christian-Conservative" character of the master-artisan movement had become entirely impossible.[46] For the first time in years the meeting heard openly anti-Semitic speeches, and greeted Adolf Stöcker's rhetoric with "thundering applause."[47] Once again the masters abandoned a moderate conciliatory position in order to take a militant social-reactionary and anti-Semitic line.

The estrangement of the master-artisan movement from the government and the major parties of order grew considerably after the publication of the draft of the governments' handicraft bill. In the summer of 1893 von Berlepsch began to solicit public support for his legislative proposal. The plan was a curious mixture of elements, attempting to satisfy all and eventually satisfying no one.[48] It included a

[45] *Steno. Berichte*, November 24, 1891.

[46] *Protokoll über die Verhandlungen, Berlin 1892*, p. 47.

[47] Ibid., p. 41.

[48] On von Berlepsch's draft see the supplement to the *Protokoll über die Verhandlungen, Berlin 1894*.

proposal for the establishment of compulsory vocational associations (Fachgenossenschaften) with special journeymen divisions holding a veto power over all matters concerning their affairs, topped by a network of handicraft chambers supervising the activities of both the new associations and the existing free guilds. Significantly, the principle of compulsory association was thus accepted by the government. It was not, however, applied to the guilds, but to new and strictly controlled vocational associations. Furthermore, the proposed bill did not include any provision for compulsory masters' examinations, and thus avoided instituting any administrative control over the social composition of the revived Handwerkerstand. The precise relationship between the new vocational associations, the guilds, and the handicraft chambers, as well as the division of labor among them, remained unclear. At first sight the bill seemed extremely complicated and its details insufficiently thought out; it aroused a torrent of protests and complaints.

The most vehement opposition to the von Berlepsch bill came first from the liberal segment of the handicraft masters, organized in the various regional industrial chambers, and then from the militant conservative wing of the masters' movement represented by the Westphalian Handwerkerbund. In a national congress of industrial chambers at Eisenach in October 1893, the majority announced its disappointment with the government bill and rejected the capitulation to what it considered a "state-socialist" notion of compulsory vocational association.[49] Moreover, the industrial chambers felt the attempt to create separate handicraft organizations to be a danger to themselves, and were strongly against official and independent representation for small industrial enterprises. At the other end of the political spectrum master-artisan Möller from Dortmund and his associates in the Westphalian Handwerkerbund were quick to raise the battle cry against the new proposal: "Never, at

[49] See the reports in *Jahresbericht der Hamburgerischen Gewerbekammer für 1893*, pp. 57-58; and in the *AHZ*, October 20, 1893.

any time shall we let ourselves agree to it, and whoever accepts it will be regarded by us as an archenemy."[50] Initially the guild movement in Berlin reacted less adamantly, but within a few weeks, it too was swept into the campaign against the bill, prompted by uneasiness about the proposal for a duplicate organizational structure of the handicrafts and for limiting the independence of the existing guilds. Eventually, in a joint call for a national master-artisans' congress in Berlin, on April 9, 1894, both the Central Guild Committee and the executive committee of the Handwerkerbund expressed their unyielding opposition to the government proposal. What eventually unified them was their common resistance to a fundamental concept of the new bill, which had declared the principle of compulsory masters' examinations to be "incompatible with the present structure of the economy." It was precisely the masters' examinations, the combined leadership of the masters' organizations now argued, that could serve "as the best protection for the entire handicraft organization of the future."[51] The Bund had always considered the Befähigungsnachweis as its major reform demand, but by the 1890s the Central Guild Committee also refused to compromise on this point.

The opposition of the master-artisans' movement to the government initiative enabled it to overcome its internal strife. After years of bitter mutual recrimination and personal conflicts the two organizations were joined in their opposition to the government. From the ideological standpoint this rapprochement meant in effect a victory for the position of the Bund. Paradoxically, it was the artisans' organizations from the relatively unindustrialized areas that gained the upper hand within the masters' organized national movement, as industrialization proceeded unabated in all parts of the country. With the onset of the new depression, the moderate position of the Berlin-centered guild

[50] *AHZ*, September 8, 1893.

[51] The joint call was reprinted in *Protokoll über die Verhandlungen, Berlin 1894*, pp. 3-4.

movement during the 1880s appeared useless. The entire movement was finally uniting in an effort to preserve the independent economic and social position of small master artisans. Confronting a government plan for the compulsory organization of all practicing independent craftsmen, the guild movement now realized the weakness of its own previous position. Such a comprehensive organization, lamented their representative, master-shoemaker Beutel from Berlin, would in fact mean the inclusion of men who were not "real Handwerker," and would imperil the uniqueness and homogeneity of the craft masters as a social group. Compulsory guilds without obligatory masters' examinations would be meaningless under the social conditions prevailing in Germany, and the proposed journeyman division, the masters argued, were certain to fall under the control of Social Democracy.[52]

At this stage the master-artisan movement openly took it upon itself to represent the small, skilled, master employers —most of them guild members—against both medium- and large-scale producers and against other poor, unorganized craftsmen and the masses of handicraft journeymen. In the face of a growing trade-union movement and a strong Socialist party, and in an era dominated by the power of big industry, the Mittelstand master artisans closed their ranks in opposition to both capital and labor. As a result they also found themselves in open conflict with the Reich government and with all the major political parties in Germany.

Bitterness, Defiance, and Discord

The political homelessness of the militant conservative master artisans from 1890 to 1895 was greatly aggravated by what may be loosely called the psychological stand of their movement. Their attitude toward the old issue of industrial freedom was symptomatic and therefore deserves

[52] Ibid., pp. 35; 54-60.

special attention. For all practical purposes, the master-artisan movement in Germany waged a battle against the principle of Gewerbefreiheit as soon as it was made into law. But the heat and energy this issue managed to generate among the small masters throughout the last quarter of the century can hardly be explained either with reference to the actual conditions of the economy as a whole, nor in relation to the specific economic situation of the small masters. The precise effect of Gewerbefreiheit on the various handicrafts in Germany was a topic for endless debate throughout the century. Undoubtedly, however, though it may have had some impact during the experimental pre-March years, it was definitely of little significance as German industry matured during the Great Depression.[53] In the 1870s and 1880s, further structural transformation of the handicrafts resulted from the changing conditions of the market, the development of new machines, and other aspects of industrialization. Measures of economic policy were of little consequence, and normally only served to give legal sanction to existing conditions. For decades the small master artisans engaged in a quixotic offensive against industrial freedom—deaf to the arguments of others and oblivious of the evidence of their own daily lives.

In 1895, bookbinder-master Nagler from Munich, the second president of the Handwerkerbund, delivered the opening address at the Eighth General Congress of master artisans in Halle. After twenty-five years of political and legal battle, he still found it necessary to dedicate his speech to the hated Gewerbefreiheit.[54] A couple of sentences in the federal industrial law, he claimed in all seriousness, meant the destruction of the ancient guilds, the debasement of the concept of Handwerk, and immeasurable damage to the

[53] See chap. 1, n. 6; and the section on the masters' ambivalent liberalism in chap. 5.

[54] *Protokoll über die Verhandlungen zu Halle 1895*, pp. 18-20. Also the opening remarks in the 1894 congress in Berlin, *Protokoll über die Verhandlungen, Berlin 1894*, p. 27.

most vital element of the nation, the handicraft estate. Industrial freedom, he continued, opened the field for the competition of Jews and other unrespectable groups, whose only motto was, "Wealth and well-being at all costs." The new freedom, exclaimed another speaker at the congress, picking up this theme again, was a degrading Jewish institution, a veritable Raubtierfreiheit (freedom of beasts of prey).[55] Nagler gave the tone to the entire conference by demanding: "Give us true social legislation, an honest and just industrial law; banish the demon of gold, the devil of false profit, from the thresholds of the fatherland; expel false freedom, and give us instead a real one, since without *real* freedom there is no nobility and no well-being."[56]

The false Gewerbefreiheit had to be abolished, the masters' journals and their delegates to numerous meetings and congresses demanded repeatedly. These emotional calls however, could not have been seriously regarded by the government and the bureaucracy nor by the major political parties. By the 1880s, Germans had for two decades witnessed the gradual abolition of all laissez-faire policies through the introduction of protectionist legislation and administrative supervision of the economy. But despite the fact that during the years of the depression, the laws protecting industrial freedom were being continuously undermined, the master-artisans' attack upon industrial freedom lost none of its bitterness. Indeed, it seemed to become increasingly more violent and emotional with the years, indicating the masters' collective misconception of reality, and their pathological attachment to a simplified and erroneous explanation of their misfortune.

Even the remedies proposed by the masters remained the same throughout these years. For two decades the organized master-artisan movement demanded the introduction of obligatory guilds and the compulsory masters' examination. By 1890, these two demands had acquired exclusive promi-

[55] *Protokoll über die Verhandlungen zu Halle 1895,* p. 87.
[56] Ibid., p. 29.

nence in their public discussions, agitation, and political activity. No other method of alleviating the conditions of craftsmen in Germany was ever seriously considered. The cooperative movement was vehemently rejected by these "freedom-loving" men.[57] Even the special credit cooperative scheme, proposed by the trustworthy Conservative, von Broich, in 1894, received only partial support from the guild movement's official newspaper, and eventually came to naught. The entire plan, wrote the *DHZ*, was based on a false view of human nature. Complete economic independence, explained the article, was a fundamental principle of German life and should not be impinged upon.[58] All liberal suggestions for the development of artistic handicrafts were waved away contemptuously. Government statistical investigations, designed to study the problems of the artisans so as to be better equipped to offer appropriate cures, were deemed entirely useless.[59] "We hear the message," protested the masters immediately following the January 1895 debate in the Reichstag on the problem of the handicrafts, "but we lack the faith."[60] All the talk and different suggestions, argued the leaders of the master-artisan movement, led to the blurring of the masters' two simple demands: the institution of obligatory guilds and compulsory masters' examinations. No sophism on the part of those unsolicited advisers, they continued, could possibly alter their stand. Obviously the entire issue had become an idée fixe for the masters. They were therefore unable to reevaluate their difficulties or judge the solutions proposed with any degree of objectivity.

[57] See the discussion in the section on master artisans and other Mittelständler in chap. 4.

[58] *DHZ*, January 20, 1894. For von Broich's campaign see also the articles on March 16 and August 17, 1895.

[59] For other details see the section on the masters' social isolation in chap. 4.

[60] "Aufruf zum besuche des VIII. allgemeinen deutschen Handwerkertages," reprinted in the *Protokoll über die Verhandlungen zu Halle 1895*, p. 3.

In a joint call, published immediately after the 1891 Reichstag debate, the leaders of the master-artisan movement declared: "We wish to speak directly, openly, and straightforwardly: we remain loyal to the Kaiser and the Reich, to throne and fatherland; but we strongly cling to our holy rights."[61] And in an even darker mood they added: "We German artisans feel ourselves as one of the strongest protections of an orderly state system, but we German artisans also fear no one in the world but God, who is the relentless and trustworthy avenger of all injustice upon the earth."[62] The prevailing social situation, as it was perceived by the small master artisans, indeed required intervention from above. The overall disintegration they believed they were witnessing was not merely a matter of an unfortunate political constellation, but a general and catastrophic cultural collapse. "Everything has become questionable," mourned the *DHZ* in its 1894 opening issue, "and no one can provide the answers."[63] Man had indeed captured the elements and harnessed them to his service, continued the editorial, but the result turned out to be a severe and pervasive disease, infecting the entire human race. Men could have been "submerged in plenty," but instead they were increasingly impoverished and enslaved to the power of capital, to debts, and to moneylenders.

A feeling of political homelessness and a prevalent cultural pessimism gave rise to a general sense of crisis among the master artisans. Consequently their collective solidarity was reinforced, and they developed a position of general defiance and hostility. "Only strong men, harmoniously cooperating, impress the legislature and the masses of hypocrites and phrase-mongers," exclaimed the *AHZ*, and it persisted tirelessly in its call for unity and self-sufficiency.[64] In the face of this rising militancy, however, unity was all the more difficult to achieve. During 1894-95, the Berlin master-artisans' organ, the *Deutsche Handwerker Zeitung*, came

[61] Ibid., p. 4.

[62] Ibid.

[63] *DHZ*, January 6, 1894.

[64] *AHZ*, July 14, 1888.

under the influence of a group of militant Social Conservatives, anti-Semites, and supporters of the Deutsche Reformpartei. They attacked both the Bund and the Central Guild Committee, and rekindled the strife within the master-artisan movement. The Bund leadership in Munich was accused of being nothing but an instrument of the Catholic-Center party and of being lax in its anti-Semitism and indecisive in its political action. The members of the Central Guild Committee were personally attacked, as it happened by their own official journal, for exploiting the movement for their own aggrandizement and enrichment, and for consistently betraying their own supporters. The Berliners were accused of supporting a legal patchwork, designed to divert public attention from the specific demands of the masters' movement. The verbal battle between the leaders of the Bund and the Central Guild Committee appeared to have acquired new dimensions. The mood of the movement was one of bitterness, defiance, and discord.[65]

By 1895, however, as the government temporarily abandoned its legislative efforts on behalf of the artisans and the economic crisis appeared to be subsiding, the leadership of the artisan movement regained a measure of composure. Government apathy was the pretext for the Berlin masters to resume a more militant, oppositional attitude, thus approaching more closely the stand of their counterparts in the artisans' Bund. The Central Guild Committee in Berlin managed to silence its internal opposition and by the mid-nineties was again in basic agreement with the leadership of the Bund on matters of both ideology and tactics. The two bodies finally seemed able to present a common front against the government, the parties, and the educated pub-

[65] *DHZ*, January 13 and 20; November 3, 10, 17, and 24; December 22, 1894. In July 1895, government officials met again with representatives of the master artisans, but apparently only with those who were members of the small-business divisions of several industrial chambers. This was the cause of renewed bitterness on the part of the guild-movement leaders. See *DHZ*, September 7 and 21; October 5, 12, and 19, 1895.

lic. Their unity was founded on a joint hostility to all three. The tone and style of the masters' speeches, petitions, and resolutions indicated a growing defiance. By the mid-nineties the masters' isolation was at its peak. Even the passage of the new guild law in 1897 did not allay their fears and suspicions. The bill provided for obligatory guilds in cases where a majority of local artisans supported such an arrangement; it strengthened the authority of the guilds in matters of apprenticeship education and combined them all under a network of special handicraft chambers.[66] It meant in effect a far-reaching concession to the demands of the masters for social privileges and state protection. The bureaucracy was prepared to set up and support masters' organizations, openly providing them with some protection against their competitors. But the initial response of the master-artisans' organizations was lukewarm. As long as the effects of the Great Depression were still felt and remembered, no legal measure could reassure them. They did not share the hope for a better future that inspired the workers' movement, nor the faith in the existing capitalist economy that encouraged the supporters of industrialization even during the hard times of the depression. For them, the Golden Age was relegated to a somewhat vaguely defined past, and the chance of its reconstruction extremely dim; the present appeared objectionable and distasteful.

[66] See "Gewerbegesetzgebung" and "Innungen" in *HBS*, 4th ed.

ELEVEN

POPULAR ANTIMODERNISM

Social and Sociopsychological Background

By the third phase of the Great Depression the masters' sense of isolation had reached a new peak. Neither the rhetoric of government officials, nor the high-sounding verbiage of Conservative and Liberal politicians helped them to overcome their growing alienation. Following a period of political searching and organizational experimentation they had gradually regained a group consciousness and formulated a series of loosely related ideas expressing their attitudes toward state and society. Their unique mental state and the ideological and political posture that had been based on it is the subject matter of this last chapter. It intends to recapture and summarize the masters' unique stand and relate it to the overall social history of Germany during this period.[1]

The establishment of the new German Reich in 1870 was conceived of as a solution to the problem of German unification, an attempt to assert in political terms the existence of a single German nation. It was an effort to go beyond a linguistic, cultural, and historical unity by creating a modern nation-state. Bismarck's solution to the problem of German unity, however, never received unanimous approval. By opting for the military and Prussia-oriented version of the "lesser Germany" solution, Bismarck, it was argued both at the time and by later historians, had divided rather than united Germany.[2] Moreover, his style of politics and the

1 See the earlier version of this chapter: "Popular Anti-Modernism. Ideology and Sentiment among Master-Artisans during the 1890's"; also the author's "The Social and Political Function of Anti-Semitism."

2 See Wolfgang Sauer, "Das Problem des deutschen Nationalstaates," especially pp. 407-409; 427-429. Also Wehler, *Das Deutsche Kaiserreich*, pp. 96-100; 105-180.

constitution he had introduced made it impossible to unite even that part of the nation that found itself within the boundaries of the new Reich. Bismarck's sham parliamentarism and the authoritarian and paternalistic nature of his government played a major role in the process that eventually made Germany a country deeply divided, concealing its multifarious rifts under a veil of nationalistic rhetoric. Germany of the late nineteenth century, and especially Germany without Bismarck, was a country torn by internal controversies over the most basic public issues. These controversies concerned not merely the tactics of government but the very structure of German society and its relationship with the state. These were conflicts between contrasting and hostile ideals.[3]

Rainer M. Lepsius has suggested a model for understanding the composition of German society from the last decade of the nineteenth century until the Nazi seizure of power that divides the society into four major milieus, each representing a unique subculture, an overall Weltanschauung, and a specific political direction. Within each of these milieus, culture and life style, interests and ideology, political action and organization overlapped and reinforced each other. The conservative, liberal, socialist, and Catholic milieus each developed great cohesion and a unique pattern of interaction with the others.[4] In addition, however, a fifth milieu was slowly taking shape, becoming discernible, and gaining significance within German society. It was composed of groups and individuals who, for a variety of reasons, did not succeed in becoming associated with any of the other milieus. It constituted a mixture of leftover social elements, comprising about 10 percent of Germany's adult

[3] The use of "ideal" to denote roughly a "Weltanschauung" is taken from Perkin, *The Origins of Modern English Society*, in which the author describes the social, economic, and ideological struggle in England during the first half of the nineteenth century in terms of "the struggle between the ideals." See especially pp. 218-270.

[4] Rainer M. Lepsius, "Parteiensystem und Sozialstruktur," pp. 371-393.

male population—a small but expandable and susceptible contingent. Many of the urban traditional master artisans in Germany came to be associated with this milieu. While the Catholic masters normally managed to feel themselves a part of the large, influential Catholic milieu, the traditional Protestant masters in the north and in the mixed Catholic-Protestant regions remained chronically unattached—culturally, socially, and politically. It was these men who most readily responded to demagogues and rabble-rousers, and who tended to cling to distorted historical memories and develop general social resentment and a hostility toward everything modern.

Together with other Mittelstand groups in Germany, and later also with other déclassé and unattached social elements, these men constituted the fifth milieu. In addition to a unique subculture, a life style, and a specific Weltanschauung, they finally also developed their own political orientation. By the late nineteenth century the formation of this milieu as a coherent and recognizable social element was still incomplete. The main social and ideological struggle of the nineties was still fought between the conservative agrarians on the one hand and the progressive industrializers on the other, and was focused upon the future character of the German state.[5] At the margin of the arena, however, two other groups increasingly influenced the controversy and prepared to enter the struggle: the working class armed with a Social-Democratic ideology, and the Mittelstand with a popular version of antimodernism. By the 1890s the proletarian Social-Democratic milieu already had an elaborate organizational network and a relatively clear political purpose. The popular antimodern bloc, however, was still dispersed, unorganized, and above all, unconscious of its potential strength. Only the outline of its ideology was emerging. Two more decades were necessary before the flexibility of its social ideal and its attractiveness for a grow-

[5] See especially Barkin, *The Controversy over German Industrialization*, and Lebovics, "'Agrarians' vs. 'Industrializers.'"

ing number of Germans made it into a central force in German society, and a thoroughly destructive one.

Antimodern sentiment, directed against all forms of industrialism, against the social implications of the new economy, and against the various democratic impulses that came to be associated with it, was widespread in the Germany of the 1890s. It was formulated in respectable intellectual terms by distinguished men in the scientific and cultural community, and gained a certain influence in German public life and policy-making during those years. However, the lasting impact of this sentiment on the course of German history lay in its tremendous power to attract not just a small group of intellectuals and academicians, but a considerable segment of the general public as well. Parallel to the trend of cultural pessimism there arose an indigenous popular movement. Its origins were varied, as was the intensity with which it was supported by the different social groups in Germany. It did not develop a unified organizational base, but nonetheless emerged as a distinct popular trend of thought and eventually also as a motive force for a unique type of political action.

The adherents of popular antimodernism had little contact with the writings of the intellectual cultural pessimists. They rarely borrowed directly from their ideas, nor were they normally aware of the similarity of their thinking. The various sophisticated expressions of social conservatism, the mood of cultural despair, and the ideology of agrarianism rarely reached men of little education. These men, however, developed their own patterns of thought, unsystematic to be sure, but basically similar to those of their educated contemporaries. Ties between the two elements naturally existed. A host of second-rate writers and journalists worked to popularize the ideas of Carl Rodbertus, Hermann Wagener, Adolf Wagner, and Werner Sombart, and through such indirect channels many readers, especially from the Mittelstand, became roughly familiar with the intellectual version of antimodernism. That this process often led to distortions and occasionally to complete misrepresentation of the original ideas is not surprising. Popular antimodernism, however, cannot be explained away as a mere vulgarization of better and subtler ideas. It was to a large measure a spontaneous creation of a unique popular movement. In many ways scholars such as Gustav Schmoller and Max Sering, artists such as Richard Wagner, and half-baked philosophers like Julius Langbehn, affected the popular ideology as much as they were influenced by it.

The term "antimodernism" indicates a whole range of loosely related ideas. They do not add up to a systematic philosophy. Logic was never a strong point with the men who believed, articulated, and propagated them. The affinity among these views is at first sight only accidental: they were all held by the same people at the same time. Beyond that, however, they constituted a whole by virtue of the fact that all of them expressed the same sentiment and had a common sociopsychological origin.

The popular version of antimodernism grew spontaneously during the early nineties, especially among the members of the German Mittelstand. It may be detected in the ideology of small peasants and in the public posture of small retailers, lower officials, white-collar employees, and small independent handicraft masters. The handicraft masters provide a particularly appropriate subject for the investigation of this general trend, though their organized movement was by no means the only public body then expressing this peculiar agglomeration of ideas and sentiments. In addition to other interest-group organizations representing other elements within the Mittelstand, the various anti-Semitic, social-conservative parties, which then mushroomed, were certainly as vocal and unambiguous in their attitudes. They were, however, one step away from the grass roots of the popular antimodern movement itself. They participated directly in the political process and were led by experienced professional politicians and organizers. The voice of the electorate was obscured by the demagoguery of men like

Stöcker, Liebermann von Sonnenberg, Hermann Ahlwardt, or Otto Boeckel. The Bund der Landwirte, another proponent of antimodern ideas, was somewhere between a conventional political party and a socioeconomic interest group. Its antimodernism was primarily the product of the BdL's aristocratic leadership. Its ideology was no doubt designed to appeal to the German peasants but served at the same time as a tool for gaining popular support for the interests of the Prussian landowning elite. The case of the small master-artisan movement was different. In spite of continuous efforts, the masters never managed to organize their own independent political party, nor to form a permanent link with any of the existing ones. They did not succeed in enlisting effective support from outside their own ranks, and their local and national associations remained essentially social-cultural bodies, only occasionally managing to operate as modern, organized interest groups. Consequently, their movement remained essentially independent of the direct influence of Conservative politicians, ambitious Junkers, or high-ranking reactionary officials.

The master artisans repeatedly expressed their opposition to everything modern—in the economic order, in the structure of society, in the political sphere, and in the moral and cultural world around them. Furthermore, they opposed any ideology that seemed to encourage and support modernization. The majority appears to have been antiliberal, antisocialist and anticapitalist, antidemocratic, and antiparliamentarian. They were anti-Semitic and authoritarian, monarchists, and fervent patriots. Their antimodernism was not a dogma; it lacked a positive reform program or a clear political objective. It was an expression of undifferentiated hostility, a rejection of all facets of the prevailing social reality. Like the sentiment that had engendered it, it was often vague and confused, but at the same time radical and powerful. It abounded in internal tensions, and heightened rather than alleviated the desperation of its followers.

Opposition to Political Liberalism and Democracy

Antiliberalism predominated in all the versions of antimodernism throughout the 1890s. Fritz Stern wrote of the antimodernism of Germany's cultural desperados: "They attacked liberalism because it seemed to them the principal premise of modern society; everything they dreaded seemed to spring from it: The bourgeois life, Manchesterism, Materialism, parliament and the parties, the lack of political leadership. Even more they sensed in liberalism the source of all their inner sufferings."[6] This assessment is equally applicable to the position of the small traditional handicraft masters. In their case too, liberalism gradually came to stand for everything they despised, for all the antitraditional, internationalist, and individualistic trends in the Germany of their day.

As has been shown, the masters' opposition to liberalism can be traced back to the early years of the century.[7] From the reform era on, some of them consistently opposed the introduction of complete freedom of trade and movement. But what had emerged as a series of complaints against the practice of certain measures of liberal economic policy developed over the years into fundamental criticism of the entire liberal Weltanschauung. Under the conditions of late nineteenth-century Germany the masters' antiliberalism came to encompass a variety of complaints not only against prevailing socioeconomic practices but also against the emerging political order.

The main attack of the handicraft masters was leveled against the liberal concept of freedom. It was likened to the freedom of the wild beasts, denounced as a fraud perpetrated upon the public, rejected as a mere cover for the supposedly catastrophic "process of social dissolution."[8]

[6] Stern, *The Politics of Cultural Despair*, p. 2.

[7] See the section on the masters' ambivalent liberalism in chap. 5.

[8] See, for instance, speeches in the *Protokoll über die Verhandlungen zu Halle 1895*, pp. 29, 87, 140.

Gradually, opposition to "liberal freedom" became more radical. In 1896, at a congress of master artisans in southwestern Germany, a delegate from Württemberg, the renowned center of German liberalism, denounced freedom as being "a word and nothing more,"[9] and in a long editorial, "On Freedom," published by the *Deutsche Handwerker Zeitung* in March 1894, the editor, perhaps inadvertently, revealed the real source of the master-artisans' discontent with liberalism.[10] The error of the "modern idea of freedom," he explained, originated in the Enlightenment when freedom was proclaimed as the right of *every* individual human being. It was the association of freedom with equality, so often indeed problematical for even the most outspoken and committed liberals, that was now so deeply resented by the master artisans.

Still enamored of the guild tradition of a community of equals, the masters found it difficult to come to terms with a concept of freedom that emphasized the unattached, independent individual. Their conflict with liberalism in and around 1848 sprang from their insistence on the preservation of such community spirit, which could accommodate liberty only when taken together with a certain conception of equality and fraternity.[11] Toward the end of the century it was once again the liberal individualistic concept of freedom that the masters found uncongenial. Now, however, it was not its opposition to a collectivity that they rejected but its implications with regard to the universal equality of men. As long as civil society consisted solely of solid middle-class elements, the traditional master artisans objected to the liberal-inspired process of atomization within its boundaries. Now that the benefits of society were demanded and seemed gradually to be acquired by all men, the master artisans were disturbed by its all-inclusiveness. Freedom, they believed, could not be granted to all men because not all of

[9] *Protokoll über die Verhandlungen zu Heidelberg 1896*, p. 60.

[10] *DHZ*, March 31, 1894.

[11] See the section on the masters' ambivalent liberalism, chap. 5.

them possessed the degree of honesty, competence, and industry that the proper exercise of freedom required.[12] Having abandoned their liberal premises and moved toward conservatism, they could now cite the natural inequality of men to give moral backing to their sense of social superiority and to the existing system of social inequality. Together with other conservatives they now objected to the liberal concept of freedom because of the threat it posed to their privileged position and authority. These were their most cherished values now that they found themselves confronting the pretensions of a new class of successful industrialists and the opposition of the organized working-class movement. For the liberal, individualistic model of society the masters now wished to substitute not a community of free and equal independent men, but a social order based on the privileges of competence and the "natural hierarchy" among human beings.

A vision of a hierarchical society was now the center of the masters' world outlook. It appealed to them above all because it reflected the social reality they believed to have prevailed during the medieval period, the glorified Golden Age of the guilds. In addition, hierarchy was deemed essential as the organizing principle of the traditional handicraft workshop in which masters, journeymen, and apprentices fit into a rigid framework, based upon an uneven distribution of social respectability, economic prosperity, and professional competence. Considering themselves a select aristocracy of skill and virtue, the masters came also to believe in the need to preserve a national aristocracy as an indispensable element in the life of a "healthy people." Increasingly they saw the handicraft workshop as the manifestation of all good qualities and sought to transfer the principles inherent in it to the larger social context.

Yet the glorification of an aristocracy remained problematic for the small masters. They repeatedly felt compelled to provide their own definition of aristocracy so as to

[12] *DHZ*, March 3 and 11, 1894.

prevent a possible misunderstanding. An aristocracy, they explained, was nothing but "a community of the best in the nation."[13] Its superior social position was based neither on birth nor on wealth but on competence and skill. As such this superiority was equivalent to that of a master craftsman over his assistants. This concept of hierarchy helped to perpetuate a version of conservatism suited to the taste of the "small man." It recommended the acceptance of social inequality, seeking at the same time to keep society open to talent. As men of low social status the masters could appreciate the advantages of egalitarianism and democracy, but since they felt they were fighting to prevent a further deterioration of their social position, they preferred to fight for inequality vis-à-vis their social inferiors rather than greater equality vis-à-vis their superiors.

Occasionally, however, they still found themselves demanding equality. With some regret the masters' newspaper analyzed the basic weakness of modern liberalism as being "the contradiction between political equality and economic inequality."[14] This tension, it argued, must bring about a collapse of the entire liberal system from within. Undoubtedly, however, the masters did not intend to defend the interests of the propertyless masses of workers but to draw attention to their own straits. A total endorsement of a hierarchical society based on the medieval model would have meant a betrayal of the masters' most fundamental interests, but by the 1890s an acceptance of the democratic model seemed equally dangerous. To the majority of the master artisans it meant an abandonment of the sacred principles of competence, achievement, and conceivably even of private property itself. Facing this dilemma, the masters chose to advocate a form of government that was to be led by a "responsible monarch," assisted by a "responsible nobility," and in which, nonetheless, everything was to be "by and for the people."[15] How such a form of government could

[13] Ibid., November 11, 1894. [14] Ibid., January 25, 1887.
[15] Ibid., November 11, 1894.

be brought about or how it might then function, the small masters never asked, let alone answered.

Despite the apparent choice that the master artisans had made in favor of hierarchy and against egalitarianism, the tension between the two continued to disturb them. It made their desertion of liberalism uncomfortable, and perpetually partial. Characteristically, at times of improved economic conditions and in areas of less acute socioeconomic pressure, many of them turned back to their left-liberal democratic convictions. But at the height of the last phase of the Great Depression, the masters' hostility to liberalism and its social and political implications appeared to be unrelenting. At that time they valued privilege far above freedom for all men, and their varying degrees of vocational and moral competence above their equality.

From Anticapitalism to Antisocialism

The devotion with which the masters carried on their campaign against liberal industrial freedom and against the abolition of guild privileges never diminished. By the nineties, however, some of the heat that had accompanied this campaign was gradually directed elsewhere. Capitalism came to replace Manchesterism as the main enemy of the small traditional craftsmen. Both were conceived of as facets of the same development, but since the 1870s the focus of attention had swung from one to the other. The attack against Manchesterism gradually lost its effectiveness, and anticapitalism emerged as a far more promising propaganda device and a potentially better instrument for obtaining government protection against immediate economic difficulties.[16]

[16] These attitudes and the gradual shift in the masters' focus of attention can be judged from the articles in the masters' weeklies. See, for example, *AHZ*, January 25, March 25, 1887; March 7, 1890; May 23, 1891; February 3, March 10, 1894; *DHZ*, January 6, March 31, 1894. See also the remarks in the *Protokoll über die Verhandlungen zu Halle 1895*.

Anticapitalism was associated in the masters' minds with their long battle against big business—industrial, commercial, and financial. They employed the term "capitalism" to indicate the entire spectrum of business activity peculiar to the new economy. Instead of attacking specific economic policies and the manner in which the government was handling economic problems, the masters began to take a more comprehensive view of the entire modern economic system. They proceeded to place the blame for their difficulties on the operation of this system as a whole, rather than on isolated, and usually ineffective and unenforced, economic measures. This, no doubt, represented a trend toward greater realism on their part. The masters were finally prepared to launch a principled attack on the entire economic order, operating militantly and occasionally showing real revolutionary fervor.

Their enthusiasm, however, was soon curbed. In the early 1890s, after the repeal of the anti-Socialist legislation and with the ever-spreading effects of industrialization, the masters' anticapitalism suddenly seemed to be working to their own detriment. Like other social conservatives, they gradually realized the potential affinity between their own anticapitalism and that of the socialists. Both camps were in fact well aware of this affinity. Friedrich Engels had often warned the Social Democrats of this danger, and at the 1892 congress of the Social-Democratic party in Berlin, Wilhelm Liebknecht delivered a long address designed to emphasize the fundamental distinction between conservative state socialism and revolutionary Social Democracy. The two, he argued passionately, were irreconcilable opposites, which had nothing at all in common.[17] This was the central theme in the subsequent debate, in which the moderate parliamentary position of a segment within the party, led by Georg von Vollmar, the leader of Bavarian Social Democ-

[17] *Protokoll über die Verhandlungen des Parteitages der SPD, Berlin 1892*, pp. 173 ff.; see also Vernon L. Lidtke, "German Social Democracy and State Socialism."

racy, was vehemently attacked. The need for a clear-cut distinction between anticapitalism of the left and anticapitalism of the right was equally urgent for the social conservatives, and it seemed particularly pressing for the small employers in the master-artisan movement. Their criticism of the economic inequality inherent in capitalism and their emphasis on the value of productive labor brought them dangerously close to the socialist position and forced them to find a formula in which a principled anticapitalism could be combined with an equally principled antisocialism.

The "capitalist workshop," declared a master-artisan newspaper in one of its editorials, presumably referring to large factories, was the reversal of all natural order and inherent rights, while the alternative utopian socialist organization was equally unacceptable. In both, ran the argument, personal freedom and true individualism were crushed.[18] Only the coexistence of economic independence and productive labor could protect man from the slavery of capitalism and the inhuman utopia of socialism. This coexistence was unique to the master artisan, who both owned the means of production and engaged in manual, productive labor. Handicraft as a form of social organization, argued another article, should become a model for the entire nation, for all occupations and social groups.[19]

The emphasis on the preservation of personal liberty sounded strange indeed in the mouths of such ardent antiliberals as the editors of the masters' weekly and the leaders of the guild movement. On the one hand, the master artisans blamed liberalism and personal freedom as such for all revolutionary activities in the country and especially for the rise of revolutionary socialism; on the other, they opposed both capitalism and socialism on the grounds that these two systems of production were inimical to the individual's complete freedom.

[18] *DHZ*, January 6, 1894.

[19] *AHZ*, April 4, 1890; *DHZ*, February 24, September 8, November 11, 1894.

Characteristically, however, the masters appeared to be undisturbed by the feeble logic of their argument. Liberalism, capitalism, and socialism were not really rejected on the basis of a rational and realistic diagnosis of existing circumstances and future possibilities, but as various aspects of modernity. The logic twisting necessary to accommodate a principled opposition to contradictory and hostile creeds was of little moment, since it was not logic but emotion that had inspired the entire movement. Conversely, the apparent logical connection between the elements of the masters' ideology should not be taken at face value. Their anticapitalism, like their antiliberalism and antisocialism, originated in the need to express a general disaffection with the course of economic and social developments. The question of the historical relationship between liberalism and socialism or the causal connection of either to the masters' actual difficulties was only of marginal interest, and usually conveniently disregarded.

By the early 1890s, the growing power of the socialist working-class movement and the masters' antagonism toward it made reconciliation with capitalism increasingly urgent. Under the pressure of social and political reality it became necessary to make a choice. Only one of the two rivals, capitalism or socialism, could be fought without reserve. The affiliated masters found it essential to define their enemies with greater precision. It was not capitalism as such, they concluded, that was objectionable, but specific capitalist practices; not capitalism itself, but a corrupt and misused capitalism.[20] While the master-artisans' antiliberalism moved from an opposition to a series of legal measures to a general, principled opposition, their anticapitalism de-

[20] A striking exposition of the masters' ambivalence toward capitalism is given in the opening article of the *DHZ* on January 6, 1894, which explains the details shown in the new front-page picture of the journal. In it an armed knight draws his sword but hesitates before stabbing the "dragon of capitalism." See also the *Protokoll über die Verhandlungen zu Heidelberg 1896*, p. 8.

generated into a continuing attack on the stock market and on big business, and tended to merge with virulent anti-Semitism. As early as 1882, a group of masters from Würzburg in Bavaria, formulated their position as follows: "Our enemies are industrial freedom and capitalism. It is not private property, nor the private ownership of the means of production, that are responsible for the present calamity. It is the misuse, the unlimited exploitation of private property that is the source of the decline. Private property *within its proper boundaries* is the basis for every real cultural development."[21] It was not property as such to which the masters objected, explained the *Allgemeine Handwerkerzeitung* in January 1894, but excessive wealth.[22] By September 1896, the president of the Handwerkerbund was perfectly clear on this point. In his opening address to the annual Bavarian master-artisans' congress he stated: "We reject entirely the approach that assaults only capitalism, since it is on this ground that Social Democracy expands. Our battle is waged not against capital, but against the overgrowth of capitalism."[23]

Their growing fear of socialism extinguished the potential radicalism of the masters' anticapitalist campaign, and gradually led to their absorption into the reactionary "alliance of fear" uniting the various elements of the German ruling elite.[24] Back in the 1880s the masters had often seen themselves as the strongest protectors of the existing order against the "revolutionary tide of socialism." In the Westphalian master-artisans' congress of February 1888, the Center-party Reichstag member from Bensberg, master-tailor Euler, assured his audience that "in all walks of life it is agreed today that the handicraftsmen are the best protec-

[21] *Fränkisches Volksblatt,* November 11, 1882. (Italics added.)

[22] *AHZ,* January 13, 1894.

[23] *Protokoll über die Verhandlungen zu Aibling 1896,* p. 8.

[24] For this concept see H. Rosenberg, *Grosse Depression,* pp. 178-191; 201-202; 222-227; and Wehler, *Das Deutsche Kaiserreich,* pp. 100-105.

tion against Social Democracy."[25] Only a powerful Mittelstand, the masters believed, could stand against the onslaught of socialism. The official artisans' journal argued that Social-Democratic propaganda was in fact completely ineffectual against the persistence of private property and the advantages of economic independence demonstrated by the masters' traditional way of life.[26]

After 1890, however, when the Social-Democratic party was finally operating in the open throughout the country, this confidence seemed to evaporate. Fear of the growing power of socialism made the masters increasingly incapable of supporting any demand of the socialist workers, and ever more anxious to retain the protection of the state against the power of the trade-union movement. Even the Bavarian masters began to feel the pressure. By 1893, there was not an issue of the two major master-artisans' weeklies that did not publish an attack on socialism. The growing indolence of the workers and their hostility toward their masters were repeatedly denounced, and Social Democracy was accused of destroying the work ethic and all forms of morality. Socialism was attacked for its antireligiousness, for its lack of patriotism, and for its disrespect toward the traditional institution of the family. Between 1890 and 1896 socialism gradually became the major enemy of the organized master artisans. It was socialism that came to represent everything modern in the prevailing social order, and that was to become increasingly abhorrent because it supported industrialism and declared its intention of pursuing modernization with special vigor.

While the master-artisans' antiliberalism lost much of its relevance, and their anticapitalism its militancy, they developed a fresh radical stand in opposition to socialism. Their antisocialism, like their antiliberalism, combined practical grievances with ideological arguments. It was an outcome both of their fear of organized labor and of their con-

[25] *AHZ*, March 4, 1888. [26] Ibid., April 11, 1890.

tempt for the entire socialist movement as representative of the new industrial society. Socialist opposition to the established order was based on a desire to draw the social, political, and cultural conclusions from the irreversible process of modernization. The masters' opposition grew out of their disaffection with modern society, and their almost desperate desire to halt its course and contain its repercussions. As long as there was still some doubt as to the nature, extent, and social implications of modernization, liberalism—as the propagator of the new system—was the major enemy of the masters. When, however, after half a century of rapid industrialization, social change, and periodic cyclical depressions, the process was recognized for what it was, socialism as the representative of the drive to fulfill its promise became the major villain. At the same time antiliberalism and anticapitalism often relapsed into anti-Semitism, giving vent to the whole range of the masters' undefined resentment, frustration, and hate.

Anti-Semitism and Militant Nationalism

The late 1870s and early 1880s saw the first wave of organized political anti-Semitism in Germany. Throughout these years, however, the grass-roots support of this movement remained limited. For many former Liberals, anti-Semitism provided a necessary transitional stage between liberalism and conservatism. During the early eighties, most of the anti-Semitic Reichstag members gradually merged with the conservative parliamentary parties, and it is most likely that the majority of their supporters likewise became more or less permanent conservative voters. An independent militant anti-Semitic movement emerged in Germany only in the early 1890s. As in the late 1870s, this time, too, it was nurtured by insecurity in the face of continuing economic fluctuations, and derived its strength from men who felt betrayed by the established political forces within the Reich, and were increasingly aware of being left outside of Germany's social mainstream.

After a somewhat shadowy existence during the years of relative economic recovery in the late 1880s, the anti-Semitic movement recovered its place immediately with the onset of the new economic downturn in 1890. During the 1870s and 1880s, anti-Semitism was primarily a form of socio-economic protest, and its strength was directly related to that of popular antiliberal sentiment. At the time, explicit anti-Semitism rarely figured in the public utterances of master artisans. Only around 1892 did it become an unmistakable driving force of their organized movement. An insight into the changing mood of the masters can be gained by examining the growing barrage of anti-Semitic propaganda specifically directed at the masters, and by reviewing their own pronouncements on the matter.

During the early years of the decade, wishing to avoid the alienation of any potential supporters, the anti-Semitic parties followed a cautious line on the handicraft question. They apparently felt that an unequivocal stand woud be unattractive to some Mittelstand groups and to certain elements outside of, or even within, the masters' interest organizations.[27] Gradually, however, impelled by the aridity of their own programs and the open enthusiasm of the master artisans, the anti-Semitic parties tended to move toward more outspoken support of the specific demands of the organized handicraft masters. In 1892, Adolf Stöcker was received with unprecedented "stormy, lengthy, and repeated applause" by the delegates to the national master-artisans' congress. Master-tailor Möller, the militant leader from Dortmund, delivering an emotional closing speech in which he attempted to summarize the master-artisans' Weltanschauung found it necessary to declare "in order to avoid misunderstanding," that "as far as we are concerned the Jewish question is solved at the moment in which only

[27] See the various anti-Semitic party-programs in Specht, *Reichstagswahlen*, pp. 503-507.

men who have learned a craft—practically and theoretically—are permitted to operate craft workshops."[28] Thus, the Jews were conveniently identified with the Pfuscher. Nine-tenths of all untrained and unqualified tailors in the country were Jews, claimed Möller, and then hastened to add that "the Jew who lives by the ten commandments is a beloved man; but when he lives by the Talmud I wish to have nothing to do with him at all."[29] Möller's speech was received with great enthusiasm, and appears to have been a true expression of the delegates' feelings. They were certainly relieved to see the problem of anti-Semitism openly discussed at their own congress. It had become so prevalent among the members of the various artisans' organizations that the national leadership could no longer disregard it.

Throughout the early 1890s, the masters made a number of attempts to avoid full and official support of the anti-Semitic parties by establishing an independent artisans' political party. Their efforts came to naught, and by 1895, they seem to have temporarily abandoned the entire enterprise. The anti-Semitic movement was the main beneficiary of the masters' organizational failure; 1893-1894 were the peak years of master-artisan anti-Semitism. The *Deutsche Handwerker Zeitung* opened its first issue of 1894 with an article entitled "The Disgrace of the Century." It presented anti-Semitism as a healthy racial impulse, and as the unavoidable outcome of a whole century of German shortsightedness and submission. For a century, it argued, honest artisans and solid shopkeepers had been faced with a constant flow of "trashy Jewish goods," which had undermined and destroyed their material well-being. With rhetorical flourish the article called upon Jews to come to the handicraft workshop in order to witness for themselves "with what power the hammer is swung, and what magnificent forms emerge from German thought and feeling, and from the skillful German hand."[30] The tone of the *DHZ*'s anti-Semitism be-

[28] *Protokoll über die Verhandlungen, Berlin 1892*, p. 61.
[29] Ibid., p. 62.
[30] *DHZ*, January 6, 1894.

came increasingly hysterical and vulgar throughout 1894. In May, the full transcript of a trial in Bonn in which two Jewish butchers had been accused of soiling meat with urine and then selling it to Christians, appeared in three full pages to show "the unbelievable rudeness and lowliness" of the accused.[31] For a whole year the paper published innumerable violent anti-Semitic articles, letters, verses, and the like.[32]

The racist leader of the Deutschsoziale Reformpartei, Paul Forster, expressed his party's support for the masters at their Halle congress in 1895. He was followed by the anti-Semitic master artisan, Jacobskötter, an organizer of the Reformverein in Leipzig, and at the time a BdL Reichstag member. A number of anti-Semitic Conservative spokesmen then mounted the podium; all were received with cheers and applause.[33] Master-builder Beyerstedt from Altona closed the opening session of the congress, giving his version of anti-Semitism: "All questions touch upon the Jewish question. Who has brought us the Gewerbefreiheit? Who has brought us the Freizügigkeit? The Jews Lasker and Bamberger have brought us all these. [Enthusiastic applause] Who has spread among the working class the well-known Social-Democratic teachings? Lassalle has done that. Why are the Jews the leaders of the SPD? Because parasites can flourish only in places of decay."[34]

Anti-Semitism fulfilled a number of important social, political, and psychological functions for the small master artisans, both as individuals and as a group. To begin with, it served as a link connecting the various aspects of their antimodernism. The destructiveness of modernization was thus explained by its association with the depravity of the Jews. Big business, urbanization, secularization, democratization

[31] Ibid., May 26, 1894.

[32] See in addition the issues of the *DHZ*, May 12 and 26, and June 16, 1894.

[33] *Protokoll über die Verhandlungen zu Halle 1895*, pp. 49; 62 ff.

[34] Ibid., p. 87.

were all the outcome of Jewish activity. Liberalism, capitalism, and socialism could all be attacked for their capitulation before the corrupting forces of Judaism. A solution to the ills of society was then also readily available: the system could easily be purified by ridding it of all Jewish elements. This was a convenient way of attacking the existing order without demanding its total overthrow and without having to offer a comprehensive alternative. Furthermore, anti-Semitism channeled the undifferentiated social hostility of the masters into an acceptable form of behavior. In Germany of the 1890s anti-Semitism provided them with a tangible target for venting their frustration, and gave them an outlet for militancy without the risk of appearing to be a revolutionary force or unduly antagonizing the powers that were. Even more important, however, was the integrative function of anti-Semitism for the masters as well as for other social groups in Germany. It proved essential for their efforts to break out of their growing isolation and regain a sense of social belonging. In comparison with the Jews, even the downtrodden small masters could appear relatively respectable, and infinitely more "German."

Anti-Semitism was never officially endorsed by the Imperial government, but its potential as an integrative force could not escape the attention of the German ruling elite. From the early 1870s Bismarck had made use of a series of internal enemies in order to overcome social divisiveness within the Reich, and his method of "negative integration" was perpetuated by his successors.[35] By 1890 the repeal of the antisocialist laws left the country for the first time in two decades without a recognized official internal enemy. By that time, however, the various elements of the Mittelstand served the government by fabricating a new target, an object of contempt and derision, thereby deflecting public anger from the responsible authorities, and pulling to-

[35] Sauer, "Das Problem des deutschen Nationalstaates," pp. 428-436; Wehler, *Das Deutsche Kaiserreich*, pp. 96-100; 105-108.

gether rival social groups into a common campaign against a "foreign" element.[36]

In late nineteenth- and early twentieth-century Germany, anti-Semitism was always associated with extreme nationalism. For a significant number of Germans the two served a complementary function. Men who felt isolated, homeless, and incapable of affecting or controlling even their own lives could, through militant anti-Semitism, feel superior by contrast to the "un-German," "oriental" Jews. A feverish nationalism complemented anti-Semitism by helping such men overlook the actual internal social disintegration of their country, and by enabling them to feel part of a powerful, glorious nation. Not belonging to any of the loose cultural, social, and political milieus, these men could at least identify themselves negatively as non-Jews and positively as proud German stock.

But like anti-Semitism, nationalism, too, was manipulated by the German rulers for their own purposes. Starting in 1848, German nationalism gradually severed its ties with liberalism. Bismarck had early realized the potential of this development, and from the time of the "wars of unification" and throughout his term of office as chancellor, he consciously manipulated nationalist sentiments against enemies within and without.[37] Emotional nationalism was a weapon in his arsenal, wielded in order to strengthen the state and perpetuate the social status quo. Following his dismissal, pan-Germanism, anti-English sentiments, and an aggressive Weltpolitik played an ever-growing role in German domestic affairs.[38] Together with anti-Semitism these variations on the theme of extreme nationalism fulfilled specific func-

[36] H. Rosenberg, *Grosse Depression*, pp. 88-117; Wehler, *Das Deutsche Kaiserreich*, pp. 110-118.

[37] For the early development of Bismarck's tactics see Otto Pflanze, *Bismarck and the Development of Germany*, especially chap. 5, pp. 111-125.

[38] See especially Kehr, *Der Primat der Innenpolitik*, pp. 87-197; H. Rosenberg, *Grosse Depression*, pp. 258-273; and Wehler, *Das Deutsche Kaiserreich*, pp. 149-192.

tions for various segments of German society, but all were skillfully manipulated by a reactionary government. They served above all to bind frustrated and alienated groups to a social order of which they actually disapproved, and to a government they often felt had ignored and betrayed them. The official endorsement of anti-Semitism by the Conservative party in its 1892 Trivoli program, the violent nationalist and anti-Semitic propaganda of the BdL, and the persistent antiforeign and often openly racist pronouncements of high-ranking bureaucrats all served to whip up prevailing sentiments among certain elements of the population and channel them toward the defense of the existing order, against the threat of democratization and revolution.[39]

The Popular Antimodern Ideal

The masters' nationalism on the one hand, and the social protectionism of the Imperial government on the other, moderated the formers' basic opposition to the rapidly modernizing German state. Following a long tradition of loyalty to the authorities and facing the danger of revolution, they eventually preferred to be counted among the forces of order and stability. These two values became sacred for them, although in practice they only served to preserve and perpetuate an unsatisfactory system. The masters prided themselves on being the "only bulwark against dissatisfaction" in the Reich, the most loyal "state-preserving element" in society, and above all the most ardent "protectors of the crown."[40] From the mid-seventies on, the master-artisans'

[39] For the Tivoli program see Salomon, *Die deutschen Parteiprogramme*, vol. 2, pp. 71-72. See also Puhle, *Agrarische Interessenpolitik*, pp. 111-140; and Wehler, *Das Deutsche Kaiserreich*, pp. 110-114.

[40] See the comments in the *Verhandlungen des zweiten deutschen Innungstages zu Berlin 1889*, passim; *Protokoll über die Verhandlungen, Berlin 1892*, p. 62; *Protokoll über die Verhandlungen zu Halle 1895*, pp. 4, 14; *Protokoll über die Verhandlungen des Bayerischen Handwerkertages 1896*, p. 8.

national congresses always opened with a spirited "Hoch" for the Kaiser, and references to the mercy and good will of His Majesty were scattered throughout the proceedings. The masters were adherents of the idea of "social monarchy" in its most primitive form. They often appealed directly to the Kaiser on such special occasions as his birthday, and insisted on circumventing both the Reichstag and the bureaucracy, preferring to rely on the monarch's personal intervention. At the masters' 1892 congress master-tailor Möller was warmly applauded when he declared: "We desire a monarchy by the grace of God, which is for us no empty phrase, and we therefore do not want a monarchy 'by the grace of the people,' and least of all a monarchy 'by the grace of the bureaucracy.' " He then concluded: "We have such great confidence in His Majesty, that when he realizes the great need for reform of the handicrafts, he will immediately investigate in order to find out the most appropriate solution."[41] It was thus the Kaiser himself, embodying both supreme authority and fatherly love, who was expected to act for the amelioration of all social ills.

Both nationalism and monarchism were associated in the mind of the traditional master artisans with their ideal conception of the family.[42] The connection was formulated explicitly during the same congress: "We love our Christian family and our Stand, and we shall not budge from the Christian idea according to which the family begins in Heaven with the Father at its head, and communities, provinces, and states grow out of it."[43] The state was thus expected to follow the principle of the family, or more precisely, that of the *traditional* family. It was to be headed by a man acting as a strict but loving father, to whom full obedience was due in return for his just and merciful conduct of the affairs of the entire community. Ideally the

[41] *Protokoll über die Verhandlungen, Berlin 1892,* p. 62.

[42] This connection is well argued in Wilhelm Reich, *Massenpsychologie des Faschismus,* chap. 2.

[43] *Protokoll über die Verhandlungen, Berlin 1892,* p. 62.

master's personal family was so constructed, and he was continuously engaged in a struggle to preserve it. This, however, took place at a time when various aspects of modernization combined to cause far-reaching changes in the structure of the traditional family, and the masters could only view with alarm the slow disintegration of the institution under the impact of secularization, changing working patterns, and new employment opportunities. Particularly disturbing was the gradual, often imperceptible transformation in the position of women. The masters' Berlin journal, seeking to reaffirm the traditional status of women in society asserted that "woman was created by God and delivered by Him to man. It is, therefore, the first duty of every girl to marry, so that she may fulfill her mission in life as a wife, housekeeper, and mother, according to the will of her Creator."[44] The author then continues by blaming the excessive education of women for the unhealthy change in their social position and particularly in the character of their relationship to men. Providing women with a slight knowledge of music, painting, and literature seemed to him more than sufficient. The woman's role at home, idealized as an expression of God's will, was portrayed as a reflection of her delicate nature, innate devotion, and physical fragility.

In similar ways the masters defended other aspects of the traditional family. Their respect for authority, their monarchism, and their antidemocratic sentiments can all be understood within this framework. The family and the handicraft workshop had to be preserved in their old forms and their guiding principles made into generally applicable rules in the life of the nation as a whole.

Resistance to Social Democracy, insistence on the preservation of traditional German values, and opposition to everything foreign all qualified the masters in their own eyes as most reliable patriots. Patriotism was for them identical with the holy duty of preserving German tradition, and with the maintenance of German piety as an essential part of it.

[44] *DHZ*, March 12, 1894.

Nonreligious people, the masters argued as early as 1887, could not possibly be trustworthy patriots.[45] Opposition to socialism and the rejection of anything Jewish thus became the double duty of patriotic, pious men. It was their deep religious sensitivity, the masters believed, that had protected them against the tide of modernism in the guise of both liberalism and socialism. At this distance, it is difficult to assess how sincerely religious the master artisans in fact were. They were perhaps more observant and orthodox in their conduct than either the workers below them on the social ladder or their more prosperous industrial rivals above. Particularly devout were the Catholic masters, a fact that was appreciated and exploited by the Center party. In an article discussing "Handicraft and Christianity," the Catholic *Christlich-soziale Blätter* commended handicraft production as "Christian, real and of the most lasting value" and dismissed factory articles as the embodiment of "the mechanics of rapid and cheap production for the egotistical satisfaction of the moment."[46] Handicraft, continued the article, was indeed a "truly Christian industry," and handicraftsmen were thus certain to find encouragement and support in the Church. They were to be the protectors of Christianity against the tide of atheism, and Christianity was in turn to serve them in the battle against the disintegrating effects of modernity.

Even by the 1890s, the small traditional masters were unable to conceptualize a positive view of an alternative society that could give a direction to their public activity. Instead their hope for the future was based on a vague and romantic adoration of some ill-defined past. In Germany, romanticism developed as an almost exclusively conservative trend. Essentially antirevolutionary, it tended to glorify the antiliberal and antidemocratic aspects of the unique German past, often presenting the medieval handicraft

[45] *AHZ*, January 26, 1887.

[46] *Christlich-soziale Blätter*, 1895, pp. 179-190.

guilds as ideal communities based on selection and privilege. Not surprisingly, the master artisans themselves developed a special attachment to the "Age of the Guilds," seeing it as something it had certainly never been. The descriptions of the ancient guilds in the literary supplements of the masters' newspapers give the decided impression that the masters' great longing for the past was no more than the other side of their antimodernism. Their demands for the old order, for the religiosity, authority, and hierarchy it had embodied were all forms of opposition to various manifestations of modernity.

The positive elements within the master-artisans' ideology, their nationalism, monarchism, religiosity, and patriotism, did not add up to a consistent and constructive conservative vision, and certainly not to a specific program for political action. In fact, these elements served primarily as extensions of the negative elements in the masters' Weltanschauung. Nationalism and patriotism were the complementary aspects of the masters' anti-Semitism. Monarchism was for them the only known alternative to a hated democracy and despised parliamentarism. Tradition and religion were flaunted in defiance of the progressivism and agnosticism of liberals and socialists. Even the masters' nostalgic conservatism was nothing but the obverse of their overall rejection of modernity.

By the end of the nineteenth century the idea of a Berufsständestaat, perhaps unrealistic but nonetheless a comprehensive alternative to parliamentarism, so predominant in the world view of their predecessors in 1848, was disregarded by the masters.[47] At the National Congress of Master Artisans in 1895 the main speaker on government-sponsored legislation defiantly suggested submitting to the Reichstag

[47] For the master-artisans' proposed institutional reform during 1848-49 see the *Entwurf einer allgemeinen Handwerker- und Gewerbeordnung*, and some additional details given in Biermann, *Karl Georg Winkelblech*, pp. 110-152.

the social reform plan from the masters' first national congress in Frankfurt a.M., in the summer of 1848.[48] In the face of a general lack of new constructive social planning, the masters occasionally fell back on this ill-fated proposal. In this case, however, it was nothing but a rhetorical device. Between the middle and the end of the nineteenth century, the masters lost their taste for utopia. Their actual alternative legal draft, ceremoniously submitted to the government, asked for obligatory guilds and masters' examinations as measures designed to preserve the industrial Mittelstand and not as elements of a comprehensive social scheme. Even the network of handicraft chambers, which in 1848 was conceived of as the basis for a new overall state structure, was by 1895 expected only to help in revitalizing the existing guilds, a stopgap measure of social protection. Popular antimodernism had no real alternative to offer. Its sources were antagonism and disaffection, and it never emerged as a constructive force.

The continuing debate on the future of Germany conducted during the last decade of the nineteenth century between the supporters of the industrial state and the champions of the traditional agrarian state reflected the cultural and political dilemma of the age. But in fact the fate of Germany had been long decided. Continuing industrialization and a process of slow democratization were irreversible by the 1890s. The peculiarity of the German situation was that in spite of this, a powerful body of public opinion, supported by influential political and economic interest groups, was unwilling to acknowledge and accept these developments. A symbiosis had gradually evolved between the traditional conservative forces in the Reich and a growing popular antimodern movement. The tenacity of the established Conservative party helped to preserve a ray of hope in the minds of men who detested the emerging system. It provided the campaign of the small masters with a raison d'être,

[48] *Protokoll über die Verhandlungen zu Halle 1895*, p. 28.

a degree of respectability, and even some real effectiveness. The support of the Conservatives, hoping to exploit the masters' antimodernism for their own ends, kept the entire movement alive. The popular, indigenous antimodernism of the masters and other Mittelstand groups was enlisted for the last effort of the Prussian agrarian aristocracy allied with the big business oligarchy to preserve a social supremacy long outdated and ever more precarious. Instead of attempting to adjust to the emerging modern world, the traditional master artisans in Germany were encouraged to develop an ideology designed to protect them against the impact and attractions of this world, and to rationalize their deep-seated disaffection with it. The handicraft masters, together with other traditional social elements in Germany, never accepted the reality of modernization, nor its irreversibility.

Initially the popular antimodern social elements, the fifth milieu, constituted only second-line defense troops in the battle of the German ruling elite for the preservation of its power. Soon, however, they were to take the lead, whereupon their militant antimodern posture was exploited by new political forces. Their final despair and disappointment were all the more crushing, and their consequences all the more disastrous.

Epilogue

The Conditions for Popular Antimodernism: The Bipolar Model

Popular antimodernism was neither an accidental nor a passing ailment in Germany, but a deep-seated structural phenomenon. It was the mental response of men who found themselves overwhelmed by material hardship and psychological pressure, isolated from and alienated by their environment, suffering a sense of homelessness and desperately trying to overcome it. The small urban master artisans from the traditional handicrafts were among the first in Germany to display symptoms of antimodernism. A complete history of this phenomenon, however, must also take into account its roots in the mentality of other social elements; from that perspective, the history of the small masters is basically only a case study.[1] It exemplifies the difficulties that confronted traditional groups throughout the process of modernization, exposing the ways in which the pattern of their reaction and response developed. At the same time it facilitates observation of and speculation on the relationship between modernization and the growth of its popular negation in the form of the antimodern movement. It provides the necessary material for isolating the inherent features of the former that contributed to the growth of the latter.

The mood of popular antimodernism is not to be identified with a "preindustrial mentality," although preindustrial patterns of life and thought played a significant role in determining its nature.[2] As a reaction to modernity, antimod-

[1] For small retailers see Gellately, *The Politics of Economic Despair*; more comprehensive is Kocka's study of white-collar employees, *Unternehmensverwaltung und Angestelltenschaft*. See also Puhle, *Agrarische Interessenpolitik*, and his *Von der Agrarkrise zum Präfaschismus*. For a later period see especially Winkler, *Mittelstand*. No general study of the Mittelstand during the period of modernization is available.

[2] See Kocka, "Vorindustrielle Faktoren in der deutschen Indus-

ernism was itself a modern phenomenon, more or less prominent and persistent depending on local conditions. Despite its nostalgia for the past it could only flourish where that past was being continuously transformed. The social groups that tended to develop an antimodern mentality were traditional only in a limited sense, and had themselves undergone fundamental changes during the process of modernization. The small master artisans as a group, as well as such clearly traditional elements as the Prussian landowning aristocracy, preserved traits that were characteristic of the old order, but were, by both objective and subjective criteria, only pseudotraditional at the end of the nineteenth century.[3] The development of antimodernism and of the groups that adopted and spread its message was directly dependent on the pace, intensity, and nature of the process of modernization itself.

A review of both the English case and the variations that appeared within Germany, indicates that the analysis of the growth of antimodernism, like that of modernization, must take into account elements of three different stages: the premodern point of departure, the actual "passage to modernity," and the relatively modern state of affairs at the close of the period under investigation.[4] These are analytical rather than historically distinct phases. The premodern stage is nothing but the abstraction of a prolonged historical period. It is not to be identified with any ideal-type model of "traditional society," just as the final, relatively modern stage may not have embodied all the characteristics of "modernity." Instead, the starting point merely represents a rather

---

trialisierung," and H.A. Winkler, "Vom Protest zur Panik," in *Industrielles System und politische Entwicklung*, ed. Hans Mommsen et al., especially pp. 790-791. See also Robert Koehl, "Feudal Aspects of National Socialism."

3 See especially Hans Rosenberg, "Die pseudodemokratisierung der Rittergutsbesitzerklasse."

4 See Binder et al., *Crises and Sequences*, pp. 12-13. For the following discussion see also Wehler, *Modernisierungstheorie*, chaps. 1-2.

arbitrary phase in the development of premodern society, which was in itself neither static nor stagnant, while the closing state of affairs is likewise a partly arbitrary stage in the development of modern society, with no finality or perfection about it.

One crucial factor in the nature of premodern society affected significantly the emergence of antimodernism among small urban master artisans: *the content and tenacity of the local guild tradition.* A militant artisan antimodernism tended to develop particularly in places where the guild tradition was strong and affectionately preserved. This tradition dictated the masters' obstinate adherence to old forms of production and economic activity, worked to underline the importance of hierarchy, exclusiveness, and privilege in their conception of society, and implanted in them a unique set of cultural values and social norms. Most important, perhaps, the guild tradition carried within it a peculiar ambivalence toward the state and its bureaucracy, manifested by a simultaneous reliance on government support and resentment of government intervention and control. The corporate tradition restricted the range of reactions open to the small masters throughout the process of modernization. Where that heritage was strong, master artisans found it particularly difficult to organize on the basis of free associations and work together to support themselves independently of, or when necessary in opposition to, state authorities. The corporate tradition, as a whole, limited the masters' ability to adjust to the conditions of an open national market economy, compete with new forms of production, accept the reality of a new social-stratification system, adopt modern values, and learn to act as a part of a different political community. Wherever this tradition persisted, even if only as a memory of some ideal past, the small masters tended to favor mercantilist state protectionism, a society of estates subservient to an aristocratic-bureaucratic ruling elite, and the values and attitudes characteristic of that kind of society.

Four aspects of modernization affected the growth of antimodernism among artisans:

1. The speed, character, and timing of industrialization
2. The process of social restratification and the changing pattern and intensity of social mobility
3. The nature and style of both liberalism and the working-class movement, the two main proponents of the ideology and practice of change and modernization
4. The extent and the tempo of political change taking place simultaneously with other aspects of modernization

Antimodernism tended to become militant among small masters particularly in areas where industrialization was quick or distinctly uneven, and where the establishment of large-scale mechanized factories took place in the absence of a previously widespread domestic system. The combination of economic growth with recurrent and severe depressions, cyclical economic fluctuations, and a prolonged deflation made it harder for the small masters to adjust to the new economic order. Thus, the speed, comprehensiveness, and timing of industrialization proved crucial both for the development of a new group consciousness among small independent master artisans and for the prevalence of antimodernism among them. Anti-industrialism, an aspect of the masters' antimodern stand, could only develop in areas where industrialism itself was clearly discernible and of growing significance. But it was prevalent where a dominant industrialization had left pockets of rural and urban traditional economy more or less intact, and in periods of economic hardship and depression. It was the coexistence and proximity of modern and traditional economic elements during the years of crisis that proved to be the most fertile ground for the development of the masters' militant antimodernism.

Likewise, antimodernism tended to flourish where a modern pattern of social stratification did not neatly unseat the traditional one, but tended instead to coexist with it. It did not become typical for masters in areas where traditional society remained virtually intact, nor in communities in which a modern class society entirely replaced the old structure of estates. The coexistence of old and new social elements put psychological pressure especially upon men associating themselves with traditional groups, and the tension was heightened under conditions of limited social mobility, where the entry into higher social status groups with distinct modern characteristics was virtually blocked. The combination of these two elements greatly exacerbated the masters' resentment of change and contributed to their rejection of modernity as a whole.

On the ideational and political plane the intensity of the small masters' antimodernism depended primarily on the nature of their relationship with the forces that supported and encouraged the process of modernization. It was affected by the nature of liberalism and the kind of Liberal political activity in the community on the one hand, and by the character of the local working-class movement, the degree of its militancy, and the effectiveness of its trade-union activity on the other. Antimodernism grew especially where masters found it impossible to identify themselves with either of these two movements. In places where liberalism relied heavily on economic, rather than political doctrine, and stressed in particular domestic industrial freedom rather than international free trade, small master artisans gradually deserted it. They then tended to identify liberalism with change and modernity, and transformed their antiliberalism into a general antimodern position.

A working-class movement stressing its socialism and its opposition to all forms of private property, or a strong trade-union movement undermining the authority of small producers, could not provide an alternative channel for the masters' opposition to the direction of social change. Such a working-class movement only further endangered their already unstable social position and openly threatened their values and loyalties. It increased their sense of social isolation, intensified their fear of the future, and consequently strengthened their antimodernism.

Finally, it is important not to underestimate the effects of political change occurring simultaneously with the economic, social, and cultural transformations of modernization. Naturally, the process of adaptation required from such traditional social groups as the small master artisans was made all the more arduous when tension was heightened by far-reaching changes in the political nature of the community.[5] The masters had to adjust to the transition from a political system based on a traditional structure of authority to one based on rational legal principles. They had to reorganize in order to enter the battle over election rights, political influence, and economic protection. They had to internalize a new political identity required by the creation of a new national unit. These demands made the masters' overall process of adaptation particularly difficult, shook their confidence, and predisposed them to take a position of hostility toward every kind of change.

At the final stage of the investigation, one important element must be considered when an attempt is made to explain not only the rise but also the persistence of antimodernism among small master artisans even after the most fundamental transformations were completed, and modernity was substantially triumphant. That element is *the character of the emerging modern state, its level of intervention in social and economic processes, and the attitude of its ruling elite toward modernity and modernization.*

A basically negative ideological stand, antimodernism did not offer ways to adjust to change. Instead, it tenaciously opposed forces that were already dominant and clamored for the reversal of an irreversible trend. Antimodern groups therefore had to rely on state intervention and repeatedly appealed to the state for support and protection. Where

[5] See Binder et al., *Crises and Sequences*; Wehler, *Modernisierungstheorie*, pp. 34-38.

such help was not forthcoming, masters were forced to stand on their own and impelled to seek more positive solutions to their immediate problems. Conversely, an interventionist state with a policy of social protectionism designed to prop up traditional elements may at times have moderated their dissatisfaction, but in general it encouraged them to persist in their antimodernism and helped make antimodernism a permanent feature of their ideological stand and political behavior. The attitude of the ruling elite likewise influenced the longevity of antimodernism among traditional lower-class elements. Antimodernism often remained the ideology of certain social groups mainly because it was kept alive and supported by an antimodern ruling elite manipulating it for its own ends.

Taken as a whole, the conditions for the growth of radical popular antimodernism were more completely fulfilled in Germany than in England. Germany preserved a strong and highly esteemed guild tradition, which stressed industrial hierarchy, exclusiveness, and privilege. Its long bureaucratic tradition encouraged reliance on state support and prevented the urge for independent group action from developing. The country underwent a more rapid and uneven process of industrialization than did England, and a crucial phase of this process coincided with the Great Depression. The old German social-stratification system proved more persistent and more rigid than its English counterpart. Until well into the twentieth century, traditional social elements in Germany coexisted with modern ones, and upward social mobility for the lower traditional groups often became not easier, but rather more difficult to achieve. Furthermore, Germany's political liberalism was on the whole weak, and after a series of compromises with the wielders of power in the state, deteriorated to become a tool for the advancement of particular socioeconomic interests. The German working-class movement, however, emerged massive and powerful after years of oppression and underground activity. At least its rhetoric, if not always its practice, was that of a socialist, revolutionary movement, and its trade unions were large and of growing effectiveness. Political adjustments required of the German small masters during the last part of the nineteenth century were far reaching. Unlike their English counterparts they not only had to respond to the challenge of a more active political role, they also had to accommodate themselves to a new unit of government, the national one. They were expected to adjust to a number of political changes all occurring within a short period. At the same time they faced drastic social transformations and economic instability and insecurity. Finally, the emerging German state at the end of the nineteenth century was openly interventionist and its social-protectionist policy, by basically accepting the masters' demand for insurance against modernity, encouraged the development of their antimodernism, making use of it to combat the threat of social disintegration and revolution.[6] The German ruling elite of Junker landowners and large-scale industrialists soon learned to manipulate antimodernism for its own ends and make it a force for preserving the social status quo in Germany.

The guild tradition in England, on the other hand, was already partly forgotten and of relatively little importance by the late eighteenth century. For centuries the British economy operated with minimal state intervention, and even the few remnants of protectionist, mercantilist regulations still on the books were only rarely enforced. English industrialization was a slow, gradual process whose smoothness may partly be attributed to the existence of an old and well-developed putting-out system. By the time of the Great Depression it was virtually complete. The social-stratification system in England was more flexible than in Germany, absorbing new elements with greater ease and continuously preserving a certain level of mobility within it. The gradual

[6] See Jürgen Kocka, "Organisierter Kapitalismus oder Staatsmonopolistischer Kapitalismus," and H.-U. Wehler, "Der Aufstieg des organsierten Kapitalismus," both in *Organisierter Kapitalismus*, ed. H.A. Winkler.

democratization of England during the nineteenth century mainly served to mitigate the effects of the overall socio-economic development and allow it to proceed in a *relatively* nonviolent manner. English liberalism represented a mixture of political and economic demands, and was for a long time dominated by an ideology of free trade mixed with Benthamite ideas favoring state intervention on behalf of the weak. The English labor movement had a tradition of cooperation with liberalism, was non-Marxist and at least until the end of the century, moderate and reformist. Furthermore, neither the state nor the ruling elite in England had any use for antimodernism. Although measures of social protectionism were introduced in England as almost everywhere else in the industrialized West during the Great Depression, the English government never adopted social protectionism as a method of bolstering traditional elements, and the dominant social groups all had an interest in furthering modernization even when they acted with caution, attempting to direct and control it. Modernization in England did not give rise to a group-conscious small masters' community but operated to ease their absorption into other groups and smooth their adaptation to a new society. Antimodernism never became a popular trend in England. It remained merely a marginal intellectual fashion there.

The simplified form of the German-English comparison presented does not pretend to do justice to either of the two cases. It is no more than a bipolar ideal-type model serving as a tool for further research. Regional variations within these two countries, as well as the study of comparable phenomena in others, may thus be ordered upon a scale between a generalized German and a generalized English model. In this way modern German history remains within the framework of European development as an extreme but not an alien case, and aspects of it may be identified elsewhere in the modernizing countries of the West. No further international comparison will be offered here, but a quick look at some regional and local cases within Germany, not entirely identifiable with either the German or the English ideal type, may illustrate the potential of this approach.

The Conditions for Popular Antimodernism: Regional Variations

The most radical antimodern stand among small master artisans in Germany developed in the Prussian province of Westphalia. This was a highly heterogeneous area in many respects, and the position of masters within it varied from one locality to another. Dortmund, a center of the Westphalian masters' movement during the years of the Great Depression, is an interesting example.[7] The town prided itself on its long history as a member of the Hanseatic league, reaching back to the fourteenth century. It had a strong and well-preserved tradition of handicraft and commercial guilds. In 1800 it was a relatively small town, but within a few decades underwent rapid industrialization, becoming a center of mining and heavy industry. By the last quarter of the nineteenth century, Dortmund had evolved into a large industrial town, but unlike the new urban centers in the Ruhr valley, its modern industry coexisted with a large handicraft sector. Although industrialization developed early in the region as a whole and was highly advanced by the end of the nineteenth century, it had transformed only a limited number of industries, leaving others virtually intact. The putting-out system was distinctly undeveloped in Westphalia, and industrial concentration extremely uneven. Large pockets of rural and urban traditional handicraft production coexisted in this region with modern, large-scale heavy industry. Furthermore, while channels for the upward mobility of small masters were abundant in the early phases

[7] See Hans Graf, *Die Entwicklung der Wahlen in Gross-Dortmund*; Karl Meister, "Die Innungen der Stadt Dortmund"; H. Hellgrew, *Dortmund als Industriestadt*. For a comparative study of two Westphalian regions see Noll, *Sozio-ökonomischer Strukturwandel*, and for an earlier period Zunkel, *Der Rheinisch-Westfälische Unternehmer*.

of industrialization, they had become practically blocked by the last quarter of the nineteenth century. Small masters felt they were virtually locked between a prospering and influential stratum of industrial entrepreneurs and a growing working-class population. Liberalism in this region, especially after 1848, concentrated on economic issues and early became associated with the protection of the interests of large-scale, heavy industry. The working-class movement, despite its long-maintained ties with Catholicism, was rapidly becoming radical and powerful. By the early 1880s the small masters in Dortmund were antiliberal, anticapitalist, increasingly antisocialist, and often anti-Semitic. Gradually, too, as the heavy-industry interests in the region came to be identified with the economic and social objectives of both the Junker landowners and the conservative autocratic government, they also became eager to make use of the potential support of small masters. Paradoxically, the masters' emerging antimodernism was then encouraged by men representing a large-scale, modernized industrial sector. The alliance between the refeudalized industrial bourgeoisie and the small masters from traditional crafts, which finally took shape during the years of the First World War, had its roots in the conditions of the Ruhr area during the crisis years of the early 1890s.[8]

Hamburg, another Hanseatic town, represents another variation.[9] There, too, a guild tradition was old and well preserved, although within the confines of the free town the guild masters were less attached to the bureaucratic tradition characteristic of some of the larger German states. Industrialization in Hamburg, as in Dortmund, was rapid and radical, but affected significantly only the shipyards and a

[8] See Kocka, *Klassengesellschaft im Krieg*, pp. 85-93; Winkler, *Mittelstand*, pp. 65-70; and his "From Social Protectionism to National Socialism."

[9] For the economic and political development of Hamburg see Baasch, *Geschichte Hamburgs*; Laufenberg, *Geschichte der Arbeiter bewegung Hamburgs*; Comfort, *Revolutionary Hamburg*, pp. 9-29.

few related heavy industries. A large number of urban small masters remained practically untouched by it. Here again a large-scale modern industry coexisted with a sizeable traditional industrial sector. Furthermore, the rigid social hierarchy in the city proved resilient under the pressure of modernization, and while people could prosper under the new conditions, they found it extremely difficult to change their social position within the community. Hamburg's liberalism, the creed of the ruling town notables, was openly undemocratic. Its economic doctrine stressed the advantages of international free trade, and was rarely concerned with matters of domestic industrial freedom. It therefore managed to retain its appeal for at least some of the more prosperous craft masters in town well into the 1880s. The small masters' move from the liberal to the antimodern camp was motivated primarily by their fear of the socialist working-class movement. The Hamburg trade unions had originally been moderate, under the influence of a large journeymen contingent. The potential dangers of a labor movement were, however, clear to the small master employers as early as 1880, and by 1890 their fears were confirmed. A militant workers' movement emerged in Hamburg, responding to the mood and demands of the unskilled or semiskilled workers in the shipyards and the surrounding heavy industries. Nostalgic for the Golden Age of the guilds, impressed but only indirectly affected by industrialization, clearly demarcated socially from both the established prominent locals and the highly organized workers, resentful of the prolonged liberal indifference to their plight, and fearful of militant socialism, the Hamburg master artisans developed one of the most extreme antimodern elements within the national masters' movement.

The case of Berlin is a particularly complex one. The Reich capital had a long guild tradition. The early influx of workingmen into the city, however, made it practically impossible to preserve the economic privileges of the guild masters, all of which were becoming meaningless as a result of the liberal economic measures enacted by the Prussian bureaucracy. At the same time, the closeness to this same bureaucracy left a particularly strong mark on the artisan population in town, and soon proved to be the most persistent element of their premodern heritage. Industrialization in Berlin started relatively early, and by mid-century the city was a manufacturing center for much of the Prussian state.[10] Beginning in the early 1830s the city economy as a whole was fundamentally transformed under the impact of a growing national market, the construction of railroads and canals, the rapid introduction of modern machinery, and the reorganization of the production process in various industrial sectors. Even traditional crafts were greatly affected, and many small masters lost their independence, becoming a part of the relatively advanced domestic and manufacturing system in town. Recent studies have underlined again the great fluidity of social stratification in Berlin during the first half of the nineteenth century, the precarious social position of the small masters, and the early development of a working-class identity there.[11] Politically, masters and men often continued to cooperate in Berlin, supporting a left-wing democratic liberalism. Only with the gradual development of a militant industrial proletariat and the growth of the Social-Democratic movement in the last quarter of the century did the masters begin to move away from their long liberal, democratic tradition. In many ways modernization in Berlin was similar to the familiar English model, distinguished by a slow process of industrial development and a finely stratified and flexible social system preserving a relatively high degree of mobility. The case of Berlin, however,

[10] For the best material on Berlin see Büsch, ed., *Untersuchungen zur Geschichte der frühen Industrialisierung*, especially Büsch's contribution, "Das Gewerbe in der Wirtschaft des Raumes Berlin/Brandenburg"; J. Bergmann, "Das 'Alte Handwerk' "; Dieter Bergmann, "Die Berliner Arbeiterschaft."

[11] See also Frederick Marquardt, "Sozialer Aufstieg, Sozialer Abstieg," and his "A Working Class in Berlin in the 1840's?"

remained unique because of the strength of its bureaucratic tradition and the habitual dependence of the population on the authorities. The antimodernism of the Berlin masters was indeed slow to develop and remained moderate until well into the 1890s. It was, however, always attached to the concepts of social protection and state help, adjusting itself to the mood and the political needs of the bureaucracy and the ruling conservative elite.[12]

The kingdom of Saxony provides a good example of the range of variation in the behavior of small master artisans, even within a single political unit and limited geographical area.[13] The guild tradition was weak throughout Saxony, having been consistently undermined by a liberal state bureaucracy since the early eighteenth century. By the beginning of the Great Depression industrialization was well advanced in many parts of the state, but in no place was it evenly distributed or all-encompassing. In the old administrative center of Dresden, for example, modern industry and its actual and potential effects could clearly be detected during the 1870s, but handicraft production continued to flourish there. The large handicraft population in the Saxonian court town was only marginally affected by industrial change and attempted to hold on to its unique life style, values, and norms. The dominant liberalism in Dresden, of a National-Liberal variety, was never particularly attractive to the small masters, while both the Social-Democratic party and its trade-union movement had some impressive early successes there. In the midst of a rapidly modernizing country, the small masters in Dresden felt betrayed and isolated. As early as the 1880s, several anti-Semitic groups scored unexpected successes there. By the next decade the local master-artisan population was distinctly anti-

[12] See chaps. 6 and 9.

[13] For Saxony see Kötzschke and Kretzschmar, eds., *Sächsische Geschichte*; Forberger, *Die Manufaktur in Sachsen*; Donald Warren, *The Red Kingdom of Saxony*; and Strauss, *Die Lage und die Bewegung der Chemnitzer Arbeiter*.

modern, encouraged and sustained by state social protection and the promises of the conservative elite.

In the more modern urban centers of Saxony, the development of the masters' social consciousness and political attitudes followed a different path. In the Chemnitz area, for example, industrialization depended on the development of the textile trades, and there the domestic industry system slowly penetrated urban production.[14] The nature of the local textile sector began to change early, and the long, slow development of a new industrial system produced an effect reminiscent of the English model. Master artisans were gradually losing their economic independence and joining journeymen in a struggle for higher pay and better working conditions. Their struggle was at first directed against the merchant-entrepreneurs and later against modern industrial management. Throughout much of the seventies and well into the eighties left-wing liberalism was popular among the industrial workers in Chemnitz as well as among the small independent craftsmen there. Socialism, too, made rapid headway among both masters and men. Consequently, the independent master-artisan movement in the Chemnitz area remained weak, and its antimodernism mild and hesitant.

Bavaria represents another mixed case.[15] The guild tradition in many Bavarian towns was old and powerful. It was a tradition of exclusiveness and privilege, which survived well into the nineteenth century through a more or less satisfactory series of compromises with the mercantilist state authorities. In most parts of this south German state modernization was slow to penetrate. In the absence of radical symptoms of change, antimodernism had little reason to develop. The Bavarian masters were strongly antiliberal, but at least until the 1890s their antiliberalism stemmed from their continuous struggle against industrial freedom

[14] See especially Strauss, *Die Lage und die Bewegung*; also the section on the extent and the role of domestic industry in chap. 1.

[15] See Schremmer, *Die Wirtschaft Bayerns*, 236-247; 381-471; 479-482.

and small-scale nonguild production, and was heavily influenced by their social Catholicism and their attachment to the church. The militancy of the masters' Bund came primarily from the Westphalian contingent, while the Bavarians usually conducted their affairs in alliance with the Center party. This permanent link gave them a sense of security and belonging, lacking among their northern Protestant colleagues. Only in the 1890s, when industrialization had penetrated Bavaria and a socialist working-class movement began to make serious progress there, did the Bavarian masters develop typical antimodern attitudes and an increasingly more radical social-protectionist stand.

In the late nineteenth century, and for entirely different reasons, antimodernism was of little moment either among masters in the eastern Prussian provinces or in southwestern Germany. Industrialization was slow to develop in both regions. In all other respects, however, the two were conspicuously dissimilar. In much of Prussia east of the Elbe, with the exception of Berlin and its surroundings, industrialization was hardly noticeable, even by the end of the century.[16] In the large northern ports small masters long retained a left-liberal, anti-Junker orientation, while in small towns and rural areas, if politics was of any interest to them at all, they voted traditionally for the established local Conservative forces. The small masters in these regions were conservative, but not necessarily antimodern. With hardly any detectable signs of industrialization and slow or imperceptible social change, the East and West Prussian master artisans must have found the militancy of their western colleagues disturbing and incomprehensible.

In Baden and in Württemberg the militant antimodern master-artisan movement had the least success.[17] In this

[16] See Krüger, *Zur Geschichte der Manufakturen*, pp. 170 ff. Also Knut Borschardt, "Regionale Wachstumsdifferenzierung," in *Wirtschaftliche und soziale Probleme*, ed. F. Lütge, pp. 115-130.

[17] See Lang, *Die Badischen Gewerbevereine*, and for an earlier

southwestern region none of the conditions for antimodernism was satisfied. The guild tradition there was weak; industrialization was limited to a few branches of the economy and was on the whole of relatively slight significance. The southwestern liberal tradition had a strong political connotation and was explicitly democratic. It was influenced by French experiences and ideas, and was as a rule more radical and uncompromising than elsewhere in the Reich. Under the auspices of the left-liberal Deutsche Volkspartei the small masters in Baden and Württemberg remained loyal to liberalism later than handicraft groups in other regions. From the mid-eighties on they occasionally showed signs of antiliberalism and made sporadic efforts to organize guilds and join conservative national associations, but their major organizational unit was, and remained throughout the century, the liberal Gewerbeverein. Membership in the conservative Bund was small and limited to a few central towns, where the influence of Social Democracy was on the rise. On the whole, master artisans in southwestern Germany remained essentially uncommitted to the ideas of, and the organizations inspired by, antimodernism.

This preliminary review indicates once again the great diversity of the master-artisan reaction to the process of modernization. In most areas, specific local factors influenced masters' attitudes. Anti-Prussian sentiments in the Rhineland and Westphalia, in Hanover, Hamburg, and parts of Saxony, seem to have increased the political dissatisfaction of the small master artisans, sharpened their overall sense of antagonism, and intensified the militancy of their antimodernism. The proximity of the Berlin masters to the center of bureaucracy, to take a different example, reinforced their attachment to the prevailing political structure, strengthened their reliance on government social protection, and delayed the eruption of their bitterness and hostility in

---

period Wolfram Fischer, *Der Staat und die Industrialisierung in Baden.*

the form of antimodernism. Special economic circumstances, the existence of large minority groups, the level of urbanization, and other local factors all played a role in determining the exact social and political stand of the small masters. During the years of the Great Depression, however, master-artisan antimodernism in Germany as a whole tended to spread wide and far. Previous ties with liberalism were cut almost everywhere, and a growing number of small masters came to exhibit aggressive antimodernism and political behavior typical of that state of mind.

A Prelude to Fascism

Antimodernism crystallized as a dominant ideological position of small master artisans in Germany during the years of the Great Depression, and assumed its final and most militant form during the last cyclical economic downward trend, between 1890 and 1895-96. The following phase of modernization took place during a period of prosperity that extended, with only two brief interruptions, to 1913. As could be expected on the basis of the changing intensity of masters' antimodernism during the short-term economic fluctuations between 1873 and 1896, the prolonged prosperity worked to temper the masters' general antagonism to change. Government social protectionism and Conservative protestations of good will also helped reduce the masters' sense of isolation and soften their antimodern position. In addition, the masters were diverted from particular to national issues by the rhetoric of patriotism and pan-Germanism resorted to at the time by the government and the ruling elite, and were easily lured by the glories of Weltpolitik. Both the government and the Conservatives, having a vested interest in sustaining a strong opposition to liberalism and Social Democracy took the measures necessary to preserve the masters' antimodernism as a way of ensuring their continuing loyalty to, and active support of, the prevailing sociopolitical order.

Coincident with the onset of the boom years, as the opposition of big business interests slackened, the government passed the new handicraft law of 1897, introducing the "compulsory guild option" and regional handicraft chambers as institutions of public law.[18] A compulsory masters' examination was vetoed by the Bundesrat, but by 1908 the protectionist Reichstag majority managed at least to institute a measure providing that only masters who had taken that examination could train handicraft apprentices. Under conditions of prosperity these concessions appeared to have satisfied many of the masters. While some retained a militant antimodern position and demanded more far-reaching social-protectionist reforms, others took a more moderate stand, joined liberal self-help oriented associations, and occasionally even resumed ties with the liberal political parties.[19] At the eve of the First World War a considerable number of small masters rejoined the Progressive party. The influence of the liberal Hansa-Bund among them was growing, and a few of the masters' interest organizations were associated with it, either officially or through the activity of their leadership. The Hansa-Bund was then considered a serious competitor for masters' support by both the conservative-inspired and led Reichsdeutsche Mittelstandverband (The Federation of the German Mittelstand) and the more politically oriented Kartell der schaffenden Stände (Cartel of the Producing Estates).[20] Beginning in 1913, the latter attempted to reestablish solidarity among conservative agrarians, protectionist industrialists, peasants, and urban Mittelständler, but had only partial success. During the war years, however, small handicraft producers who did not go over to the left-wing opposition tended to estab-

[18] On legislative reforms during the 1890s see chap. 10.

[19] See especially Winkler, *Mittelstand*, pp. 55-57; Klaus Simon, *Die Württembergischen Demokraten*, pp. 37 ff. See also comments in Heberle, *From Democracy to Nazism*, which emphasizes, however, the voting behavior of the rural population; Lipset, *Political Man*, chap. 5; and H.-A. Winkler's "Extremismus der Mitte?"

[20] See Siegfried Mielke, *Der Hansa-Bund*, pp. 102-112.

lish a kind of alliance with big-business interests for the purpose of protecting the fatherland against democratization and revolution.[21] They were prepared to moderate their anticapitalism in order to cooperate with their former enemies on common domestic and foreign political objectives. Soon after the war, however, it became evident that big business preferred an alliance with organized labor and that masters were again isolated, squeezed as it were between these two powerful rivals.[22]

Thus, following a period characterized by a more optimistic mood among masters and some positive attempts on their part to adapt to the new standards of modernity, they found themselves once again socially isolated. Furthermore, the political system of the new republic appeared to them to have preserved all the disagreeable features of the Empire, without having the latter's claim for continuity, glory, and unity. During the fluid and uncertain early revolutionary period, Social Democracy failed to win the small masters' support.[23] In 1919 many of them, seeking a compromise to prevent the total destruction of the old order, voted for the liberal Deutsche Demokratische Partei (DDP, German Democratic party). From then on, however, they started a "long migration through the party-system of the Weimar Republic — a migration from left to right."[24] Liberalism, which for a time regained the support of many Mittelstand

[21] See the discussion in Jürgen Kocka, "The First World War and the 'Mittelstand' "; and his *Klassengesellschaft im Krieg*, pp. 85-95.

[22] In addition to Kocka's work cited in n. 21, see also Winkler, *Mittelstand*, pp. 65-70; and his "Unternehmerverbände und Nationalsozialismus," especially sections 2 and 3.

[23] On this issue see Arthur Rosenberg, *Die Entstehung der Weimarer Republik*, pp. 223-224, and his "Der Faschismus als Massenbewegung," in O. Bauer, H. Marcuse, A. Rosenberg, et al., *Faschismus und Kapitalismus*, pp. 107 ff.; also Winkler, *Mittelstand*, pp. 65 ff.

[24] Winkler, "From Social Protectionism to National Socialism." See also Wulf, *Die politische Haltung des Schleswig-holsteinischen Handwerks*; Theodor Geiger, "Panik im Mittelstand"; and Rudolf Küstenmeier, *Die Mittelschichten und ihr politischer Weg*.

voters, fast lost it after 1920. Its democratic impetus curbed, it soon proved incapable of offering a concrete plan for ameliorating the conditions of small masters and was powerless to see through any social reform policy at all. The small master artisans again turned to the conservatives. In 1924 the Deutschnationale Volkspartei (DNVP, German National People's party) attempted to broaden its popular base by proposing to reduce taxes and increase social security benefits. The Deutsche Volkspartei (DVP, German People's party) also made some unconvincing advances along similar lines. But while the Center party was relatively successful in holding its Catholic Mittelstand voters, the Protestant conservative parties of the north had only a limited and temporary success among the same social groups.[25]

In 1925, the small Wirtschaftspartei (Business party) attempted to capitalize on the political homelessness of various Mittelstand groups, master artisans included.[26] Its leaders formulated detailed reform plans and delivered fiery speeches in defense of the small handicraft masters. While the masters' national interest organizations took care not to commit themselves to the exclusive support of the Wirtschaftspartei, a great many individual masters gave it their vote. Later on, however, under the name of Reichspartei des deutschen Mittelstand (Imperial party of the German Mittelstand) this party managed to poll only 4.5 percent of the total vote, and its small size and ineffectiveness further underlined the political impotence of the masters. Then, when the 1929 crash added material hardship and economic insecurity to their social and political isolation, their feelings of anxiety and panic were reawakened.

In 1926 there were nearly 1.5 million independent small masters in Germany, employing approximately a quarter of the total labor force.[27] Their position within the new in-

[25] Winkler, *Mittelstand*, pp. 121-139.

[26] On the Wirtschaftspartei see Martin Schumacher, *Mittelstandsfront und Republik*; Winkler, *Mittelstand*, pp. 123-124.

[27] See the *Ausschuss zur Untersuchung der Erzeugungs- und Absatzbedingungen - Handwerk*, vol. 2, p. 6.

dustrial economy finally appeared to be secure. They were recuperating from the adverse effects of war and inflation when they were hit again, this time by a particularly severe depression. Then, as in 1873, the economic crisis affected short-term credit, interest rates, and the level of national consumption. Being self-employed the masters were ineligible for unemployment compensation and a number of other social security benefits; they lost trained workers to larger industries and found themselves continuously in conflict with the trade unions. At the same time they also had to compete with unemployed laborers who flooded the fast-growing crowded industrial sweatshops in all major towns.[28]

A contemporary analysis of social stratification divided the independent craftsmen in Germany into three subgroups.[29] It found that 4.5 percent of all masters had an income qualifying them as small-scale capitalist entrepreneurs, 65.5 percent lived on modest but respectable incomes, and about 30 percent could only be classified in an income category together with common industrial workers. For 1928 close to one-half of all masters registered an annual income of less than 1,500M, and the majority of the other half earned less than 3,000M per year. The number of individual self-employed masters was rising together with that of masters who apparently did not earn any income at all.

In the early 1930s, as during the years of the Great Depression, the masters continued to compare their situation with that of the large industrial shop owners on the one hand and the wage-earning workers on the other.[30] Following the crisis of 1929 their objective economic position proved to be slightly more stable. The less capital-intensive small shops often withstood the depression better than large-scale industrial entrepreneurs.[31] Continuous unemployment must

[28] On the effects of the depression on the handicrafts see Winkler, *Mittelstand*, pp. 31-39, and the bibliography cited by him, pp. 205-209.

[29] Geiger, *Die Soziale Schichtung*, p. 74.

[30] See chaps. 3 and 4.

[31] See Beckermann, "Konjunktur und Konjunkturbeobachtung," pp. 81-91.

have convinced many wage earners that they could preserve a minimal standard of living only as self-employed artisans. Despite the masters' plight, many of them could still congratulate themselves on their economic independence and the flexibility of their workshops during depression periods. Subjectively, however, they tended to exaggerate their difficulties, mixing economic with social and sociopsychological complaints. The small master may have personally felt the impact of the depression more severely than a big businessman, since his daily life was more closely dependent upon the fortune of his shop. But the masters' sense of deprivation was not directly related to these objective factors and was mainly a result of a comparison they made between their own organized socioeconomic and political position and that of their two main rivals.

Even during the years of depression, militant trade-union activity occasionally succeeded in checking the decline of wages so that it was generally less than the 18 percent decline in the overall cost of living.[32] The prices of some products remained relatively stable, as a result of the manufacturers' powerful price-controlling cartels acting in common to protect themselves in times of crisis. After the end of the war, the workers' position in German society improved as a result of the respectability and the power enjoyed by their political movement, and in a fully industrialized country, the position of large industrial employers was both respected and highly influential. Once again the master artisans found themselves in the throes of an economic crisis while they were engaged in a battle to secure public esteem and prestige.

Despite changing circumstances, the handicraft masters returned to their old campaign. They claimed a superior social position because handicraft production was the source of all "respectable labor" and the only guarantee for superior and artistic work. The German community and the German

[32] See Bry, *Wages in Germany*, pp. 254-255.

culture as a whole, they claimed, could not dispense with the handicrafts, and a true Volksgemeinschaft (people's community) was unthinkable without them. Within a "soulless civilization" they alone could become a point of departure for a new German culture of the future. The handicraft masters, they still wished to believe, had a truly historic mission as the guardians of German piety, thrift, diligence, and creativity.[33] The leaders of the organized master-artisan movement employed the same magical adjectives that had been tirelessly reiterated by their predecessors. As in the earlier period, the argument was intended primarily to boost the self-esteem of the masters themselves, since it could hardly hope to capture the attention of others. As far back as the 1870s, the gap between the masters' self-esteem and their appreciation by others had been a source of frustration and resentment. In the second and third decades of the twentieth century it became even larger and acted again as a motive force in the development of the master-artisans' political attitudes and behavior.[34]

By the end of the 1920s, the small master artisans once again displayed all the symptoms of militant antimodernism. They looked back with nostalgia to the glorious past of the medieval guilds; they vehemently attacked all aspects of modern life and assigned themselves the task of preserving and upholding true, traditional, German virtues. The cult of the Volk, so popular at the time, only lent additional support to this attitude. By 1930, a large portion of the small independent master artisans in Germany were nostalgic conservatives, antiliberal, anticapitalist, and more than ever antisocialist and anti-Semitic. Predictably, they were extreme nationalists, fervent patriots, antidemocratic and antiparliamentarian; ready to endorse the politics of National Socialism.

[33] See *Handwerk tut Not*, a publication of the Reichsverband des deutschen Handwerks und Gewerbekammertag, pp. 40-62; also Winkler, *Mittelstand*, pp. 65-70.

[34] See chap. 4.

The relationship between modernization and the rise of fascism has often been discussed in recent literature.[35] Opposition to modernity is now also occasionally considered pertinent to this development. But when antimodernism is introduced as an element in explaining either the phenomenon of fascism in general or that of National Socialism in particular, it has usually been applied to the analysis of ideas and ideologies.[36] Thus, National-Socialist ideas have been related to the various aspects of the "conservative revolution" as well as to the development of social conservatism during the Weimar period. H.A. Turner, stressing the goal rather than the methods of National Socialism, has gone as far as to characterize its stand as an extreme form of "utopian antimodernism."[37] From another perspective fascism has been defined as "the reaction of the lower-class losers" to industrialization.[38] Sociological studies of the supporters of National Socialism all confirm the thesis that Mittelstand elements were overrepresented among members of the Nazi party and among those who voted for it.[39] However, these two issues—the antimodern aspect in the ideology of National Socialism and the attractiveness of the movement to Mittelstand groups—have rarely been treated together. Such an integrative approach, combining intellectual and social history, is necessary for the development of a new theory of fascism that may finally dispense with both the totalitarianism concept and the orthodox Marxist model.

The ideology of the Nazi party was eclectic and often

[35] See the discussion in Jürgen Kocka, "Recent Historiography of Germany and Austria," pp. 110 ff.

[36] See especially Lebovics, *Social Conservatism and the Middle Classes*; Stern, *The Politics of Cultural Despair*; Klemens von Klemperer, *Germany's New Conservatism*; Kurt Sontheimer, *Antidemokratisches Denken in der Weimarer Republik*.

[37] See his "Faschismus und Anti-Modernismus," in *Faschismus und Kapitalismus*, pp. 161-162.

[38] See Wolfgang Sauer, "National Socialism: Totalitarianism or Fascism?" pp. 417-422.

[39] For literature see the introduction, n. 4.

contradictory. Undoubtedly, antimodern elements were always a part of it. However, to rely completely on the pronouncements of Nazi leaders as proof that their antimodern ideas were vital to them and that they had only temporarily postponed the implementation of their antimodern reform plans, is to overestimate their sincerity and underestimate their ability to carry out even the most impractical projects in the name of sacred principles.[40] For the Nazi party leaders antimodernism was at most only one aspect of a rather incoherent social philosophy, and at worst nothing but a propaganda device. The main goals of the Nazi movement were an unlimited expansion and a "final solution" to the Jewish question. The latter objective was carried out eventually under the improbable conditions of a war on several fronts, requiring great expenditures of scarce manpower and material resources. Plans for the creation of a consciously antimodern society always remained empty talk. Soon after the Nazis' seizure of power it became evident that the much-discussed "artisan socialism" was a distinct obstacle when modern rearmament and the preparation for war were the main political objectives. Large industrial enterprises were clearly indispensable. An increased flow of verbiage and a heightened anti-Semitic campaign served to obscure the fact that the new National-Socialist party intended to consistently neglect the interests of its staunchest supporters.

Initially the slogans of National Socialism were not particularly attractive to the small master artisans. Only toward the end of the twenties did the Nazis turn in earnest to the task of attracting the Mittelstand, and only then did they unequivocally support the Mittelstand demand for further state protection and bring to the fore the antimodern spirit they ostensibly shared with it.[41] In a speech before a national master-artisans' congress, Alfred Rosenberg attempted to reaffirm the alliance between the various traditional forces in

[40] See the discussion in Turner, "Faschismus und Anti-Modernismus," in *Faschismus und Kapitalismus*, pp. 156-177.

[41] Winkler, *Mittlestand*, pp. 157-182.

Germany. "The nobles," he declared, "established the German town; the handicraftsmen made it into a home."[42] Hitler, too, found it wise to proclaim his wish "that the German handicrafts, rooted in a dignified tradition, will proceed to a new blooming, sheltered by Volk and Staat."[43] Nazi officials repeatedly promised to work for the development of new corporations based on the best characteristics of the medieval guilds: loyalty, discipline, competence, and solidarity. To this list was now added the great virtue of "purity of blood," and the old guilds were hailed as the earliest German institutions that had orthodoxly upheld that purity throughout the ages.

The Nazis' social-protectionist promises were certainly important in attracting small master artisans to their ranks. These promises, however, would have been treated with greater skepticism by the masters, accustomed to the empty promises of opposition parties, had there not been a further affinity between themselves and the National Socialists. Nazi antimodernism was closer to the master-artisans' variety than to that of social conservatives and despairing intellectuals. It was not based on a well thought-out plan for reform or a lucid social vision, but was primarily a manifestation of general hostility and a resentment of modernity. It expressed the vague and unrealizable desire to stop the clock. During the 1890s, such hopes could still be made to appear realistic and therefore gave rise to a feverish but controllable kind of reactionary politics. By the second decade of the twentieth century, a return to traditional society was nothing but a dream, and the politics of antimodernism acquired a desperate, hysterical tinge. The full force of modern technology was to be applied to the destruction of modern society, and indeed came alarmingly close to achieving this task. The magnitude of the effort, the enormity of the means adopted, and above all the extent of the crime

[42] Quoted in Wilhelm Wernet, *Soziale Handwerksordnung*, p. 451.

[43] Quoted in Ferdinand Schramm, *Der Reichsstand des deutschen Handwerks*, p. 1.

and of the resulting dehumanization of society were all phenomena peculiar to the twentieth century. But it was the intensity and not the content that gave the antimodern movement of the twentieth century its unique character. In a new setting and under different circumstances the master artisans' early alliance with twentieth-century fascism was essentially a reenactment of their late nineteenth-century ties with political anti-Semitism, radical social conservatism, or, in a word, with the various organized forces of antimodernism.

In the 1920s as well as in the 1890s, antimodernism was the response of an unintegrated, insecure, and resentful segment of society, supported in varying degrees by established conservative forces. Throughout the Imperial period the conservatives managed to manipulate this sentiment in their own interests. Under the leadership of National Socialism, however, they lost control. The Nazis proved capable of transforming popular antimodernism into a powerful independent political force, but ultimately they, too, only made use of it in their own way and for the fulfillment of their own destructive goals.

National-Socialist propaganda must have sounded strangely familiar to the small master artisans in Germany of the 1920s. Some of them could actually remember the experience of the late nineteenth century and recall the attitudes of their predecessors. Others responded in a similar fashion to similar pressures. They reacted to objective economic difficulties, social tension, and political disorientation as well as to their subjective fears of further modernization, an unfulfilled need to belong, and a deep-seated feeling of homelessness.

Bibliography

1. GOVERNMENT ARCHIVAL COLLECTIONS

Deutsches Zentralarchiv, Abt. I: Potsdam

Reichsamt des Innern:

6297-6299: Die Hebung der wirtschaftlichen Lage des Handwerks, Kleingewerbes und Kleinhandels (Mittelstandsbewegung), 1881-1896

6332-6338: Die Organisation des Handwerks, 1881-1897

6341-6345: Eingaben in Bezug auf die Organisation des Handwerks, 1881-1897

Reichskanzlei:

485-489: Innungswesen und Organisation des Handwerks, 1878-1898

Deutsches Zentralarchiv, Abt. II: Merseburg

Ministerium für Handel und Gewerbe:

I. Reform der Gewerbegesetze

1. Generalia

no. 13 Die Petitionen und nichtamtlichen Äusserungen wegen Abänderung der Gewerbegesetzgebung

(116) Bd. 2 1863-1865

(117) Bd. 5 1880-1881

(118) Bd. 6 1881-1882

(119) Bd. 7 1882-1884

(120) Bd. 8 1885-1886

(121) Bd. 9 1886-1890

VI. Gewerbekammern

1. Generalia

no. 1 Die Organisierung einer wirtschaftlichen Interessenvertretung resp. die Errichtung von Gewerbekammern

(626) Bd. 1 1869-1883

VII. Gewerbegehilfen, Gesellen, Lehrlinge, Fabrikarbeiter

1. Im allgemeinen

no. 8 Die Gewerkvereine

(1001) Bd. 1 1868-1879

(1002) Bd. 2 1880-1892

Bayerisches Hauptstaatsarchiv
Handel-Ministerium:
14636-14661 Innungswesen 1881-1891

Badisches Generallandesarchiv
Staatsministerium:
Abt. 233/10023
Innenministerium:
Abt. 236/96724: Innungen
Abt. 236/17081: Polizei
Finanzministerium:
Abt. 237/25013-14: Gewerbevereine
Abt. 237/24656

Staatsarchiv Münster:
369: Innungswesen
742: Status der Innungen

Stadtsarchiv Köln:
Abt. III, 4: Innungen.

2. PUBLISHED MINUTES

Entwurf einer allgemeinen Handwerker- und Gewerbeordnung für Deutschland. Berathen und beschlossen vom deutschen Handwerker- und Gewerbekongress zu Frankfurt a.M. in den Monaten Juli und August 1848. Frankfurt a.M., 1848.

Jahresberichte der Hamburgerischen Gewerbekammern, Hamburg, 1873-96.

Offener Brief an alle Innungsgenossen Deutschlands so wie zugleich an alle Bürger und Hausväter. Von zweiundzwanzig Innungen zu Leipzig. Leipzig, 1848.

Protokoll über die Verhandlungen auf dem achten Delegiertentage des Innungs-Verbandes deutscher Baugewerkmeister zu Hannover, am 16., 17. und 18. Juli 1893.

Protokoll über die Verhandlungen des VIII. allgemeinen deutschen Handwerkertages und des X. Delegiertentages des allgemeinen deutschen Handwerkerbundes, zu Halle a.S. 21., 22., 23. und 24. April 1895. Munich, 1895.

Protokoll über die Verhandlungen des Delegiertentages des Vereins selbständiger Handwerker und Fabrikanten Deutschlands:
zu Quedlinburg, am 27., 28. und 29. August 1874. Berlin, 1874.
zu Köln, am 2., 3., 4. und 5. August 1876. Berlin, 1876.
zu Darmstadt, am 8., 9., 10. und 11. August 1877. Berlin, 1877.

Protokoll über die Verhandlungen des deutschen Innungs- und allgemeinen Handwerkertages
vom 14. bis 17. Februar 1892 in Berlin. Berlin, 1892.
am 9. und 10. April 1894 in Berlin. Berlin, 1894.

Protokoll über die Verhandlungen des XIII. allgemeinen Bayerischen Handwerkertages und des XIII. Delegiertentages des Bayerischen Handwerkerbundes zu Aibling am 19., 20. und 21. September 1896. Munich, 1896.

Protokoll über die Verhandlungen des I. Südwestdeutschen Handwerkertages zu Heidelberg, am 23. und 24. August 1896. Heidelberg, 1896.

Protokoll über die Verhandlungen des Parteitages der Sozialdemokratischen Partei Deutschlands in Berlin 1892. Berlin, 1892.

Stenographische Berichte über die Verhandlungen der deutschen constituierenden Nationalversammlung zu Frankfurt a.M. Edited by Franz Wigard. 9 vols. Frankfurt a.M., 1848-49.

Stenographische Berichte über die Verhandlungen des deutschen Reichstags, 1873-97.

Verhandlungen auf dem neunten Delegiertentage des Verbandes deutscher Baugewerksmeister zu Danzig am 4., 5. und 6. September 1881.

Verhandlungen des 8. Evangelisch-sozialen Kongresses (10. und 11. Juni 1897). Göttingen, 1897.

Verhandlungen des allgemeinen deutschen Handwerkertages
zu Magdeburg, am 31. May, 1. und 2. Juni 1882. Berlin, 1882.
zu Hannover, am 21. und 22. Mai 1883. Berlin, 1883.
zu Kösen, am 15. und 16. September 1886. Berlin, 1886.

Verhandlungen der ersten Abgeordneten Versammlung des norddeutschen Handwerker- und Gewerbestandes zu Hamburg, den 2.—6. Juni 1848. Edited by G. Schirges. Hamburg, 1848.

Verhandlungen des ersten deutschen Handwerker- und Gewerbekongresses gehalten zu Frankfurt a.M. vom 14. Juli bis 18. August 1848. Edited by G. Shirges. Darmstadt, 1848.

Verhandlungen des zweiten deutschen Innungstages zu Berlin am 9., 10., 11. und 12. September 1888. Berlin, 1888.

Der zweite deutsche Handwerkertag zu Frankfurt a.M. von 25. bis 28. September 1863. Frankfurt a.M., 1863.

3. OFFICIAL STATISTICAL SOURCES

Die Bevölkerungs- und Wohnungsaufnahme von Dezember 1885, 1890, 1895 in der Stadt Berlin. Städtische Deputation für Statistik. Berlin, 1896.

Erhebung über die Lage des Kleingewerbes in Baden, 1885. 3 vols. Karlsruhe, 1887-88.

Erhebung über die Verhältnisse im Handwerk. Veranstaltet im Sommer 1895. Bearbeitet im Kaiserlichen Statistischen Amt. Part i and ii. Berlin, 1895.

Erhebung über die Wirkung des Handwerkergesetzes 1897, und über die Tätigkeit und Erfolg der Handwerkerkammern 1907. Berlin, 1908.

Jahrbuch für die amtliche Statistik des Preussischen Staats.

Statistik des Deutschen Reichs.

Statistisches Jahrbuch der Stadt Berlin. 1874 ff.

Statistisches Jahrbuch deutscher Städte. 1890-96.

Statistisches Jahrbuch für das Deutsche Reich.

Statistisches Jahrbuch für das Königreich Sachsen. 1873 ff.

4. BOOKS AND ARTICLES

Excluded from this list are entries in handbooks and encyclopedias and articles concerning single local crafts that are included in the VSP *Untersuchungen, Schriften* 62-70 (1895-97).

BIBLIOGRAPHY

Abel, Wilhelm. "Der Pauperismus in Deutschland am Vorabend der industriellen Revolution." In *Festschrift F. Lütge*, edited by W. Abel et al. Stuttgart, 1966.

———. "Zur Ortsbestimmung des Handwerks vor dem Hintergrund seiner Geschichte." In *Das Handwerk in der modernen Wirtschaft und Gesellschaft.* Bad Wörrishofen, 1966.

———. *Massenarmut und Hungerkrisen im vorindustriellen Deutschland.* Göttingen, 1972.

Abel, Wilhelm et al. *Handwerksgeschichte in neuer Sicht.* Göttingen, 1970.

Abrams, Karl. *Der Strukturwandel im Handwerk in der ersten Hälfte des 19. Jahrhunderts und seine Bedeutung für die Berufserziehung.* Cologne, 1955.

Albrecht, H. "Die Volkswirtschaftliche Bedeutung der Kleinkraft Machinen." *Schmollers JB* 12 (1889): 490-497.

Alexander, Edgar. "Church and Society in Germany." In *Catholic Social and Political Movements 1789-1950*, edited by Joseph M. Moody. New York, 1953.

Allen, G.C. *The Industrial Development of Birmingham and the Black Country 1860-1927.* London, 1929.

Allmann, O. *Geschichte der deutschen Bäcker- und Konditorenbewegung.* Hamburg, 1910.

Anderson, Eugene N. *The Social and Political Conflict in Prussia 1858-1864.* Lincoln, Neb., 1954.

Arnold, Philipp. *Das Münchener Bäckergewerbe.* Stuttgart, 1895.

Ashton, T.S. *An Economic History of England: The Eighteenth Century.* London, 1961.

Assmann, Klaus, and Stavenhagen, Gerhard. *Handwerkereinkommen am Vorabend der Industriellen Revolution. Materialien aus dem Raum Braunschweig - Wolfenbüttel.* Göttingen, 1969.

Aubin, Hermann and Zorn, Wolfgang, eds. *Handbuch der deutschen Wirtschafts- und Sozialgeschichte.* Stuttgart, 1971.

Ausschuss zur Untersuchung der Erzeugungs- und Absatz-

bedingungen der deutschen Wirtschaft. III Unterausschuss, 8. Arbeitsgruppe (Handwerk). Berlin, 1930.

Baar, Lothar. *Die Berliner Industrie in der Industriellen Revolution.* Berlin, 1966.

Baasch, Ernst. *Geschichte Hamburgs.* 2 vols. Gotha, 1924.

Badtke, Walther. *Zur Entwicklung des deutschen Bäckergewerbes.* Jena, 1906.

Barkin, Kenneth D. "Adolf Wagner and German Industrial Development." *JMH* 41 (1969): 144-159.

———. *The Controversy over German Industrialization, 1890-1902.* Chicago, 1970.

Basner, Emil. *Die Schneiderbewegung in Deutschland.* Berlin, 1913.

Bauer, O.; Marcuse, H.; and Rosenberg, A. et al. *Faschismus und Kapitalismus.* Frankfurt a.M., 1967.

Beales, H.L. "The Great Depression in Industry and Trade." *EHR* 5 (1934): 65-75.

Beckermann, Theodor. "Konjunktur und Konjunkturbeobachtung." In *Das Handwerk in der modernen Wirtschaft und Gesellschaft.* Bad-Wörrishofen, 1966.

Behr, Friedrich. *Die Volkswirtschaftliche Bedeutung der technischen Entwicklung in der Schuhindustrie.* Leipzig, 1909.

Behr, Paul. *Die Katholischen Gesellenvereine in Deutschland.* Berlin, 1882.

Bendix, Reinhard. *Work and Authority in Industry.* New York, 1956.

———. "Tradition and Modernity Reconsidered." *Comparative Studies in Society and History* 9 (1967): 292-346.

Bendix, Reinhard and Lipset, S. M., eds. *Class, Status and Power. Social Stratification in Comparative Perspective.* 2d ed. New York, 1966.

Bergmann, Dieter. "Die Berliner Arbeiterschaft in Vormärz und Revolution 1830-1850." In *Untersuchungen zur Geschichte der frühen Industrialisierung*, edited by Otto Büsch. Berlin, 1971.

Bergmann, Jürgen. "Das 'Alte Handwerk' im Übergang." In *Untersuchungen zur Geschichte der frühen Industrialisierung*, edited by Otto Büsch. Berlin, 1971.

Bernstein, Eduard. *Die Voraussetzungen des Sozialismus und die Aufgaben der Sozialdemokratie*. Stuttgart, 1899.

———. *Die Geschichte der Berliner Arbeiterbewegung*. 2 vols. Berlin, 1907.

Biermann, W.E. *Karl Georg Winkelblech (Karl Marlo)*. Leipzig, 1909.

Binder, Leonard et al. *Crises and Sequences in Political Development*. Princeton, N.J., 1971.

Bismarck, Otto von. *Die Gesammelten Werke*. 15 vols. Friedrichsruh, 1924-35.

Black, C.E. *The Dynamics of Modernization. A Study in Comparative History*. New York, 1966.

Blank, R. "Die soziale Zusammensetzung der sozialdemokratischen Wählerschaft." *ASS* 20 (1905): 507-550.

Block, Hermann. *Die parlamentarische Krisis der nationalliberalen Partei, 1879-80*. Münster, 1930.

Böhmert, Victor. *Beiträge zur Geschichte des Zunftwesens*. Leipzig, 1862.

Bopp, Hartwig P. *Die Entwicklung des deutschen Handwerkergesellentums*. Paderborn, 1932.

Born, Karl-Erich. *Staat und Sozialpolitik seit Bismarcks Sturz, 1890-1914*. Wiesbaden, 1957.

Böttger, Hugo. *Das Programm der Handwerker*. Brunswick, 1893.

Bowen, Ralph H. *German Theories of the Corporative State*. New York, 1947.

Bowley, A.L. "The Survival of Small Firms." *Economica* 1 (1921): 113-115.

Box, Steven, and Ford, Julienne M. "Some Questionable Assumptions in the Theory of Status Inconsistency." *Sociological Review* 17 (1969): 187-201.

Bramsted, Ernst K. *Aristocracy and the Middle-Classes in Germany. Social Types in German Literature 1830-1900*. Rev. ed. London, 1964.

Brauer, Theodor. "Mittelstandspolitik." *Grundriss der Sozialökonomik* 9 (1927): 369-410.

Brentano, Lujo. *Die Arbeitergilden der Gegenwart.* Vol. 1: *Zur Geschichte der englischen Gewerkvereine*. Leipzig, 1871.

Briggs, Asa, ed. *Chartist Studies.* London, 1951.

Briggs, Asa, and Saville, John, eds. *Essays in Labour History. In Memory of G.D.H. Cole.* London, 1960.

Brodnitz, George. "Betriebskonzentration und Kleinbetrieb in der englischen Industrie." *JNS* 35 (1908): 173-218; 36 (1909): 51-86; 145-184.

Broszat, Martin. "Die Antisemitische Bewegung im Wilhelminischen Deutschland." Ph.D. dissertation, University of Cologne, 1952.

Bry, Gerhard. *Wages in Germany 1871-1945.* Princeton, N.J., 1960.

Bücher, Karl. *Die gewerbliche Bildungsfrage und der industrielle Rückgang.* Eisenach, 1877.

———. *Die Arbeiterfrage im Kaufmannsstande.* In *Deutsche Zeit- und Streitfragen*, no. 181, edited by Franz Holtzendorf and Hermann Oncken. Berlin, 1883.

———. "Einkommenverhältnisse der Leipziger Handwerker." *Schriften* 67 (1896) : 699-705.

———. *Industrial Evolution.* London, 1901.

Büsch, Otto, ed. *Untersuchungen zur Geschichte der frühen Industrialisierung vornehmlich im Wirtschaftsraum Berlin/Brandenburg.* Berlin, 1971.

Calwer, Richard. "Zur Entwicklung des Handwerks in den Jahren 1882 bis 1895." *Die Neue Zeit* 15, part ii (1897): 597-600.

Clapham, J.H. *An Economic History of Modern Britain.* Cambridge, 1926.

Clark, Evelyn A. "Adolf Wagner : From National Economist to National Socialist." *Political Science Quarterly* 45 (1940): 378-411.

Cole, G.D.H. *British Trade and Industry.* London, 1932.

———. *Chartist Portraits.* London, 1941.
Comfort, R. *Revolutionary Hamburg: Labor Politics in the Early Weimar Republic.* Stanford, Cal., 1966.
Conze, Werner. "Vom 'Pöbel' zum 'Proletariat.' Sozialogeschichtliche Voraussetzungen für den Sozialismus in Deutschland." *VSWG* 41 (1954): 333-364.
———. *Möglichkeiten und Grenzen der liberalen Arbeiterbewegung in Deutschland.* Heidelberg, 1965.
———, ed. *Staat und Gesellschaft im deutschen Vormärz, 1815-1848.* 2d ed. Stuttgart, 1970.
Correspondenzblatt der Generalkommission der Gewerkschaften Deutschlands. Berlin, 1890–.
Croner, Fritz. *Die Angestelltlen in der modernen Gesellschaft.* Frankfurt a.M., 1954.
———. *Soziologie der Angestellten.* Cologne, 1962.
Crouzet, François. "England and France in the Eighteenth Century : A Comparative Analysis of Two Economic Growths." In *The Causes of the Industrial Revolution in England,* edited by R.M. Hartwell. London, 1967.
Curtius, J. *Bismarcks Plan eines deutschen Volkswirtschaftsrates.* Heidelberg, 1910.
Die Demokratische Partei und die Handwerker. Munich, 1883.
Derry, T.K. "The Repeal of Apprenticeship Clauses of the Statute of Apprentices." *EHR* 3 (1931): 67-87.
Desai, Ashok V. *Real Wages in Germany, 1871-1913.* Oxford, 1968.
Droz, Jacques. *Les Révolutions allemandes de 1848.* Paris, 1957.
Drunsel, Adam. *Die Geschichte der deutschen Töpferbewegung.* Berlin, 1911.
Duverger, Maurice. *Parties politiques et Classes sociales en France.* Paris, 1955.
Eckert, Hugo. *Liberal- oder Sozialdemokratie. Frühgeschichte der Nürnberger Arbeiterbewegung.* Stuttgart, 1968.

Elm, Ludwig. *Zwischen Fortschritt und Reaktion. Geschichte der Parteien der liberalen Bourgeoisie in Deutschland, 1873-1918*. Berlin, 1968.

Engels, Friedrich. *The Conditions of the Working-Class in England in 1844*. London, 1926.

Engelsing, Rolf. *Sozial- und Wirtschaftsgeschichte Deutschlands*. Göttingen, 1973.

Faust, Hellmut. *Geschichte der Genossenschaftsbewegung*. Frankfurt a.M., 1965.

Fechenbach, Friedrich Carl von. *Ein Beitrag zur Lohn- und Arbeiterfrage*. Berlin, 1882.

———. *"Gouvernmental" und "Conservativ"; die Partei Bismarck "sans Phrase."* 5th ed. Osnabrück, 1885.

Fischer, Wolfram. *Der Staat und die Industrialisierung in Baden*. Berlin, 1962.

———. "Soziale Unterschichten im Zeitalter der Frühindustrialisierung." *Int. Rev. of Soc. Hist.* 8 (1963): 415-435.

———. "Das deutsche Handwerk in den Frühphasen der Industrialisierung." *ZGS* 120 (1964): 686-712.

———. "Innerbetrieblicher und sozialer Status der frühen Fabrikarbeiterschaft." In *Die wirtschaftliche Situation in Deutschland und Österreich um die Wende vom 18. zum 19. Jahrhundert*, edited by F. Lütge. Stuttgart, 1964.

———. "Die Rolle des Kleingewerbes im wirtschaftlichen Wachstumsprozess in Deutschland, 1850-1914." In *Wirtschaftliche und soziale Probleme der gewerblichen Entwicklung im 15., 16. und 19. Jahrhundert*, edited by F. Lütge. Stuttgart, 1968.

———. *Wirtschaft und Gesellschaft im Zeitalter der Industrialisierung*. Göttingen, 1972.

Fogarty, Michael P. *Christian-Democracy in Western Europe 1820-1953*. London, 1957.

Forberger, Rudolf. *Die Manufaktur in Sachsen vom Ende des 16. bis zum Anfang des 19. Jahrhunderts*. Berlin, 1958.

Fraenkel, Ernst. *Deutschland und die westlichen Demokratien*. Stuttgart, 1964.

Die Fraktion der Antisemiten im Reichstag. Berlin, 1890.

Francke, Ernst. *Die Schuhmacherei in Bayern.* Stuttgart, 1893.

Frank, Walter, *Hofprediger Adolf Stöcker und die Christlichsoziale Bewegung.* Hamburg, 1935.

Frantz, Constantin. *Der Nationalliberalismus und die Judenherrschaft.* Munich, 1874.

Gabler, Hans. "Die Entwicklung der deutschen Parteien auf Landschaftlicher Grundlage von 1871 bis 1912." Ph.D. dissertation, University of Berlin, 1934.

Geiger, Theodor. "Panik im Mittelstand." *Die Arbeit* 7 (1930): 637-654.

———. *Die Soziale Schichtung des deutschen Volkes.* Stuttgart, 1932.

Gellately, Robert, *The Politics of Economic Despair. Shopkeepers and German Politics 1890-1914.* London, 1974.

George, Dorothy. *London Life in the Eighteenth Century.* 3rd ed. London, 1965.

———. *England in Transition.* 2d ed. London, 1969.

Gerlach, Hellmut von. *Von Rechts nach Links.* Zurich, 1937.

Gerschenkron, Alexander. *Bread and Democracy in Germany.* Berkeley, Cal., 1943.

Geschichtliche Grundbegriffe. Historisches Lexikon zur politisch-sozialen Sprache in Deutschland. Stuttgart, 1972–.

Gewerbefreiheit und Innungen. Heidelberg, 1886.

Giessen, Paul. "Die Preussische Handwerkerpolitik unter Otto von Manteuffel." Ph.D. dissertation, University of Cologne, 1933.

Glagau, Otto. *Der Bankerott des Nationalliberalismus und die "Reaktion."* 8th ed. Berlin, 1878.

———. *Deutsches Handwerk und historisches Bürgertum.* 5th ed. Osnabrück, 1879.

Glass, David V. ed., *Social Mobility in Britain.* London, 1954.

Goldschmidt, Ernst Friedrich. "Die deutsche Handwerkerbewegung bis zum Sieg der Gewerbefreiheit." Ph.D. dissertation, University of Munich, 1915.

Goldthorpe, John H., and Lockwood, David. "Affluence and the British Class Structure." *Sociological Review* 11 (1963): 133-163.

Graetzer, Rudolf. *Organisation der Berufsinteressen.* Berlin, 1890.

———. "Zur Statistik der deutschen Innungen." In *Bayerische Handelszeitung.* Munich, September 14, 1895.

Graf, Hans. *Die Entwicklung der Wahlen in Gross-Dortmund.* Hanover, 1958.

Grandke, Hans. "Die vom 'Verein für Sozialpolitik' Veranstalteten Untersuchungen über die Lage des Handwerks in Deutschland." *Schmollers JB* 21 (1897): 1,031-1,088.

Groh, Dieter. *Negative Integration und revolutionärer Attentismus. Die Sozialdemokratie am Vorabend des Ersten Weltkrieges.* Frankfurt a.M., 1973.

Grünberg, Emil. *Der Mittelstand in der kapitalistischen Gesellschaft.* Leipzig, 1932.

Habermas, Jürgen. *Strukturwandel der Öffentlichkeit. Untersuchungen zu einer Kategorie der bürgerlichen Gesellschaft.* Neuwied, 1962.

Habersbrunner, Franz. *Die Lohn- Arbeits- und Organisationsverhältnisse im deutschen Baugewerbe.* Leipzig, 1903.

Hamerow, Theodore S. *Restoration, Revolution, Reaction. Economics and Politics in Germany, 1815-1871.* Princeton, N.J., 1958.

———. "The German Artisan Movement, 1848/49." *Journal of Central European Affairs* 21 (1961): 135-152.

———. *The Social Foundations of German Unification 1858-71.* Princeton, N.J., 1969.

Hampke, Thilo. *Der Befähigungsnachweis im Handwerk.* Jena, 1892.

———. *Handwerker- oder Gewerbekammern? Ein Beitrag zur Lösung der gewerblichen Organisationsfrage.* Jena, 1893.

Handwerk tut Not! Fordert das Handwerk! Das Büchlein fur Alle! Published by the Reichsverband des deutschen Handwerks und deutscher Handwerks- und Gewerbekammertag. Berlin, 1931.

Handwörterbuch der Sozialwissenschaften. Stuttgart, 1953-1968.

Handwörterbuch der Staatswissenschaften. 3rd ed., 1907-1911; 4th ed., 1924-1928.

Hansen, Alvin H. *Business Cycles and National Income.* 2d ed. New York, 1964.

Hardach, Karl W. *Die Bedeutung wirtschaftlicher Faktoren bei der Wiedereinführung der Eisen- und Getreidezölle in Deutschland, 1879.* Berlin, 1967.

Harms, Bernhard. *Zur Entwicklung der deutschen Buchbinderei in der zweiten Hälfte des 19. Jahrhunderts.* Tübingen, 1902.

———, ed. *Strukturwandlungen der Deutschen Volkswirtschaft.* 2 vols. Berlin, 1928.

Haushofer, M. *Das Kleingewerbe in seinem Existenzkampf gegen die Grossindustrie.* Berlin, 1885.

Hausindustrie und Heimarbeit in Deutschland und Österreich. Schriften 87 (1899).

Heberle, Rudolf. *From Democracy to Nazism. A Regional Case Study of Political Parties in Germany.* Baton Rouge, La., 1945.

Heffter, Heinrich. *Die deutsche Selbstverwaltung im 19. Jahrhundert.* 2d ed. Stuttgart, 1969.

Held, Adolf. *Zwei Bücher zur sozialen Geschichte Englands.* Leipzig, 1881.

Hellgrew, H. *Dortmund als Industrie- und Arbeitsstadt.* Dortmund, 1951.

Henning, Friedrich Wilhelm. "Die Einführung der Gewerbefreiheit und ihre Auswirkungen auf das Handwerk in Deutschland." In *Handwerksgeschichte in neuer Sicht,* edited by Wilhelm Abel et al. Göttingen, 1970.

———. *Die Industrialisierung in Deutschland 1800 bis 1914.* Paderborn, 1973.

Henrici, Ernst. *Was ist der Kern der Judenfrage*. Berlin, 1881.

Herberger, Karl Valerius. "Die Stellung der preussischen Konservativen zur sozialen Frage." Ph.D. dissertation, University of Leipzig, 1914.

Herrfahrdt, Heinrich. *Das Problem der Berufsständischen Vertretung von der Französischen Revolution bis zur Gegenwart*. Berlin, 1921.

Hertling, Georg Freiherr von. *Aufsätze und Reden Sozialpolitischen Inhalts*. Freiburg, 1884.

———. *Erinnerungen aus meinen Leben*. 2 vols. Munich, 1919.

Herzfeld, Hans. *Johannes von Miquel. Sein Anteil am Ausbau des deutschen Reiches bis zur Jahrhundertswende*. Detmold, 1938.

Hicks, John R. *A Theory of Economic History*. Oxford, 1969.

Hintze, Otto. *Staat und Verfassung. Gesammelte Abhandlungen zur allgemeinen Verfassungsgeschichte*. 2d ed. Göttingen, 1962.

Hitze, Franz. *Kapital und Arbeit und die Reorganisation der Gesellschaft*. Paderborn, 1880.

———. *Schutz dem Handwerk*. Paderborn, 1883.

Hobsbawm, E.J. *Labouring Men. Studies in the History of Labour*. New York, 1964.

———. "From Social History to the History of Society." *Daedalus* 100 (1971): 30-45.

Hočevar, Rolf K. *Stände und Repräsentation beim jungen Hegel. Ein Beitrag zu seiner Staats- und Gesellschaftslehre sowie zur Theorie der Repräsentation*. Munich, 1968.

Hoffmann, Stanley. *Le Mouvement Poujade*. Paris, 1956.

Hoffmann, Stanley et al. *In Search of France. The Economy, Society and Political System in the Twentieth Century*. New York, 1963.

Hoffmann, Walther G. *Das Wachstum der deutschen Wirtschaft seit der Mitte des 19. Jahrhunderts*. Berlin, 1965.

International Encyclopedia of the Social Sciences. New York, 1968.

Jäger, Eugen, *Die Handwerkerfrage. Geschichte der Handwerkerbewegung bis zum Jahre 1884.* Berlin, 1887.

Jantke, Carl, and Hilger, Dietrich. *Die Eigentumslosen. Der deutsche Pauperismus und die Emanzipationskrise in Darstellungen und Deutungen der Zeitgenössischen Literatur.* Freiburg, 1965.

John, A.H. "Aspects of English Economic Growth in the First Half of the Eighteenth Century." *Economica* 28 (1961): 176-190.

Kaehler, Siegfried. "Stöckers Versuch eine christliche-soziale Arbeiterpartei in Berlin zu begründen (1878)." In *Deutscher Staat und deutsche Parteien, Beiträge zur deutschen Partei- und Ideengeschichte*, edited by Paul Wentzcke. Munich, 1922.

Kaelble, Hartmut. *Industrielle Interessenpolitik in der Wilhelminischen Gesellschaft. Centralverband deutscher Industrieller 1895-1915.* Berlin, 1967.

———. *Berliner Unternehmer während der frühen Industrialisierung. Herkunft, Sozialer Status und politischer Einfluss.* Berlin, 1972.

———. "Sozialer Aufstieg in Deutschland 1850-1914." *VSWG* 60 (1973): 41-71.

Kampmann, Wanda. "Stöcker und die Berliner Bewegung." *Geschichte in Wissenschaft und Unterricht* 13 (1962): 558-579.

Kater, Michael H. "Zur Soziographie der frühen NSDAP." *VZ* 19 (1971): 124-131.

Kaufhold, Karl Heinrich. *Das Handwerk der Stadt Hildesheim im 18. Jahrhundert. Eine wirtschaftsgeschichtliche Studie.* Göttingen, 1970.

———. "Das preussische Handwerk in der Zeit der Frühindustrialisierung." In *Beiträge zu Wirtschaftswachstum und Wirtschaftsstruktur im 16. und 19. Jahrhundert*, edited by W. Fischer. Berlin, 1971.

Kautsky, Karl. "Der Untergang des Kleinbetriebs." In *Das Erfurter Programm.* 14th ed. Stuttgart, 1919.

Kehr, Eckart. *Schlachtflottenbau und Parteipolitik, 1894-1901.* Berlin, 1930.

———. *Der Primat der Innenpolitik. Gesammelte Aufsätze zur preussisch-deutschen Sozialgeschichte im 19. und 20. Jahrhundert.* Edited by H.-U. Wehler. Berlin, 1965.

Kellenbenz, Hermann, ed. *Agrarisches Nebengewerbe und Formen der Reagrarisierung im Spätmittelalter und 19./20. Jahrhundert.* Stuttgart, 1975.

Kelly, K. Dennis, and Chambliss, William J. "Status Consistency and Political Attitudes." *Am. Soc. Rev.* 31 (1966): 375-382.

Kenkel, William F. "The Relationship between Status Consistency and Political Attitudes." *Am. Soc. Rev.* 21 (1956): 365-368.

Kermann, J. *Die Manufaktur im Rheinland 1750-1833.* Bonn, 1972.

Kimbel, Wilhelm. *Unser Handwerk in Not.* Berlin, n.d.

Kisch, Herbert. "The Textile Industries in Silesia and the Rhineland." *JEH* 19 (1959): 541-564.

Klein, Ernst. *Von der Reform zur Restauration.* Berlin, 1965.

Klemperer, Klemens von. *Germany's New Conservatism: Its History and Dilemma in the Twentieth Century.* Princeton, N.J., 1957.

Klinkenberg, Hans-Martin. "Zwischen Liberalismus und Nationalismus im 2. Kaiserreich (1870-1918)." In *Monumenta Judaica,* edited by Konrad Schilling. Cologne, 1963.

Kocka, Jürgen. *Unternehmensverwaltung und Angestelltenschaft am Beispiel Siemens 1847-1914.* Stuttgart, 1969.

———. "Vorindustrielle Faktoren in der deutschen Industrialisierung. Industriebureaukratie und 'neuer Mittelstand.'" In *Das kaiserliche Deutschland,* edited by M. Stürmer. Düsseldorf, 1970.

———. "Sozial- und Wirtschaftsgeschichte." *Sowjetsystem und Demokratische Gesellschaft* 6 (1972): 3-7.

———. "Theorieprobleme der Sozial- und Wirtschaftsgeschichte." In *Geschichte und Soziologie*, edited by H.-U. Wehler. Cologne, 1972.

———. "The First World War and the 'Mittelstand': German Artisans and White-Collar Workers." *JCH* 8 (1973): 101-124.

———. *Klassengesellschaft im Krieg. Deutsche Sozialgeschichte 1914-1918.* Göttingen, 1973.

———. "Entrepreneurship in a Late-comer Country." Paper read at the International Conference on Business History. Shizuoka, Japan, 1975.

———. "Recent Historiography of Germany and Austria. Theoretical Approaches to Social and Economic History of Modern Germany: Some Recent Trends, Concepts and Problems in Western and Eastern Germany." *JMH* 47 (1975): 101-119.

———. "Theorien in der Sozial- und Gesellschaftsgeschichte." *GG* 1 (1975): 9-42.

———. *Unternehmer in der deutschen Industrialisierung.* Göttingen, 1975.

Koehl, Robert. "Feudal Aspects of National Socialism." *American Political Science Review* 54 (1960): 921-933.

Köllmann, Wolfgang. "Grundzüge der Bevölkerungsgeschichte Deutschlands im. 19. und 20. Jahrhundert." *Studium Generale* 12 (1959): 381-392.

———. "Industrialisierung, Binnenwanderung und 'Soziale Frage.'" *VSWG* 46 (1959): 45-70.

———. *Sozialgeschichte der Stadt Barmen im 19. Jahrhundert.* Tübingen, 1960.

———. "Bevölkerung und Arbeitskräftepotential in Deutschland, 1815-1865. Ein Beitrag zur Analyse der Problematik des Pauperismus." *Jahrbuch des Landesamtes für Forschung Nordrhein-Westfalen* (1968): 209-254.

Koselleck, Reinhart. *Preussen zwischen Reform und Revolution, 1791-1848.* Stuttgart, 1967.

Kötzschke, Rudolf, and Kretzschmar Hellmut, eds. *Sächsische Geschichte*. Dresden, 1935.

Krahl, Willi. *Der Verband deutscher Buchdrucker, 50 Jahre gewerkschaftlicher Arbeit, mit einer Vorgeschichte*. Berlin, 1916.

Krüger, Horst. *Zur Geschichte der Manufakturen und der Manufakturarbeiter in Preussen*. Berlin, 1958.

Kuczynski, Jürgen. *Die Geschichte der Lage der Arbeiter in Deutschland von 1800 bis in die Gegenwart*. 2 vols. Berlin, 1954.

Küstenmeier, Rudolf. *Die Mittelschichten und ihr politischer Weg*. Potsdam, 1933.

Lambi, Nikolai Ivo. *Free Trade and Protection in Germany 1868-1879*. Wiesbaden, 1963.

Landes, David S. "Technological Change and Development in Western Europe, 1750-1914." In *The Cambridge Economic History of Europe*, edited by H.J. Habakkuk and M. Postan, vol. 6, part 1. Cambridge, 1966.

———. *Prometheus Unbound*. Cambridge, 1969.

Lang, Alexander. "Die Badischen Gewerbevereine und Handwerkerverbände und ihre Stellungnahme zum neuen Handwerkergesetz." Ph.D. dissertation, University of Heidelberg, 1900.

Laslett, Peter. *The World We Have Lost*. London, 1965.

Laufenberg, Heinrich. *Geschichte der Arbeiterbewegung Hamburgs*. Hamburg, 1931.

Laveleye, Emil von. *Die sozialen Parteien der Gegenwart*. Tübingen, 1884.

Lebovics, Herman. "'Agrarians' versus 'Industrializers.' Social Conservative Resistance to Industrialism and Capitalism in Late 19th Century Germany." *Int. Rev. of Soc. Hist.* 12 (1967): 31-65.

———. *Social Conservatism and the Middle Classes in Germany 1914-1933*. Princeton, N.J., 1969.

Lederer, Emil. *Die wirtschaftlichen Organisationen und die Reichstagswahlen*. Tübingen, 1912.

Lenski, Gerhard E. "Status Crystallization: A Non-Vertical

Dimension of Social Status." *Am. Soc. Rev.* 19 (1954): 405-413.

Leppert-Fögen, Annette. *Die deklassierte Klasse. Studien zur Geschichte und Ideologie des Kleinbürgertums.* Frankfurt a.M., 1974.

Lepsius, Rainer M. "Parteiensystem und Sozialstruktur. Zum Problem der Demokratisierung der deutschen Gesellschaft." In *Festschrift für F. Lütge*, edited by W. Abel et al. Stuttgart, 1966.

Levy, Richard S. *The Downfall of the Anti-Semitic Political Parties in Imperial Germany.* New Haven, Conn., 1975.

Lexis, Wilhelm. *Gewerkvereine und Unternehmerverbände in Frankreich.* Leipzig, 1879.

Lidtke, Vernon L. "German Social Democracy and German State Socialism 1876-1884." *Int. Rev. of Soc. Hist.* 9 (1964): 202-225.

———. *The Outlawed Party. Social Democracy in Germany 1878-1890.* Princeton, N.J., 1966.

Lipset, Seymour Martin. *Political Man. The Social Bases of Politics.* New York, 1960.

Löbner, Arthur. *Wie das deutsche Kleingewerbe über die Innungsfrage und die Reform der Reichsgewerbeordnung denkt.* Berlin, 1879.

Lütge, Friedrich. *Die Wirtschaftliche Situation in Deutschland und Österreich um die Wende vom 18. zum 19. Jahrhundert.* Stuttgart, 1964.

———. *Deutsche Sozial- und Wirtschaftsgeschichte.* 3rd ed. Heidelberg, 1966.

———. *Wirtschaftliche und soziale Probleme der gewerblichen Entwicklung im 15., 16. und 19. Jahrhundert.* Stuttgart, 1968.

Maenner, Ludwig. *Deutschlands Wirtschaft und der Liberalismus in 1879.* Berlin, 1929.

Mantoux, Paul. *The Industrial Revolution in the Eighteenth Century: An Outline of the Beginning of the Modern Factory System in England.* 2d ed. London, 1961.

Marbach, Fritz. *Theorie des Mittlestandes.* Bern, 1942.

Marquardt, Frederick D. "*The Manual Worker in the Social Order in Berlin Under the Old Regime.*" Ph.D. dissertation, University of California, 1973.

———. "A Working Class in Berlin in the 1840's?" In *Sozialgeschichte Heute*, edited by H.-U. Wehler. Göttingen, 1974.

———. "Sozialer Aufstieg, Sozialer Abstieg und die Entstehung der Berliner Arbeiterklasse, 1806-1848." *GG* 1 (1975): 43-77.

Marr, Wilhelm, ed. *Die Deutsche Wacht.* Berlin, 1879-80.

Marshall, T.H. *Class, Citizenship and Social Development*, Garden City, N.Y., 1965.

Marx, Karl and Engels, Friedrich. *Werke.* Berlin, 1961-1971.

Mascher, H.A. *Das deutsche Gewerbewesen von der frühsten Zeit bis auf die Gegenwart.* Potsdam, 1866.

Massing, Paul W. *Rehearsal for Destruction. A Study of Political Anti-Semitism in Imperial Germany.* New York, 1949.

Mathias, Peter. *The First Industrial Nation.* London, 1969.

Mayer, Arno J. "The Lower Middle Class as Historical Problem." *JMH* 47 (1975): 409-436.

Mayer, Gustav. *Die Trennung der Proletarischen von der Bürgerlichen Demokratie in Deutschland, 1863-70.* Leipzig, 1911.

Mehring, Franz. *Geschichte der deutschen Sozialdemokratie.* 2d ed. Stuttgart, 1922.

Meister, Karl. "Die Innungen der Stadt Dortmund." Ph.D. dissertation, University of Munich, 1904.

Mendels, F. "Proto-Industrialization: The First Phase of the Industrialization Process." *JEH* 32 (1972): 241-261.

Meusch, Hans. *Die Handwerkerbewegung von 1848/49.* Alfeld, 1949.

Meyer, Rudolf. *Was Heisst Konservativ Sein? Reform oder Restauration.* Berlin, 1873.

———. *Der Emancipationskampf der Vierten Standes.* 2 vols. Berlin, 1874-75.

Michels, Robert. "Die deutsche Sozialdemokratie: Parteimitgliederschaft und soziale Zusammensetzung." *ASS* 23 (1906): 471-556.

Mieck, Ilja. *Preussische Gewerbepolitik in Berlin 1806-1844.* Berlin, 1965.

Mielke, Siegfried. *Der Hansa-Bund für Gewerbe, Handel und Industrie 1909-1914.* Göttingen, 1976.

Miquel, Johannes von. *Reden.* Edited by Walther Schultze and Friedrich Thimme. Halle, 1913.

Mommsen, Hans et al., eds. *Industrielles System und politische Entwicklung in der Weimarer Republik.* Düsseldorf, 1974.

Mommsen, Wilhelm, ed. *Deutsche Parteiprogramme.* Munich, 1960.

Moody, Joseph M. ed. *Catholic Social and Political Movements 1789-1950.* New York, 1953.

Moring, Karl-Ernst. *Die Sozialdemokratische Partei in Bremen 1890-1914.* Hanover, 1968.

Müffelmann, Leo. *Die Wirtschaftlichen Verbände.* Leipzig, 1912.

———. *Die politische Mittelstandsbewegung.* Berlin, 1913.

Müller, Edith. "Die Katholische Wirtschafts- und Gesellschaftsidee in der Politik des Zentrums im Reichstag 1871-1879." Ph.D. dissertation, University of Frankfurt a.M., 1955.

Müller, Hugo. "Der Preussische Volksverein." Ph.D. dissertation, University of Berlin, 1914.

Neues ABC-Buch für freisinnige Wähler. Berlin, 1884.

Nipperdey, Thomas. "Interessenverbände und Parteien in Deutschland vor dem Ersten Weltkrieg." *PVS* 2 (1961): 262-280.

———. *Die Organisation der deutschen Parteien vor 1918.* Düsseldorf, 1961.

Noll, Adolf. "Wirtschaftliche und Soziale Entwicklung des Handwerks in der Zweiten Phase der Industrialisierung." In *Zur soziologischen Theorie und Analyse des 19. Jahrhunderts,* edited by Walter Rüegg and Otto Neuloh. Göttingen, 1971.

———. *Sozio-ökonomischer Strukturwandel des Handwerks in der Zweiten Phase der Industrialisierung.* Göttingen, 1975.

Noyes, P.H. *Organization and Revolution. Working-class Associations in the German Revolutions of 1848-49.* Princeton, N.J., 1966.

Oelsner, Ludwig. "Die wirtschaft- und sozialpolitischen Verhandlungen des Frankfurter Parlaments." *Preussische Jahrbücher* 87 (1897): 81-96.

O'Lessker, Karl. "Who Voted for Hitler: A New Look at the Class Basis of Nazism." *Am. J. of Soc.* 74 (1968): 63-69.

Ossowski, Stanislaw. *Class Structure in the Social Consciousness.* London, 1963.

Perkin, Harold. *The Origins of Modern English Society 1780-1880.* London, 1969.

Perrot, F. *Das Handwerk, seine Reorganisation und seine Befreiung von der Übermacht des Grosskapitals.* Leipzig, 1876.

Pesl, L.D. "Mittelstandsfragen." *Grundriss der Sozialökonomik* 9 (1926): 70-121.

Pflanze, Otto. *Bismarck and the Development of Germany.* Princeton, N.J., 1963.

Phelps-Brown, E.H., and Hopkins, Sheila V. "The Course of Wage Rates in Five Countries 1860-1939." *Oxford Economic Papers* 2 (1950): 226-296.

Pinkney, David H. "The Crowd in the French Revolution of 1830." *AHR* 23 (1961): 1-17.

Pinson, Kopel S., ed. *Essays on Anti-Semitism.* New York, 1946.

Pollard, Sidney. *A History of Labour in Sheffield.* Liverpool, 1959.

———. *The Genesis of Modern Management. A Study of the Industrial Revolution in England.* London, 1965.

Puhle, Hans-Jürgen. *Agrarische Interessenpolitik und preussischer Konservatismus im wilhelminischen Reich, 1893-1914.* Hanover, 1966.

———. "Parlament, Parteien und Interessenverbände 1890-1914." In *Das kaiserliche Deutschland*, edited by M. Stürmer. Düsseldorf, 1970.

———. *Von der Akrarkrise zum Präfaschismus. Thesen zum Stellenwert der agrarischen Interessenverbände in der deutschen Politik am Ende des 19. Jahrhunderts.* Wiesbaden, 1972.

Pulzer, Peter G.J. *The Rise of Political Anti-Semitism in Germany and Austria.* New York, 1964.

Rauchberg, Heinrich. "Die Berufs- und Gewerbezählung im Deutschen Reich vom 14.6.1895." *ASS* 14 (1899): 603-657.

Redlich, Fritz. *Der Unternehmer. Wirtschafts- und sozialgeschichtliche Studie.* Göttingen, 1964.

Reich, Wilhelm. *Massenpsychologie des Faschismus.* Copenhagen, 1933.

Richter, Eugen. *Gegen die Zwangsinnung.* Berlin, 1896.

Riehl, Wilhelm H. *Die bürgerliche Gesellschaft.* 6th ed. Stuttgart, 1866.

Ringer, Fritz K. "Higher Education in Germany in the 19th Century." *JCH* 2 (1967): 123-138.

———. *The Decline of the German Mandarins. The Academic Community 1890-1933.* Cambridge, Mass., 1969.

Ritter, Emil. *Die Katholisch-soziale Bewegung Deutschlands im 19. Jahrhundert und der Volksverein.* Cologne, 1954.

Ritter, Gerhard A. *Die Arbeiterbewegung im Wilhelminischen Reich.* Berlin, 1959.

———, ed. *Entstehung und Wandel der modernen Gesellschaft. Festschrift für Hans Rosenberg zum 65. Geburtstag.* Berlin, 1970.

Roberts, Cecil E. "Handwerk und Handwerker in der deutschen Erzählung vom Ausgang des 18. Jahrhunderts bis zur Gegenwart." Ph.D. dissertation, University of Breslau, 1939.

Röhl, John C.G. *Germany without Bismarck. The Crisis of*

Government in the Second Reich 1890-1900. London, 1968.

Rohr, Donald G. *The Origins of Social Liberalism in Germany*. Chicago, 1963.

Rosenberg, Arthur. *Die Entstehung der Weimarer Republik*. Frankfurt a.M., 1961.

Rosenberg, Hans. "Die Pseudodemokratisierung der Rittergutsbesitzerklasse." In *Moderne deutsche Sozialgeschichte*, edited by H.-U. Wehler. Cologne, 1966.

———. *Grosse Depression und Bismarckzeit. Wirtschaftsablauf, Gesellschaft und Politik in Mitteleuropa*. Berlin, 1967.

———. *Die Weltwirtschaftskrise 1857-1859*. 2d ed. Göttingen, 1974.

Rosenblatt, Frank F. *The Chartist Movement in its Social and Economic Aspects*. 2d ed. London, 1967.

Rostow, W.W. *British Economy of the 19th Century*. Oxford, 1949.

Roth, Gunther. *Social Democrats in Imperial Germany. A Study in Working-Class Isolation and National Integration*. Totowa, N.J., 1963.

Rothfels, Hans, *Theodor Lohmann und die Kampfjahre der Staatlichen Sozialpolitik, 1871-1905*. Berlin, 1927.

———. *Prinzipienfragen der Bismarckschen Sozialpolitik*. Königsberg, 1935.

———. "Bismarck's Social Policy and the Problem of State-Socialism in Germany." *Sociological Review* 30 (1938): 81-84; 288-302.

Rude, Fernand. *Le Mouvement Ouvrier à Lyon de 1827-1832*. Paris, 1944.

Rudé, George. *The Crowd in the French Revolution*. Oxford, 1959.

———. *The Crowd in History. A Study of Popular Disturbances in France and England 1730-1848*. New York, 1964.

Rüegg, Walter, and Neuloh, Otto, eds. *Zur soziologischen*

Theorie und Analyse des 19. Jahrhunderts. Göttingen, 1971.

Runciman, Walter G. *Relative Deprivation and Social Justice.* Berkeley, Cal., 1966.

———. *Sociology in its Place and Other Essays.* Cambridge, 1970.

Rürup, Reinhard. "Kontinuität und Diskontinuität der 'Judenfrage' im 19. Jahrhundert. Zur Entstehung des modernen Antisemitismus." In *Sozialgeschichte Heute,* edited by H.-U. Wehler. Göttingen, 1974.

Rush, Gary B. "Status Consistency and Right-Wing Extremism." *Am. Soc. Rev.* 32 (1967): 86-92.

Saile, Wolfgang. *Hermann Wagener und sein Verhältniss zu Bismarck. Geschichte des konservativen Sozialismus.* Tübingen, 1958.

Saldern, Adelheid von. "Gewerbegerichte im Wilhelminischen Deutschland." In *Festschrift für W. Treue,* edited by Karl-Heinz Manegold. Munich, 1969.

Salomon, Felix, ed. *Die deutschen Parteiprogramme.* Leipzig, 1912.

Sauer, Wolfgang. "Das Problem des deutschen Nationalstaates." In *Moderne deutsche Sozialgeschichte,* edited by H.-U. Wehler. Cologne, 1966.

———. "National Socialism: Totalitarianism or Fascism?" *AHR* 73 (1967): 404-424.

Saul, S.B. *The Myth of the Great Depression.* London, 1969.

Schmidt, Karl-Heinz. "Die Rolle des Kleingewerbes in regionalen Wachstumsprozessen in der zweiten Hälfte des 19. Jahrhunderts." In *Festschrift für Wilhelm Abel zum 70. Geburtstag,* edited by Ingomar Bog et al., vol. 3. Hanover, 1974.

Schmoller, Gustav. *Zur Geschichte der deutschen Kleingewerbe im 19. Jahrhundert.* Halle, 1870.

———. "Was verstehen wir unter dem Mittelstande? (Hat er im 19. Jahrhundert zu- oder abgenommen?)" Vortrag

auf dem Evangelisch-sozialen Kongress in Leipzig am 11. Juni 1897. Göttingen, 1897.
Schoenbaum, David. *Hitler's Social Revolution. Class and Status in Nazi Germany 1933-1939.* New York, 1966.
Schoeps, Hans-Joachim. "Hermann Wagener—Ein konservativer Sozialist. Ein Beitrag zur Geschichte des konservativen Sozialismus." *Zeitschrift für Religions- und Geistesgeschichte* 8 (1956): 214-215.
———. "CDU vor 75 Jahren: Die Sozialpolitischen Bestrebungen des Reichsfreiherr Friedrich Carl von Fechenbach (1836-1907)." *Zeitschrift für Religions- und Geistesgeschichte* 9 (1957): 266-277.
Schramm, Ferdinand. *Der Reichsstand des deutschen Handwerks.* Berlin, 1941.
Schremmer, Eckart. *Die Wirtschaft Bayerns. Vom hohen Mittelalter bis zum Beginn der Industrialisierung. Bergbau. Gewerbe. Handel.* Munich, 1970.
Schulthess, Heinrich. ed. *Europäischer Geschichtskalender.* Nördlingen, 1872-96.
Schulz, Gerhard. "Über Entstehung und Formen von Interessengruppen in Deutschland seit Beginn der Industrialisierung." *PVS* 2 (1961): 124-154.
Schumacher, Martin. *Mittelstandsfront und Republik. Die Wirtschaftspartei—Reichspartei des deutschen Mittelstandes 1919-1933.* Düsseldorf, 1972.
Schumpeter, Joseph A. *Aufsätze zur Soziologie.* Tübingen, 1953.
Schwabe, Hermann. *Die Königliche Haupt- und Residenzstadt Berlin in ihren Bevölkerungs-, Berufs- und Wohnungsverhältnissen.* Berlin, 1874.
Schweitzer, Arthur. "The Nazification of the Lower Middle-Class and Peasants." In *The Third Reich.* London, 1955.
Seeber, Gustav. *Zwischen Bebel und Bismarck. Zur Geschichte des Linksliberalismus in Deutschland 1871-1893.* Berlin, 1965.
Segall, J. *Die beruflichen und sozialen Verhältnisse der Juden in Deutschland.* Berlin, 1912.

Sell, Friedrich C. *Die Tragödie des deutschen Liberalismus.* Stuttgart, 1953.

Shanahan, William O. *German Protestants Face the Social Question.* Notre Dame, Ind., 1954.

Shapiro, David, ed. *The Right in France 1890-1919. Three Studies.* London, 1962.

Sheehan, James J. "Liberalism and Society in Germany 1815-48." *JMH* 45 (1973): 583-604.

Shorter, Edward. "Middle-Class Anxiety in the German Revolution of 1848." *Journal of Social History* 2 (1969): 189-215.

Simon Klaus. *Die Württembergischen Demokraten, ihre Stellung und Arbeit im Verfassungssystem in Württemberg und im deutschen Reich 1890-1920.* Stuttgart, 1969.

Simon, Oskar. *Das Gewerbliche fortbildungs- und Fachschulwesen.* Berlin, 1903.

Smelser, Neil J. *Social Change in the Industrial Revolution. An Application of Theory to the British Cotton Industry.* Chicago, 1959.

———. *Theory of Collective Behavior.* New York, 1962.

———. "Personality and the Explanation of Political Phenomena at the Social-System Level: A Methodological Statement." *Journal of Social Issues* 24 (1968): 111-125.

Snyder, Louis L. *From Bismarck to Hitler.* New York, 1935.

Soboul, Albert, *Les sans-culottes parisiens en l'an II.* Paris, 1958.

———. *The Parisian Sans Culottes and the French Revolution, 1793-4.* Oxford, 1964.

Sombart, Werner. *Die deutsche Volkswirtschaft im neunzehnten Jahrhundert.* 7th ed. Berlin, 1927.

Sontheimer, Kurt. *Antidemokratisches Denken in der Weimarer Republik. Die politischen Ideen des deutschen Nationalismus zwischen 1918 und 1933.* Munich, 1962.

Die Sozialpolitik der deutschen Zentrumspartei. Gesammelte sozial-politische Flugblätter des Volksvereins. München-Gladbach, 1907.

Specht, Fritz. *Die Reichstagswahlen von 1867 bis 1897.* Berlin, 1898.

Stadelmann, Rudolf. *Soziale und politische Geschichte der Revolution von 1848.* Munich, 1948.

Stadelmann, Rudolf, and Fischer, Wolfram. *Die Bildungswelt des deutschen Handwerkers um 1800.* Berlin, 1955.

Stegmann, Dirk. *Die Erben Bismarcks. Parteien und Verbände in der Spätphase des wilhelminischen Deutschlands.* Cologne, 1970.

Sterling, Eleonore. *Judenhass. Die Anfänge des politischen Antisemitismus in Deutschland (1815-1850).* 2d ed. Frankfurt a.M., 1969.

Stern, Fritz. *The Politics of Cultural Despair: A Study of the Rise of Germanic Ideology.* Garden City, N.Y., 1965.

Stieda, Wilhelm. "Die Innungsenquete." *JNS* 3rd ser., 12 (1896): 1-35.

———. *Die Lebensfähigkeit des deutschen Handwerks.* Rostock, 1897.

Stillich, Oskar. *Die Politischen Parteien in Deutschland.* Berlin, 1911.

Stock, Erich. *Wirtschafts- und Sozialpolitische Bestrebungen der deutsch konservativen Partei unter Bismarck 1876-1890.* Breslau, 1928.

Stöcker, Adolf. *Christlich-Sozial. Reden und Aufsätze.* Bielefeld, 1885.

Strauss, Rudolf. *Die Lage und die Bewegung der Chemnitzer Arbeiter in der ersten Hälfte des 19. Jahrhunderts.* Berlin, 1960.

Stürmer, Michael, ed. *Das kaiserliche Deutschland. Politik und Gesellschaft 1870-1918.* Düsseldorf, 1970.

Tal, Uriel. *Christians and Jews in Germany; Religion, Politics and Ideology in the Second Reich, 1870-1914.* Ithaca, N.Y., 1975.

Teuteberg, Hans J., and Wiegelmann, Gunter. *Der Wandel der Nahrungsgewohnheiten unter dem Einfluss der Industrialisierung.* Göttingen, 1972.

Thier, Erich. *Rodbertus, Lassalle, Adolf Wagner. Ein Beitrag zu Theorie und Geschichte des deutschen Staatssozialismus.* Jena, 1930.

Thompson, E. P. *The Making of the English Working Class.* London, 1963.

Thrupp, Sylvia L. "The Guilds." In *The Cambridge Economic History of Europe*, edited by H.J. Habakkuk and M. Postan, vol. 3. Cambridge, 1963.

Todt, Rudolf. *Der Radikale deutsche Sozialismus und die Christliche Gesellschaft.* Wittenberg, 1877.

Toury, Jacob. *Ka'wim Le'cheker k'nissat Ha'yehudim La'chaim Ha'ezrachiym Begermania (Prolegomena to the Entrance of Jews into German Citizenry).* Tel-Aviv, 1972 (Hebrew).

Turner, Henry Ashby. *Faschismus und Kapitalismus in Deutschland.* Göttingen, 1972.

Untersuchungen über die Lage des Handwerks in Deutschland mit besonderer Rücksicht auf seine Konkurrenzfähigkeit gegenüber der Grossindustrie. In *Schriften* 62-70 (1895-97).

Valentin, Veit. *Geschichte der deutschen Revolution von 1848-49.* Frankfurt a.M., 1930-31.

Voigt, Paul. "Die Hauptergebnisse der neuesten deutschen Handwerkerstatistik von 1895." *Schmollers JB* 21 (1896): 997-1,030.

———. "Das deutsche Handwerk nach den Berufszählungen von 1882 und 1895." *Schriften* 70 (1897): 629-669.

———. "Die neue deutsche Handwerkergesetzgebung." ASS 11 (1897): 39-87.

Volkov, Shulamit. "The 'Decline of the German Handicrafts'—Another Reappraisal." *VSWG* 61 (1974): 165-184.

———. "Popular Anti-Modernism. Ideology and Sentiment Among Master-Artisans During the 1890's." *Jahrbuch des Instituts für deutsche Geschichte* 3 (1974): 203-225.

———. "The Social and Political Function of Late 19th Century Anti-Semitism. The Case of the Small Handicraft Masters." In *Sozialgeschichte Heute*, edited by H.-U. Wehler. Göttingen, 1974.

Waentig, Heinrich. *Gewerbliche Mittelstandspolitik. Eine rechtshistorisch-wirtschaftspolitische Studie auf Grund österreichischer Quellen*. Leipzig, 1898.

———. "Die Gewerbepolitischen Anschauungen in Wissenschaft und Gesetzgebung des 19. Jahrhunderts." In *Festschrift für Gustav Schmoller*. Leipzig, 1908.

Wagener, Hermann. *Erlebtes; Meine Memoiren aus der Zeit von 1848 bis 1866, und von 1873 bis jetzt*. Berlin, 1885.

———. *Die kleine aber mächtige Partei*. Berlin, 1885.

———. *Die Mängel der christlich-sozialen Bewegung*. Berlin, 1885.

Walker, Mack. "Home Towns and State Administrators: South German Politics, 1815-30." *Political Science Quarterly* 82 (1967): 35-60.

———. *German Home Towns. Community, State and General Estate*. Ithaca, N.Y., 1971.

Walterhausen, A. Sartorius von. *Deutsche Wirtschaftsgeschichte 1815-1914*. Jena, 1920.

Warren, Donald. *The Red Kingdom of Saxony. Lobbying Grounds of Gustav Stresemann*. The Hague, 1964.

Was hat das Zentrum für die Handwerker getan. Munich-Gladbach, 1910.

Wawrzinek, K. *Die Entstehung der deutschen Antisemitenparteien (1872-1890)*. Berlin, 1927.

Webb, Sidney and Beatrice. *History of Trade Unionism*. Rev. ed. London, 1926.

Weber, Max. *Wirtschaft und Gesellschaft*. 2 vols. Tübingen, 1922.

———. *Gesammelte politische Schriften*. Edited by V.J. Winckelmann. 2d ed. Tübingen, 1958.

Weber, Rolf. *Die Kleinbürgerliche Demokraten in der deutschen Einheitsbewegung 1863-66*. Leipzig, 1958.

———. "Die Beziehungen zwischen sozialer Struktur und politischer Ideologie des Kleinbürgertums in der Revolution von 1848/49." *ZG*, part 7 (1965): 1,186-1,193.

———. "Zur Geschichte der kleinbürgerlichen Demokraten." *Beiträge zur Geschichte der Arbeiterbewegung* 7 (1965): 491-496.

Wehler, Hans-Ulrich, ed. *Moderne Deutsche Sozialgeschichte*. Cologne, 1966.

———. *Bismarck und der Imperialismus*. Cologne, 1969.

———. *Das Deutsche Kaiserreich 1871-1918*. Göttingen, 1973.

———, ed. *Sozialgeschichte Heute. Festschrift für Hans Rosenberg zum 70. Geburtstag*. Göttingen, 1974.

———. *Modernisierungstheorie und Geschichte*. Göttingen, 1975.

Wellmanns, Hermann. *Das deutsche Handwerk im Gemeinsamen Markt*. Bonn, 1960.

Wernet, Wilhelm. *Soziale Handwerksordnung. Aufriss einer deutschen Handwerksgeschichte im Hinblick auf die Sozialtätigkeit der Handwerklichen Berufsorganisation*. Berlin, 1939.

———. *Handwerkspolitik*. Göttingen, 1952.

Wernicke, Johannes. *Kapitalismus und Mittelstandspolitik*. Jena, 1907.

Wilmanns, C. *Die goldene Internationale und die Notwendigkeit einer sozialen Reformpartei*. Berlin, 1876.

Wilson, C. "The Entrepreneur in the Industrial Revolution." *Explorations in Entrepreneurial History* 7 (1954/55): 129-145.

Winkler, Heinrich August. "Bürgertum." *Sowietsystem und Demokratische Gesellschaft* 1 (1964): 934-953.

———. "Unternehmerverbände zwischen Ständeideologie und Nationalsozialismus." *VZ* 17 (1969): 341-371.

———. "Der rückversicherte Mittelstand: Die Interessenverbände von Handwerk und Kleinhandel im deutschen Kaiserreich." In *Zur soziologischen Theorie und Analyse des 19. Jahrhunderts*, edited by Walter Rüegg and Otto Neuloh. Göttingen, 1971.

———. "Extremismus der Mitte? Sozialgeschichtliche Aspecte der nationalsozialistischen Machtergreifung." *VZG* 20 (1972): 175-191.

———. *Mittelstand, Demokratie und Nationalsozialismus. Die politische Entwicklung von Handwerk und Kleinhandel in der Weimarer Republik.* Cologne, 1972.

———. *Pluralismus oder Protektionismus? Verfassungspolitische Probleme des Verbandswesen im deutschen Kaiserreich.* Wiesbaden, 1972.

———, ed. *Organisierter Kapitalismus. Voraussetzungen und Anfänge.* Göttingen, 1974.

———. "From Social Protectionism to National Socialism: German Small Business Movement in Comparative Perspective." *JMH* 48 (1976): 1-18.

Wischnitzer, Mark. *A History of Jewish Crafts and Guilds.* New York, 1965.

Wulf, Peter. *Die politische Haltung des Schleswig-holsteinischen Handwerks 1928-1932.* Cologne, 1969.

Zang, Hans. "*Die Gartenlaube* als politisches Organ. Belletristik, Bilderwerk und literarische Kritik im Dienste der liberalen Politik 1860-1880." Ph.D. dissertation, University of Coburg, 1935.

Zorn, Wolfgang. "Typen und Entwicklungskräfte deutschen Unternehemertums im 19. Jahrhundert." *VSWG* 44 (1957): 57-77.

Zunkel, Friedrich. *Der Rheinisch-Westfälische Unternehmer 1834-1879.* Cologne, 1962.

Zwing, Karl. *Geschichte der deutschen freien Gewerkschaften.* 2d ed. Jena, 1926.

Index

Library of Congress Cataloging in Publication Data

Volkov, Shulamit, 1942-
The rise of popular antimodernism in Germany.

Bibliography: p.
Includes index.
1. Artisans—Germany—Political activity—History.
2. Middle classes—Germany—Political activity—History.
I. Title.
HD2346.G3V64 323'.2'0943 77-85571
ISBN 0-691-05264-6